Old Testament Theology

AN INTRODUCTION

The Library of Biblical Theology

LIBRARY OF BIBLICAL THEOLOGY

OLD TESTAMENT THEOLOGY

AN INTRODUCTION

WALTER BRUEGGEMANN

Abingdon Press
Nashville

OLD TESTAMENT THEOLOGY
AN INTRODUCTION

This book is printed on acid-free paper.

Library of Congress Cataloging-in-Publication Data

Brueggemann, Walter.
Old Testament theology : an introduction / Walter Brueggemann.
p. cm. — (Library of biblical theology)
Includes index.
ISBN 978-0-687-34090-3 (v. 1 : pbk. : alk. paper)
1. Bible. O.T.—Theology. I. Title.

BS1192.5.B777 2008
230′.0411—dc22

2008036528

Ancient language fonts were developed in the public domain for scholars who comprise the Society of Biblical Literature, including SPTiberian for Hebrew, SPIonic for Greek, and SPAtlantis for transliteration.

9 10 11 12 13 14 15 16 17—10 9 8 7 6 5 4 3 2

MANUFACTURED IN THE UNITED STATES OF AMERICA

CONTENTS

For M. Douglas Meeks

PREFACE

In my *Theology of the Old Testament: Testimony, Dispute, Advocacy* (Fortress Press, 1997), I have offered my primary extended interpretive statement about Old Testament theology. I have worked with the thick metaphor of "testimony" and have sought to develop the theme and metaphor in terms of the unsettled, open-ended pluralism of the text itself. As it happens, the attempt to listen carefully to the rich variety of voices of faith in the Old Testament (which cannot be easily brought together) served well the appeal to a postmodern hermeneutical perspective. I have had and now have no desire to be postmodern except as the polyvocal character of the text itself indicates such an interpretive perspective.

On the whole, that book has been well received. The primary objections to the book have come, as might be expected, from those who continue to be committed to modernist historicist assumptions, in which they have more confidence than do I. In any case, the present volume does not seek to respond to criticisms of that volume nor to emend any of those arguments. (It is, in my judgment, important to notice that the shrillest modernist critiques of my book in fact have exhibited no interest in the argument of the book nor have they paid any attention to the interpretive gains offered therein.) But that statement is as it is, and I am content to leave it at that.

The present volume has a quite different intention, namely, to provide an entry point into the Library of Biblical Theology, the ambitious, multivolume project edited by Leo Perdue. I have understood my task in this volume with reference to the projected series. Thus, I have attempted no new programmatic statement, nor have I sought to offer a particularly novel angle on any of the topics I have discussed. Rather, I have sought to state a more-or-less straightforward consensus view, with openness to colleagues in other disciplines. As is usual in my work, I have kept one eye on the immense contemporaneity of the text. My judgment is that U.S. society in general, and mainline church life in particular, face enormous challenges and must undertake great risks for the sake of our common faith and our common humanness. It is my conviction that the biblical text offers a place from which to mount such a risky venture of faith. Such a venture requires thoughtful critical grounding, passionate trust in the truth disclosed in the text, and a wisdom about the world in which the text is to be lived out. I have sought to offer my exposition from that perspective.

I am pleased to be included in the series and am grateful to Leo Perdue and to the editorial staff that have seen the book through. As is regularly the case, I am grateful to Tia Foley for bringing the manuscript to fruition. I trust the discussion offered here will contribute in useful ways to our continuing interpretive task.

I am pleased to dedicate this book to M. Douglas Meeks, my long-time friend, colleague, companion, and teacher. Doug, more than anyone else, introduced me to the thickness and urgency of theology in the service of the church. Through our long years of team teaching, he introduced me to the mysteries of critical hermeneutics and has been, all this time—along with Blair—a good and trustworthy friend. My vocation has been strengthened because of his presence in my life, and I am grateful.

Walter Brueggemann
Holy Week 2007

I. INTRODUCTION

CHAPTER ONE

INTRODUCTION TO THE TASK

The aim and task of Library of Biblical Theology series is to offer a coherent, wholistic presentation of the faith claims of the canonical text in a way that satisfies the investigations of historical-critical scholarship and the confessional-interpretive needs of ongoing ecclesial communities. That same aim and task of course pertain to a subset of biblical theology: Old Testament theology or, alternatively, theology of the Hebrew Scriptures, the subject of this present volume. From the rich ferment of recent and current study of Old Testament theology, it is evident (a) that there are many alternative legitimate ways of enacting such an aim and task, (b) that there is no one single right way to perform such a task to the exclusion of other presentations, even if a particular perspective receives passionate and high-minded advocacy, and (c) that in order to offer such articulation, one must adopt an interpretive perspective that has some particularity to it. It is not possible, so present study would evidence, to proceed in a given way without some antecedent interpretive perspective.[1] Thus it is proper that we begin with a recognition on some viable alternatives that have claimed some significant adherence.[2]

We may identify three general variables that are characteristically present in efforts at Old Testament theology. First, it is clear that the Old Testament did not originate in a historical-cultural vacuum, but was formed fully within the matrix of ancient Near Eastern culture and history. The archaeological gains of the past 200 years have given scholarship what seems to be a reliable sense of that culture and history that in large sweep consisted in a series of empires to the north of the land of Israel that rose and fell through various political encounters and military ambitions. To the south, the several dynasties of Egypt maintained a coherence and stability that anchored the southern end of the Fertile Crescent. The land of Israel that primally concerns the Old Testament is endlessly an arena of contestation between Egyptian power in the south and the sporadic imperial ambitions of the powers in the north. In the Old Testament period, this latter concerned the sequence of Assyrian, Babylonian, and Persian Empires, culminating at the end of the Old Testament period with the conquest of Alexander and the cultural domination of Hellenism.

It is clear, moreover, that these significant political-cultural establishments over the many centuries were not simply concentrations of power; they were, at the same time, of necessity, centers of artistic and cultural reflection, for human communities are inescapably symbol-constructing and symbol-practicing enterprises. As a consequence, the cultural-liturgical legacy of these centers of power and meaning produced an important and abidingly influential literature. In addition to a legacy of law and wisdom, the great political centers were also the great liturgical centers that generated, practiced, and preserved great liturgies through which the ruling regime was made legitimate and, derivatively, through which the world was made safe. Such liturgies that are at the same time theologically serious and politically interested regularly celebrated the ruling God as creator and preserver of the world, and the ruling king (dynasty) as the proximate regent and shepherd of the realm.

A specific subset of this general liturgic-mythic practice that pertains especially to the Old Testament is the *Canaanite religion* evidenced by the ancient library at Ugarit (Ras Shamra) that details the liturgic-mythic practice of religion of Israel's closest neighbors whereby, Baal, the God of generativity, presides over the well-being of the agricultural economy (Hosea 2).[3]

This liturgic material is now reasonably well known. There is no doubt that in context the practice of such liturgic generativity was taken with great seriousness. There is also no doubt that over time, the community that produced the Old Testament appropriated much of this common material and made use of it in its liturgic practice and in its theological self-understanding. The issue for Old Testament theology is the question of the extent to which Israel *appropriated* such material, the extent to which it radically *transformed* the material, and the extent to which it *rejected* the material that it found inimical to its own theological commitments. The answer to these questions determines the extent to which the Old Testament reflects *common theology* that was generic in the ancient Near East and the extent to which Israel's faith is distinctive and without parallel in its cultural environment.[4] The issue admits of no single, one-dimensional answer, because it is clear that appropriation, transformation, and rejection were all strategic possibilities in any given point in the theological articulation of Israel. This cultural-liturgical reality amounts to a crucial issue for Old Testament theology, because it concerns what is definitive in Old Testament faith, that is, what are the core claims that characterize the God of Israel and Israel as the people of that God. Over the stretch of the twentieth century—largely due to the confessing situation of the church in Germany and the decisive influence of Karl Barth mediated through Gerhard von Rad and G. Ernest Wright—Old Testament theology placed the accent characteristically upon Israel's distinctiveness, and so emphasized the contrast between the faith of Israel and the religious claims of its cultural environment.[5] Since the 1970s however, much of Old Testament scholarship has retreated from the boldest claims of theological distinctiveness and has more or less accepted that Israel's faith is best understood in close relation to that cultural-religious environment. It is evident, moreover, that one might acknowledge decisive accent points in Israel's faith, that is, God as Creator, and nonetheless recognize in such a theological theme a common theological heritage that is widely shared in the ancient Near East.[6]

Second, Old Testament theology, in the mainstream of modern Western critical scholarship, must take into account the critical tradition of scholarship, for decisions about the date, context, and sequence of the literature will be important for theological interpretation. Whereas much theological interpretation tends to disregard these critical matters and treat the material as an undifferentiated mass, scholars within the field of Old Testament study cannot disregard these differentiations but characteristically proceed on the assumption that *the date and context of a piece of literature* will inescapably *reflect the interpretive interests of that time and place*. For that reason, it has been a primary task of critical study to locate and situate distinct pieces of literature, in the conviction that the text characteristically reflects not the situation *reported* in the text, but the situation of the *reporting* tradition.

In taking up the critical tradition that is indispensable for theological interpretation, we may begin with the older critical consensus that goes under the label of *Wellhausianism.* This consensus was reached over two centuries of scholarship that was largely German and Protestant, and was given its normative articulation by Julius Wellhausen.[7] This consensus, known as the *documentary hypothesis*, proposed *a series of redactions* (editions) *of the narrative and legal material of the Pentateuch* that stretched from the early days of the monarchy to the exile. While that literary analysis is now critiqued and refined, the distinction of layers of literary material in the text continues to be a widely held assumption of critical scholars. But the hypothesis of Wellhausen is not concerned primarily with a sequence of literary redactions, even though such layers of traditions are readily acknowledged. Rather the important matter that is attached to the theory of literary editions was a hypothesis about *the course of Israelite religion*, so that the "early sources" were correlated with *primitive religion*, middle range sources with *ethical monotheism*, and later sources with *punctilious legalism*. That is, the hypothesis about *the history of the literature* was pressed into the service of *a history of religion*. While scholarship continues to practice some form of *source analysis*, the theory of the evolutionary development of Israelite religion in a unilinear fashion is now largely rejected. There is no doubt that this nineteenth-century hypothesis was deeply influenced by evolutionary categories of interpretation rooted in Hegel and maximized by Darwin. It is now clear that Israel's faith did not develop in such a unilinear way, but was in every setting of its life, complex and pluriform in practice and in expression.[8] While acknowledging this critique of the hypothesis, it is fair to say that the most elemental assumptions of Israel's religious history in the hypothesis continue to hold great sway among scholars, even though the assumptions have been shown to be imposed upon the material in a most inappropriate way. That is, there is still a widespread assumption of the move from primitive to ethical to legalistic. Aside from the specificity of the hypothesis, the crucial learning is that the fundamental assumptions of the interpreter that may lie beneath any critical judgment that is decisive for interpretive outcomes.

It is now clear that the documentary hypothesis, of course including a hypothesis concerning the history of Israelite religion, was not an innocent scholarly matter, as our hypotheses characteristically are not innocent. This is true even though scholars in the rising modern period no doubt proceeded in what they took to be an *objective* manner. It is evident that the hypothesis has a distinct Christian bias with an inchoate supersessionism implied, for the evolutionary dynamism of the hypothesis assumed that Israelite religion would keep moving until it "arrived" at a "better" faith, in the instant, Christian faith. Thus, taken at its worst, the hypothesis had an anti-Jewish tilt; for what was readily labeled as belated priestly legalism constituted what in fact was the funding of Judaism, albeit portrayed in Christian usage in a caricature. It is the case that this scholarship was largely the work of German Protestants who had a vigorous bias against cultic discipline and practice, and a great bias for ethical concerns. This bias, positively and negatively, permitted a less than critical, less than self-aware hypothesis that has dominated scholarship. The problem in critiquing the hypothesis has been to value the discernment of literary layers in the tradition, without attaching to those several layers *stages* in Israel's religious history.

The truth of the hypothesis is that the tradition of Israel's faith that became the Old Testament is complex, multilayered, and multivoiced; that it has a dynamism that is intrinsic to the substance of faith; that that dynamism moreover changes over time and through circumstance, and each such fresh articulation in a new circumstance, while rooted in what is remembered and treasured as normative, creates something of a theological novum. The attempt to order that dynamism and to identify the layers of that dynamism—the work of the dominant hypothesis—is hazardous indeed; but it is also an inescapable effort. Thus we are left, as theological interpreters, with the residue of that erstwhile critical consensus. The hypothesis has been committed to a certain notion of evolutionary dynamism, but it is important to recognize that the developmental dynamism, voiced in the hypothesis has enough of truth in it to have given credence to the hypothesis over a long period of time.[9] Alongside that credence, however, the hypothesis has conveniently served a propensity to *explain away* whatever is found to be objectionable in the tradition as *superseded* by what comes later.

By the 1970s, the consensus hypothesis of Wellhausianism began to collapse; by the turn of the century, the primary attention given to the hypothesis is by precritical scholars who continue to assault the hypothesis even though it now has few advocates. The collapse of the hypothesis was produced by a variety of factors and forces, but in general was a subset of the general collapse of the dominant paradigm of the West that featured the Vietnam War, the assassinations of the Kennedys and Martin Luther King, Paris student revolt, and the rise of a *liberation consciousness* that refused dominant paradigms of power and truth. In Old Testament studies, the key factor has been a widespread loss of confidence in the older claims made for archaeology as having a capacity to connect, in some detail, text and alleged context.[10] The earlier work of John Van Seters and Thomas Thompson, followed by the so-called minimalists, has made a strong case, in part embraced even by William Dever, that the claims made for the historicity of events and therefore the historicity of a context for the literature cannot be demonstrated, or in some measure even made credible.[11] The effect of this scholarly judgment that is now widely shared—though not unanimously—is to suggest that the early history of Israel is a quite belated memory (invention, fabrication) and not reportage. The critical conclusion that the ancestral narratives in Genesis are not historical has been followed by a widely shared critical judgment that the events of the thirteenth–eleventh centuries (Moses, Joshua, Samuel) are not historical, and the existence of David and Solomon is now widely contested. More radical critics, drawn to more negative critical judgments, raise issues about the historicity of Hezekiah and Josiah, so that clear historical ground for what the Bible asserts is at the earliest, for the most radical judgments, in the sixth or even fifth centuries.

The effect of this loss of confidence in historical reportage is the capacity to make the judgment that the several traditions concerning the "early period" of Israel's biblical history are ideological constructs that are precisely designed to fund the faith of the later community in the sixth or fifth century. And what was taken as *religious development* over the centuries is now best viewed as side-by-side renditions of faith that evidence profound and ongoing contestation about the character of God, the nature of faith, and the identity of Israel.

The critical matters in Old Testament scholarship that surround Old Testament theology are now deeply contested and unsettled. The influence of the old hypothesis persists because it did, in its own interpretive context, make a coherent sense of the text available. But whatever persists now about that hypothesis makes its way in a new situation in which historical claims are deeply problematic. As a consequence, the older phrase, "God acts in history," is problematic as it is now is to be taken as a confessional (or an ideological) statement that for the most part is seen to be constructive and not reportage. It is clear that such constructive confessionalism was multisided in ancient Israel and certainly in the period of emerging Judaism that Christians have long preferred to view in a simplistic reductionism. These continuing and unsettling critical problems of course concern Old Testament scholars more than they do other biblical interpreters. But other biblical interpreters as well, including theologians, cannot, in present circumstance, proceed without reference to these problems. As I shall indicate below, the conviction that what was taken as historical reportage in some sense constructed still leaves open important interpretive possibilities, notably that the text is constituted as a *canonical* claim with immense normative authority or that it is an *ideological* claim with a self-serving agenda barely concealed in the formation and transmission of the tradition. If we were to agree, as the minimalists now claim, that the formative work on the tradition was to serve the community that emerged from the deportation in the sixth and fifth centuries, this makes historical critical work no less urgent. Only now that critical work is not to hypothesize about the long development of religious tradition, but to focus on the more specific context of the post-deportation Judaism to try to learn the meaning of the contestation that is reflected in the complexity of the text. Old Testament theology, even in such a context, still depends upon historical-critical judgments that we make as best we can. It is the case, I suspect, that historical critical judgments operate either openly or covertly, even among those who seek to bracket out such vexed questions.

Third, alongside critical readings of the Old Testament that are crucial for Old Testament theology, there is no doubt that much theological interpretation is done in confessional, ecclesial communities that may be informed by critical study but in the long run intend to serve a particular community of faith. It is clear that the relationship between critical and confessional reading is always an uneasy one that admits of no final settlement. We may identify three such undertakings that pertain to biblical theology.

First, it is clear that Old Testament theology, in mainstream scholarship, has been, until recently, almost an exclusively Protestant Christian domain, or more particularly a German Protestant domain.[12] It was only after Karl Barth and the Confessing Church in Germany that Old Testament theology as a distinct and self-conscious discipline developed. In the wake of Barth, it is not surprising that such work was German and Protestant. Its strong representative figures in the mid-twentieth century were the Lutheran scholar Gerhard von Rad and the Calvinist scholar Walter Eichrodt.[13] It was a common assumption with Eichrodt and von Rad (and many less influential interpreters in the same period) that Old Testament interpretation led inescapably to the New Testament and to the affirmation of the gospel of Jesus Christ. Both von Rad and Eichrodt were of course alert to the complexity of the move from the Old Testament to the New and did not make a simple-minded connection between the two. Nevertheless, the connection is definitional for Old Testament theology in the mid-twentieth century, because their interpretive work was in *the Old Testament,* a designation that clearly and unapologetically implied the defining connection to the New. It is right to say that such a characteristic interpretive move was not intended or understood by them to be supersessionist or anti-Jewish, but was simply an unexamined interpretive maneuver that was taken for granted in Protestant Germany, given a lack of other conversation partners! The connection between the Old and New Testaments is characteristically made either as a "promise-and-fulfillment" scheme or as "salvation history" for which Jesus Christ is the fulfillment and culmination.[14]

Well through the twentieth century this common practice and unexamined interpretive maneuver held sway in the discipline. It was only with the direct and sharp challenge of Jon Levenson that scholars began to become alert to the implicit supersessionism that was embodied in this characteristic interpretive maneuver.[15] Indeed, Levenson's defining question, "Why Are Jews Not Interested in Biblical Theology?" is answered that biblical theology does not interest or engage Jewish interpreters because the regnant categories of interpretation are relentlessly and uncompromisingly Christian. Levenson's programmatic alert has, over time, had an immense impact upon the field.[16] While Christian scholars of course continue to write in and for the church, and so toward the distinctive Christian claim made for the gospel, there is a growing awareness among Christian scholars that claims made for the connection between the Old and New Testaments cannot be made in absolutist and exclusive terms.[17] Alongside such Christian claims, it must be readily acknowledged that other readings, of course specifically Jewish readings that eventuate in Judaism, are equally valid and so must be taken seriously by Christian interpreters.

Such an acknowledgment does not preclude Christian interpretation, but invites modesty and humility that knows other legitimate readings stand alongside such convinced readings. How we are to write as church theologians with an uncompromising allegiance to the gospel and at the same time acknowledge the equal legitimacy of Jewish reading is an open issue with which we will continue to struggle. In any case, we are a long distance now away from Bultmann's dictum that Old Testament history is "a history of failure."[18] The move toward the New Testament will inescapably be made in church interpretation; but it surely is now recognized that it is not the only interpretive move that can be made. Given the long history of Christian domination, moreover, room must be made for readings that place our own readings off center.

Second and conversely, in the latter part of the twentieth century the task of biblical theology has been freshly undertaken by Jewish scholars.[19] Levenson has forcefully called attention to Christian hegemony in the discipline; but it is also Levenson more than anyone else who has made significant contributions to biblical theology that exhibit a characteristic move from the text itself to the rabbinic tradition in a way that parallels, *mutatis mutandis*, Christian moves from the text to the New Testament.[20] While it is deeply rooted in Jewish tradition, Levenson's work offers the sort of compelling interpretation that evokes the engagement of interpreters well beyond the Jewish community.[21] That is, it is work to which informed Christians must pay attention. Particular attention should also be called to the programmatic essay of Goshen-Gottstein, who has reviewed the historical problem of Jews doing biblical theology and then concludes that the undertaking of such a task is a high priority for the next phase of scholarship:

> It was probably necessary to wait for the first half-century of Jewish academic Bible study to pass until we could allow ourselves the luxury of facing the bias on each side and put the question afresh: "What is Tanakh all about?" I have my ideas as to how a future Tanakh theology would be organized, based on the evaluation of *legoumena* on the relationship between God, people, and land, and how such a base line might contrast with later Jewish theologies. These and many other issues of content and method could not be raised in the first English outline which cannot be more than an attempt to direct our attention to what to me is a central and urgent issue of biblical studies. I can only hope that this essay will help to set the stage for a more realistic and deeply truthful atmosphere in the common work of Christians and Jews in the academic study of biblical religion.[22]

The new opening suggested by Goshen-Gottstein and pursued by Levenson has taken place in a slowly changing social context after the Shoah. The brutal elimination of Jews with the silent permit of Christians has required a new humility among Christians about hegemonic claims, both political and exegetical.[23] That new humility has permitted a recognition of the legitimacy of Jewish exegesis—not to say

Jewish existence—which exhibits the shame of every Christian "Final Solution," even final solutions of an exegetical variety. Many factors have helped to create a new situation in which Jews may be regarded, by Christians, as important companions in the interpretive process, without a compromise on either side about the seriousness of confessional, ecclesial commitments.[24] The new environment that makes fresh critical reading possible is strikingly articulated in the statement of Jewish scholars, Dabru Emet.[25] This is a most welcome reference point for future work. That welcome reference point both requires and invites Christian interpreters to position themselves alongside Jewish readers and not in a position of dominance over as has been mostly assumed in actual practice. Such alongsidedness, when taken seriously, makes it possible to recognize that many Christian interpretive efforts have in fact been deceptively self-serving and quaintly parochial in ways that do not have to do with core confessional commitments.

Alongside conventional Protestant dominance in Old Testament theology and newly emerging Jewish engagement with the discipline, we may identify as a third confessional, ecclesial practice of recent interest in what has come to be called *canonical criticism*.[26] The term is notoriously elusive and the meaning of the phrase is not agreed upon. Taken generically, the task of so-called canonical criticism is to consider the biblical text in the way it is given us through the traditioning process that has been shaped by the believing community without excessive regard to the complicated prehistory of the text or excessive preoccupation with critical study that has tended to break the wholistic theological intentionality of the text by analytic fragmentation. This work tends to be *postcritical*, taking criticism into account but moving beyond it with confident theological nerve approximating what Ricoeur terms a *second naiveté*.[27] We may distinguish two more-or-less programmatic efforts at such a canonical approach. First, James Sanders has been occupied with the ongoing and open-ended dynamism of the text and the textual-interpretive tradition that is always pushing toward the normative. At the same time, however, that push toward the normative is always being challenged by dialogic openness that responds to the particular environment in which the text is being formed, transmitted, and interpreted. Most recently Sanders has written:

> The Bible is a dialogical literature that in turn gave rise to two dialogical religions based on it. The issue of the date of closure of the various canons of the two religions, the Tanak and the Talmud, and the

> double-testament Christian Bible, is elusive and difficult to pinpoint, now that we are freed of the Yavneh/Jamnia or conciliar mentality. Is it so important after all? Whatever a church council has done to declare its canon closed served to recognize and ratify what had come to be practiced in the majority of believing communities, as well as to curb the intra-canonical dialogue. Any such effort within Rabbinic Judaism would simply have become part of further debate. The closures enveloped enough internal dialogue for the process of repetition/recitation, which had started it all, to continue unabated in the communities that find their embracing identity in their canon. No closure can curb the dialogue that is inherent in a canon of scripture, which, over against the *magisteria* and *regulae fidei* that developed after closure in all churches, mandates dialogue about its continuing relevance and authority. A canon is basically a community's paradigm for how to continue the dialogue in ever changing socio-political contexts. Leaders within a community, the scribes, the translators, the teachers, the preachers, the midrashists and the commentators, precisely those convinced of its continuing relevance, have been and are tradents of the text, those who bring the text's past into the present in the contemporary terms of their ongoing community.[28]

Sanders's concern is to resist the notion that the canon—the normative text—is flat, closed, and one-dimensional in a way that precludes the work of ongoing dialogue.

Second, and by far the more influential, is the work of Brevard Childs in which the notion of canon has evolved to different understandings over time.[29] The initial impetus for Childs's programmatic work has been his awareness that critical study had not only fragmented the text, but has weakened if not nullified the large theological claim of the text that governs all parts of the text and that delivers the text, within the community of faith, as a wholistic, normative, theological statement. Thus his work is initially a response to the outcomes of historical critical work that eventually has detracted from the theologically normative character of the biblical text.

In important ways Childs stands in continuity with the work of the great German Protestant interpreters of the twentieth century and is peculiarly and gladly indebted to Barth in his readiness to take on the core theological task of interpretation, even at the cost of overriding historical critical interest. But Childs is also deeply critical of the great German scholars who were his teachers, because they permitted the critical issues to detract from a definitive and intentional theological focus.

In his major and formidable book of 1993, Childs offered what is for now the culmination of his canonical reflection, that the Old Testament and New Testament are two witnesses to Jesus Christ. It is clear that Childs is, without compromise or apology, doing Christian theology; he is of course aware of Jewish biblical theology, but understands that as a quite distinct task in which he has no interest and with which he has no quarrel. Childs of course is a master of historical criticism as is evident in his several commentaries; but his work is to move beyond critical study and not to be deterred by it. I suggest that with Childs the task of relating *critical study* and *theological exposition* to each other is not of great interest, but continues to be in any case an unresolved issue. In his work of 1993, Childs offers a full exposition of "The Discrete Witness of the Old Testament" (95–207) and "The Discrete Witness of the New Testament."[30] This is followed, after a small pause, by "Theological Reflection on the Christian Bible."[31] It is clear that Childs, along with the rest of us, has not found a compelling way to integrate those "discrete witnesses" to his reading of "The Christian Bible." That work of integration is a task that requires our continuous attention, even while we receive important clues from Childs.

We may distinguish three terms that are crucial for Childs that will serve us well as we consider the task of theological interpretation:

1. *The Final Form of the Text.* By this Childs evidences his lack of interest in the prehistory of the text that has been a primary preoccupation of guild scholarship. The text as we have it is the product of the believing community, so that the very form of the text as given in the canon is itself a defining theological datum. This focus of interpretive attention will be appealing to theological interpreters outside the world of Old Testament scholarship who incline to take the text as it is.

2. *The Plain Meaning of the Text.* In this usage, Childs stands within a long tradition that takes *plain meaning* not to refer to a surface impression of the text, but the meaning that has been found in Christian practice, meaning that points characteristically to Jesus Christ as the true subject of the text. This point has been made especially clear in his recent study of the history of interpretation of the book of Isaiah; characteristically Christian theology has read the book of Isaiah with reference to Jesus, even though it is clear in Childs's own commentary on Isaiah that Childs does not disregard more conventional historical interpretation.[32]

3. *The Rule of Faith.* This phrase, though admittedly somewhat enigmatic, refers to the normative confessional presuppositions of the church

with reference to the Christological and trinitarian claims formulated in the great early councils of the church. It is Childs's insistence that in the end, biblical theology of the Old and New Testaments must focus on the Rule of Faith that gives center, focus, and coherence to all of the canon:

> The church struggles with the task of continually discerning the truth of God being revealed in scripture and at the same time she stands within a fully human, ecclesiastical tradition which remains the tradent of the Word. The hearing of God's Word is repeatedly confirmed by the Holy Spirit through its resonance within the church's christological rule-of-faith.
>
> In sum, the proposal being made is not that of developing a canon-within-the-canon, nor is it of identifying the canon with accumulated ecclesiastical tradition. Rather, the complete canon of the Christian church as the rule-of-faith sets for the community of faith the proper theological context in which we stand, but it also remains continually the object of critical theological scrutiny subordinate to its subject matter who is Jesus Christ. This movement from the outer parameters of tradition to the inner parameters of Word is constitutive of the theological task.[33]

Childs's powerful advocacy seeks to establish that proper biblical interpretation is not only within an ecclesial community—as distinct from the critical guild—but also with a theological intentionality that characteristically submits the elements and details of the text to the larger theological claim that pervades the whole, a claim that is its *canonical* sense.

While Childs's proposal is highly contested and easily critiqued for its reductionism, he has posed primal questions for the task of biblical theology. While I am deeply impacted by the work of Childs, I have not, even as he judges, fully subscribed to his way of reading the text. I believe that much of what he attributes to the text is an imposition that fails to take the text in terms of its own seriousness. I find much more congenial to my own perspective the dynamism of Sanders that keeps the *normative* in some tension with the adaptable. It is clear that in the formation of the canonical text, the canonizing pressure so accented by Childs was not able to overcome the detail of the text that does not conform to that intentionality. One may judge that the material was so intransigently powerful that the canonical intention was not able to prevail; or alternatively one may conclude, as do I, that such overcoming was not such a grand intention as Childs proposes. In any case, these are elements of the current discussion that need to be taken into serious account.

It is not surprising that the subject of Old Testament theology encompasses a rich array of experimentation that stretches all the way from *ancient Near Eastern parallels* to the classical formulations of church faith under the heading *of "Rule of Faith."* I have traced in brief form the impact of *ancient Near Eastern culture and liturgy, the classical tradition of criticism,* and *the compelling power of the ecclesial confessional community.* And yet, after all of that, it remains to be said that the *world* attested in the Old Testament is so *strange* and so *new*—beyond all of our horizons and categories—that it will not readily or fully submit to any of our preferred themes or categories, either historical or theological or canonical.[34] After we have done our best work and vigorously pursued our most passionate modes of reading, the text—and the God featured in the text—remain inscrutable and undomesticated. Partly the reason for that inscrutability and lack of domestication is that the text in its final form is complex and pluralistic, hosting a variety of traditioning and interpreting voices that become normative traditions. More than that, however, the inscrutability and lack of domestication in the text are a consequences of the God attested in these pages who is Holy Other. This God, in the end, is no more accommodated to the normative traditions of the church than to what was culturally hegemonic in the ancient Near East. However this strangeness and newness are to be understood, it is evident that articulation in Hebrew rhetoric and grammar serves this elusive, irascible God well; the rabbis have always seen that there is a curious, playful, undecipherable dimension to this God and to the way in which the canonical voice brings that God to articulation. Old Testament theology has as its task the attempt to make some coherent sense out of this material; but such coherent sense is characteristically hazardous because our explanatory modes of discourse run immediately in the direction of idolatry, of producing a God who is discernable, explicable, and therefore to some extent manageable. The one who meets us here, however, is as hidden as discernable, as inscrutable as explicable, and as subversive as manageable. The attempt to write an Old Testament theology is a risky business, as risky as touching the ark of the covenant (see 2 Samuel 6:6-8).

It follows, does it not, that every risky attempt at Old Testament theology including this one, disciplined and informed as it might be, is a quite personal effort, even if lined out from and toward responsible scholarship and serious faith. It is personal and to that extent inescapably subjective, even if it is cast in the sure tone of infallibility that tempts both academic and ecclesial interpreters. This characterization of our work is fully and variously acknowledged:

> It needs only to be mentioned at this juncture that no one is in a position to know in which direction a possible new consensus may lead. However, since this outlook is not likely to change in the near future, the following discussion will dare to venture an opinion here and there about debated issues (e.g., the existence or dating of the so-called Yahwist). While taking such a position is risky, the attempt will still be made. This effort proceeds with the full recognition of the danger that the presentation is both its entirety and each of its parts cannot be "fully informed by the current (and perhaps a very particular) scholarly stance." However, one cannot simply throw up one's hands in despair at either lagging behind the contemporary scholarly understandings of various issues or, having assimilated them, finding that the discussion has moved forward.[35]

> In a Christian context there exists today a field of inquiry within Old Testament studies that cannot be divorced from personal position or even axiomatic attitudes, and I do not think I am far off the mark if I suggest that this inquiry plays a much larger role within the total academic activity than we like to admit to ourselves in our idealized picture of what modern nondenominational scholarly biblical study is about. . . . Yet the more we deal with aspects of meaning, of the biblical text in its final form—from textual unit to canon and message—the less can we avoid our personal background and attitude.[36]

Given that severe reality that evokes humility, the interpreter must nonetheless proceed as best he or she can in an intrepid way. I do so with a full heart, enormous indebtedness to many colleagues, and hope for freshness yet to be given.

II. THE PRIMAL DISCLOSURES

CHAPTER TWO

A PRIMAL REVELATION (EXODUS 3:1–4:17)

YHWH appeared abruptly to Moses at Horeb (Exodus 3:1-6). It is this reassuring, demanding, summoning meeting that sets in motion the narrative of the exodus emancipation of the slaves and from that the entire account of Israel's life with YHWH. It could well be argued that this meeting is the decisive one for all of Old Testament faith. I will not insist upon that, but only that it is a characteristic meeting of disclosure, arguably the most definitive, that exhibits many of the most characteristic elements of Israel's faith.

Our beginning focus is upon the theophanic encounter (Exodus 3:1-6), but that encounter is embedded in the larger narrative of Exodus 2:25–4:17 that will eventually concern us. The theophany itself amounts to an abrupt intrusion into the life of Moses and the life of Israel, unexpected and inexplicable. That of course is precisely the nature of YHWH who, in the narrative of Israel, is an originary character without antecedents. YHWH appears in the narrative fully identified and established. There are, of course, many religious antecedents to YHWH and a religious environment of the ancient Near East, and scholars have used great energy on that data.[1] In the narrative, however, YHWH is underived and capable of direct intrusion into the narrative life of Israel without preparation or antecedent. Thus there is, in the purview of Israel, no *prehistory* to YHWH.

The theophanic report permits us to make four observations that pertain to the general project of Old Testament theology:

1. YHWH's appearance to Moses is not self-exhibit. It is rather purposeful, summoning, and demanding. Thus the very first utterance of YHWH in this narrative is the double address to Moses to which Moses must give prompt and submissive response: "Here I am" (v. 4). YHWH's initial utterance is as a sovereign who dominates the situation, who will impose a purpose on Moses, and who will be obeyed.

2. YHWH's self-commitment concerns YHWH's holiness that derivatively causes the ground on which YHWH stands to be holy (v. 5). The utterance of the term *holy* at the outset makes a primal claim for YHWH. YHWH is not, as the other gods of Moses' environment, useful or available for any human intention. YHWH is for YHWH's self and YHWH's purposes, and is on that account unapproachable as an ominous presence. Moses is put on notice that this is no user-friendly God. While the term *holy* is used almost in passing, this beginning point leads to a trajectory of holiness that includes the well-known song of the divine counsel in Isaiah 6:3: "And one called to another and said: / '*Holy*, *holy*, *holy* is the LORD of hosts; / the whole earth is full of his glory' " (emphasis added).

Through the course of Israel's life YHWH is an overwhelming and demanding presence, a presence that is capable of life and death, of judgment and rescue. The term *holy* is used twice more in the Exodus narrative. In Exodus 12:16, the Passover and celebration of unleavened bread is a *holy convocation*, marking Israel's distinctiveness as YHWH's rescued people. And in Exodus 15:13, the term "holy abode" refers to the goal of the exodus trek, referring either to the *holy land* or to the Jerusalem temple. These latter usages are, of course, derivative from YHWH's own unparalleled self.

3. Related to YHWH's holiness is Moses' fear at seeing God (v. 6). This refusal on Moses' part is a characteristic acknowledgment in Israel that YHWH is a fully embodied, fully visible person. For the project of Old Testament theology, it will not do to spiritualize away the fully embodied character of YHWH, for Israel's theological articulation has no fear of or embarrassment about such an embodied sense of God. That is, there is no apology for what modern categories apologetically label *anthropomorphisms*. This embodied sense of YHWH is, of course, commensurate with an Old Testament affirmation of the goodness of embodied creation and a fully embodied human personhood. A great deal of unfortunate mischief has been caused by modern embarrassment about such so-called anthropomorphisms of Old Testament rhetoric, a practice that constitutes no problem or awkwardness for Israel's own discourse in faith. The

materiality of the entire project is of immense importance; theological interpretation must resist rightly every effort to overcome such "primitive" materiality. And of course for Christian interpretation and its commitment to the *incarnation*, this embodiment of YHWH is acutely important.

4. YHWH, in addressing Moses, identifies YHWH as the God of the Genesis ancestors (v. 6). Common critical judgment holds that the ancestral narratives developed without connection to the Mosaic tradition.[2] It is clear, however, that the canonical tradition takes great care to make an intrinsic connection. The importance of that connection in this instant is that it is the *God of Promise* who now addresses Moses; in the verses that follow, the old promises made to the family of Abraham are now deployed to the community of Moses. And because the core promise is to the land, the Moses tradition can now anticipate the deportation from Egyptian slavery as the beginning of the journey to the land. The slaves and all the generations that follow are now recipients of YHWH's promissory fidelity.

Thus the narrative of theophany gives us primal themes for the larger task of Old Testament theology:

- YHWH as a God of purposeful summons
- YHWH as holy in all the ominous severity of that term
- YHWH as fully embodied as an acute agent in the life of the world and the life of Israel
- YHWH's promissory commitment to the community of Moses that is focused on the gift of the land

The theophanic report, in fact, continues through verse 10, but the divine statement of verses 7-10 will be held in abeyance until we consider the premise of the theophanic narrative in Exodus 2:23-25.

The theophanic entry of YHWH into the life of Moses and Israel is to be understood in context where it is clear that the entry of YHWH into the life of Israel is not simply by "divine initiative." Exodus 2:23-25 makes clear that YHWH's entry is in fact a response to human utterance; the initiative is taken by Israel's address to YHWH in 2:23. The recognition of verse 23 as the beginning of the exodus plot is of enormous importance; it makes clear that Israel can take an initiative, can break its silence and announce itself, and can evoke a response from the holy God. This narrative arrangement suggests a profoundly dialogical structure to Old

Testament faith and speaks against any conventional theological notion of the exclusive reality of divine initiative. The importance of this narrative beginning can hardly be overstated for all that follows.

The Israelites were held a long time in slavery, ever since their father Joseph sold them out to Pharaoh (see Genesis 47:13-27). The memory of that long travail is obscure, and we do not know the names or dates of any of the pertinent pharaohs. (And, in any case, by the time of this text, "pharaoh" has become a cipher for every oppressive power. The narrative needs to be read as Eric Voegelin has suggested, as "paradigmatic.")[3] The regime of Pharaoh is remembered as stifling and exploitative in every regard, whereby the underlings in their pain and resentment are completely silenced.

Such silencing, as every abusive regime eventually discovers, cannot finally be sustained. At the death of Pharaoh, as often happens with regime change, the slaves find voice. Israel, the slave community, enters history when it finds its voice.[4] Their initial utterance, after a long, unbearable silence, is the raw, unrestrained, undifferentiated shriek of pain. Israel "cried out" and so began its history. The cry is not aimed at anyone; it is not addressed anywhere. It is the most elemental human insistence, the rawest bottom-line sense of entitlement that is given "airtime" for all to hear. We do not know, in this case, if the slaves knew anything of YHWH or of the Genesis promises. If they do, they do not here make an appeal to YHWH or to YHWH's promises. Matters are too raw and inchoate for such a particular reference.

The dramatic leap in the middle of Exodus 2:23 is remarkable and should not be passed over easily. "The Israelites . . . cried . . . . their cry . . . rose up to God." The slaves did not raise up a cry to God. But the cry had its own intentionality. The cry knew, all on its own, that it was precisely addressed to "God." The "God" so addressed is not named. In context, the reference is unmistakably to YHWH. YHWH is like a magnet that draws such cries, for it is YHWH who receives, is affected by, and responds to the cry of those uncredentialed nobodies that now begin their history. In commenting on Psalm 82, James Kugel comments:

> It says that hearing the victim's cry is a god's duty and God's duty. It says that if that job is not properly performed, the very foundations of the earth will shake. . . . It was simply any god's job to be compassionate and merciful, and this truth was so universally assumed in the Bible that, as we have seen, it underlies the dozens of passages that speak of the victim's cry. Yet here, in Exodus, this cliché is presented as a revelation.

> God's ultimate self-revelation to Moses: I am by nature *ḥannun* and *raḥum* (despite all evidence to the contrary). I hear the cry of the victim; I can't help it.[5]

The response of YHWH is full and complete (Exodus 2:23-24). God *heard*! God *remembered*; the statement permits the judgment that YHWH had not until now remembered the Genesis promises; it was only the *cry of the silenced* that evoked an active divine remembering. The divine response concludes tersely, "God *saw*, God *knew*." YHWH is now fully attentive to the situation of the silenced who now have voice. It is this exchange of "cry-hear" that evokes the theophany in chapter 3 that we have already considered.

It is impossible to overstate the importance of the "cry-save" dialogue for the faith of Israel.[6] The pattern recurs often in the narratives. It is, moreover, the dominant dialogic structure of Israel's prayer practice in the book of Psalms. The pattern assumes that Israel's faith is deeply and pervasively dialogical. This pattern assures, on the one hand, that Israel is a fully entitled and fully empowered partner in the exchange who is able to take initiative and has legitimate ground for addressing YHWH with imperatives (though here, there are no explicit imperatives). The narrative exchange assumes, on the other hand, that YHWH is readily and regularly drawn into an interactive relationship with Israel and is summoned and evoked to do what YHWH would not do, except for Israel's complaint. This articulation of YHWH, of course, flies in the face of much theology that is rooted in classical understandings that does not want to imagine God so much at risk in the transaction of faith. Against the safer assumption of classical formulation, Karl Barth can conclude about prayer that prayer causes God to do what God would not otherwise do: "God is not deaf, but listens; more than that, he acts. God does not act in the same way whether we pray or not. Prayer exerts an influence upon God's action, even upon his existence."[7]

Thus in the context of these verses, we may imagine that it is the cry of Israel that evoked the exodus rescue of YHWH; without the cry then, there would have been no exodus.

In the dramatic introduction of "cry-save," it is also the case that the drama provides grounds for the option of unresponsiveness and infidelity, for the possibility that YHWH may be absent, silent, and indifferent.[8] But of course such absence, silence, or indifference is not present here! Here YHWH is fully responsive and fully engaged in a way that causes a decisive turn in history.

On the basis of this initial *cry* and *divine response*, the theophany is enacted that evokes the promissory power of the family of Abraham, a promise already mentioned in 2:24. The linkage between *Abrahamic promise* and the *Mosaic community of slaves* is an important interpretive maneuver, thus connecting YHWH's most elemental promises to Israel with nondescript "rabble" now become the bearers of that promise (Exodus 12:38).[9]

The theophanic declaration of Exodus 3:5-6 is continued in verses 7-9, a divine oracle dominated, as was Exodus 2:24-25, by first-person verbs: "I have observed; I have heard; I know; I have come down." The first three verbs are reiterated from 2:24-25. The fourth verb, "came down," is an advance in divine speech. This verb, in spatial imagery, remarkably traces the condescension of God into the pain of human history, a descent that will figure powerfully in Christian articulation of the significance of Jesus. Attached to that fourth verb are two crucial verbs that summarize the core narrative of Israel's faith: "to *deliver*... to *bring out*... to *bring up*."[10] Thus the narrative stretches from slavery to the land of well-being, and anticipates the total reversal of the fortunes of Israel wrought singularly by YHWH's own commitment.[11] Verse 9 offers a reprise on the whole; the primary weight of divine commitment in verses 7-8 is to assure the transformation of Israel from a rabble of slaves to a community secure in a blessed land.

The powerful sequence of verbs in 2:24-25 and 3:7-9 with YHWH as subject indicate YHWH's deep resolve; given that sequence, we are scarcely prepared for verse 10: "So come, I will send you to Pharaoh to bring my people, the Israelites, out of Egypt" (Exodus 3:10).

After the divine resolve of the preceding, that resolve now turns abruptly into human mandate. It is Moses, not YHWH, who will make a demanding, risky approach to Pharaoh. To be sure, YHWH will "be with you," but Moses is the point person. This move is a most important one for Old Testament theology; it attests that Israel's faith is not intoxicated with *supernaturalism*, but in a realistic way understands the decisiveness of human agency for newness in the historical process. It is possible to think in terms of a *double agency*, but in the end human history is made by human agency.[12] The result is that the reality and *activity* of YHWH are in fact distanced from specific salvific events. This has immense importance for biblical theology:

- Long ago Gerhard von Rad discerned the way in which David emerges as a historical agent and YHWH recedes into a surreptitious governance behind the scene, for which 2 Samuel 17:14 is an importance reference point.[13]

■ The capacity to "stir up" agents in the world scene, especially concerning Nebuchadnezzar and Cyrus, in order to enact decisive change in international politics, is yet another example of the cruciality of human agency (Isaiah 41:2, 25).

■ In Christian derivation, the role of Jesus as the embodiment and agent of YHWH's will and purpose in the world is decisive for faith. Indeed the relationship of "the Son" to "the Father," however the language is understood, is of course a characteristic double agency in the bringing of the new regime in the earth.

It is no stretch to see that Karl Marx's notion of "man come of age" as "actors in their own history" is a derivation from this fundamental mandate of YHWH.[14] In the purview of biblical faith, human history is a scene of human action propelled by the authority, legitimacy, and empowerment of YHWH's will. The remainder of this text in Exodus 3:11–4:17 is a negotiation to secure the acceptance of the divine mandate for human agency. This text consists in five reservations on the part of Moses, and five insistent responses on the part of YHWH, yet another clear presentation of the dialogic work of biblical theology.

■ The first objection of Moses receives an assurance of divine accompaniment (Exodus 3:12). The Bible characteristically affirms such an affirmation in the form of a salvation oracle (Isaiah 41:8-13; 43:1-5); but also characteristic is the refusal to say how such accompaniment works and what difference it may make.

■ The second question of Moses (Exodus 3:13) receives an extended and complex divine response (Exodus 3:14-22). As much as any other text, this text struggles to articulate the identity of YHWH and recognizes the complexity, hiddenness, and inscrutability of that name before which "every knee shall bow" (Isaiah 45:23). Two responses are given to Moses' question concerning name and identity. First, the name is given full enigmatic play in Exodus 3:14: "God said to Moses, 'I AM WHO I AM.' He said further, 'Thus you shall say to the Israelites, I AM has sent me to you.' "

This formulation is notoriously difficult. It may be, as Frank Cross has urged, related to YHWH as "creator," playing on the verb *hayah*, "to be," or in the causative, "to cause to be."[15] However the grammar be taken, the formula asserts YHWH's full distinctive, peculiar self without handing over the mystery of YHWH to Moses or to Israel. The God who dispatches Moses remains undeciphered and undomesticated. The enigmatic formula of this verse has been a long practiced field day for all sorts of speculation, most especially by more philosophic theologians who push the text toward a notion of *being*.[16] The text is open to such a reading, though it seems remote from the rhetorical field of Israel's own discourse. Better to leave the phrase enigmatic as is the God named by the formula, and to let the inscrutability of the formula be filled out, as it is in the text, by the more familiar formulation of verse 15. It is as though the God who utters verse 14 is immediately aware that Moses needs more clues and so the formula is properly followed by, "God also said to Moses." The "also" of divine self-disclosure is YHWH as the God of the ancestors in Genesis, the one who makes and keeps promises. It is of this formula (and not that of v. 14) that God says: "This is my name forever, / and this my title for all generations" (Exodus 3:15).

That reference to the ancestors has already been articulated in Exodus 2:24 and 3:6, and will be repeated again in 3:16. There is little doubt that the ancestral stories that testify to divine presence and divine fidelity are a distinct tradition in ancient Israel and have no original linkage to the Moses community. Yet there is also no doubt that the ancestral narratives of promise were fully incorporated into the horizon of Mosaic faith. For the larger purposes of Old Testament theology, we can see in this incorporation a characteristic dynamism of biblical faith that preserves, respects, and takes seriously older remembered tradition and causes it, in new usage, to serve new purposes. Now in Exodus 3:15 the ancestral references place the exodus narrative of Moses under the rubric of promise. Moses is yet one more human agent recruited by YHWH to move Israel and the life of the world toward YHWH's larger intention; the dynamism of incorporation and reinterpretation is everywhere characteristic of this theological tradition. It is the promissory God of the Genesis tradition who now sets postslave life in motion for Israel:

> I have given heed to you and to what has been done to you in Egypt. I declare that I will bring you up out of the misery of Egypt, to the land of the Canaanites, the Hittites, the Amorites, the Perizzites, the Hivites, and the Jebusites, a land flowing with milk and honey. (Exodus 3:16b-17)

The divine oracle extends to the end of the chapter (vv. 18-22). In addition to the characteristic and normative promises made to the slaves concerning the land of promise, the oracle anticipates (a) the confrontation with the king of Egypt, (b) a refusal on the part of Pharaoh to allow the worship of YHWH, and (c) a resolve on YHWH's part to do "wonders" that will accomplish the release of the Hebrews. The identity of YHWH in terms of the ancestors places all of Israel's history under promise.

The identity of YHWH permits an anticipation of "wonders" that will overpower the defiant pharaoh. In context the term refers, first of all, to the plagues that will be enacted in Exodus 6–11 in a way that will astonish Pharaoh and eventually defeat him. Taken in larger scope, Israel's tradition of doxology is essentially a recital of a normative list of divine wonders, that is, explicable and inscrutable shows of power that ran beyond human capacity or human imagination. In its doxologies, Israel has a rich vocabulary for such *impossibilities*, for the miracles are central to the faith of Israel:[17]

> I will extol you, my God and King,
> and bless your name for ever and ever.
> Every day I will bless you,
> and praise your name for ever and ever.
> Great is the LORD, and greatly to be praised;
> his greatness is unsearchable.
>
> One generation shall laud your works to another,
> and shall declare your mighty acts.
> On the glorious splendour of your majesty,
> and on your wondrous works, I will meditate.
> The might of your awesome deeds shall be proclaimed,
> and I will declare your greatness.
> They shall celebrate the fame of your abundant goodness,
> and shall sing aloud of your righteousness. (Psalm 145:1-7)

It is typical that the inventory of miracles, so well attested in Israel's hymns, characteristically refers to YHWH's manifestation of sovereignty in both *nature* and *history*, both spheres that are ultimately presided over and responsible to YHWH. The plague in exodus narratives that follow, as Fretheim has demonstrated, constitute a contest between Pharaoh *the destroyer of creation* and YHWH *the generator and protector of creation* who as God of life prevails over the regime of brutality and death.[18] The outcome of that contest is reported in Exodus 16—just after the departure—when the gifts of the creator's abundance are enacted for Israel even in the wilderness where there is no life-sustaining infrastructure.[19] The defeat of Pharaoh by "miracles" makes possible the restoration of creation in its fruitfulness, given precisely to those who are now beyond the deathliness of slavery under Pharaoh. All of this is anticipated in the promise of triumphant "wonders" that will override Pharaoh's regime: "I know, however, that the king of Egypt will not let you go unless compelled by a mighty hand. So I will stretch out my hand and strike Egypt with all my *wonders* that I will perform in it; after that he will let you go" (Exodus 3:19-20, italics added).

The category of "wonders" concerns an inscrutable capacity on the part of YHWH that lies beyond the explanatory power of the learned regime of Pharaoh. There is nothing here violating *natural order*, but only the doxological conviction that YHWH's rule pertains in decisive ways to the future and well-being of the earth.

Finally in this second part of Moses' resistance in Exodus 3:13, YHWH responds that Israel will not leave slavery empty-handed, but will depart with the jewelry and clothing of the empire. It is possible that this reference (see also Exodus 11:2) relates to Israel's "year of release" where the poor are not to be left "empty-handed" (Deuteronomy 15:13). Thus the God who responds to Moses is

- *an enigmatic God* who will not disclose God's self fully, even to Moses;
- *a promissory God* already known among the ancestors;
- *a releasing God* who makes provision for those who depart slavery to enter an emancipated economy.

The enigmatic, promissory, releasing God is one who enacts "miracles" that confound the wisdom and power of the established order of the earth (see Isaiah 19:11-15).

Moses' third objection to YHWH concerns Israel's capacity to trust him in his advocacy of departure from slavery (Exodus 4:1). The term *amen*, rendered in the New Revised Standard Version (NRSV) as "believe," means to rely upon enough to act boldly in the face of pharaonic power. Moses' question reminds us that the intention of YHWH is completely "outside the box" of thinkable, political options for the slaves. And, of course, YHWH's inimitable response to Moses concerns manifestations of power through two "miracles" with the prospect of even a third (vv. 2-5). Most important, the God who summons Moses upon whom Israel is to rely is, yet again, the God of the Genesis ancestors. Reliance upon this God as an alternative to conventional imperial slavery is foundational to all that follows. That reliance is d and so it is attested in Exodus 14:30-31 by a great man inscrutable power that decisively overturns the power of the also 4:31).[20]

Moses' fourth objection concerns his ineptness at the kind of speech that will be required before Pharaoh (Exodus 4:10). YHWH's response, not unlike that made to Jeremiah but more fully expressed (see Jeremiah 1:4-10), is that it is YHWH, the creator God, who gives speech and who determines the status of all human beings. That is, YHWH is capable of doing whatever YHWH pleases, including making the mute speak. This sweeping claim is echoed in the later narrative text of Daniel:

> You shall be driven away from human society, and your dwelling shall be with the wild animals. You shall be made to eat grass like oxen, you shall be bathed with the dew of heaven, and seven times shall pass over you, until you have learned that the Most High has sovereignty over the kingdom of mortals, and gives it to whom he will. . . . You shall be driven away from human society, and your dwelling shall be with the animals of the field. You shall be made to eat grass like oxen, and seven times shall pass over you, until you have learned that the Most High has sovereignty over the kingdom of mortals and gives it to whom he will. (Daniel 4:25, 32)

YHWH is unencumbered and presides over human power in complete and effective freedom. Thus Moses' inadequacy is no impediment, given divine resolve.

The fifth reservation of Moses in 4:13 is a feeble one. Most remarkably, YHWH, in a response, seems to concede a point to Moses' cowardice or ineptness; YHWH authorizes Aaron to speak instead of Moses. Conversely, this provision would seem to subvert the claim of verse 11. But perhaps if we juxtapose the two responses of YHWH we may see that YHWH is capable of *strident sovereignty* (v. 11) and of *compassionate accommodation* (vv. 14-17). The narrative is terse, but there is no doubt that YHWH is agile and free, free enough either to override Moses or to accommodate Moses, surely a rich characterization of this deeply engaged alternative to Pharaoh.

The exchange between Moses and YHWH is one of both remarkable intimacy and bold recognition. The outcome of this exchange is that *divine purpose*, which intends to curb the pharaonic pretension of human power, is now allied with *human designation*. The paradigmatic encounter is between YHWH and Pharaoh or YHWH and the Egyptian gods (see Exodus 12:12). But the primary agent in the encounter, according to the narrative, is Moses. The narrative exhibits a characteristic capacity in the Old Testament to speak at the same time of *divine intention* and *human engagement*. The two are never confused; except in quite late texts in the Old Testament, the Old Testament eschews one-dimensional supernaturalism and focuses upon human agency to accomplish divine intent.[21]

This initial self-disclosure of YHWH contains within it the primary motifs that are likely to dominate any Old Testament theology. We may summarize these themes in three groupings:

1. *The narrative functions to serve YHWH's self-disclosure as one who arrives on the scene of Egyptian oppression without antecedent or explanation.*

■ YHWH is offered in an originary self-disclosure; YHWH's entry into the life of the world and into the life of Israel requires no explanatory antecedents. YHWH is characteristically beyond the explanatory power of Israel and will be contained in none of the conventional categories of ancient Near Eastern religion. Thus if we think theologically (rather in terms of the history of religion), it is not credible to explain YHWH as derived or emergent from the religious environment of the ancient Near East. Israel is left always dazzled by YHWH. For this reason, Israel's characteristic mode of faith is not explanatory theology but yielding doxology.[22] The faith of Israel is grounded in awe and voiced as praise.

■ YHWH is holy... unapproachable, awesome, even ominous... and so derivatively holy is whatever YHWH touches or occupies. YHWH's inapproachability and the danger of being in YHWH's presence set Israel on a long, rigorous, critical reflection about holiness.[23] Among the outcomes of this reflective process is the "holiness tradition" of the Priestly stretch of literature that seeks to sort out holy and profane, clean and unclean, a practice also undertaken in some prophetic traditions, notably Ezekiel:

> Its priests have done violence to my teaching and have profaned my holy things; they have made no distinction between the holy and the common, neither have they taught the difference between the unclean and the clean, and they have disregarded my sabbaths, so that I am profaned among them. (Ezekiel 22:26)[24]

■ YHWH is fully bodied but not to be seen. This double claim on the one hand assures that Israel will avoid excessive "spiritualizing" of its faith, precluding any flight into gnostic directions or toward what we have come to call *New Age options*. Israel's faith, grounded in the corporeal reality of YHWH, is preoccupied with the materiality of all that is. On the other hand, the ominous threat of "seeing God" causes Israel to ponder the proper practice of cultic presence, and to guard against coziness or user-friendliness. Direct, face-to-face contact with YHWH is rare; presence is characteristically mediated through designated agents (priests) and through the cultic apparatus.

■ YHWH is not easily or wholly available even in moments of willing self-disclosure. Thus the enigmatic name of in Exodus 3:14 assures that even in disclosure YHWH remains hidden, inscrutable, and unavailable: "Am I a God near by, says the LORD, and not a God far off?" (Jeremiah 23:23).

This awesome quality of YHWH that is not to be violated is implemented in the second and third commands of the Decalogue concerning "graven images" and the utilization of YHWH's name (see Exodus 20:4-7). YHWH has no usefulness and will not be taken up into any human purpose. This is a God who is preoccupied with "getting glory" for YHWH's own self (see Exodus 14:4, 17; Isaiah 42:8; 48:11; Ezekiel 36:22-23, 32). In sum, God is for God's self and will be glorified. It is Israel's primal task to give YHWH glory, to enhance YHWH in the eyes of the world and in the eyes of the other gods. In the interest of this task, other nations are summoned as well to join the doxology that is so peculiarly appropriate to YHWH: "Praise the LORD, all you nations! / Extol him, all you peoples!" (Psalm 117:1).

And beyond the nations, "all creatures of our God and king" are summoned to join in adoring lyrics toward YHWH:

> Praise the LORD!
> Praise the LORD from the heavens;
> praise him in the heights!
> Praise him, all his angels;
> praise him, all his host!
>
> Praise him, sun and moon;
> praise him, all you shining stars!
> Praise him, you highest heavens,
> and you waters above the heavens!
>
> Let them praise the name of the LORD,
> for he commanded and they were created.
> He established them forever and ever;
> he fixed their bounds, which cannot be passed.

Praise the LORD from the earth,
    you sea monsters and all deeps,
fire and hail, snow and frost,
    stormy wind fulfilling his command!

Mountains and all hills,
    fruit trees and all cedars!
Wild animals and all cattle,
    creeping things and flying birds! (Psalm 148:1-10)

2. *The God, so resolved to be honored and praised, is the God who purposefully and actively presides over the processes of creation and history; this God who will be glorified looks beyond self-concern to be concerned for and engaged in the world:*

■ This God presides over the affairs of all of the nations and will reorder the public domain according to divine purpose. This is continually evident in the resolve to dispatch Moses to Pharaoh and to deliver the slaves from the slave economy of Egypt (Exodus 3:10). The ensuing narrative exhibits YHWH in a contest with pharaonic power with a clear intent (and outcome) that Pharaoh should be an obedient subject of YHWH.[25] That same expectation is implicit in the awareness that the erstwhile slave community is being sent to occupy and claim the land already held by "the Canaanites [and] the Hittites" (Exodus 3:8). This theme of governance of the world and all worldly power is crucial to the prophets and most particularly to the prophetic oracles against the nations.[26] In the tradition of oracles against the nations, the focus is eventually upon Nebuchadnezzar the Babylonian who is "my servant" (Jeremiah 25:9; 27:6). Thus Old Testament theology is a meditation on the ways in which the governing claims of YHWH are articulated and imposed on powers that imagine themselves to be autonomous in the world.

That claim of autonomy made by the nations is countered in a less developed way in the narrative by the claim that YHWH presides over the whole of creation. This is inchoately affirmed in the anticipation of "a land flowing with milk and honey," a land where abundance is guaranteed by the creator God (see Exodus 3:8). Put negatively, the threat against the Nile River in Exodus 4:9 concludes that YHWH can dispatch the creaturely order as YHWH chooses. This is more fully developed in Exodus 7:14-25 (see Isaiah 19:5-10).[27] The Nile, moreover, becomes a subject of Pharaoh's immense arrogance wherein the king of Egypt does not recognize and acknowledge that it is YHWH who gives the Nile:

Speak, and say, Thus says the Lord GOD:
I am against you,
Pharaoh king of Egypt,
the great dragon sprawling
in the midst of its channels,
saying, "My Nile is my own;
I made it for myself." (Ezekiel 29:3)

■ YHWH is the Lord of the future that takes place completely under the aegis of YHWH's durable and certain promises. Thus the repeated references to the ancestral promises of Genesis include the claim that the entire process of world history enacts YHWH's intention; resistance to the promises is futile and self-destructive. The force of the promise asserts that human history is not ultimately shaped by human plan and human ingenuity. Divine commitment makes human intention penultimate. This ultimate reliance upon divine intention will become a *leitmotif* in the great promissory oracles of the exilic prophets (Isaiah 40:55; Jeremiah 30–33; Ezekiel 33–47). The promises are the ground on which newness emerges in human history that is beyond human hope as well as beyond human capacity. The world will come to YHWH's intention, which eventually is twofold, the peaceable settlement of Israel that Israel may know and trust: "So that they may believe that the LORD, the God of their ancestors, the God of Abraham, the God of Isaac, and the God of Jacob, has appeared to you" (Exodus 4:5).

The future is well set on YHWH's horizon and eventually all creatures—and all human powers—will acknowledge that abiding reality.

■ YHWH's mode of governance is through "wonders" that lie beyond human possibility, to permit the emergence of the utterly new in the processes of nature and history. It is the "wonders" of YHWH that become the grist of Israel's doxologies; see Psalm 136:4 that utilizes the term wonder which is followed by an extended recital of YHWH's characteristic acts.

These inexplicable emergents in the life processes of the world are known in Israel to be quite public. The same "impossible possibility" is evident in the detailed life of individuals who give thanks for YHWH's gift of life in venues of despair:

Then they cried to the LORD in their trouble,
and he delivered them from their distress;
he led them by a straight way,

until they reached an inhabited town.
Let them thank the LORD for his steadfast love,
for his wonderful works to humankind.
For he satisfies the thirsty,
and the hungry he fills with good things. . . .
Let them thank the LORD for his steadfast love,
for his wonderful works to humankind.
For he shatters the doors of bronze,
and cuts in two the bars of iron. . . .
He made the storm be still,
and the waves of the sea were hushed.
Then they were glad because they had quiet,
and he brought them to their desired haven.
Let them thank the LORD for his steadfast love,
for his wonderful works to humankind. (Psalm 107:6-9, 15-16, 29-31)

■ The last note of Exodus 3:21-22, however it is to be understood, evidences YHWH as the one who intends and provides abundance. In this instant, the abundance is the reassignment of the economic goods from the powerful Egyptians to the needy Hebrew slaves. Thus the divine intention of abundance would seem to contain a revolutionary impetus that gives even as it takes away.

■ The reference in Exodus 3:20 and 4:9 suggest that in inchoate ways YHWH will confound the Egyptian "wise men" who are representative of the technical capacity of worldly knowledge.[28] While not too much should be made of it, the reference permits an opening toward *wisdom traditions*; for wisdom in the Old Testament is never simply a pragmatic "know-how," but also is rooted in the awareness of the governance of YHWH who has ordered the world alternatively. Thus the Egyptian "intelligence community," like every human concentration of power, has had to learn that the intention of YHWH, engrained in the very structure of creation, cannot be violated with impunity. The wisdom traditions of Proverbs and especially of the book of Job are a study in the life-giving intention of YHWH and the limit of human capacity to do otherwise:

Hear instruction and be wise,
and do not neglect it.
Happy is the one who listens to me,
watching daily at my gates,
waiting beside my doors.

For whoever finds me finds life
    and obtains favor from the LORD;
but those who miss me injure themselves;
    all who hate me love death. (Proverbs 8:33-36)

And he said to humankind,
"Truly, the fear of the Lord, that is wisdom;
    and to depart from evil is understanding." (Job 28:28)

In sum, the world, all of its creatures and all of its capacity, belong to YHWH and will, soon or late, serve YHWH's intention. In its praise, Israel focuses upon the inexplicable ways in which the intention of YHWH prevails in the world, an intention that turns out to be good, abundant, and restorative (Genesis 50:20). Resistance to that divine intentionality is an application for death.

3. *In this originary narrative, we meet the God of Israel who "gets glory" and who exercises sovereignty by keeping promises, overthrowing recalcitrant powers, and bringing Israel to a new future. It is clear that YHWH's glorious sovereignty is a rule that is deeply committed to the processes of history:*

■ It is of utmost importance for Israel's faith that YHWH is drawn into the drama that eventuates in the exodus by the cries of Israel. Indeed, as the story stands the "miracle" of liberation is not through "divine initiative." Rather, the initiative is taken by the erstwhile slaves who evoke YHWH to act by their groans. The God of Israel is one who responds to hurt and need and who intervenes in order to transform such circumstances. YHWH is a God who answers hurt, who is attentive to the voiced pain of Israel. We may see this paradigmatic reality made concrete in the entire tradition of complaint and lament that is so powerfully represented in the Psalter.[29] This truth about direct address in prayer tells powerfully about the character of YHWH who is concerned not only for God's own self.

■ This response to Israel's groan marks YHWH as a genuinely dialogical God who engages with Israel as partner, who is put at risk by such exchanges, and who responds in freedom to the prayers of YHWH's people. This dialogic capacity is also on exhibit in the extended exchange of YHWH with Moses (Exodus 3:11–4:17). In general YHWH seeks to meet Moses' resistances and objections; but most spectacularly in the fifth Mosaic objection, YHWH concedes the point to Moses and makes an alternative arrangement.

The dialogic character of YHWH is not only evident in YHWH's responsiveness to Israel's prayer. Alongside divine responsiveness toward *human need* there is also divine initiative toward *human vocation*. In Exodus 3:10, it becomes Moses' mandate to confront pharaonic power, and to enact the departure of his people from slavery. To be sure, Moses' bold action is accompanied by the power of YHWH in Exodus 6–12; but Moses, human agent, is the point person. It is characteristic of Old Testament faith that divine intentionality is carried by human agency.

Beyond Moses, of course, the same divine designation of human agency is evident throughout the Old Testament. As Moses is *called* to perform divine intentionality, so the prophets characteristically are summoned to confront worldly power, as was Moses. Alongside prophetic mandate, this mode of divine impingement is evident in the public arena through the summoning and designation of royal power. Most especially is this on exhibit in David who is identified in a narrative of intimate designation (1 Samuel 16:1-13) that is in turn legitimated and given public forum in a more formal prophetic oracle (2 Samuel 7:1-16; see Psalm 89:19-37). As YHWH may summon worldly power in Israel, so beyond Israel YHWH works by human agency. Beyond Nebuchadnezzar, who becomes a cipher for anti-YHWH power in the Old Testament, Cyrus the Persian more positively is designated "my messiah" (Isaiah 45:1) whom YHWH "stirs up" to accomplish the well-being of Israel (Jeremiah 50:9-10; 2 Chronicles 36:22-23). In Christian reading, moreover, this divine designation of human agency is the taproot of an understanding of Jesus as Messiah, a claim that formally came to be expressed in trinitarian formulation. The Old Testament, in its core articulation of YHWH's power, does not doubt YHWH's sovereignty. That sovereignty, however, is not for the most part—until the belated development of apocalyptic thought and imagery—articulated as direct supernaturalism. Thus Moses is a paradigmatic figure in Old Testament faith who embodies this extraordinary convergence of *divine intention* and *human enactment*. It is for this reason, of course, that Moses delays his task so long and resists it as far as he is able; for enactment of such revolutionary and divine purpose is characteristically at odds with established worldly power and characteristically at risk before such power.

In sum, this originary narrative makes clear that YHWH, for all of YHWH's self-regard, is not a God who exists for God's self. This God is known from the outset to be deeply resonant with the human-historical reality, deeply responsive to human need, and deeply passionate for human capacity in a transformation of the historical environment of the world. This motif of *God-for-the-world*, *God-for-Israel*, *God-for-freedom*, *God-for-us* distinguishes this God from those of the surrounding religious environment. Thus, at the same time, the God who is *glorified in holiness* is also *engaged in and for the historical process*. The narrative form of Israel's faith manages to articulate both these claims at the same time. It is evident that the themes encountered in this dramatic and dialogic self-revelation become the themes that pervade the Old Testament, including YHWH's *narrative art*, *the prophets*, *the kings*, *wisdom*, and Israel's *hymnody* in both doxologies of praise and laments of pain. The narrative provides an entry point for all of the rich literature that follows in the Old Testament.

CHAPTER THREE

A SECOND PRIMAL REVELATION (EXODUS 19:1–24:18)

The confrontation of YHWH with Moses just considered in Exodus 3:1–4:17 occurred at "Horeb, the mountain of God" (3:1). The second text we consider, the meeting of YHWH with Israel, occurred in "the wilderness of Sinai" (Exodus 19:1). Since *Horeb* and *Sinai* are reckoned by scholars to be two names in variant traditions for the same holy mountain, we proceed on the assumption that the two meetings, with Moses and then with Israel, are intimately connected in their testimony about YHWH's authoritative and generative intervention into the life of Israel. Thus I shall take Exodus 19:1–24:18 as a second primal revelation of YHWH as the God of Israel.[1] This text on the one hand is complex, and scholars have suggested that it consists in the conflation of several strands of tradition. On the other hand, this text has figured prominently in the argument that Israel's covenant is patterned after international treaties, either of a Hittite or Assyrian model.[2]

For purposes of theological exposition, we may consider in sequence the several rhetorical units that constitute this quite distinct corpus.[3] The text begins with a divine word given to Moses in 19:4-6, an oracle that summarizes much of the faith of Israel. Verse 4 connects the Sinai meeting with the exodus deliverance, a connection that will be decisive in giving the commands of Exodus 20:1-17. The grounding for the covenant to follow is YHWH's powerful "wonder" of the overthrow of the state slave system of Pharaoh. What follows in verses 5-6 is a summons to obedience to YHWH who has replaced Pharaoh as the master to whom Israel is accountable. The summons includes two quite strong verbs, "to listen and to keep (covenant)," thus binding Israel into a new and defining relationship.[4] Verse 6 defines Israel's peculiar identity and vocation as "a priestly kingdom and a holy nation," vis-à-vis other peoples in "the whole earth." Thus the *redeemer of Israel* is acknowledged in the same sentence as the *creator and sovereign* over all that is. Israel's peculiar relationship with YHWH is accented, but without denying that YHWH has a decisive relationship with all that is outside and beyond Israel. The phrase "priestly kingdom" is notoriously enigmatic but may suggest that Israel is to have a priestly function vis-à-vis other people as an intercessor. [5] The most remarkable thing about this divine summons is that Israel's response in verse 8 is complete and without reservation. Even before Israel hears the commands that are yet to come, Israel is prepared for obedience. Israel's eagerness to sign on with YHWH likely reflects an awareness that the demands of YHWH, whatever they will be, are better, lighter demands than the oppressive requirements of Pharaoh, on which see Exodus 5. This new allegiance to YHWH amounts to nothing less than a regime change whereby Israel ascends to a new defining loyalty.

Thus three basic themes are announced: (a) a linkage to the exodus, (b) a summons to obedience with a peculiar identity, and (c) a ready response of assent that signifies the establishment of a covenantal relationship that is now to be narrated in some detail. On the basis of this preliminary exchange of command and obedience, Israel is now ready to approach the holy mountain, an approach that is filled with danger and risk. In Exodus 19:10-25, two narrative elements are offered, both of which parallel the encounter of Exodus 3:1-6. The most poignant part of the narrative is the theophanic coming of YHWH to be on the mountain (Exodus 19:16-25). The characterization of the coming of God expressed in a way that is characteristic in Israel is of a loud, disturbing intrusion that is immensely disruptive. Verses 16-25 communicate the danger and threat of divine presence. In dramatic language, this theophanic description parallels YHWH "in the bush" but stretches the description in extreme rhetoric. By verse 25 we have no doubt that YHWH is fully, sovereignly present in the mountain.

As in 3:1-6, the meeting at the mountain is no casual matter. The mountain is holy because the God who comes there is holy; entry into such a presence requires preparation and qualification and that is the second item of this narrative that moves toward chapter 20. Such preparation is reported in 19:10-15 with an admonition to "consecrate" (make holy) themselves (v. 10). While Israel is to make themselves holy, in verse 14 it is Moses who consecrates them. The Israelites wash and are so made clean. Verse 15 reports specifically on the avoidance of sexual contact and the repeated verb "touch" (*nagha*ʿ) suggests that the wrong "touching" is dangerous and may contaminate or destroy. The rhetoric of the paragraph effects a priestly agenda, otherwise lined out in the traditions of the book of Leviticus in which approach to the presence of YHWH must be done with punctilious attentiveness.[6] The interface of *careful preparation* and *disruptive intrusion* is strikingly incongruous, unless we recognize that priestly interpreters have drawn *theophanic rhetoric* into the disciplined work of *cultic practice*. By doing so, the tradition makes clear that the theophany is not a one-time report; it is rather a replicatable cultic event wherein Israel may repeatedly enter into the presence of this dangerous God, but may do so only with great attentiveness. This paragraph concerning preparation thus displaces *theophany* into *cult*. In doing so, the report adumbrates the careful and detailed traditions of holiness that follow in the development of the Sinai material. The interpretive accomplishment of this juxtaposition of theophany and disciplines of holiness is to assure that the practice of covenant making is cast as a sacramental activity, conducted repeatedly by qualified leadership and participated in by the qualified community.[7]

The theophanic report of Exodus 19:16-25 provides an opening frame for the Decalogue that is now to follow (20:1-17). The juxtaposition of *theophany* and *Decalogue*, not unlike *theophany* (Exodus 3:1-6) and *summons* (Exodus 3:10), assumes that the mandate of the Decalogue—like the earlier mandate to Moses—is originary, directly from YHWH with all of YHWH's authority and without mediation. The Decalogue is voiced by the sovereign Lord of covenant, the one who has overpowered and overthrown Pharaoh with wonders (Exodus 20:1), and the one attested in Exodus 20:11 as creator of heaven and earth. The commands that follow are the *rules of emancipation* by the redeemer God and, at the same time, the *rules for a viable order of life* by the creator God. While there are many parallels and analogues in the ancient Near East to other legal materials in the Old Testament, there is no parallel to this utterance from the holy mountain.[8] These commands that require total and uncompromised obedience are a radical alternative to the commands of Pharaoh issued in Exodus 5. Whereas those commands are in the interest of production for the state economy, the Decalogue issues commands that lie outside the state and outside the usual agenda of the economy.[9]

The Decalogue, as is commonly recognized, has two points of accent. First, the Decalogue asserts the distinctive claim of YHWH to be the sole subject of Israel's worship and obedience, a subject not to be domesticated or contained in any act of human artistic imagination (Exodus 20:4-6), not to be harnessed or utilized for any human agenda (Exodus 20:7). YHWH is articulated here in YHWH's completely unfettered selfhood before which Israel must yield in radical and uncompromising obedience. This God, and no other, will jealously judge and punish (Exodus 20:5), this God will act in covenant fidelity for all imaginable time to come (Exodus 20:6). Israel's life, in this relationship, is placed on a wholly new foundation.

Second, the God who will be unrivaled in Israel is the God who wills and orders a viable and sustainable human community (Exodus 20:12-17). This cryptic set of commands sets rigorous limits on exploitative abuse of the neighbor, and guarantees that the neighbor who cannot defend life or property is defended and guaranteed by divine sanction.

This neighborly ethic is, of course, decisive of Old Testament faith. We may see it worked out in some detail in the particular commands of Deuteronomy 21–24 in which rules are provided for the protection of the vulnerable and the economically needy. Beyond the traditions of Deuteronomy, it is fair to say that this neighborly ethic reaches its fullest and most complete articulation in Job 31 in which Job states his innocence with reference to enacting care for his community.[10] It is not clear about the way in which a *covenantal ethic* relates to such a *sapiential inventory*. It is surely fair to say, nonetheless, that even Israel's wisdom materials are shot through with covenantal awareness; it is clear all through the wisdom teaching that members of society are all deeply responsible with and for one another and that the cohesion of the community is derived from the rule of the creator-redeemer God. In Job 31, moreover, it is affirmed, as is characteristic in the Old Testament, that the covenantal ethic is indeed doable. A righteous man or a righteous woman can indeed practice such an ethic and is held accountable for it: "Surely, this commandment that I am commanding you today is not too hard for you, nor is it too far away. . . . No, the word is very near to you; it is in your mouth and in your heart for you to observe" (Deuteronomy 30:11, 14).

The accent on *YHWH alone* (20:1-7) and *the neighbor* (20:12-17) of course represent the primary foci of biblical ethics (see Mark 12:28-31).

It is the dramatic and nonnegotiable juxtaposition of the two parts that constitutes the defining character of Old Testament ethics. In the modern world, it is most often preferred to focus on "the second tablet" of neighborly concern while disregarding the first set of commands as a more-or-less primitive sectarianism. But of course in Israel's horizon it is precisely the requirements concerning YHWH that fund and ground the neighborly vision that follows. Conversely, it will not do, as is often a religious temptation, to be so preoccupied with "love of God" that there is no neighborly mandate in a religious vista that is myopic and without a social dimension (see 1 John 4:20-21).

The requirements are of course articulated for what must have been a small, likely agricultural community (witness "ox and donkey" in v. 17). Unfortunately some forms of ethical interpretation, especially among conservative Christians, persist in seeing the commands only in terms of face-to-face neighborliness without reference to systemic issues in society. It is clear that the radical ethic of the dialogue is transposed in the prophetic tradition of Israel into a large-scale systemic analysis and demand. On the one hand, the neighborly commands in verses 12-17 are transposed in prophetic imagination into an acute systemic analysis of the politics and economics of the Jerusalem apparatus. That is explicitly evident in two prophetic utterances:

> Swearing, lying, and murder,
> and stealing and adultery break out;
> bloodshed follows bloodshed. (Hosea 4:2)

> Will you steal, murder, commit adultery, swear falsely, make offerings to Baal, and go after other gods that you have not known? (Jeremiah 7:9)

Beyond these two uses, however, the entire theme of "righteousness and justice" concerns neighborly practice in the economy (Isaiah 5:7; Amos 4:24); in prophetic tradition the royal regime and the urban establishment receive heavy prophetic speeches of judgment precisely from this tradition.

On the other hand, when the prophetic tradition concerns the international scene and the abusive arrogant autonomy of other nation states, then it is from the first commands concerning the unrivaled sovereignty of YHWH that is brought into play; characteristically such arrogant autonomy that issues an exploitation is said to be "mocking" of YHWH (Isaiah 37:4, 17). As the prophetic tradition is linked to the covenantal ethics of the Decalogue, so the wisdom traditions are in the same way informed by such an ethic (Proverbs 17:5). It may well be that the ancient Near Eastern *sapiential* tradition developed separately from *covenantalism* and was grounded in a discerning pragmatism. There is no doubt, however, that in the formation of the Old Testament the sapiential teaching is understood to be connected to the covenantal ethic of Sinai.[11]

As with the prophetic tradition and the sapiential tradition, there is no doubt that the Psalms are deeply permeated with Torah instruction.[12] Thus the first Psalm situates the Psalter within the horizon of the Torah as a condition of prosperity:

> Happy are those
> who do not follow the advice of the wicked,
> or take the path that sinners tread,
> or sit in the seat of scoffers;
> but their delight is in *the law of the LORD*,
> and on his law they meditate day and night. (Psalm 1:1-2, italics added)

While the notation in Psalm 1 remains general and undifferentiated, the more specific portrayal of "the righteous" concerns the neighborly practice of care and justice:

> They rise in the darkness as a light for the upright;
> they are gracious, *merciful, and righteous*.
> It is well with those who deal generously and lend,
> who conduct their affairs with *justice*. . . .
> They have distributed freely, they have given to the poor;
> their righteousness endures forever;
> their horn is exalted in honor. (Psalm 112:4-5, 9, italics added)

The keeping of such a neighborly Torah rooted in the commands of Sinai is the prerequisite and the guarantee of a life of well-being and prosperity:

> They are like trees
> planted by streams of water,
> which yield their fruit in its season,
> and their leaves do not wither.
> In all that they do, they prosper. (Psalm 1:3)

Wealth and riches are in their houses,
    and their righteousness endures forever. . . .
For the righteous will never be moved;
    they will be remembered forever.
They are not afraid of evil tidings;
    their hearts are firm, secure in the LORD.
Their hearts are steady, they will not be afraid;
    in the end they will look in triumph on their foes. (Psalm 112:3, 6-8)

Thus it is no stretch to see that the prophetic, sapiential, and psalmic traditions are all informed by the covenantal ethic of Sinai in the final form of the text. It may be that in some cases the traditions are impacted directly by the Decalogue that surely exercised great authority. It is not, however, necessary to claim such a direct connection. It is enough to see that the Decalogue offers an authoritative summary of the covenantal ethic that everywhere pervaded Israel's venturesome ethical reflection.

The "first tablet" (Exodus 20:1-7) concerns YHWH's *sovereignty* and tells against *arrogant autonomy*. The "second tablet" (Exodus 20:12-17) concerns *neighborliness* rooted in YHWH's alternative government that precludes pharaonic exploitation and tells against *socioeconomic oppression*. Lodged exactly between the "two tablets," though usually assigned to the second tablet, is the command concerning sabbath (Exodus 20:8-11). This provision commands work stoppage from all productive systems—in context surely with reference to the productive system of the state economy of Egypt. The purpose of such work stoppage is to assert that human existence in covenantal form is not defined by productivity and is not subject to the imposed quotas of an economy of demand. Most important for Old Testament theology is the fact that the command to sabbath rest is grounded in the restfulness of the creator God (Exodus 20:11; Genesis 2:1-4a), so that the sabbath provision is not socially imposed but is inherent in the very fabric of creation. It is in keeping sabbath rest that Israel . . . and the human community . . . most directly imitates the creator and practices the same restfulness as does YHWH the creator God. This reference to the creator God at the center of the Decalogue makes clear that the commands of Sinai are not simply Israelite devices for a community alternative to pharaonic exploitation, though they are that. Beyond that claim, the Decalogue implies the much larger claim that the commands correspond to structures of creation ordered by the creator God. Obedience to them brings the community into sync with the most elemental and nonnegotiable realities of creation. Thus H. H. Schmid has compellingly argued that the commands cohere with the ordering of the world, the violation of which brings death.[13] It is for that reason that Walter Harrelson concludes his splendid exposition of the Decalogue with reference to the Helsinki declaration on human rights.[14] It is evident that the Sinai declaration makes a radically new beginning in ethics in the history of the world that stretches well beyond the Israelite community. Self-disclosure of YHWH stands as an abiding critique of all anticovenantal forms of power, and as a warrant for covenantal forms of power that enhance the human community and that resist reduction of human life to power and wealth.

When the assertion of the commandments is completed, it is clear in the present form of the text that this was an awesome, dread-filled moment in the memory of Israel that could not be replicated. As the tradition reports, this is a one-time disclosure that has brought Moses and Israel into dangerous contact with what is most revolutionary in YHWH's rule of the world. In response to that dangerous moment, Israel responds immediately by requesting a mediator so that there need not be in time to come such a raw exposure to the reality and rule of YHWH (Exodus 20:18-21). The request indicates that Israel knew that the encounter at the mountain with YHWH was life-threatening. The request is immediately granted; Moses will now be the go-between, while YHWH recedes into "thick darkness," a term that bespeaks hidden cultic remoteness.

Two dimensions of this provision for a mediator are to be noted. First, the text is arranged so that the declaration of the Decalogue (Exodus 20:1-17) is placed singularly between the *theophany* (Exodus 19:16-25) and the *provision for mediator* (Exodus 20:18-21). This arrangement brackets the Decalogue and sets it apart as the *single direct utterance* of YHWH at Sinai, thus evidencing the primacy and unparalleled importance of the Ten Commandments. This is *the* foundational divine utterance upon which everything rests for Israel as a community sworn to YHWH and granted life outside the grasp of pharaonic oppression. The Ten Commandments characterize and protect that alternative status in covenant.[15]

Second, the provision of Moses as mediator is of immense importance for the development of the textual tradition and for the interpretive dynamism that characterizes Israel's self-understanding and that identifies the larger text as a product of ongoing imaginative hermeneutical activity. All that follows at Sinai is now mediation by Moses, that is, exposition in commentary on the Ten Commandments. This provision provides an enormous freedom and elasticity to the function of the commandments in Israel. The mediation of Moses is evident in the enormous growth of commandments beyond the Decalogue in the Sinai materials (Exodus–Numbers) and beyond the Sinai material in the tradition of Deuteronomy that is "expounded" by Moses (Deuteronomy 1:5).[16] Beyond that, it is clear that the Mosaic *function* of reinterpretation to adapt the Torah to new time, new place, and new circumstance is not limited to the person and lifetime of Moses; rather, that function continued over the generations as new agents occupied the Mosaic "office" of exposition and commentary. This dynamism is evident in the text itself in the several layers of tradition that address different contexts.

It is, moreover, clear in the peculiar role of Ezra as a second founder of Judaism in his interpretive work in Nehemiah 8:7-8. It is clear beyond the canonical text in ongoing rabbinic work, evidenced for example in the "old-new" antitheses of Jesus (Matthew 5:21-48). The ongoing process of mediation is alive in the several interpretive practices of both Judaism and Christianity. Thus it is clear that while the Ten Commandments provide the absolute, nonnegotiable foundation of covenantal ethics, that nonnegotiable foundation receives, in the tradition, a dynamic afterlife whereby the will and rule of YHWH, Lord of the covenant, is kept pertinent and germane to every circumstance of this alternative community of covenantal obedience.[17] Clearly the ongoing, disputatious ethical reflection of the community of faith, even in our own time, is a continuation of the practice set in motion by the mediating function of Moses. In the midst of every such disputatious encounter, it is important to remember that such mediating work is the only alternative to direct meeting with YHWH through which "we will die" (Exodus 20:19). The generous allowance of a provision for a mediator constitutes the assurance that in the encounter with YHWH it may boldly be said, "Do not fear" (Exodus 20:20).

In the present form of the text, the appearance of the *mediator* (Exodus 20:18-21) is promptly followed by a collection of laws commonly designated the *Book of the Covenant*, on which see Exodus 24:7 (Exodus 20:22–23:33).[18] This corpus of material is commonly thought to be an independent collection that had no original relationship to the Sinai covenant. But the fact that it has been incorporated into the Sinai tradition and functions as an offer of the mediation of Moses demonstrates the dynamic capacity of the covenant tradition to incorporate fresh materials into the normative ethic of Israel by the process of interpretation. Two observations about the "Book of Covenant" may be made. First, the several commandments therein reflect a simple face-to-face agricultural community that must manage concrete realistic disputes and contested claims. The quotidian quality of these rules is sharply contrasted with the grand absolutes of the Decalogue. That, however, is the way in which the large claims of the Decalogue must characteristically be parsed for the sake of concrete obedience. The concreteness of these commands, as they are incorporated into the covenant tradition, has the effect of bringing every detail of daily life under the aegis of YHWH. Who would have thought, for example, that the great God of Sinai would have an intention for how to handle a cow that grazes in a neighbor's field (Exodus 22:5)! But that, of course, is the detail required in instruction that governs daily life.

Second, as Paul Hanson has made clear, there are mixed genres and mixed claims that are operative in this corpus;[19] these several detailed claims, however, are all drawn in the formulation of the text to the central vision of a community that in every sphere of life is responsive to the Lord of the Covenant. This is not to deny that the incorporating process on occasion takes up material that is inimical to the grand vision of covenant. Thus the canonical claims of command are a mixed lot that requires ongoing critical review; there can be no doubt, however, of the central commitment to covenant that seeks to pervade all of the adapted materials, albeit with varying degrees of success. This tension between *core vision* and *quotidian reality* is a powerful case in point of James Sanders's claim that the "monotheizing tendency" of the material is powerful, but not so powerful as to rule out a flexibility toward materials that do not easily yield to the central covenantal claim.[20] That inescapably is the nature of ethical material that is gathered disputatiously over time, an outcome that precludes any simplistic presentation. It is futile to imagine that the voice of normative Yahwism could easily dictate the terms of incorporation of new materials or readily silence teachings that did not conform to the core vision of covenant. These recalcitrant materials, of course, are among the most interesting in the text and recurringly the most problematic for an ongoing reflection and interpretation.[21] The move from grand "policy" statement to detailed "technique" is never easy or obvious or simple.[22] It is nonetheless the interpretive move that the mediating tradition must, perforce, continually make. The large legal corpus of Sinai (and beyond Sinai in the book of Deuteronomy) is the literary legacy of the practice of negotiating *large absolute claims of covenant* and *detailed practicality in daily life*.

The culmination of the Book of Covenant in Exodus 23:20-33 is a meditation upon the land of promise where the details of covenant command are to be practiced. Yet again the tradition is clear: the trek from Sinai through the wilderness is to come to the land long since promised to Israel (see Exodus 3:8, 17), though reference to the Genesis ancestors is noticeably absent here. The land is the culmination of the promise; in the starchy world of Sinai claims, however, everything depends upon radical allegiance to the Lord of Sinai. The threat constituted by the worship of other gods and the violation of the first commandment placed the promise at risk. One can see in this passage the intrusion of the conditionality of covenant to be voiced extensively in the Deuteronomic tradition. The effect is to underscore the conditionality of covenant obedience, a conditionality to which Israel is already on notice in the dominant "if" of Exodus 19:5-6.

If we understand the Book of Covenant to be a more-or-less belated incorporation into the text of Sinai, it is possible to read directly from chapter 20 to chapter 24. But since the Book of Covenant is present in the final form of the text, we may take "the Book of Covenant" as the specific terms of the covenant now about to be completed. In Exodus 24, the narrative of covenant making is found in verses 3-8. Three dimensions of covenant making are to be noted:

- The "Book of Covenant" sets the terms of agreement (Exodus 24:8). Israel is summoned to an alternative neighborly existence.
- Israel takes a solemn oath of allegiance and obedience to the Lord of the Covenant, thus foreswearing any autonomous life or any allegiance to the pharaonic system of productivity (Exodus 24:3, 7). The solemn oath of Israel is a reiteration of Exodus 19:8. The transaction would seem to be a unilateral commitment to YHWH. In the later, fuller articulation of Deuteronomy, however, it is clear that the binding commitment is bilateral; YHWH also is now bound in loyalty to Israel:

> Today you have obtained the LORD's agreement: to be your God; and for you to walk in his ways, to keep his statutes, his commandments, and his ordinances, and to obey him. Today the LORD has obtained your agreement: to be his treasured people, as he promised you, and to keep his

> commandments; for him to set you high above all nations that he has made, in praise and in fame and in honor; and for you to be a people holy to the LORD your God, as he promised. (Deuteronomy 26:17-19)

- While the oath has overtones of the formality of a juridical procedure, the reference to the "blood of the covenant" (Exodus 24:8), as well as the offer of sacrifices (Exodus 24:4-5), evidences a sacramental dimension to covenant making that gives the process even more gravitas than the juridical. The action of covenant making is performative; a profound *novum* now emerges in the historical process, a people created by and for the God of covenant who stands over against all pharaonic power in the world.

The *covenant-making* process in Exodus 24:3-8 is set in the midst of a quite different accent (Exodus 24:1-2, 9-17). Here the key matter is not *covenant* but *presence*, and it is the tradition of cultic presence that provides a context in Exodus 24 for covenant making. In this differently nuanced tradition, Israel "goes up" to "behold God," a presence that is indicated by "the appearance of the glory of God."[23] In this tradition there is nothing bilateral; here YHWH is singularly the focus and Israel is, at best, observer, worshiper, and suppliant who must carefully keep distance from YHWH. While *the covenant tradition* has received much more scholarly attention and seems more available for contemporary theological usage, *the tradition of presence* that stands in tension with it is by no means of lesser importance.[24] The remarkable juxtaposition of the two in chapter 24 makes clear that these parallel traditions, surely reflecting competing interpretive claims in the Israelite community, are both important and are never easily resolved.

The tradition of presence insists that interaction with YHWH is fundamentally a sacramental act that requires a well-ordered venue of worship. The dialectic of *worship* and *civic life* is an important one in Israel, one that is extrapolated in the Priestly and Deuteronomic traditions. And even in the contemporary life of the church, those competing interpretive accents on *purity* and *justice* replicate the old tension that is present in the initial voicing of the tradition.[25] Both are there together; neither prevails, neither is excluded. From the outset, the tradition of life with YHWH is bivocal and must be kept so.

This second primal revelation in Exodus 19–24 is intimately linked to the episode of the burning bush in Exodus 2:23–4:17. It is nonetheless clear that this second episode at Sinai is an important advance beyond the initial confrontation with Moses, a move from *personal summons* to *communal formation*. In the covenant-making interaction of Sinai, in the context of awesome Holy Presence, these accents are clear:

- YHWH is sovereign and presides over the life of Israel and of the larger territory (land-earth) to be entrusted to Israel.
- YHWH is profoundly committed to Israel, both to keep very old promises made to the ancestors and to institutionalize for the long term the emancipatory realities of the exodus.
- YHWH's passion for Israel is to be practiced in the context of a legal framework of commands.
- Israel's assent to YHWH's commands makes a new life possible outside the regime of Pharaoh; while the demands of YHWH are massive and become more so in the ongoing tradition, they are clearly alternative to Pharaoh. Israel willingly signs on for this alternative mode of existence.
- The acknowledgment of Moses as mediator establishes Moses (and the ongoing "office" of Moses) as structurally defining for Israel. There cannot be an Israel without a Mosaic practice of ongoing interpretation. The office of mediator ensures a dynamism to the substance and process of covenantal command that leaves the absolute commands of Sinai open-ended and subject to ongoing interpretive variation.
- The covenant is nonnegotiable in its Yahwistic singularity; in order to live in any social environment, however, Israel must foster and participate in "a culture of interpretation" that is generative and inescapably disputatious.
- The tradition of presence, only expressed in Exodus 24 but given full play in the Priestly traditions of Exodus 25–31, 35–40, assures that the bilateral relationship of covenant is definingly incommensurate. For all of the commitment to mutuality, YHWH is unmistakably beyond the reach of Israel's capacity. By the end of the Sinai pericope in Exodus 24, Israel can only be awed and dazzled by the God whom it sees. For all the hints of partnership, Israel dare not draw closer to YHWH.

CHAPTER FOUR

A THIRD PRIMAL REVELATION (EXODUS 32–34)

In the first primal self-disclosure of YHWH in Exodus 3:1-6, Moses has been summoned to confront Pharaoh; in the ensuing narrative the exodus has been enacted (Exodus 5–15) and Israel has traversed its difficult way to the Holy Mountain, sustained by YHWH's "wonders" (Exodus 16–18). In the second primal self-disclosure of YHWH in Exodus 19–24, a new alternative community has been formed, bound in singular loyalty to YHWH. With the *oath of allegiance* (Exodus 24:3, 8) and the *vision of God* (Exodus 24:9-11), the process of community formation is complete. We might expect after Exodus 24 that Israel would promptly depart Sinai en route to the land of promise that is the goal of the trek from slavery.

But of course Israel, according to the tradition, does not promptly depart from Sinai but lingers until Numbers 10:11. The long stretch of material from Exodus 25:1 to Numbers 10:10 is characterized almost exclusively by more commands that are situated at Sinai according to the Priestly tradition. The only exception to the Priestly instruction in Exodus 25:1 to Numbers 10:10 is found in Exodus 32:1–34:28, a narrative account that connects directly to Exodus 24 and is commonly reckoned as a part of the more normative testimony featured in the Sinai Pericope of Exodus 19–24. While Exodus 32–34 is after and derivative from the covenant-making initiative at Exodus 19–24, I will here treat Exodus 32–34 as a third primal self-disclosure of YHWH, for in these chapters something fresh and different about YHWH is evidenced that is surely definitive for our understanding of the God of Israel.[1] The distinct corpus of Exodus 32–34 begins in a crisis. Moses had disappeared into the Holy Mountain for forty days and forty nights (Exodus 24:18), too long for a community completely reliant on his mediation. The crisis of perceived absence is countered by the initiative of Aaron, priestly brother and rival of Moses (see Exodus 4:14-17).[2] The narrative no doubt contains a polemic against the priestly leadership, for Aaron either does not understand or take seriously the initial commands of Sinai. He proceeds to "make other gods," thus violating the first command of Exodus 20:3 and to do so with visible imagery, thus violating the second command of Exodus 20:4-6. The narrative begins with the initial, seemingly intentional violation of the Decalogue. And if we read directly from Exodus 24–32, overlooking the intervening Priestly material, the *violation of covenant* happens immediately upon the *making of covenant.* From day one, Israel's covenant with YHWH is a *broken covenant.* This is the crisis of the narrative, paradigmatic of the characteristic crisis in Israel, a broken covenant with YHWH who will tolerate no violation!

The response of YHWH to the crisis of violated command does not in fact surprise (Exodus 32:7-10). YHWH is a sovereign who will not be mocked; the violation of covenant is a radical rejection of YHWH's sovereignty that evokes YHWH's harsh reaction. The tradition exhibits no awkwardness about YHWH's harshness. In the developing tradition of the prophets, this combination of *covenant violation* and *divine judgment* is a staple of biblical faith and becomes the *leitmotif* of the theology of the tradition of Deuteronomy.[3]

YHWH's response is not surprising. What is surprising is Moses' role in the ensuing tradition. In Exodus 32:10, YHWH bids Moses to leave him alone in anger, for YHWH is not free to be recklessly angry in the presence of Moses. By his very presence Moses is a curb on YHWH's ferocious self-regard, so that Moses promptly emerges in the narrative as a definitive force in the life of Israel's covenant. We are able to see, in the petition of Moses in Exodus 32:11-13, why YHWH in verse 10 wants to be left alone without Moses. In his prayer, Moses addresses YHWH to "turn" YHWH from his immense anger toward disobedient Israel. The petition is grounded in two matters: (a) appeal to YHWH's reputation, suggesting that YHWH will be shamed if Israel is destroyed, and (b) appeal to YHWH's promises to the ancestors. Both the pragmatic appeal to shame and the affirmation of YHWH's fidelity count enough that YHWH "changed his mind."[4] YHWH is responsive to the advocacy of Moses on behalf of Israel! In the remainder of the narrative, Moses now becomes directly aware of Aaron's transgression, as YHWH was previously aware. And like YHWH, Moses is deeply indignant and undertakes fresh judgment against disobedient Israel. The reliance upon the Levites to implement divine wrath no doubt reflects rivalry between that priestly group and the Aaronides (Exodus 32:25-29).

The outcome of Exodus 32, taken immediately after chapter 24, is that the covenant of Sinai is profoundly violated. Moses bids for YHWH's forgiveness (v. 32); YHWH, however, is hard-nosed and unwilling to forgive. YHWH still intends that the community should proceed to the land of promise, but those to receive the new land are only the Torah keepers. All others are disqualified (see Numbers 14:22-24). Thus the narrative effect of chapter 32, with some opening to the future, is the reality of judgment that is intensely harsh. YHWH is unforgiving!

The verdict of YHWH in Exodus 32:9 that Israel is "stiff necked" becomes the harsh opener of chapter 33 (v. 3). Moses is now intimate with YHWH (33:7-11); in Exodus 33:12-23, Moses becomes a demanding advocate on the part of Israel. The narrative report suggests that Moses loves Israel more than does YHWH, and Moses is more committed to Israel than is YHWH. For YHWH, Israel is quite dispensable! The initial declaration of YHWH in this chapter is that YHWH will not accompany Israel on its way to the land of promise: "Go up to a land flowing with milk and honey; but I will not go up among you, or I would consume you on the way, for you are a stiff-necked people" (Exodus 33:3). Moses, however, is adamant that YHWH must accompany Israel. Thus it is Moses who insists upon the cruciality and indispensability of YHWH's accompaniment of Israel: "And he said to him, 'If your presence will not go, do not carry us up from here. For how shall it be known that I have found favor in your sight, I and your people, unless you go with us? In this way, we shall be distinct, I and your people, from every people on the face of the earth'" (Exodus 33:15-16). It is clear that Moses understands that the story line of Israel's faith is not simply arrival in the promised land; it is rather arrival in the promised land *with the God of covenant*. Thus the relationship is more important to Moses than is the real estate. By verse 17, YHWH completely reverses field and concedes to Moses' primary demand: "The LORD said to Moses, 'I will do the very thing that you have asked; for you have found favor in my sight, and I know you by name'" (Exodus 33:17).

The remainder of chapter 33 is a grudging conversation between YHWH and Moses in which YHWH concedes much to Moses, but not everything. Moses will know YHWH's "goodness" and will see the backside of YHWH's "glory"; but Moses will not see YHWH's face (v. 20). The verdict is a surprise in light of verse 11; verse 11, however, concerns cultic regulation, whereas verse 20 is a point in an interpersonal narrative. What is most important in this exchange for Old Testament theology is the unmistakable fact that Israel's faith is articulated in raw narrative in which YHWH is a real character and a genuine participant in the plot with all of the risks and possibilities pertaining thereto.

By the end of chapter 33, YHWH remains unforgiving; except that Exodus 33 leaves an opening for grace and mercy that is YHWH's peculiar prerogative. YHWH is characterized as "gracious and merciful," but his grace and mercy is one option among many options for YHWH as YHWH in freedom decides. Chapter 33 has advanced the negotiation between YHWH and Moses well beyond chapter 32, but with no clear resolution. By the end of chapter 33, we still do not know. YHWH makes concessions to Moses but they do not seem to be very great in scope. The text requires that the reader wait until chapter 34 to see how Israel will have a future . . . if at all.

In chapter 34, without any explanation, YHWH takes a new initiative. YHWH proposes to Moses the offer of new tablets of the commandments thus to articulate the demands of covenant and thus to reestablish the covenant. YHWH does not need to explain YHWH's actions or intentions. Now without forewarning, YHWH is prepared to begin with Israel again beyond the anger of chapter 32 and beyond the strictures and limitations of chapter 33. In YHWH's initial word to Moses in this new chapter, YHWH acknowledges that the new tablets replace the old tablets "which you broke" (v. 1). In the midst of tablet giving, YHWH issues an announcement of self-disclosure. It is as though, in the midst of the crisis of the broken tablets (broken covenant) and the project of new tablets (new covenant), YHWH wants to go behind the tablets (and the commands) to YHWH's own life in order to make YHWH's very self available as YHWH had not been willing to do in the previous chapter. A new beginning is offered for Moses in verses 6-7 after the deep violation of the covenant in the foregoing. The ground for any possible future must be in YHWH's self-resolve, which, of course, depends upon YHWH's own character.

The words of verses 6-7 provide in summary form the essential characteristics of YHWH as the Lord of the covenant. [5] The cluster of terms in this self-disclosure of YHWH is not unlike the cluster of terms in Psalm 36:5, 7 that concern YHWH's mercy, truth, righteousness, and loving kindness, which Calvin terms the "four cardinal attributes of the Deity":

> David, nevertheless, maintains that the world is full of the goodness and righteousness of God, and that he governs heaven and earth on the strictest principles of equity. And certainly, whenever the corruption of the world affects our minds, and fills us with amazement, we must take care not to limit our views to the wickedness of men who overturn and confound all things; but in the midst of this strange confusion, it becomes us to elevate our thoughts in admiration and wonder, to the contemplation of the secret providence of God. David here enumerates four cardinal attributes of Deity, which, according to the figure of speech called *synecdoche*, include all the others, and by which he intimates, in short, that although carnal reason may suggest to us that the world moves at random, and is directed by chance, yet we ought to consider that the infinite power of God is always associated with perfect righteousness.[6]

In verse 6, YHWH is self-characterized by five terms, each of which bespeaks YHWH's fidelity and will to be in a relationship of fidelity:

- *merciful* (*rakhum*). The term is related to "womb" and with Phyllis Trible is translated "womb-like mother love," the kind of love a mother has for a child (see Isaiah 49:14-15).[7]
- *gracious* (*khanan*). The term means to care for gratuitously, without merit on the part of the one loved and without any conditions or prerequisites for graciousness.
- *slow to anger* (*ʾerekh ʾappayim*). The phrase in Hebrew means "with a long nose," suggesting that YHWH's fiery anger will cool and will not remain hot and destructive by the time it moves to the end of the fiery nose (see Psalm 103:9).
- *steadfast love* (*khesedh*). This is the principal term for covenant fidelity, which asserts that YHWH will stand by YHWH's covenant commitments even in the face of infidelity by the covenant partner.
- *faithfulness* (*ʾemeth*) bespeaking YHWH's utter reliability.

The five terms together bespeak a God of abiding fidelity, a faithfulness that is not disrupted by the fickleness of the other party. The sum of these terms would suggest that not even the aberration of Aaron in chapter 32 would diminish or interrupt YHWH's deep commitment to Israel. This stunning and elemental affirmation is arrived at only in chapter 34. In the earlier narrative account of chapters 32 and 33, that characterization of YHWH does not yet seem to be the case. It is as though YHWH has moved into and through YHWH's anger to the more underlying truth of YHWH's abiding fidelity. The claim made for YHWH is in some tension with the narrative development of these chapters, but testifies to the theological outcome upon which the future of Israel depends.

The divine self-disclosure continues in verse 7 by reiterating the term *steadfast love* (*khesedh*) and relating it to forgiveness, the capacity of YHWH to overrule and overlook the affront of the covenant partner. Verse 7 continues with the sobering acknowledgment that iniquity, transgression, and sin are taken seriously by YHWH, very seriously indeed. The tension in verse 7 that addresses the crisis of these chapters consists in the juxtaposition of *punishment* to the third and fourth generation, but *steadfast love* to a thousand generations. This statement does not abrogate severe punishment, but surely asserts that punishment is in the context of abiding and generous fidelity that is expressed as forgiveness. The sum of the self-disclosure of YHWH in verses 6-7 is a stunning presentation of the thickness of YHWH's inclination toward Israel that is marked not only by generosity but also by uncompromising self-regard on the part of YHWH.

In response to divine self-disclosure of covenantal thickness in verses 6-7 that assures *grace beyond judgment*, Moses prays yet again to YHWH (v. 9). The prayer petitions YHWH to "go with us," again stressing that Moses cares primally about the durability of the relationship. The prayer of Moses acknowledges YHWH's verdict of Israel as "stiff-necked" and seeks pardon, a prayer back to the divine assurance of forgiveness.[8] In this prayer, Moses makes no case for Israel, does not deny the shattering affront to YHWH in the preceding chapters, and offers no ground for new possibility. Indeed, Moses throws himself and his people completely on the mercy, generosity, and graciousness of YHWH that has just been announced.

After Moses' daring petition that relied completely upon YHWH's willingness to make new, the text offers a breathtaking moment of waiting before the divine response in verse 10. Now YHWH answers and completely meets Moses' expectation. The petition of Moses is fully and positively answered in two parts. First, YHWH will make a covenant! This is the covenant "which you broke" (v. 1). The covenant will be remade. Nothing is said now of the transgression of Israel or of Aaron. It is the will of YHWH to act in mercy, graciousness, steadfast love, and faithfulness, as in verse 6. The Sinai connection begins again; most remarkably there is no hint of punishment. There is a renewal grounded only in YHWH's generous and inexplicable inclination.

But the second half of verse 10 is even more astonishing! YHWH will enact "marvels" (*nifla'oth*) that are awesome (*nora'*). The term *marvel* is the same term we have seen in Exodus 3:20, an act of sovereign power that will confound all conventional notions of how the world is ordered. These miracles, moreover, are completely unprecedented anywhere in creation or in the international community (see Exodus 9:24). That is, YHWH's best, most impressive miracles are reserved for Israel. It is especially important that the term rendered *performed* in the NRSV is the spectacular term for "create" (*bara'*). Thus the miracles pertain to creation and witness to the power and authority of the creator God. The same term is used in the same reflexive form exactly concerning creation (see Genesis 2:4):

> Male and female he created them, and he blessed them and named them "Humankind" when they were created. (Genesis 5:2)

> When you send forth your spirit, *they are created*;
> and you renew the face of the ground. (Psalm 104:30, italics added)

> Praise him, sun and moon;
> praise him, all you shining stars!
> Praise him, you highest heavens,
> and you waters above the heavens!
> Let them praise the name of the LORD,
> for he commanded and *they were created*. (Psalm 148:3-5, italics added)

The response of YHWH to the petition of Moses is on a very large scale. Israel's future is now explicitly situated in the massive, generous governance of the creator God. In this divine utterance, nothing specific is said to identify the miracles; as close as the narrative comes to specificity are the plagues in Exodus 7–11 that are regularly massive and ferocious, and the miracle of bread given in the wilderness. The use of the term *bara*ʾ coheres with Terrance Fretheim's important judgment that the exodus narrative is exactly on the horizon of creation.[9] The *novum* now to be wrought out of YHWH's mercy and graciousness is a *novum* that is of the proportion of creation, albeit for the specific benefit of Israel.

Following the pledge of YHWH to Moses to act in covenantal fidelity toward Israel who has violated covenantal fidelity, YHWH now issues a new set of commands that are variously taken by scholars as a new Decalogue or as parallel to the Decalogue of Exodus 20 (Exodus 34:11-26).[10] Covenant with YHWH characteristically exhibits the requirements of the sovereign, covenant Lord. The conclusion of the narrative in Exodus 34:27-28 picks up the theme of "forty days and forty nights" from Exodus 24:18, and explicitly refers to the Decalogue of 20:1-17. This reference to the "ten words" at the end of the narrative makes clear that the narrative is self-consciously playing against the Sinai pericope of Exodus 19–24. The play against the earlier text sets in tension in a paradigmatic way the initial covenant and the broken-remade covenant.

It is impossible to overstate the cruciality of Exodus 32–34 for Old Testament theology. When these chapters are twinned with the antecedent text of Exodus 19–24, we are able to observe the dramatic wholeness of the text that pivots around Exodus 32 and the verdict concerning, "the former tablets, which you broke" (Exodus 34:1). The overriding theme of the entire drama is not *covenant making* but it is *remaking broken covenant*. Israel can, to be sure, remember the original covenant making at Sinai. But the characteristic mode of Israel's life with YHWH and YHWH's life with Israel is *broken covenant being renewed in YHWH's mercy*. The recognition of this fact shifts the center of interpretive gravity from the *covenant making* of Exodus 19–24 to the *covenant remaking* of Exodus 32–34. Thus the pattern is evident,

- covenant making;
- covenant breaking;
- covenant remaking.[11]

This pattern that depends completely upon YHWH's will to covenant is a most characteristic pattern in Old Testament theology. We may identify four arenas in which this pattern is operative, because in every sphere of life Israel comes to understand that a visible future is possible only in the gift of YHWH.

First, this pattern is exactly reflective of Israel's life around its core symbol of *Jerusalem.* Jerusalem—temple and monarchy—was in the tradition taken as a sign of YHWH's generous fidelity to David and through David to Israel. There is no doubt, however, that the city of David was destroyed and, in the imagination of Israel, left dormant and abandoned. The "exile" of Israel was understood for the most part to be a result of Israel's sin, sin about which the prophets had warned Israel incessantly (see 2 Kings 17:13). But the formation of the Old Testament canon around the leadership of Ezra is itself attestation that YHWH provides for the rebuilding and restoration of the holy city, albeit in a more modest Judaism: "Thus says King Cyrus of Persia: The LORD, the God of heaven, has given me all the kingdoms of the earth, and he has charged me to build him a house at Jerusalem, which is in Judah. Whoever is among you of all his people, may the LORD his God be with him! Let him go up" (2 Chronicles 36:23). Thus the lived reality of Israel in the city is understood as a drama *gifted city . . . destroyed city . . . rebuilt city,* exactly paralleling the covenant drama of our text.

The dramatic building, unbuilding, and rebuilding of the city of Jerusalem as the core symbol of Davidic faith is lined out in the liturgical materials of the Psalter.[12] On the one hand, the songs of Zion, most especially Psalms 46, 48, 76, and 84, celebrate and validate the theological claims of Jerusalem as the city of God. On the other hand, the communal laments of Psalm 74 and Psalm 79 bespeak the disaster that came upon Jerusalem, at the hands of the Babylonians. (In prophetic discourse, unlike that of the Psalter, the work of the Babylonians was at the behest of YHWH as divine judgment.) The balance of the *songs of Zion* and the *communal laments* is unmistakable in the Psalter; it is, however, the case in popular church usage that the songs of Zion are much used and celebrated, whereas the communal laments concerning the city are neglected and have, for the most part, fallen out of the repertoire. The retention and utilization of both kinds of psalms is important to understand in a full way the precariousness of the city of Jerusalem and the wonder of its life as a gift from YHWH.

Second, the large dramatic field of *Israel's prophets* follows the same movement of *judgment* against a people who violate the covenant and *hope* for a people who have been judged and are given a new future by YHWH. Ronald Clements has seen how this pattern is evident in the prophetic texts:

> In such fashion we can at least come to understand the value and meaning of the way in which distinctive patterns have been imposed upon the prophetic collections of the canon so that warnings of doom and disaster are always followed by promises of hope and restoration.... The final result in the prophetic corpus of the canon formed a recognizable unity not entirely dissimilar from that of the Pentateuch.... The Former and Latter Prophets...acquired an overarching thematic unity. This centered on the death and rebirth of Israel, interpreted theologically as acts of divine judgment and salvation.[13]

Nowhere is this twofold presentation more evident than in the book of Jeremiah. In its first twenty chapters, the book of Jeremiah is largely preoccupied with the oracles of judgment that anticipate that the violation of covenant will lead to harsh public historical judgment. Alongside Ezekiel, Jeremiah is the most intense in voicing the common concern of the preexilic prophets that Jerusalem and Judah are on a course of self-destruction. In the final form of the text, the prophets understand violation of Torah to be the ground of divine judgment.

What is most remarkable about the prophets, however, is that in the midst of such harsh declarations about the termination of the YHWH-Israel connection, promises and hopes for a future well up that are characteristically grounded in nothing more than YHWH's good and faithful intention.[14] This is articulated in the promises of Isaiah 40–55 about YHWH's "new thing" after judgment, and in Ezekiel's new vision of restoration in Ezekiel 33–48 after harsh judgment. The promise of restoration is sounded in Lamentations 3:20-24 that utilizes the great terms of Exodus 34:6, "steadfast love, mercy, faithfulness."

That turn toward newness is nowhere more powerfully stated than in the "Book of Comfort" in Jeremiah 30–31 and specifically in the promise of covenant making in Jeremiah 31:31-34. In that divine oracle, the remaking of the covenant concerns the "covenant that they broke" (Jeremiah 31:32), a covenant intimately linked in the oracle to the exodus. The language of breaking covenant is closely paralleled to the language of shattering in Exodus 34:1, even though there the breaking concerns *tablets* and not covenant. The point, however, is the same in Exodus 34:1 and Jeremiah 31:32. The subject in both cases is the *remaking* of what has been *broken* between YHWH and Israel. As Moses bid for forgiveness as a ground for the remaking of covenant (Exodus 34:9), so the remade covenant in Jeremiah 31:34 is grounded only and precisely in divine forgiveness. In sum, the prophetic message of *judgment and hope* concerning the city of Jerusalem and the covenant of YHWH with Israel closely parallels and echoes the dramatic movement of Exodus 19–24; 32–34.

Third, the use of the verb *create* (*bara*ʾ) in Exodus 34:10 invites us to notice YHWH's larger creative activity, even while we focus upon the specifics of Israel's covenant.[15] We may see the same drama of *brokenness and remaking* in the text of Genesis 1–9. In this text, the initial gift is taken to be the goodness of creation (Genesis 1:31). That initial goodness, however, is disrupted by "corruption" that evokes a divine resolve to "make an end of all flesh" (Genesis 6:12-13). The flood narrative, YHWH's massive response of judgment against a corrupt earth, functions not unlike the wrath of YHWH (and Moses) in Exodus 32 that causes many deaths and the termination of the covenant.

But of course the wonder of the flood narrative is the "turn" of YHWH after judgment in order to reestablish the fruitful ordering of the earth (Genesis 8:22) and the establishment of a new covenant with "every living creature" (Genesis 9:10). The drama of *initial goodness, sin that brings destruction*, and a *new diving initiative* is the same as in Exodus 19–24; 32–34. Again the newness is possible because YHWH wills a relationship of fidelity that is not precluded by the recalcitrance of the object of YHWH's fidelity. Thus Rolf Rendtorff can conclude:

> To summarize: the primeval history in Genesis 1–11 and the Sinai story in Exodus 19–34 show a parallel structure. In both cases the first gift of God (creation/covenant) is endangered by human sin and threatened with destruction because of God's wrath. In both cases God changes his mind because of (the intervention of) one man (Noah/Moses). In both cases God promises not to bring destruction again (on humanity/on Israel), and in order to confirm that he (re)establishes his covenant (*berith*). Now neither humanity nor Israel lives in the original situation of creation or covenant, but in a restored one, which is spoiled by human sin but whose continuous existence, nevertheless, is guaranteed by the *berith* God himself has established.[16]

The quite distinct spheres of YHWH's appearance—in creation and in history—both rely completely upon YHWH's fidelity that is in the end not disrupted by either the recalcitrance of Israel or by the corruption of creation.

Fourth, and in a less direct way, the same pattern of brokenness and newness is evident in the Psalter, especially in the laments that evoke divine acts of rescue and divine oracles of assurance.[17] Because of that regular evocation, laments characteristically culminate in praise and thanksgiving for YHWH's readiness to rescue and begin again.

We may take the four episodes of Psalm 107:4-32 as a characteristic drama of brokenness and newness in the life of Israel. The four episodes feature four crises in the life of human persons, presumably Israelites, in disarray in the desert (vv. 4-9), in prison (vv. 10-16), through sickness (vv. 17-22), and during storm at sea (vv. 23-32). In each case, those who are at risk cry out to YHWH in their need, and in each case YHWH hears and rescues. Thus the transaction is the very same as in the initial exchange of Exodus 2:23-25. In two of these cases, the crisis is understood as evoked by transgression against YHWH. In verse 11, they had "rebelled against the words of God"; in verse 17, sickness was "through their sinful ways." In the other two cases, no explanation for the trouble is given. Thus the "fracture" of viable life is either linked to disobedience or is left without comment or explanation. Either way, Israel's only resource in circumstances that overwhelm is to cry out to YHWH and to rely upon YHWH.[18] In each case, so it is said in the Psalm, YHWH responds positively. Thus the pattern of *break and restoration* is enacted in each case.

What interests us further is the juxtaposition of two words at the end of each case (vv. 8, 15, 21, 31). On the one hand, it is affirmed that the rescue is grounded in YHWH's "steadfast love" (*khesedh*). On the other hand, YHWH's rescue is accomplished through YHWH's "wonderful works" (*nifle᾽oth*). YHWH's steadfast love is abiding and durable in and through the several crises of Israel's life; that steadfast love, however, in particular circumstances requires a dazzling exhibit of divine power that overrides the threat that is made against human life.

We may summarize the pattern that persists in various articulations of Israel's faith:

Break from initial goodness	**Restoration by YHWH's faithful grace**
Exodus 32 in violation of covenant	Exodus 34:10 new covenant exhibited in "marvels"
Jerusalem destroyed	Jerusalem restored
prophetic judgment	prophetic promise
flood is punishment on corrupt creation	new covenant with "every living creature"
a cry of need in crisis	rescue by a "wonderful work" rooted in "steadfast love"

The recurring pattern that attests to YHWH's decisive and generous fidelity is evident in every sphere of life: (a) Israel's narrative memory of *Sinai*, (b) the life and destiny of the city of *Jerusalem* that is (c) imagined through *prophetic declarations* of judgment and hope, (d) *creation* that fractured in corruption and was given new life in covenant, and (e) *personal existence* that relies upon YHWH's responsive care and intervention. It is evident that the pattern of *break and remake* permeates all of Israel's imaginative construals of reality and was no doubt a dominant template of Israel's cultic practice that sustained the community over the generations.[19] As a result of such liturgical activity, the Israelites were prepared and able to reconstrue much of its life and experience through this imaginative taxonomy. While this is not the only such template in the Old Testament, it is certainly a central and dominant one.

The importance of this pattern of imaginative interpretation is all the more powerful when it is recognized that in two ways the claim of this pattern is profoundly *countercultural* in almost every circumstance. In the Old Testament itself, both the claim of a *break made in judgment* and the claim of a *genuine novum* challenge dominant cultural assumptions. The assertion that divine judgment may be severe and lead to termination is a part of the core pattern. Thus in Exodus 32 the tablets (and the covenant) are indeed totally shattered . . . as was Jerusalem . . . as was creation. (In Christian tradition, it is no doubt that this radical break is taken up in the narrative of the crucifixion of Jesus.)[20]

That utter termination that is present in all of these scenarios is challenged by the *shalom prophets* who refuse the depth of prophetic judgment and who voice the perennial conviction of dominant culture. The assertion of the *shalom* prophets is that YHWH is so deeply committed to Israel (and to Jerusalem) that termination is unthinkable. Thus reference may be made to Hananiah (Jeremiah 28:3-4, 11) and those prophets critiqued by Ezekiel:

> My hand will be against the prophets who see false visions and utter lying divinations; they shall not be in the council of my people, nor be enrolled in the register of the house of Israel, nor shall they enter the land of Israel; and you shall know that I am the Lord GOD. Because, in truth, because they have misled my people, saying, "Peace," when there is no peace; and because, when the people build a wall, these prophets smear whitewash on it. (Ezekiel 13:9-10)

Those who deny such deep disruption—and so deny the judging work of YHWH—continue to announce *shalom* over Jerusalem because they believe the city is protected by YHWH's presence and is immune to judgment:

> For from the least to the greatest of them,
> everyone is greedy for unjust gain;
> and from prophet to priest,
> everyone deals falsely.
>
> They have treated the wound of my people carelessly,
> saying, "Peace, peace,"
> when there is no peace.
>
> They acted shamefully, they committed abomination;
> yet they were not ashamed,
> they did not know how to blush.
> Therefore they shall fall among those who fall;
> at the time that I punish them, they shall be overthrown,
> says the LORD. (Jeremiah 6:13-15) (see 8:10-12)

That is, they engage in denial and believe that radical judgment "cannot happen here." The tradition we have traced from Exodus 32 counters such an illusion with a conviction about YHWH's severity and the conditionality of all human existence, including the people and the city that YHWH loves.

Second, the assertion that YHWH will work a newness is countercultural in every culture of despair. Those who despair about the future (who may be buoyant managers of the present) do not believe that YHWH could enact a radical *novum* that is beyond human reasonableness. They may believe that the world is closed and not open to miracle (a quite "modern conviction") or they may believe that YHWH is weak, powerless, or indifferent. This counsel of despair, so richly countered by Second Isaiah, is evident in the sentiments assigned to the adversaries of the prophetic poet:

> Why do you say, O Jacob,
> and speak, O Israel,
> "My way is hidden from the LORD,
> and my right is disregarded by my God"? (Isaiah 40:27)

> But Zion said, "The LORD has forsaken me,
> my Lord has forgotten me." (Isaiah 49:14; see Jeremiah 8:20)

> Is my hand shortened, that it cannot redeem?
> Or have I no power to deliver? (Isaiah 50:2; see Isaiah 59:1)

These articulations of despair that echo the laments of Israel are statements of resignation about the future. This despair doubts the capacity and willingness of YHWH to do anything radically new. Clearly the claim made for YHWH in Israel, so evident in Exodus 34:10, allows that YHWH can indeed work a newness beyond Israelite possibility or explanation. (There is no doubt in Christian tradition it is this capacity for YHWH to do a *novum* in the history of the world that eventuates in churches' confession of the resurrection of Jesus.[21])

The twinned resistances of *denial* and *despair* are deeply rooted even in ancient Israel. It is abundantly clear, moreover, that these are also quite contemporary options. The core tradition of Israel *refuses such denial* and is honest about the break. The core tradition of Israel is *resistant to despair* and is buoyant about new possibility for YHWH's own intention. The counter to both denial and despair is the confessed reality of YHWH as remembered, portrayed, imagined, and anticipated in the text of Israel.

III. GOD AS PRIMAL CHARACTER AND AGENT

CHAPTER FIVE

YHWH AS SOVEREIGN GOD

YHWH, according to the testimony of the Old Testament, is a sovereign who presides in power and authority over heaven and earth, over all creation, and over the historical processes of human affairs. In characterizing YHWH in this way as the Old Testament pervasively does, the Old Testament participates in the "common" religious affirmation of ancient Near Eastern culture in which every state and tribe acknowledges and exalts in a high God who is credited with power and authority.[1] Indeed it is clear that the Old Testament not only shares this perspective, but makes use of antecedent liturgical and theological materials in order to make the theological claim that it makes. Insofar as YHWH is described in such common categories, YHWH is not unlike the gods of the ancient Near East who are variously understood as active agents for whom the preferred mode of discourse is narrative, characteristic mythic articulation in liturgic context. Such a God of whom YHWH is one (a) is credited with immense power and authority, (b) governs broadly but at the same time in the interest of a particular social community (state), and (c) presides over an assembly of lesser gods who submit to and perform the will of the High God.[2] The God featured in this common theology is the Creator God who maintains the world through edicts that enact sanctions of rewards and punishments, and who acts as is necessary to preserve the world and its just order. This God of common theology appears in many forms; in contemporary popular religion this God shows up as the "enforcer" of a *quid pro quo* morality, as a source of patriarchal authoritarianism, as the champion of the religion of the state with its self-assured military capacity, and even as the Santa Claus figure who "knows who has been bad or good."

There is no doubt that the God of the Old Testament participates to some large extent in this common theology. However common theology is construed, it does not provide adequate categories through which to present the God of the Old Testament; what interests us in Old Testament theology is the narrative particularity of the presentation of YHWH whereby the distinctiveness of YHWH is made evident, and nuance is given to common theology that sets the faith of Israel apart from the high theologies of its religious environment.[3] In order to consider the narrative particularity of the God of Israel, this discussion of YHWH's sovereignty will pursue two lines of investigation. First, I will consider *the narrative particularity of YHWH* in the three "primal self-disclosures" that I have considered in Exodus 2:23–4:17, Exodus 19–24, and Exodus 32–34. On that basis, second, I will consider the ways in which the articulation of YHWH is developed in the Old Testament in terms of dominant metaphors for YHWH.

The three narratives of divine self-disclosure—and the account of the exodus—exhibit YHWH's sovereignty through faithful imagination, connecting YHWH to every dimension of life in the world.

■ YHWH is the *sovereign creator* who presides over the earth and over all creatures—human and nonhuman—that inhabit the earth. This affirmation is explicitly stated in Exodus 20:11 but is everywhere implied.[4] The citation in Exodus 20:11 clearly alludes back to the creation liturgy of Genesis 1:1–2:4a. It calls attention, moreover, to the observance of the sabbath, as in Genesis 2:2-3, as a sign that YHWH's creation is well ordered, stable, and peaceful, free of restless chaos and anxiety. Exodus 19:5, in making a signal claim for YHWH's connection to Israel, does so in a sweeping assertion that the "whole earth belongs to me" (see Psalm 24:1-2). The reason that the whole earth is a possession of YHWH is that YHWH has caused the earth to be. The earth is precisely the domain of YHWH's sovereignty. The large claims of Exodus 19:5 and 20:11 are given particularity in the plague narrative of Exodus 7–11 wherein YHWH evokes "natural disasters" (wonders) in order to bring Pharaoh reluctantly to obedience. Indeed, it is possible to see that the "wind" (*ruakh*) that causes the disturbance of the waters is precisely YHWH's "spirit" (*ruakh*) that broods over the earth in sovereign ways as it did in the initial account of creation (Genesis 1:2). Most specifically, it is YHWH's ability to transpose the Nile River into a channel of death that makes YHWH's capacity as creator unmistakable (Exodus 7:14-25).[5] YHWH manages creation in order to accomplish YHWH's end, which is to "get glory" over Pharaoh (Exodus 14:4, 17). The prophetic poem of Isaiah 19:5-10 reflects on YHWH's disturbance of the Nile that attests both that the Nile is subject to the whim of YHWH, and that Pharaoh has no autonomous power. Pharaoh may indeed flaunt his supposed autonomy and even make the claim that he is the creator of the Nile: "My Nile is my own; / I made it for myself" (Ezekiel 29:3). But the exodus narrative says otherwise. And what the narrative asserts of YHWH's sovereignty over the Nile is everywhere extended in prophetic faith to all of creation. The God who creates is the God who may uncreate (Jeremiah 4:23-26)!

■ YHWH is *sovereign over the affairs of kingdoms, states, and empires* and presides over the international scene.[6] The exodus story, of course, narrates the way in which YHWH exercises sovereignty over Pharaoh and eventually brings Pharaoh to recognize that sovereignty (Exodus 9:27; 10:16). In a less dramatic way, the repeated inventory of the seven small nations in Exodus 3:8, 17; 23:23; 33:2 makes clear that YHWH presides over all nations and can reassign and redeploy territory from other nations to Israel precisely because "all the earth belongs to me." As dominion over Pharaoh stands at the beginning of the Old Testament, so dominion over Nebuchadnezzar plays a large role at the end of the Old Testament. Nebuchadnezzar is reckoned, in prophetic discourse, to be "my servant" (Jeremiah 25:9; 27:6); but in the end Nebuchadnezzar is only YHWH's recalcitrant servant who must be "brought low" in order to accept YHWH's sovereignty (Isaiah 47). The narrative of Daniel 4, quite late in the Old Testament, is not unlike the exodus concerning Pharaoh, wherein Nebuchadnezzar eventually must learn to praise and submit to YHWH:

> At that time my reason returned to me; and my majesty and splendor were restored to me for the glory of my kingdom. My counselors and my lords sought me out, I was re-established over my kingdom, and still more greatness was added to me. Now I, Nebuchadnezzar, praise and extol and honor the King of heaven,
> for all his works are truth,
> and his ways are justice;
> and he is able to bring low
> those who walk in pride. (Daniel 4:36-37)

Between Pharaoh and Nebuchadnezzar, it is clear that the Old Testament everywhere reckons the international process to be an arena of YHWH's rule.[7] Thus the prophets—both in their citation of foreign nations as instruments of YHWH's judgment on Israel and in the Oracles Against the Nations dismiss autonomous imperial power—regularly assert YHWH's rule and YHWH's purpose. In a defiant and dismissive tone, Isaiah, for example, derides Assyria's pretension to autonomous power:

> The LORD of hosts has sworn:
> As I have designed,
> so shall it be;
> and as I have planned,
> so shall it come to pass:
> I will break the Assyrian in my land,
> and on my mountains trample him under foot;
> his yoke shall be removed from them,
> and his burden from their shoulders.
> This is the plan that is planned
> concerning the whole earth;
> and this is the hand that is stretched out
> over all the nations.
> For the LORD of hosts has planned,
> and who will annul it?
> His hand is stretched out,
> and who will turn it back? (Isaiah 14:24-27)[8]

- *YHWH's intention ("plan") cannot finally be thwarted by human pride or self-assertion*. In the end, it is imagined that all nations of the people will submit to YHWH's Torah in a way that will bring disarmament and peace in the world (Isaiah 2:2-4; Micah 4:1-4). It is on this basis, in Christian tradition, that there is hope for all "nations and tongues" to join in common worship and common peace (Revelation 5:9; 7:9; 10:11; 11:9; 13:7). It is on this basis that the church prays that YHWH's rule may come on earth as in heaven.
- *YHWH's overriding intentionality is that YHWH's sovereignty will create new futures of well-being*. YHWH is sovereign over the future. This claim is articulated in the regular citation in our primal text concerning the promise to the ancestors, that YHWH will be with Israel to bring Israel to the good land (Exodus 2:24; 3:6, 16; 4:5). YHWH has made the promise, and it is a source of abiding hope that the promise persists because YHWH is faithful. The specific promise that is accented in our text is that YHWH has promised the ancestor's *land* and well-being derived from

the land that is fertile and peaceable. In Exodus 23:31, the anticipation of a "Greater Israel" is intimately linked to the covenantal promise made to Abraham in Genesis 15:18-21: "I will set your borders from the Red Sea to the sea of the Philistines, and from the wilderness to the Euphrates; for I will hand over to you the inhabitants of the land, and you shall drive them out before you" (Exodus 23:31).

It is impossible to overstate the importance of the land promise that hovers over all of the Old Testament.[9] It is clear that the remembered promise of land became decisive for Israel in the deportation of the sixth century when Jews experienced displacement from the land.[10] In the great prophetic promises of the sixth century, the promise to the ancestors continues to be a source of buoyancy amid debilitating circumstance:

> Listen to me, you that pursue righteousness,
> you that seek the LORD.
> Look to the rock from which you were hewn,
> and to the quarry from which you were dug.
> Look to *Abraham* your father
> and to *Sarah* who bore you;
> for he was but one when I called him,
> but I blessed him and made him many.
> For the LORD will comfort Zion;
> he will comfort all her waste places,
> and will make her wilderness like Eden,
> her desert like the garden of the LORD;
> joy and gladness will be found in her,
> thanksgiving and the voice of song. (Isaiah 51:1-3, italics added)

> Thus says the LORD: Only if I had not established my covenant with day and night and the ordinances of heaven and earth, would I reject the offspring of Jacob and of my servant David and not choose any of his descendants as rulers over the offspring of *Abraham, Isaac, and Jacob*. For I will restore their fortunes, and will have mercy upon them. (Jeremiah 33:25-26, italics added)

> Mortal, the inhabitants of these waste places in the land of Israel keep saying, "*Abraham* was only one man, yet he got possession of the land; but we are many; the land is surely given us to possess." (Ezekiel 33:24, italics added; see Leviticus 26:40-45)

That land promise persists as a powerful force in current politics in the Near East, sometimes taken up in harsh ideological form.[11] (As with all such religious claims, interpretation of Old Testament theology must be alert to ideological dimensions of tradition, for no tradition is innocent in its formulation of faith.)

There is, of course, a second dimension to the ancestral promises, namely, that Israel would be a blessing to the nations (Genesis 12:3; 22:18; 26:4; 28:14).[12] Because our texts of primal disclosure of YHWH are primarily preoccupied with Israel's destiny in moving from slavery to land, this motif of a blessing to the nations is not given much attention in these texts. There is, however, one most remarkable text that Hans Walter Wolff has read in relationship to the larger scope of blessing. In Exodus 12:31-32, Pharaoh's final word to Moses and to the departing Israelite slaves is a word of dismissal: "Then he summoned Moses and Aaron in the night, and said, 'Rise up, go away from my people, both you and the Israelites! Go, worship the LORD, as you said. Take your flocks and your herds, as you said, and be gone.'" But then, remarkably, Pharaoh adds an imperative to Moses: "And bring a blessing on me too!" In the moment of that utterance, there is a dramatic role reversal between the great imperial power and the vulnerable slave community. Now the empire acknowledges that the slave community identified with YHWH is a carrier of blessing for the nations (see Ezekiel 32:31-32).[13] This bid by Pharaoh for a blessing would seem to echo the Abrahamic assurance, though it is to be noted, perhaps pointedly, that Moses makes no response to Pharaoh's request for a blessing. At this point in the narrative Pharaoh remains unblessed as Moses withholds a blessing. The exodus narrative only leaves the implied claim that Moses has the capacity to bless Pharaoh, were he prepared to do so.

The second text that may be related to the Abrahamic theme of blessing the nations is the enigmatic identification of Israel as "a priestly kingdom" (Exodus 19:6).[14] In the text the phrase is not at all explicated. If, however, we take the modifier *priestly* with seriousness, the phrase suggests that Israel may *mediate* the need of the nations to God by intercession and *mediate* the blessing of God to the nations that stand in need of blessing. None of that is spelled out here. Nonetheless, the phrasing suggests an awareness that in the sovereignty of YHWH, Israel is linked to the other nations and has responsibility and opportunity to impact the other nations according to the intention of YHWH. Both texts, Exodus 12:32 and Exodus 19:6, fall far short of anything that could be construed as missional; at the same time, these uses suggest that Israel's life with YHWH is not lived in a vacuum, precisely because YHWH's sovereign rule encompasses all nations and is not confined to the well-being of Israel. In the end, YHWH's rule for the sake of new futures of well-being encompasses Israel and the world that Israel inhabits.[15]

YHWH's sovereignty concerns all of creation and all peoples within creation. Nonetheless, it is inescapably the case that in these narratives of primal disclosure, *YHWH's sovereignty is fully devoted to the creation and deliverance of Israel* as YHWH's "treasured possession" (Exodus 19:5).[16] Though the governance of YHWH pertains to creation and to the peoples of the earth, there is no doubt that the narratives that cluster around these three primal disclosures concern Israel, a people whose destiny runs from slavery through wilderness to the land of promise long since intended for the chosen heirs of Abraham. What has been called the *election*—better *chosenness*—of Israel is a central conviction of Old Testament theology, a particularity that is characteristically scandalous to more generic religion.

Out of the rich material on this theme, we may make the following observations:

■ The "chosenness of Israel" in the narrative of Moses begins in divine attentiveness to the suffering of Israel, an attentiveness that causes YHWH to notice, to remember, and to come down:

> God heard their groaning, and God remembered his covenant with Abraham, Isaac, and Jacob. God looked upon the Israelites, and God took notice of them. (Exodus 2:24-25)

> Then the LORD said, "I have observed the misery of my people who are in Egypt; I have heard their cry on account of their taskmasters. Indeed, I know their sufferings, and I have come down to deliver them from the Egyptians, and to bring them up out of that land to a good and broad land, a land flowing with milk and honey, to the country of the Canaanites, the Hittites, the Amorites, the Perizzites, the Hivites, and the Jebusites." (Exodus 3:7-8)

"Chosenness" here bespeaks YHWH's resolve to rescue Israel from unbearable suffering and to offer to Israel an alternative life of dignity, security, and well-being. This commitment on YHWH's part is enacted through the contestation of the exodus narrative and continues through the wondrous provisions made for the wilderness sojourn.

■ It is the insistence of Sinai, as just noted above, that the intention of YHWH is to form for YHWH's own self "my treasured possession" out of all the peoples over whom YHWH presides. This phrase suggests that whereas YHWH governs all peoples in a public way, YHWH's attachment to Israel is of a different sort, an attachment bespeaking intimacy, peculiar passion, and entitlement for Israel that are not extended to other peoples who are also YHWH's subjects. The entire narrative faith of Israel pivots on this special relationship that has no parallel elsewhere and ultimately has no explanation.

The way in which Israel is to become and remain YHWH's "treasured possession," however, is not simply by divine designation, but by vigorous, intense, intentional adherence to YHWH's commands given in the Torah of Sinai. By situating "chosenness" at Sinai, we can see that the tradition witnesses to the *unconditional* commitment of YHWH to Israel that is *conditioned* by Torah obedience. Thus the status of Israel as YHWH's chosen people participates in the riddle of conditionality and unconditionality, or we may better say, that the categories of unconditionality and conditionality are unhelpful for this relationship that moves in its wonder beyond all explanatory categories.

The status of Israel as YHWH's chosen people depends upon Israel being "holy," that is, being singularly and uncompromisingly devoted to YHWH.[17] Thus the term *holy* in Exodus 19:6 pertains to Israel's peculiar status. It is fair to say that the remainder of Torah exposition at Sinai is intended to explicate a notion of holiness. The root meaning of the term is that Israel *belongs exclusively* to YHWH and has no other competing loyalty. It remained for subsequent mediation and interpretation, both at Sinai and beyond Sinai, to propose what Israel's holiness might entail. Most prominently, the Priestly tradition urged Israel as a "holy people": "Speak to all the congregation of the people of Israel and say to them: You shall be holy, for I the LORD your God am holy" (Leviticus 19:2). The Priestly tradition proposed and advocated a community of purity without disturbance or disorder.

At the same time, in other traditions, it was recognized that Israel could not "qualify" for chosenness; rather chosenness was YHWH's inexplicable decision rooted in YHWH's own inclination:

> It was not because you were more numerous than any other people that the LORD *set his heart* on you and chose you—for you were the fewest of all peoples. It was because the LORD loved you and kept the oath that

> he swore to your ancestors, that the LORD has brought you out with a mighty hand, and redeemed you from the house of slavery, from the hand of Pharaoh king of Egypt. (Deuteronomy 7:7-8, italics added)

The crucial word is *set his heart* (*khashaq*), reiterated in Deuteronomy 10: "Although heaven and the heaven of heavens belong to the LORD your God, the earth with all that is in it, yet the LORD *set his heart* in love on your ancestors alone and chose you, their descendants after them, out of all the peoples, as it is today" (vv. 14-15). Lest Israel imagine that it was in any way "qualified" to be YHWH's intimate treasure, the tradition of Deuteronomy refutes the notion:

> When the LORD your God thrusts them out before you, do not say to yourself, "It is because of my righteousness that the LORD has brought me in to occupy this land"; it is rather because of the wickedness of these nations that the LORD is dispossessing them before you. It is not because of your righteousness or the uprightness of your heart that you are going in to occupy their land; but because of the wickedness of these nations the LORD your God is dispossessing them before you, in order to fulfill the promise that the LORD made on oath to your ancestors, to Abraham, to Isaac, and to Jacob. (Deuteronomy 9:4-5)

Thus Israel's status before YHWH remains, even to Israel itself, something of an inexplicable reality. In the prophetic tradition, the status of Israel as YHWH's chosen people caused severe judgment against Israel, a judgment that is rooted exactly in Israel's special status and in YHWH's special expectation of Israel:

> You only have I known
> of all the families of the earth;
> therefore I will punish you
> for all your iniquities. (Amos 3:2)

Given much harsh judgment on the lips of the prophets, the question inescapably arises whether Israel can, by habitual disobedience, forfeit its relationship with YHWH. That question arose acutely in the sixth century exile, and in imaginative metaphor is refuted by the prophet:

> But Zion said, "The LORD has forsaken me,
> my LORD has forgotten me."

Can a woman forget her nursing child,
or show no compassion for the child of her womb? (Isaiah 49:14-15)[18]

Thus the very chosenness that evokes harsh divine *judgment* is chosenness that becomes the ground of *hope* during the most acute crisis of ancient Israel.

There is no doubt that the object of YHWH's exodus work is precisely the "liberation" of *slaves* from Egypt, so that they may become "servants" (*slaves* of YHWH), a transposition accomplished at Sinai (see Leviticus 25:42).[19] It is the case that YHWH responds in powerful ways to the suffering and cries of the slaves in order to create a new community of obedience to YHWH, that is, the story is concretely about the people of Israel.[20]

There also can be no doubt that divine attentiveness to the slaves has become paradigmatic for many peoples who have claimed the Yahwistic "revolution" as the ground of subsequent revolutionary activity.[21] The move from the *particularity of Israel* to a *paradigmatic model* that pertains to many subsequent peoples is a tricky one, as is evidenced in the strictures of Jon Levenson's critique of the work of Jorge Pixley.[22] As I understand it, Levenson is concerned not only with the loss of Jewish particularity in Pixley's paradigmatic approach, but also with the confusion over or displacement of covenantal attentiveness by modern autonomous notions of freedom and liberation. The emancipated people of Israel were not emancipated in order to live autonomously in the world; rather they are destined to go to Sinai, and there to submit in willing obedience to the purpose of the creator God. Given Levenson's thoughtful and severe critique, it is clear that the move from the *particular* to the *paradigmatic* needs to be made with extreme care.

But it is nonetheless a move that will readily be made by any oppressed people that finds in the holy power of YHWH an openness in history to a new existence. Such interpretive moves can be critiqued as Levenson has done when carelessly made, but they cannot be stopped or silenced. YHWH is inextricably drawn to suffering Israelites; but *mutatis mutandis*, YHWH is characteristically drawn to suffering peoples. Carefully nuanced we may indeed, with reference to these texts, speak of YHWH's "preferential option" for the poor and the suffering.[23] At the very edge of the Old Testament, we may notice two texts that daringly suggest that alongside Israel as "treasured possession," alongside but not in place of Israel, YHWH may have other treasured possessions as well. In Amos 9:7, it is imagined that as YHWH has enacted the deliverance of Israel, so

YHWH conducts other exoduses with other peoples whom YHWH notices and to whose cries YHWH answers:

> Are you not like the Ethiopians to me,
> O people of Israel? says the LORD.
> Did I not bring Israel up from the land of Egypt,
> and the Philistines from Caphtor and the Arameans from Kir?
> (Amos 9:7)[24]

In Isaiah 19:24-25, moreover, it is anticipated that alongside Israel and not in place of Israel, there will be other preferential peoples on the horizon of YHWH, one termed *my people* and one named *the work of my hands*: "On that day Israel will be the third with Egypt and Assyria, a blessing in the midst of the earth, whom the LORD of hosts has blessed, saying, 'Blessed be Egypt my people, and Assyria the work of my hands, and Israel my heritage'" (Isaiah19:24-25). Such imaginative texts do not detract from the core claim of Israel's status with YHWH. They do, however, speak powerfully against the temptation to religious monopoly, a temptation in Israel to imagine the privileged entitlement that is exclusive. The dominant narrative focuses on Israel to be sure; its sense of the large sovereignty of YHWH, however, eventually tells against inclusivism. There is no way in which all of these claims about Israel's chosenness can be made consistent, for the claim of chosenness is a supple one that requires many different nuances in different circumstances, nuances that run from grand entitlement to severe judgment. The rich interpretive alternatives attached to Israel's chosenness are not unexpected, given the claim that the one who chooses Israel is at the same time the active sovereign Lord of all, "God of gods and Lord of lords" (Deuteronomy 10:17).[25]

YHWH's sovereignty, as attested in these primal narratives of self-disclosure, is as the decisive ruler over *creation*, over *the nations*, over *Israel*, and over *the future*. As the decisive ruler whose word and action function to determine the status of every creature in the realm of creation, YHWH is a "High God" not unlike the high gods of the common theology of the ancient Near East and not unlike the high god of much conventional, classical Christianity. But of course such a capacity to govern decisively is not the whole story of this sovereign, for YHWH's sovereignty is *sovereignty in relationship*, an inexplicable mystery that is at the heart of biblical testimony. As Israel attests, relationships of fidelity and loyalty to which YHWH is committed do not lessen or diminish YHWH's capacity for governance. But they do decisively change the character of sovereignty so that YHWH is not disinterested in or unaffected by the reality of the partners in the relationship.[26] Here I will call attention to three texts that nicely summarize the claim of *sovereignty in relationship*:

■ In Exodus 2:24-25 and Exodus 3:7-8, YHWH is impinged upon and responsive to the cries and sufferings of Israel; in response to these cries, YHWH acts to set in motion the primal action that constitutes Israel's core memory of faith. On behalf of the sufferings of Israel in slavery, YHWH sets out to overthrow and delegitimate the powerful regime of Pharaoh. That is, YHWH's sovereignty is on exhibit precisely in response to the need of those with whom YHWH has intensely related. The testimony is clear that this is a free inclination on YHWH's part, in no way evoked by any "quality" on the part of Israel, not its size or its virtue. That free act of commitment is because YHWH "set his heart" on Israel and thereby distinguished this divine governance from every other divine governance, for no other god has committed to a people... as distinct from a state or a regime.

The Bible is not able or willing to say why this relationship is undertaken that so decisively reshapes divine sovereignty. It is possible to say that YHWH is a God peculiarly attentive to and responsive to suffering, a thought that gives rise to the notion of "God's preferential option for the poor." Of course, the Old Testament does not attest that YHWH is allied with every such community of suffering, but only with this particular community of suffering. The attestation in the text is the affirmation that YHWH's attentiveness to enslaved Israel is because of the antecedent commitment that YHWH has made to the ancestors in Genesis.[27] But that explanation of course only pushes our wonderment back in time, for we are given no reason for YHWH's initial attachment to the ancestors. More cannot be said; the attachment is a given of biblical faith. Characteristically, YHWH's sovereignty is enacted with primal attentiveness to Israel, not least when YHWH's judgment comes most harshly on recalcitrant Israel.

■ In YHWH's self-declaration of Exodus 34:6-7, the accent is all on relatedness.[28] The five basic terms of "merciful, gracious, slow to anger, steadfast love, faithfulness" all concern the way in which YHWH will relate to Israel—and by interference to all of creation—in ways of fidelity. The future anticipated by these terms is short-term judgment and long-term forgiveness. To be sure, the power that makes such related sovereignty viable is here and everywhere in Israel assumed. It is not doubted that YHWH has as much power as any high god whom YHWH replicates or rivals. But *divine power per se* is not very interesting in Israel or the subject of much critical reflection. Rather the accent, characteristically, is upon the deployment of divine power in the interest of relatedness. Thus Job, at the far reach of Israel's critical reflection, can readily concede divine power:

> "Indeed I know that this is so;
> but how can a mortal be just before God?
> If one wished to contend with him,
> one could not answer him once in a thousand.
> He is wise in heart, and mighty in strength
> —who has resisted him, and succeeded?—
> he who removes mountains, and they do not know it,
> when he overturns them in his anger;
> who shakes the earth out of its place,
> and its pillars tremble;
> who commands the sun, and it does not rise;
> who seals up the stars;
> who alone stretched out the heavens
> and trampled the waves of the Sea;
> who made the Bear and Orion,
> the Pleiades and the chambers of the south;
> who does great things beyond understanding,
> and marvelous things without number.
> Look, he passes by me, and I do not see him;
> he moves on, but I do not perceive him.
> He snatches away; who can stop him?
> Who will say to him, "What are you doing?" (Job 9:2-12)

What preoccupies Job, however, is not divine power that is fully and gladly affirmed. Rather the issue is about relatedness, justice, innocence, blamelessness, and guilt. On these questions, according to Job, YHWH receives low marks:

> It is all one; therefore I say,
> he destroys both the blameless and the wicked.
> When disaster brings sudden death,
> he mocks at the calamity of the innocent.
> The earth is given into the hand of the wicked;
> he covers the eyes of its judges—
> if it is not he, who then is it? (Job 9:22-24)

Eventually the enigma of *divine power* and *divine fidelity* will lead to the question of theodicy.[29] But long before that question is formally posed, Israel utilizes its critical energy and its faithful passion to engage the relatedness of YHWH. YHWH, moreover, does not dissent from the issue of relatedness, but asserts YHWH's self precisely in terms of fidelity.

■ Alongside Exodus 34:6-7, the interaction of Moses with YHWH in light of the broken tablets and the broken covenant culminates in YHWH's high-handed negotiation with Moses in Exodus 33:12-21. Moses makes demands; YHWH grants some of those demands and resists others. For our purposes the decisive utterance of YHWH concerning sovereignty in relationship is YHWH's self-declaration in verse 19: "And he said, 'I will make all my goodness pass before you, and will proclaim before you the name, "The LORD"; and I will be gracious to whom I will be gracious, and will show mercy on whom I will show mercy'" (Exodus 33:19).

It belongs to the very character of YHWH to be a God of "graciousness and mercy," the same words that are central in the self-proclamation of Exodus 34:6. That declaration of divine fidelity is the ground for Israel's hope in light of its alienation from YHWH. Thus the fidelity question is settled on the grounds of divine grace and mercy. Except that in this formulation in 33:19, grace and mercy are not unconditionally guaranteed in Israel as a possession on which Israel can count. Rather, the double use of *khanan* and *rakham* turn back to YHWH's sovereign freedom and self-regard. YHWH is not mindlessly everywhere and unconditionally committed to grace and mercy; rather the grace and mercy of YHWH cohere with and result from YHWH's inclination in the practice of YHWH's unfettered self-assertion. Beyond this Israel (or YHWH) will not go. As a consequence, we come full circle to conclude that *grace and mercy* are *functions of free divine sovereignty*. At points in Israel's attestation YHWH's self-interested sovereignty overrides the possibility of grace and mercy; at other points, grace and mercy are the full embodiment of YHWH's sovereignty. The delicacy of grace and mercy practiced by YHWH maintains YHWH's freedom to be YHWH in every circumstance; this same delicacy assures that Israel's obligation to imaginative interpretation is completely open-ended. Israel will never finish in its discernment of or attestation to YHWH's sovereignty in relationship, because YHWH will not finish being YHWH's own self in and for Israel, in and for creation, but always YHWH in full sovereignty.

CHAPTER SIX

YHWH AS SOVEREIGN—IN METAPHOR

From these primal narratives of self-disclosure Israel learns that approach to YHWH is dangerous and requires care (Exodus 3:5; 19:10-13), that YHWH will not be seen (Exodus 33:20), and that YHWH is free to act without obligation according to YHWH's own inclination (Exodus 33:19). The texts make clear that YHWH is hidden and inscrutable, beyond domestication into any of Israel's categories. For that reason there can be no images of YHWH (Exodus 20:4-6; see Deuteronomy 4:15-20), and even attempts to describe YHWH verbally are hazardous and sure to be inexact. The result is that Israel's characteristic speech concerning YHWH, expressed in song, oracles, and narrative, is according to image and metaphor that proceed playfully and imaginatively without any claim to being descriptive. At best, Israel's speech concerning YHWH is elusive and suggestive, thereby congruent with the most intense encounters with YHWH that Israel is permitted.[1]

The field of metaphors through which Israel gives testimony to YHWH is rich, varied, and complex; but all such speech seeks to articulate this God who is *sovereign in relationship*.[2] From that rich, varied, and complex field of discourse, I will mention four of the dominant metaphors used by Israel to articulate YHWH, each of which makes a claim for YHWH, but makes a claim even while it concedes that the claim is inadequate to the reality of YHWH.

1. In the exodus narrative, Israel articulates YHWH as *the divine warrior* who forcefully participates in combat with the armies of Pharaoh in order that YHWH may yet get glory and in order that the Israelite slaves

may leave bondage.[3] We may identify four accent points in Israel's appeal to YHWH's warrior, and then reflect on the claim of the metaphor.

■ The exodus narrative requires an agency of ferocious power to overcome the might and resolve of Pharaoh. It is Israel's attestation that the exodus departure is not made possible through human agency, even though Moses is prominent in the narrative. The claim of the exodus narrative is that it is YHWH who fights for Israel and who defeats the state power of Pharaoh:

> But Moses said to the people, "Do not be afraid, stand firm, and see the deliverance that the LORD will accomplish for you today; for the Egyptians whom you see today you shall never see again. The LORD will fight for you, and you have only to keep still." . . . [YHWH] clogged their chariot wheels so that they turned with difficulty. The Egyptians said, "Let us flee from the Israelites, for the LORD is fighting for them against Egypt. (Exodus 14:13-14, 25)

There is no doubt that the military imagery is intimately connected to the mythic imagery of creation and chaos, for the warrior God also manages and manipulates the waters of the sea:

> So Moses stretched out his hand over the sea, and at dawn the sea returned to its normal depth. As the Egyptians fled before it, the LORD tossed the Egyptians into the sea. The waters returned and covered the chariots and the chariot drivers, the entire army of Pharaoh that had followed them into the sea; not one of them remained. But the Israelites walked on dry ground through the sea, the waters forming a wall for them on their right and on their left. (Exodus 14:27-29)

Israel's earliest songs attest that YHWH is "a man of war" (Exodus 15:3). Miriam sings of the triumph of YHWH over Pharaoh: "And Miriam sang to them: / 'Sing to the LORD, for he has triumphed gloriously; / horse and rider he has thrown into the sea'" (Exodus 15:21).

The Song of Moses, moreover, celebrates the dramatic defeat of Pharaoh because of the overwhelming power of YHWH:

> Pharaoh's chariots and his army he cast into the sea;
> his picked officers were sunk into the Red Sea.
> The floods covered them;
> they went down into the depths like a stone.
> Your right hand, O LORD, glorious in power—

your right hand, O LORD, shattered the enemy.
In the greatness of your majesty you overthrew your adversaries;
you sent out your fury, it consumed them like stubble.
At the blast of your nostrils the waters piled up,
the floods stood up in a heap;
the deeps congealed in the heart of the sea.
The enemy said, "I will pursue, I will overtake,
I will divide the spoil, my desire shall have its fill of them.
I will draw my sword, my hand shall destroy them."
You blew with your wind, the sea covered them;
they sank like lead in the mighty waters. (Exodus 15:4-10)

This exodus imagery pervades the Bible, stretching the capacity of YHWH from historical enemies to cosmic, spiritual enemies that, in New Testament witness, make us "more than conquerors" (Romans 8:37).
■ The mighty capacity of YHWH in the exodus is, in the Song of Moses, extended to the conquest of the land of promise:

The peoples heard, they trembled;
pangs seized the inhabitants of Philistia.
Then the chiefs of Edom were dismayed;
trembling seized the leaders of Moab;
all the inhabitants of Canaan melted away.
Terror and dread fell upon them;
by the might of your arm, they became still as a stone
until your people, O LORD, passed by,
until the people whom you acquired passed by. (Exodus 15:14-16)

This lyrical affirmation lies behind the narrative account of land seizure in the book of Joshua. In Joshua 10–12; the seizure of the "land of Canaan" is massive and brutal. In contrast to the exodus narrative, the conquest narrative allows much more credit to human agents, as Joshua and his army are seen to be effective agents in the destruction of the resident population: "The following are the kings of the land whom Joshua and the Israelites defeated on the west side of the Jordan, from Baalgad in the valley of Lebanon to Mount Halak, that rises toward Seir (and Joshua gave the land to the tribes of Israel as a possession according to their allotments)" (Joshua 12:7). Nonetheless there can be no doubt that the whole of the narrative features YHWH as the leader of the army of Joshua and as the legitimator of the brutality enacted against the indigenous population. Indeed, it is possible to see the conquest as a twin event that reenacts the exodus in a new venue, both times featuring YHWH as the aggressive perpetrator of the new order. The twinning of the two events that feature YHWH as warrior is evident in the "as" of the theologically self-conscious statement of Joshua:

> For the LORD your God dried up the waters of the Jordan for you until you crossed over, *as* the LORD your God did to the Red Sea, which he dried up for us until we crossed over, so that all the peoples of the earth may know that the hand of the LORD is mighty, and so that you may fear the LORD your God forever. (Joshua 4:23-24, italics added)

It is clear that the land is taken by violent force, a violence that is, according to the text, at the behest of the warrior God of the exodus.

■ The treasured traditions of Israel are agreed that "YHWH fights for Israel," YHWH's chosen people and treasured possession. It is equally clear, however, in the subsequent witness of the prophets, that the military capacity of YHWH is also turned against Israel when Israel is judged and punished by covenantal sanctions for the violation of covenant Torah. In prophetic discourse, YHWH the enforcer enforces covenant sanctions most vigorously against Israel.[4]

By and large, prophetic themes of judgment allow that military threat against Israel is by identifiable military agents, most especially the Assyrians (see Isaiah 10:5-6) and then most decisively the Babylonians (Jeremiah 25:9; 27:6).[5] In such prophetic discourse, however, it is clear that human perpetrators of military violence act at the initiative of YHWH who dispatches such armies. At the same time, prophetic rhetorical can speak as though YHWH is the direct military agent. Thus in Jeremiah 21:4 the prophet anticipates the coming of the Babylonians, but then in verse 5 presents YHWH as the direct actor in military threat: "I myself will fight against you with outstretched hand and mighty arm, in anger, in fury, and in great wrath" (Jeremiah 21:5). In that declaration, moreover, the rhetoric echoes exactly the phrasing of Exodus language, so that the God who in Exodus *fights for Israel* is now to be the God who *fights against Israel.*[6] And in the telling of the normative story of ancient Israel, it is YHWH, via the Babylonians, who brings the Holy City to devastating termination.

■ We might anticipate that such an inversion of the metaphor of divine warrior would lead to the culmination of the image. The God who fought *for* now fights *against*... to the finish. Most remarkably, however, the metaphor survives the crisis of the destruction of the city and resurfaces in subsequent exilic literature to assert again that YHWH will fight for Israel. Thus in Isaiah 40:10, YHWH is again the mighty warrior on behalf of Israel. In Isaiah 40:26, YHWH marshals the stars to fight as the heavenly armies. Above all in Isaiah 43:16-17, the "new thing" that replicates and displaces the old exodus will be done by YHWH with military effectiveness:

> Thus says the LORD,
> who makes a way in the sea,
> a path in the mighty waters,
> who brings out chariot and horse,
> army and warrior;
> they lie down, they cannot rise,
> they are extinguished, quenched like a wick. (Isaiah 43:16-17)

The old claim of YHWH as warrior provides a rhetoric of hope in the sixth century, even after the divine warrior has decisively assaulted the chosen people.

There is no doubt that the imagery of divine warrior is problematic for biblical faith, as we have become increasingly aware that the Bible is permeated with violence in which YHWH is deeply enmeshed. G. Ernest Wright, in a quite old fashioned way, has indicated why this imagery is crucial for faith; it is essential to have a God of power who is known to act decisively against the strong power of evil.[7] Since the time of Wright's presentation, however, we are of course much more aware of the ways in which such imagery is a huge liability, for it serves willy-nilly to authorize and legitimate all sorts of military adventurism in the name of God; and of course at this point in time the United States propensity to use such imagery as theological justification for military adventurism is immense.

Regina Schwartz, in her programmatic analysis of violence in the Bible, has seen that the exodus-conquest traditions and the recurring premise of the warrior God are enduringly problematic in biblical faith.[8] Wright has seen that a God of power is indispensable in faith; it follows in the text and seemingly for Wright that such power of necessity comes as violence. Schwartz shows that the afterlife of the text of violence featuring the warrior God has provided a rationale for many subsequent acts of political violence:

> In the end, whether the people who generated the myth were empowered or disempowered—and making ethics contingent upon power makes a mockery of ethics as an independent court of judgment—whether they were conquerors or oppressed victims seeking liberation, they have bequeathed a myth to future generations that is ethically problematic at best, a myth that advocates the wholesale annihilation of indigenous peoples to take their land.[9]

There are, of course, interpretive strategies that can lessen the toxin of these traditions. Biblical theologians, however, must take care not to "explain away" what is so definitional for the textual tradition. This imagery is something that we must live with, albeit with awkwardness and embarrassment. We might wish for another, better theological tradition. This, however, is the one we have. The presentation of this God is not marginal to the Bible nor can it be justified simply as human projection among the disinherited, nor can it be easily resolved by a "developmental hypothesis," the preferred strategy of Old Testament scholarship. It is there; self-critical reflection requires of course critique of the very God whom Jews and Christians confess. While we make our awkward, self-aware confession, we cannot fail to notice, even among us, the ways in which this theological tradition continues to fund that which we rightly abhor.

2. When the warrior makes war—as YHWH against Pharaoh—the purpose is to overthrow entrenched power and establish a new order governed by the new intentionality of the victorious warrior. This of course is what happened as YHWH made war; YHWH went from *warrior in Egypt* to *King at Sinai*. Kings are warriors who succeed; the Old Testament is saturated with the language of "YHWH as king," the one who has overcome powers and arrangements that are inimical to YHWH's will, in order that YHWH's "kingdom and power and glory" may come to efficacious fulfillment.

The Song of Moses in Exodus 15:1-18, as we have seen, begins with a characterization of YHWH as a man of war (v. 3). By the end of the poem, Israel's drama from slavery to land is completed; the poem culminates with YHWH celebrated as king with a characteristic doxology of enthronement: "The LORD will reign forever and ever" (Exodus 15:18). The God who fought with Pharaoh now, in Israel's lyrical imagination, rings unchallenged in Jerusalem. The poem is an early articulation of Israel's characteristic connection between the temple in Jerusalem and the rule of YHWH over all the nations (see Isaiah 2:2-4). That doxological affirmation, together with many repetitions and liturgical reenactments, stands at the center of Israel's faith. Through its lyrical, doxological articulation, Israel claims YHWH's royal rule over all of creation and over all of human history.

The formula of enthronement in Exodus 15:18 is a taproot for the principal theological trajectory of the Jerusalem tradition that dominates the worship of Israel and, consequently, the Psalter in its celebration of YHWH's kingship: "Exodus 15:1-18 is the parade example of this scenario and furnishes a full paradigm for the others. When the horizon of inquiry is the canon, it stands as introductory to all other cases in the psalms and elsewhere."[10] The enthronement Psalms celebrate the liturgical reality that YHWH is king of the gods, king of creation, king over the nations including Israel (Psalms 47; 93; 96–99). Sigmund Mowinckel, moreover, has urged that this doxological reality was regularly reenacted and dramatized in the Jerusalem liturgy, a hypothesis that has recently been given new vitality by the analysis of J. J. M. Roberts.[11] This dramatic, liturgical generation of divine sovereignty reaches back into the old myths that are antecedent to Israel. In Christian tradition, the same liturgical, dramatic, doxological claim is exhibited in Christmas and Easter celebrations whereby the kingship of Jesus is celebrated and given liturgical renewal.

Less directly, the reference in Exodus 19:6 to a "priestly kingdom" also indicates royal categories of thought, though the modifier "priestly" may suggest a theocratic ideal of governance. Whatever may be the nature of the "priestly community" that is to exercise governance, behind that human arrangement is the king God who can boast of possessing the whole earth. The sweeping assumption of this text is the universal kingship of YHWH who has no rivals or competitors for legitimate power.

In both the exodus (Exodus 15:18) and at Sinai (Exodus 19:6), YHWH's royal authority is the premise and dominating reality. It is an authority gained by the defeat of Pharaoh and exercised by the enunciation of Torah. We may identify three spheres of YHWH's rule as king:

a. The first dimension of the rule of the God-king, according to the common theology of the Near East, is presiding authority over the council of the gods, and assembly in heaven of all the gods who are, in the end, subservient to and committed to the rule of the High God, YHWH. This divine kingship is articulated in the great state myths and eventually in Israel in the state myth of Jerusalem. The "divine council" is no doubt an effective poetic way to manage the reality of polytheism, while still affirming the singular preeminence of YHWH as High God.[12] This interpretive strategy is evident, for example, in Psalm 82 that envisions the divine assembly presided over by the High God: "God has taken his place in the divine council; / in the midst of the gods he holds judgment" (Psalm 82:1).

By such a poetic stratagem, Israel asserts that all powers of divinity are mobilized according to the will of YHWH:

> By myself I have sworn,
> from my mouth has gone forth in righteousness
> a word that shall not return:
> "To me every knee shall bow,
> every tongue shall swear." (Isaiah 45:23)

b. Because YHWH rules among the gods, YHWH is acknowledged to be the creator God who has made and governs heaven and earth. When it is recognized that "creation" in the Old Testament pertains consistently to the *ordering* of preextant chaos, then it is understandable that the king is the creator who by edict can compel chaos to "come to order." In Genesis 1:1-2 and in many places in the Old Testament, unshaped chaos takes the form of the raging uncontained sea that surges in damaging and intimidating ways. It is the doxological affirmation of Israel that YHWH is capable of taming the surging powers of chaos and so to make possible a safe, fruitful environment for creatureliness, both nonhuman and human. Creation faith, then, is a celebration of divine royal authority and is not at all interested in the explanatory questions that currently preoccupy the "religion-science debates" in U.S. society.

The taming of the waters of chaos is a theme that appears in the initial notice of "formless and void" (*tohu wabohu*) in Genesis 1:1-2 and, alternatively, in the capacity of YHWH to manage the seawaters in the exodus (Exodus 14:27-29; 15:4-10) and in the parallel wonder of the Jordan River (Joshua 4:18). It is affirmed in the Jeremiah tradition that the creator God set a boundary and limit on the waters (Jeremiah 5:22), and in Psalm 104:25-26 it is acknowledged that all the threat of the evil sea monster has been tamed by YHWH. Thus the work of the king is to provide *order* against every threat of chaos that makes viable, sustained, peaceable, faithful life possible.

A quite different manifestation of faith in the creator-king is evident in the wisdom traditions. These teachings, rooted in simple proverbial sayings, observe the reliable order and givenness of all reality—including social reality—that cannot be violated with impunity. Thus for good reason that wisdom teaching is reckoned to be creation theology, for wisdom focuses on the bedrock of reliable order that makes viable life possible.[13] Because "wisdom" is a discernment of created order, there is good reason that "wisdom" should declare:

> By me kings reign,
> and rulers decree what is just;
> by me rulers rule,
> and nobles, all who govern rightly. (Proverbs 8:15-16)

This statement makes clear that human kings and their capacity for order are in fact quite penultimate, for beneath such human arrangements is the guaranteed order given by the creator king.

c. When Israel reaches Sinai, the *mythic claim* of divine kingship and the *cosmic claim* of creation are assumed and implied. At Sinai, however, the agenda of the divine king now has become *political and historical*, looking to the formation of an alternative social community that coheres with the covenantal intentionality of the creator king. It is clear that YHWH is offered and received as an alternative to the kingship of Pharaoh, with an alternative vision of social reality, an alternative set of requirements and sanctions of enforcement. In Old Testament studies the articulation of this new theo-politics in Exodus 19–24 has, since the initial work of George Mendenhall, been understood in terms of a treaty-covenant that is not unlike the international treaties known in the ancient Near East.[14] While Mendenhall's initial proposal found the parallels in the Hittite treaties of the thirteenth century, more recent scholarship has found more plausible parallels in Assyrian treaties from the ninth through the seventh centuries.[15] The shift from Hittite to Assyrian models has the effect of dating the parallel evidence much later, in Israel's monarchal period.

According to either parallel and according to Israel's own texts, most notably in the full expression of the book of Deuteronomy, the covenant established by YHWH with Israel binds the client community of Israel to the will and purpose of the High God who will preside over Israel as over all nation-states as over all of creation. The covenant is grounded in YHWH's initial act of rescue (noted in Exodus 20:2 and narrated in Exodus 1–15). The covenant includes the commands of YHWH (stipulations, conditions) upon which the covenant is based (Exodus 20:1-17), an oath of allegiance on the part of Israel, and a set of sanctions (blessings and curses) that assume compliance.[16] The outcome of the transaction of Sinai is the formation of a new historical entity, Israel, that participates in the sociopolitical, economic, military life of the world, but that does so in response to the invisible king who in power and splendor transcends all the conventional limitations of human kingship. This strange interface of *political realism* and *theological foundation* is characteristic of Israel and is without parallel in the world. It is this combination that provides the dynamics of Israel's life and faith and that assures that Israel remains something of an enigma in the world of international realism. *Mutatis mutandis*, it is this same enigmatic combination that is contained in the contemporary state of Israel as it participates both in the theological claims of Judaism and is organized according to the power and risks of *realpolitik*.[17]

While scholars continue to contest the historical dating of the covenant texts, there can be no doubt that the covenant is definitional for the faith of Israel and for its self-understanding in the world. In the final form of the text, there is no doubt that the prophets are to be understood in the wake of the covenant, so that the dangers and possibilities of the historical process for the community of Israel are understood in terms of compliance to or violation of the Torah demands of covenant that thereby subject Israel to covenantal sanctions. Thus the prophetic speech of judgment among the preexilic prophets consists in an *indictment* (that amounts to violation of covenant conditions) and *sentence* (that enacts covenant sanctions).[18] In broad sweep the destruction of Jerusalem and of the historical community of Israel is understood in prophetic tradition as a consequence of broken covenant:

> There they made offerings on all the high places, as the nations did whom the LORD carried away before them. They did wicked things, provoking the LORD to anger; they served idols, of which the LORD had said to them, "You shall not do this." Yet the LORD warned Israel and Judah by every prophet and every seer, saying, "Turn from your evil ways and keep my commandments and my statutes, in accordance with all the law that I commanded your ancestors and that I sent to you by my servants the prophets." They would not listen but were stubborn, as their ancestors had been, who did not believe in the LORD their God. They despised his statutes, and his covenant that he made with their ancestors, and the warnings that he gave them. They went after false idols and became false; they followed the nations that were around them, concerning whom the LORD had commanded them that they should not

> do as they did. They rejected all the commandments of the LORD their God and made for themselves cast images of two calves; they made a sacred pole, worshiped all the host of heaven, and served Baal. They made their sons and their daughters pass through fire; they used divination and augury; and they sold themselves to do evil in the sight of the LORD, provoking him to anger. Therefore the LORD was very angry with Israel and removed them out of his sight; none was left but the tribe of Judah alone. (2 Kings 17:11-18)

The same pattern of *indictment and sentence*, the acts of the great king who presides over covenant, is clear in a variety of prophetic texts:

> Hear this word, you cows of Bashan
> who are on Mount Samaria,
> who oppress the poor, who crush the needy,
> who say to their husbands, "Bring something to drink!"
> The Lord GOD has sworn by his holiness:
> The time is surely coming upon you,
> when they shall take you away with hooks,
> even the last of you with fishhooks.
> Through breaches in the wall you shall leave,
> each one straight ahead;
> and you shall be flung out into Harmon,
> says the LORD. (Amos 4:1-3)

> Hear the word of the LORD,
> O people of Israel:
> for the LORD has an indictment
> against the inhabitants of the land.
> There is no faithfulness or loyalty,
> and no knowledge of God in the land.
> Swearing, lying, and murder,
> and stealing and adultery break out;
> bloodshed follows bloodshed.
> Therefore the land mourns,
> and all who live in it languish;
> together with the wild animals
> and the birds of the air,
> even the fish of the sea are perishing. (Hosea 4:1-3)

> Hear this, you rulers of the house of Jacob
> and chiefs of the house of Israel,

who abhor justice
  and pervert all equity,
who build Zion with blood
  and Jerusalem with wrong!
Its rulers give judgment for a bribe,
  its priests teach for a price,
  its prophets give oracles for money;
yet they lean upon the LORD and say,
  "Surely the LORD is with us!
  No harm shall come upon us."
Therefore because of you
  Zion shall be plowed as a field;
Jerusalem shall become a heap of ruins,
  and the mountain of the house a wooded height. (Micah 3:9-12)

The King's policies will prevail and cannot be circumvented by any effort of wisdom or power.

The covenant that becomes *the ground for punishment* and destruction when the king's covenant is mocked also becomes *the ground for new possibility* in the sixth century after the destruction of Jerusalem. In addition to the renewal of the covenant as the new foundation of Judaism in Jeremiah 31:31-34, the oracles of Isaiah in the exile appeal to King YHWH as the crown for Israel's future (see Isaiah 41:21; 44:6):

I am the LORD, your Holy One,
  the Creator of Israel, your King. . . .
How beautiful upon the mountains
  are the feet of the messenger who announces peace,
who brings good news,
  who announces salvation,
  who says to Zion, "Your God reigns." (Isaiah 43:15; 52:7)

Thus the king of the covenant is the one who punishes the covenant people and the one who makes newness possible for that punished people.

Alongside prophetic appeal to the covenant and to the king who presides over it, scholars have identified Psalms 50, 81, and 95 as liturgical presentations of the covenant broken and the covenant restored; thus the community that violates the will of the king is presented as the community that may yet again be YHWH's people.[19] In at least one of these psalms, the Lord of the covenant is named king:

> O come, let us sing to the LORD;
> let us make a joyful noise to the rock of our salvation!
> Let us come into his presence with thanksgiving;
> let us make a joyful noise to him with songs of praise!
> For the LORD is a great God,
> and *a great King above all gods*.
> In his hand are the depths of the earth;
> the heights of the mountains are his also.
> The sea is his, for he made it,
> and the dry land, which his hands have formed. (Psalm 95:1-5, italics added)

This king is ruler of "all gods," creator of sea and dry land, but counts Israel as "the people of his pasture . . . the sheep of his hand." This psalm, moreover, ends with a severe warning to those who do not "listen" (v. 7b-11) who thereby miss the blessing of the Lord of the covenant.

The king of the covenant may perform two characteristic functions of kingship. First, kings may redeploy and reassign land over which the king exercises sovereignty.[20] While the point is not explicit, the conquest of the land in the book of Joshua may be understood as such a royal act. And certainly behind the book of Joshua the promise of the land to the ancestors in Genesis, as Moshe Weinfeld has shown, is an act of royal designation.[21]

Second, and more important, it is a primary task of the king to maintain justice. Whether actual policies of justice are enacted or not, every king employs the rhetoric of justice. In the case of YHWH, Psalm 82 evidences YHWH as king among the gods, insisting that justice is indeed a nonnegotiable mark of godness:

> "How long will you judge unjustly
> and show partiality to the wicked?
> Give justice to the weak and the orphan;
> maintain the right of the lowly and the destitute.
> Rescue the weak and the needy;
> deliver them from the hand of the wicked." (Psalm 82:2-4)

The lesser gods are, in the end, condemned because they have failed to do justice.

The prophetic tradition articulates a primary accent on justice as the will of the High King. Nowhere is this clearer than in the remarkable prophetic oracle of Ezekiel 34. Human kings (shepherds) are condemned and dismissed for their failure to do justice (vv. 3-4), a failure that led to the deportation of Jews (vv. 5-6). As a stunning alternative, the High King resolves to establish *direct rule* so that YHWH personally commits to the practice of justice, thereby assuring a viable community:

> For thus says the Lord GOD: I myself will search for my sheep, and will seek them out. As shepherds seek out their flocks when they are among their scattered sheep, so I will seek out my sheep. I will rescue them from all the places to which they have been scattered on a day of clouds and thick darkness. I will bring them out from the peoples and gather them from the countries, and will bring them into their own land; and I will feed them on the mountains of Israel, by the watercourses, and in all the inhabited parts of the land. I will feed them with good pasture, and the mountain heights of Israel shall be their pasture; there they shall lie down in good grazing land, and they shall feed on rich pasture on the mountains of Israel. I myself will be the shepherd of my sheep, and I will make them lie down, says the Lord GOD. I will seek the lost, and I will bring back the strayed, and I will bind up the injured; and I will strengthen the weak, but the fat and the strong I will destroy. I will feed them with justice. (Ezekiel 34:11-16)

The work of the High God as king is implemented and made more complex by the appearance of human (Davidic) kingship in Israel (see Ezekiel 34:23-24). While the interpretive route to the Davidic dynasty in 1 and 2 Samuel is complex and permeated with contradictions, there is no doubt that the Davidic house is granted legitimacy through a covenant made by YHWH with David (see 2 Samuel 7:1-16):

> Forever I will keep my steadfast love for him,
>   and my covenant with him will stand firm.
> I will establish his line forever,
>   and his throne as long as the heavens endure.
> If his children forsake my law
>   and do not walk according to my ordinances,
> if they violate my statutes
>   and do not keep my commandments,
> then I will punish their transgression with the rod
>   and their iniquity with scourges;
> but I will not remove from him my steadfast love,
>   or be false to my faithfulness.
> I will not violate my covenant,
>   or alter the word that went forth from my lips.

Once and for all I have sworn by my holiness;
    I will not lie to David.
His line shall continue forever,
    and his throne endure before me like the sun.
It shall be established forever like the moon,
    an enduring witness in the skies. (Psalm 89:28-37)

Some in Israel regarded human monarchy as an obvious instrument of the divine king; others viewed human kingship as a challenge to YHWH's rule. Either way, the reality of human kingship and the extrapolation of a notion of Messiah to come assure in Israel that history is made by human agents. It is, moreover, the task of the human king to enact justice that is a hallmark of the divine king:

Give the king your justice, O God,
    and your righteousness to a king's son.
May he judge your people with righteousness,
    and your poor with justice.
May the mountains yield prosperity for the people,
    and the hills, in righteousness.
May he defend the cause of the poor of the people,
    give deliverance to the needy,
    and crush the oppressor. . . .
For he delivers the needy when they call,
    the poor and those who have no helper.
He has pity on the weak and the needy,
    and saves the lives of the needy.
From oppression and violence he redeems their life;
    and precious is their blood in his sight. (Psalm 72:1-4, 12-14)

But of course, the human kings in Israel (with the important exceptions of Hezekiah and Josiah) are narrated as disobedient and so share in divine judgment for the failed covenant.

In Ezekiel 34 to which I have referred, YHWH will rule directly to perform the tasks of justice. In verses 23-24, however, after the condemnation and dismissal of human monarchy, a new David is imagined who will tend rightly to the tasks of kingship. It is to be noted, however, that in the designation of David in this text, he is termed *prince*, so that the title of *king* is reserved for YHWH. This "demotion" in human kingship serves to call attention to the centrality and nonnegotiability of divine kingship.

The interplay of God-king and human-king, a relationship that is complex in the Old Testament, in Christian tradition is articulated according to christological categories and eventually resolved in the language of "Father-Son" in Trinitarian formulation (see 2 Samuel 7:14; Psalm 2:7). And while Jesus as "Son" occupies the imagination in the New Testament, it is nonetheless the case that the church, as Jesus has instructed, continues to pray for the rule of the divine king: "Your kingdom come. / Your will be done, / on earth as it is in heaven" (Matthew 6:10). It is this rule, already known in Israel and anticipated for time to come, that in the faith of Israel assures a viable world and a livable history, the threats of chaos notwithstanding.

3. YHWH who is warrior and king is also articulated in Israel as *judge*. Indeed the role of judge is implicit in the office of king, for it entails the establishment and maintenance of justice, the articulation of social norms and their enforcement. For the most part YHWH as judge is implicit in the primal narratives of self-disclosure and is given more play in prophetic discourse. Given the largely implicit character of YHWH's role as judge, we may consider this metaphor for YHWH in a different way by suggesting that Pharaoh and YHWH embody two notions of justice or, with Peter Berger, they offer two distinct theodicies.[22]

The "justice" sponsored by Pharaoh was in the service of a social hierarchy enacted by an indifferent bureaucracy. That is, the social situation in Egypt, reflected in the exodus narrative, is that the privileged, powerful elite imposed abusive production quotas upon the slave community that functions as cheap labor. The privilege and entitlement of Pharaoh's elite apparatus is clear enough, already reflected in the preceding Joseph narrative (see Genesis 47). This rapacious, exploitative notion of justice is exhibited in a different context in 1 Samuel 8:10-18 wherein Samuel describes the usurpatious way of a king. In verse 11, Samuel speaks precisely of the *mišpaṭ* of the king, a phrase that is usually translated "the way of the king" or "the custom of the king." But the fact that the word *mišpaṭ* is used means that this is indeed the notion of justice that is operative even if articulated in such elite circles. By contrast, the slave population clearly has no rights, privileges, or entitlements in Egypt, but are measured and valued only for their productivity. There is no doubt that in the norming system of Pharaoh's community this was regarded as a legitimate arrangement between the powerless and the powerful, a theodicy justifying "their enjoyment of the power and privilege of their social position."[23]

The biblical narrative concerns the action of YHWH who challenges and overthrows pharaonic notions of justice and who, at Sinai, introduces an alternative theodicy that validates the social entitlements of the powerless who constitute the slave community that arrived at Sinai. In the establishment of this alternative system of justice, we may identify two actions by the divine judge. First, the judge articulates norms for an alternative society in what scholarship has come to call *apodictic law* (Exodus 20:1-17). This consists in the Ten Commandments that are absolutes that are nonnegotiable and that decisively counter the norms of pharaonic society. Second, the judge not only enunciates norms but rules on specific cases. Thus we may find the work of YHWH as judge made specific in two case laws that occur in the Book of the Covenant:

■ In Exodus 22:21-24, the judge speaks on behalf of the oppressed and aliens with direct reference to those who have been abused in Pharaoh's pattern of justice. The key issue is that the judge promises to *hear the cry* and to execute those who violate the weak and the powerless.

In Exodus 22:25-27, the judge rules in a typical case of economic exploitation enacted against the vulnerable. Again the judge promises to *hear the cry*, that is, to attend to the petition that is uttered by the abused. In this case, unlike the preceding, the judge here does not threaten punishment; rather, the judge asserts, "I am compassionate" (v. 27). The judge will act in empathy toward the vulnerable who are economically threatened and will redress the wrong done them. That statement indicates a wholly alternative practice of justice in which empathy toward the vulnerable is the key to social relationships. It may well be that the harshness of verse 24 is implied in this second case ruling, that YHWH will act *for* the vulnerable and *against* the exploiters. The claim that the judge is compassionate is a complete contrast to the pharaonic system of justice, a claim that permeates the covenantal ethic of the Bible, an ethic that comes to full expression in Job's statement of innocence.[24]

These two competing systems of justice, pharaonic and covenantal, are in profound dispute in the exodus narrative; the Sinai pericope assumes the defeat of pharaonic justice and moves on to the alternative. It is fair to say that with Solomon and his practice of "forced labor" and the more general claims of the Jerusalem establishment that pharaonic patterns of justice reappear in Israel (1 Kings 5:13-18; 10:15-22).[25] It is against the reappearance of pharaonic notions of justice in Israel that the prophets speak consistently in their sustained advocacy of justice toward the vulnerable (see for example 1 Kings 21).

The contrast between Pharaoh and YHWH is enough to justify Peter Berger's shrewd articulation of the picture of "two discrete theodicies":

> One of the very important social functions of theodicies is, indeed, their explanation of the socially prevailing inequalities of power and privilege. In this function, of course, theodicies directly legitimate the particular institutional order in question. It is important to stress in this connection that such theodicies may serve as legitimations *both* for the powerful *and* the powerless, for the privileged *and* for the deprived. For the latter, of course, they may serve as "opiates" to make their situation less intolerable, and by the same token to prevent them from rebelling against it. For the former, however, they may serve as subjectively quite important justifications of their enjoyment of the power and privilege of their social position. Put simply, theodicies provide the poor with a meaning for their poverty, but may also provide the rich with a meaning for their wealth (9). In both cases, the result is one of world maintenance and, very concretely, of the maintenance of the particular institutional order. It is, of course, another question whether the *same* theodicy can serve both groups in this way. If so, the theodicy constitutes an essentially sado-masochistic collusion, on the level of meaning, between oppressors and victims—a phenomenon that is far from rare in history. In other cases, there may be two discrete theodicies established in the society—a theodicy of suffering for one group and a theodicy of happiness for the other (10). These two theodicies may relate to each other in different ways, that is, with different degrees of "symmetry."[26]

A proper understanding of YHWH as judge requires us to notice that the same dispute between theodicies is very much at play in contemporary society. On the one hand, a singular devotion to "the market," particularly with its extreme articulation as "globalization," gives right and privilege and entitlement to the most aggressive in society who are free to seize and take and control and consume whatever they can grasp, without a thought for other members of society. That theory of justice, particularly espoused by Margaret Thatcher, now goes under the euphemistic term of *reform* that means the erosion of social obligation and the primacy of unfettered individualism. This practice is given even greater force when it is recognized that such *individualism* is in fact a function of the corporate economy that separates the *insiders* with their opulent privilege from the labor class that by law and by the uncontrolled aggressiveness of the market are cut out of the benefits produced by the system.

Alternatively, in contemporary society there is still an advocacy, though greatly weakened, for an alternative mode of justice that advocates an alliance (covenant) between the powerful and the powerless whereby the resources of society are commonly held to the benefit of all, with a prerequisite curb upon aggressive acquisitiveness.[27] It is not too much to say that the challenge offered by the communitarianism of the second model to the market model is rooted deeply and primally in the character of YHWH who in these texts is seen to offer a viable and sustainable practical alternative to pharaonic modes of power and wealth.

When we ask what makes this second, alternative mode of justice possible, it is clear that the decisive factor is the awareness in the text that YHWH is addressable and can be impacted by cries of need. This is in contrast to the gods of Egypt who silently legitimate Pharaoh's justice and who are unresponsive to the cries of the slaves. Thus the exodus narrative begins, as we have seen, in Exodus 2:23-25 and 3:7 as YHWH *hears and answers* the cries of the slaves. In the two case laws I have cited in Exodus 22:21-24 and 25-27, the pivotal point is that YHWH *hears the cries* of those in need and answers decisively on their behalf. In the highly stylized Song of Thanksgiving in Psalm 107 with its four "case studies" of need and deliverance, each case pivots on the phrase, "They cried to the LORD . . . and he delivered them" (Psalm 107:6, 13, 19, 28). In the long stretch of tradition from the initial cry in Egypt to the most polished songs of thanksgiving, Israel is characteristically the petitioner and suppliant and YHWH is the powerful judge who listens in empathy and who answers in decisive transformative power. In this articulation of YHWH, Israel's faith breaks completely with the notion of a transcendent God who is remote from need, or from an elitist God of order who is on the side of the status quo. This judge is characteristically on the side of the needy, the poor, the weak, and vulnerable and undertakes revolutionary activity to redress wrong and to transform social situations and practices in the interest of the vulnerable petitioners. The dynamism of this tradition cannot be overestimated in its concreteness, for the practice of law, and the notions of judicial advocacy. This judge is indeed "an activist on the bench." The tradition of YHWH as judge is inherently revolutionary against every pharaonic system.

The same pattern of "cry-hear" or "cry-save" that governs Israel's Song of Thanksgiving as in Psalm 107 is dominant in the narrative pattern of the book of Judges.[28] The fourfold pattern of narrative theology has often been noticed and is exemplified in the brief narrative of Othniel in Judges 3:7-11:

1. Israel sinned;
2. YHWH gave sinful Israel into oppression;
3. Israel *cried out* to YHWH;
4. YHWH responded to the cry with a rescue.

Here as in Psalm 107, it is *the cry* that causes the narrative of the destiny of Israel to turn, because YHWH is a judge who *hears and answers the cry*.

James Kugel has exposited the way in which the cry of the victim is central to the faith and practice of Israel. In commenting on Exodus 2:21-24, Kugel takes the commandment as addressed by YHWH to the perpetrators of oppression:

> It is the oppressed human's cry, in other words, that will unleash the chain of events that will ultimately result in your being punished. . . . This cry is worth considering, because it implies something about God that is at odds with our own beliefs. . . . It is addressed to the potential oppressor. If *you* do this, then *he* will cry out, and I will have to act. . . . If you victimize someone, then that someone will cry out and I will have to act against you.[29]

On Psalm 82, moreover, Kugel comments: "But we ought not to lose sight of our particular focus. It says that hearing the victim's cry is a god's duty and God's duty. It says that if that job is not properly performed, the very foundations of the earth will shake."[30] And by way of conclusion: "God's ultimate self-revelation to Moses: I am by nature *khannun* and *rakhum* (despite all evidence to the contrary). I hear the cry of the victim; I can't help it."[31]

The cry is the human act that evokes YHWH's compassion, from which YHWH moves decisively in the world as a judge who intervenes to disrupt abuse and oppression and to right wrongs that occur in the power relations of human society. YHWH is indeed the "court of last resort" for those without any other ground of appeal.

This role of YHWH as judge then is front and center in Israel's practice of lament and complaint, for it is the cry that moves the judge to transformative action:

I cry aloud to the LORD,
  and he answers me from his holy hill. (Psalm 3:4, italics added)

To you, O LORD, *I cried*,
  and to the LORD I made supplication:
"What profit is there in my death,
  if I go down to the Pit?
Will the dust praise you?
  Will it tell of your faithfulness?
Hear, O LORD, and be gracious to me!
  O LORD, be my helper!" (Psalm 30:8-10, italics added)

This poor soul cried, and was heard by the LORD,
  and was saved from every trouble. (Psalm 34:6, italics added)

I cried aloud to him,
  and he was extolled with my tongue.
If I had cherished iniquity in my heart,
  the Lord would not have listened.
But truly God has listened;
  he has given heed to the words of my prayer. (Psalm 66:17-19, italics added)

In my distress *I cry to the LORD*
  that he may answer me. (Psalm 120:1, italics added)

On the day *I called*, you answered me,
  you increased my strength of soul. (Psalm 138:3, italics added)

This warrior-king-judge is not impervious to human need, but characteristically attends to the voiced pain and need of even the most marginated voices. The entire taxonomy of the Psalter is an exhibit of YHWH as judge.

But of course the many psalms that affirm YHWH's compassionate answering propensity also require in Israel an awareness that YHWH is not an automaton who automatically answers. Israel in its candor can also recognize and make public that cries addressed to YHWH sometimes go unheeded. The most prominent case of unanswered cry is in Psalm 88:

O LORD, God of my salvation,
  when, at night, *I cry out* in your presence,

> let my prayer come before you;
> incline your ear to my cry. (Psalm 88:1-2)
>
> Every day *I call on you*, O LORD;
> I spread out my hands to you. (Psalm 88:9b, italics added)
>
> But *I, O LORD, cry out to you*;
> in the morning my prayer comes before you. (Psalm 88:13, italics added)

The context of these verses in the psalm make clear that YHWH is unresponsive and indifferent; it is for that reason that the psalm is vigorously accusatory against YHWH (see also Psalms 22:1-2; 44:23-26). It is remarkable that in Israel's practice of faith, that in the face of cries left unanswered, Israel continues to address YHWH in urgency. That is, lack of divine response does not cause a cessation in the cry. Perhaps that is because Israel has nowhere else to go. But perhaps it is also because Israel's most elemental conviction concerns YHWH's compassion, a conviction from which Israel is not dissuaded even by divine silence and indifference.

Finally, it should be noted that this model of divine judge with YHWH's remarkable commitment to the needy poor becomes in Israel a model for human judges who are to imitate the divine judge.[32] Thus in the early formulation of the Book of the Covenant Moses commands: "You shall not pervert the justice due to your poor in their lawsuits. Keep far from a false charge, and do not kill the innocent and those in the right, for I will not acquit the guilty. You shall take no bribe, for a bribe blinds the officials, and subverts the cause of those who are in the right" (Exodus 23:6-8). And in the later text of Deuteronomy, the point is the same:

> You shall appoint judges and officials throughout your tribes, in all your towns that the LORD your God is giving you, and they shall render just decisions for the people. You must not distort justice; you must not show partiality; and you must not accept bribes, for a bribe blinds the eyes of the wise and subverts the cause of those who are in the right. Justice, and only justice, you shall pursue, so that you may live and occupy the land that the LORD your God is giving you. (Deuteronomy 16:18-20)

Moses knows that money, power, and social leverage can distort justice. Thus Israel is committed to an "independent judiciary" that gives the unnamed and the powerless a fair hearing. Such a social teaching, derived from theological passion, is an important word in a society where now even the judiciary is drawn into the extremity of ideological combat. The most elemental word about the divine judge is *compassion* toward those who most need it. Israel, moreover, can imagine that a human judiciary can, in a like way, proceed with compassion toward those who need it the most. Clearly such a judge sponsors and advocates a notion of justice very different from that of Pharaoh. The divine practice of justice is anticipated in the liturgy of Jerusalem: "He will judge the world with righteousness, / and the peoples with his truth" (Psalm 96:13). YHWH as king is a "lover of justice" (Psalm 99:4) marked by compassion. Human justice can do no less in the framework of the covenant than does the divine judge.

I conclude with an extrapolation of *YHWH as judge* in Christian tradition in a parable of Jesus (Luke 18:1-8). The parable is about "the need to pray," to cry out in need to the Lord.[33] The analogue to the petition made to God is a human judge who is irresponsible and uncaring, but who eventually grants the petition of a poor widow because "she keeps bothering me." Out of the parable, Jesus admonishes that the chosen "cry to him day and night." The conclusion of the paragraph causes "faith," the capacity to trust enough to cry out, even in a world where there seems to be no response. In his interpretation of the parable, John Donahue turns particularly to 2 Chronicles 19:5-6 wherein King Jehoshaphat appoints judges:

> "Consider what you are doing, for you judge not on behalf of human beings but on the LORD's behalf; he is with you in giving judgment. Now, let the fear of the LORD be upon you; take care what you do, for there is no perversion of justice with the LORD our God, or partiality, or taking of bribes." . . . He charged them: "This is how you shall act: in the fear of the LORD, in faithfulness, and with your whole heart." (2 Chronicles 19:6-7, 9) [34]

The outcome of the process of petition (cry) is justice, even when the judge is not eager and willing to grant it. This *social practice* anticipated in Israel and the *theological foundation* in the character of YHWH importantly converge. The outcome is a theology of compassion without parallel and a derivative social practice that is against the grain of conventional pharaonic institutions.

4. There is no doubt that the three images and roles of warrior, king, and judge are preeminent in Israel's faith, all of which attest to YHWH's sovereignty. To that triad we may add a fourth image, father. This image is less central than the three already reviewed. But as our brief presentation will indicate, it is nonetheless an important facet of Israel's faith; in current discussions of gender and the awareness of the patriarchal caste of the Old Testament, moreover, the metaphor warrants consideration.

The utilization of this metaphor in our primal narratives of self-disclosure is found especially in Exodus 4:22: "Then you shall say to Pharaoh, 'Thus says the LORD: Israel is my firstborn son'" (Exodus 4:22). Without any preparation for the pronouncement, the statement provides a primal motivation in the exodus narrative that Israel should be freed enough by Pharaoh to "worship" ("serve"; *'avodah*) YHWH. In several of the demands issued by Moses to Pharaoh, the requirement is that Israel should *worship* YHWH, and in one use, "make a festival." But of course that requirement for worship or service entails extrication from Pharaoh's system, because worship of YHWH requires freedom for a life under YHWH's Torah. Thus the bid of Exodus 4:22 is that Israel leave the pharaonic system for the sake of life with YHWH. The appellation "firstborn son" of course functions to entitle Israel with particular rights and privileges (see Deuteronomy 21:15-17) and prepares the way for the tenth plague, the destruction of Pharaoh's firstborn and heir apparent (Exodus 11:5; 12:29). Thus the appellation in the narrative serves to *entitle* Israel and to *threaten* Pharaoh in a most intense way.

Our more general interest in Old Testament theology, however, looks beyond the particular narrative function to suggest that the relationship of father and (firstborn) son indicates two other important faith claims. First, the firstborn son, as heir, receives the land. This identification of Israel as firstborn connects well with the ancestral promise of the land to Israel. Israel must leave Egypt in order to claim its rightful inheritance intended by the father.

It is the second motif of sonship that concerns us in a primary way. The motivation, "that they may worship me" surely means that the son may be with the father, may attend to the father, may rely on the father, may find joy in the company of the father. Conversely, the father is the one who wants to be with the son in order to enhance the life of the son. The intervention of the father, in the enslavement of the son, is the father's act to guard, protect, and guarantee the well-being of the son. Thus one may take the metaphor of father to identify YHWH as the one who intends and guarantees well-being for the son.

This motif of fatherly care of the son Israel is articulated in two important and derivative texts. First in Hosea 11:1-9, the father speaks about the troubled relationship with the son who had become recalcitrant (see also Jeremiah 3:19). There is no doubt that Hosea 11:1-4 is a recall of Exodus 4:22 with direct reference to Egypt; the father, in uncommon practice, "taught, took up, healed, led, bent down." The series of verbs is astonishing; they suggest a self-conscious generosity on the part of the father who has foregone characteristic dignity to be completely available to the son, in order that the son might be maintained in all the ways that enhance life. The abrupt turn of the text in verses 5-7 voices the alienation between father and son, with particular reference to the nullification of the exodus and a return to Egyptian slavery. But the abrupt turn in verse 5 is not nearly as stunning as the abrupt turn of rhetoric in verse 8 wherein the father comes to deep self-awareness and resolves to absorb the rage rather than enact the rage toward the son. The recovery of the father's self-awareness after the reactive statement of verses 5-7 means that the relationship now depends completely upon the father's resolve to practice "compassion" toward the son. Thus the father, with immense authority and power to match authority, thinks now not of the dignity and respect of the father, but of the well-being of the son and the father's responsibility for the well-being of the son. That is, the father yields his just claim against the son for the sake of the son's future.

The later text is Isaiah 63:15–64:12, which also utilizes the image of YHWH as father. Whereas Hosea 11:1-9 is a divine utterance, here the utterance addressed to YHWH is on the lips of bereft Israel. The address is a lament that includes both the characterization of suffering and abuse and then a petition for help. The petition is addressed to "our father" (v. 16) who is bid to "come down" (64:1) to act in compassion (63:15) as "Redeemer" (63:16). The father is reminded that here speaks "your inheritance" (heir) who now has been abandoned (63:17). Although the prayer addressed to YHWH lacks a heavily accusatory tone, it is asserted that the son has been treated as though he had no father (vv. 18-19). In Isaiah 64:5-7, the charge against the father is turned to a confession of failure on the part of the son. These verses would suggest that the father is justified in not protecting a wayward and irresponsible son. Nonetheless the petition (after the confession) still reminds YHWH that

YHWH is indeed "our Father" and is expected to act as a protective presence:

> Yet, O LORD, you are our Father;
>   we are the clay, and you are our potter;
>   we are all the work of your hand.
> Do not be exceedingly angry, O LORD,
>   and do not remember iniquity forever.
>   Now consider, we are all your people. (Isaiah 64:8-9)

The prayer in verse 12 speaks with wistfulness that is not unlike Lamentations 5:22: "After all this, will you restrain yourself, O LORD? / Will you keep silent, and punish us so severely?" (Isaiah 64:12). The son does not know how the father will respond to the petition but the son knows that he has no alternative source of help and depends completely upon the father to rescue him from a situation of "desolation." Everything depends on the father who has both the capacity and the obligation to act for the sake of the son. The petition, along with the confession, delineates the role of the father whose obligation for the son is not voided, even by the waywardness of the son. It is the father's task to guarantee the life of the son, even when it is not merited and when the circumstance would seem to deny any such possibility. We are able to see that this image of father is not unrelated to the claims of warrior-king-judge, except that the intensity and intimacy of familial ties is in place of more formal public relationship.[35] The entire history of Israel's life with YHWH is a transaction, according to the metaphor, of a bond that is durable but often under immense strain that yields enormous tension. That tension and strain, however, do not ultimately shake Israel's deep, abiding conviction about the fidelity of the father. Israel knows that the father can be angry; but Israel also knows:

> He will not always accuse,
>   nor will he keep his anger forever.
> He does not deal with us according to our sins,
>   nor repay us according to our iniquities. (Psalm 103:9-10)

And the ground for such an assurance concerns the father's steadfast love and compassion that even profound transgression cannot override:

> For as the heavens are high above the earth,
>   so great is his steadfast love toward those who fear him;
> as far as the east is from the west,

so far he removes our transgressions from us.
As a father has compassion for his children,
so the LORD has compassion for those who fear him.
For he knows how we were made;
he remembers that we are dust. (Psalm 103:11-14)

Even when the son faces alienation from the father, that alienation is eventually in the context of the compassion and everlasting love of the father:

Let the wicked forsake their way,
and the unrighteous their thoughts;
let them return to the LORD, that he may have mercy on them,
and to our God, for he will abundantly pardon.
For my thoughts are not your thoughts,
nor are your ways my ways, says the LORD. (Isaiah 55:7-8)

The fatherhood of YHWH is fundamentally about a profound attachment to the eldest son, *Israel.* But there is a second sphere in which the same imagery is used, namely, YHWH's attachment *to the king.* Thus the Old Testament appeals to the father-son imagery that had antecedents in the great state myths that preceded Israel.[36] Indeed, it may be that the father-son imagery pertains first of all to the kingship and was transposed in Israel from king to people. In Old Testament usage, however, the process works in a reverse direction with priority given to the YHWH-Israel connection. Only in the context of Israel as son is the imagery taken over for monarchy. In that usage the imagery bespeaks YHWH's durable commitment to the Davidic dynasty, a durable commitment that is taken as seriously as the YHWH-Israel relationship. We may note three important uses of such rhetoric in the Old Testament:

■ In the founding oracle of the dynasty, it is said of David's son—and surely applied to every royal descendant of David:

I will be a father to him, and he shall be a son to me. When he commits iniquity, I will punish him with a rod such as mortals use, with blows inflicted by human beings. But I will not take my steadfast love from him, as I took it from Saul, whom I put away from before you. (2 Samuel 7:14-15)

This language suggests an unconditional durability of YHWH's commitment to the monarchy. That language is echoed in Psalm 89:

> He shall cry to me, "You are my Father,
> my God, and the Rock of my salvation!"
> I will make him the firstborn,
> the highest of the kings of the earth. (Psalm 89:26-27)

As Israel in Exodus 4:22, David is said to be firstborn among all the kings of the earth, as Israel is firstborn people among all the peoples of the earth.

■ In Psalm 2, a royal Psalm, the court language of coronation utilizes the same rhetoric: "I will tell of the decree of the LORD: / He said to me, 'You are my son; / today I have begotten you' " (Psalm 2:7). There is no doubt that the New Testament makes use of this particular psalmic formulation to voice high claims of status and authority for Jesus (Matthew 3:17; 17:5; Mark 9:7; Luke 3:22; 9:35. See also Acts 4:25-26; 13:33; Hebrews 1:5; 5:5; 7:28).

While the accent is upon the durability of YHWH's commitment to the monarchy, the history of the monarchy that was terminated in 587 B.C.E. makes the claim for the Davidic house unsustainable. Thus in Psalm 89, after the sweeping assertion of the relationship of father to son in verses 26-27, verses 38-51 must be candid about the failure of the relationship. In the end, it is clear that the father-son imagery pertains to Israel in a more profound way than it does to David. In Isaiah 53:5, the covenant with David is now reconfigured to be a covenantal commitment not to the monarchy or the dynasty, but to the whole people Israel. This verse brings into unity, by historical necessity, the fidelity language concerning Israel on the one hand and concerning David on the other. Of the transposition of the promise to David, Otto Eissfeldt comments:

> In Ps. 89 the content of the promise is interpreted exclusively in the continued existence of the Davidic dynasty—the current threat to which calls the validity of the promise into question. Second Isaiah, however, places the promise before the fate of Israel and its royal house and declares its eternal validity. In so doing, he relates the promise to the mission of Israel in the world, a mission which is Israel's destiny and which will bring her honor and recognition. Where Ps. 89 displays a static-rigid conception of the promise of Yahweh, Second Isaiah interprets it in a dynamic-activistic sense: he prevents its becoming involved in the collapse of the Davidic dynasty and thus ensures its permanent validity.[37]

The convergence of *king and people* in a single sonship recurs in Christian formulation in the Matthean birth narrative: "Then Joseph got up, took the child and his mother by night, and went to Egypt, and remained there until the death of Herod. This was to fulfill what had been spoken by the Lord through the prophet, 'Out of Egypt I have called my son' " (Matthew 2:14-15). Matthew quotes the text of Hosea 11:1 that clearly refers to the people Israel, but reclaims the reference for "my son" in christological designation of Jesus. Thus the father-son imagery is somewhat fluid, but in every usage witnesses to the transformative fidelity of the father-God.

There is yet a third way in which the Fatherhood of YHWH is used, surely as a protector, guardian, and guarantor of the most vulnerable in society. The most fundamental text for such a claim is in Psalm 68:

Father of orphans and protector of widows
    is God in his holy habitation.
God gives the desolate a home to live in;
    he leads out the prisoners to prosperity,
but the rebellious live in a parched land. (Psalm 68:5-6)

The vulnerable who are identified as vulnerable categories in society are "orphans, widows, the desolate, prisoners." The "poor" and "sojourners" are often grouped in such a category but are not mentioned here; but it is completely plausible to infer their inclusion in a generic way. God as Father takes special responsibility for and pays special attention to those otherwise neglected, forgotten, and abused by society. The attention of the Father, moreover, is from "his holy habitation," which may mean either the Jerusalem temple or God's heavenly residence. In either case, it is plausible to conclude that the "widows and orphans" mentioned in the psalm are first of all "widows and orphans" in Israel. Except, of course, that such expansive imagery, when the *Father* is surely the *creator God*, cannot be kept for one's own, even if it is heard that way in some contexts. More broadly and surely faithful to the logic of the poetry, this psalm attests the Father God of Israel actively engaged on behalf of all of the vulnerable and powerless everywhere in creation. The temple in Jerusalem is not only Israel's temple, but it is the temple for the presence of the creator God (see v. 29). Thus kings—kings of the whole earth—bring tribute to the Father-King in Jerusalem. And in return the Father-King in Jerusalem calls all kings to account concerning provisions made for widows, orphans, the desolate, and prisoners. The imagery stretches well beyond *firstborn Israel* and *last-born David* to the *last-born* and least valued of all humanity.

Two other psalms may be drawn close to this reference. In Psalm 27:10 the speaker, surely an Israelite, finds YHWH an adequate and reliable substitute parent when parents fail and in Psalm 94:6-7, it is clear that the assaults on widow, stranger, and orphan are only possible if it can be perpetrated beyond the surveillance of the God of Israel:

> They kill the widow and the stranger,
>   they murder the orphan,
> and they say, "The LORD does not see;
>   the God of Jacob does not perceive." (Psalm 94:6-7)

The inference to be drawn is that God is peculiarly attentive to the vulnerable, and they are saved as long as under the eye of YHWH (see Psalms 9–10). In every sphere of life imagined in Israel—Israel itself, kingship, all humanity—the Father God is known to be a faithful protector, sustainer, guardian, guarantor, and nourisher. The imagery of Father draws the warrior-king-judge into intimacy that is transformative of all of life. The Father embodies and enacts the truth of fidelity, without which life cannot be lived.

In Christian extrapolation from this image, we may call attention to the parable of Luke 15:11-32 that features a father of uncommon wisdom, patience, and generosity. Of course in parabolic form, the image of the father is completely congruent with the fatherly image of YHWH in the Old Testament. There is no doubt that the parable is about the father: "The father's surprising action toward both sons is the literary center where the meaning must be sought. The father shatters the self-identity of both sons."[38]

It is the work of the father to wait and watch and intervene for the sake of the son's well-being. Both sons choose each for themselves servility of a specific kind, the younger to the rapacious servitude of the market, the older to the gnawing imprisonment of his self-righteousness. In both cases the father intervenes with an offer of freedom, the same offer whereby YHWH intervened in the exodus narrative with the firstborn son. Donahue notes the connection of the probe to Paul's theology in Galatians 3–4 whereby "through God you are no longer a slave / but a son or daughter, and if so then / an heir" (Galatians 4:7).[39] His father who acts consistently even toward Israel in its waywardness and recalcitrance in generosity and emancipatory ways of course fits none of the usual strictures against "patriarchy" that are commonly and popularly associated with the term *father* in theological discussion (see Isaiah 1:2; Jeremiah 3:19). By that I do not dispute the judgment that the very use of the term *father* evokes patriarchal imagery that is often marked by authoritarianism. But the use of the term in specific texts and their context is not perforce a cipher for authoritarianism. It is rather an image bespeaking generative nurture and protectiveness toward the vulnerable.

This father, so consistently lined out in the text, is a counter-image to much of what is known, anciently and contemporarily, about fathers. I may cite the case of father David with son Absalom as the characteristic of a father who is not generative toward his son. The narrative of Absalom reports that after the murder of his brother Amnon, Absalom had to flee from his father for his life (2 Samuel 13:38). Only reluctantly is Absalom welcomed back to David's court, arriving back in the royal city two years before readmission into the king's presence (2 Samuel 14:28). And finally when allowed reentry to the court, David acts toward Absalom as king and not as father. It has been often observed that David never addresses Absalom as "son" until after he is dead; then of course there is great grief on the part of the father (2 Samuel 18:33–19:4). David is portrayed in life as an unresponsive father, even threatened by his son in rebellion, capable of deep engagement with his son only after his death. Likely this is an all-too-typical portrayal of a "patriarchal, authoritarian" father.

My point is that YHWH as father, the one portrayed in Luke's parable, is exactly the antithesis of such a character. Indeed, Sandra Schneiders has observed, surely correctly, that the father of the parable challenges such patriarchy:

> Jesus' parable about the father actually constitutes a radical challenge to patriarchy. The divine father, who had been understood as the ultimate justification of human patriarchy, is revealed as one who refuses to own us, demand our submission, or punish our rebellion. Rather, God is one who respects our freedom, mourns our alienation, waits patiently for our return, and accepts our love as pure gift.[40]

On the whole, the portrayal of YHWH as father in the Old Testament is congruent with the father of the parable. Since the exodus this father has been seeking fullness of life whether the firstborn son, whether Israel, the king, or the vulnerable and needy. It is clear that this image of YHWH tilts the strong image of warrior-king-judge in the direction of intense engagement and intimate attachment.

Each of these metaphors—warrior, king, judge, father—illuminates YHWH's sovereignty in particular ways. The narrative presentation, with its capacity for playful ambiguity, tells powerfully for a genuine interpersonal agent and against any flat, one-dimensional ruler remote from the life, needs, and hopes of the ruled community.

CHAPTER SEVEN

ISRAEL'S CONFESSION OF ONE GOD

The Old Testament is a complex testimony of faith that is everywhere dominated by YHWH and by Israel's uncompromising adherence to YHWH who is the creator of heaven and earth, Lord of lords and God of gods, and savior and patron of Israel (Deuteronomy 10:14-18). Israel's impulse toward the singularity of YHWH is not an academic or theoretical one; it is rather a quite practical affirmation rooted in the conviction and informed by the experience that it is only YHWH who can save and who can guarantee a livable future for Israel and for the world.[1] It is not possible to know how or when or in what way such a conviction arose and was articulated in Israel.[2] For purposes of Old Testament theology, we may say that it was "always" "everywhere" known to be so in Israel from the earliest oracles and songs of Israel to the later and more self-conscious urbane affirmations. Israel is to worship only YHWH.

In making this remarkable claim, it is useful to refer in particular to two paramount affirmations that are at the core of Israel's testimony. First, Deuteronomy 6:4-5, the famous *shema*, stands at the core of Old Testament faith: "Hear, O Israel: The LORD is our God, the LORD alone. You shall love the LORD your God with all your heart, and with all your soul, and with all your might" (Deuteronomy 6:4-5).[3] This statement by Moses has dominated the faith of Judaism and is central to the ethical instruction of Jesus (Mark 12:29-30).

We may note three important matters about this summons to Israel. First, the opening word *shema*, an imperative, is a summons to Israel to radical obedience to the will and purpose of YHWH. While the specificity of YHWH's commands is voiced in the Decalogue (Deuteronomy 5:6-17) and further exposited in the corpus of Deuteronomy 12–25, the importance of the opening summons is that Israel's position *before YHWH* is defined as one of urgent and complete obedience.[4] Second, the statement in verse 4 is open to more than one reading, more than one nuance, and interpreters are not yet agreed on the point. One reading asserts that "YHWH is one, that is, has integrity and moral unity, so that YHWH's will and purpose is everywhere the same.[5] Such an affirmation may mean to counter the multiple local YHWHs who occupy different shrines or different subcommunities with different agenda. Or it may mean to counter the notion that YHWH is morally unreliable and wills alternative matters in alternative contexts. The other rendering of Deuteronomy 6:4 that has been more prominent in rabbinic Judaism is that "you shall worship *only* YHWH," as distinct from other gods. This rendering insists on absolute, uncompromising loyalty to YHWH, and has an existential urgency to it concerning the exclusionary summons of the covenant God and the rejection of any other gods who might also compete for Israel's loyalty and service. Either way, the confession concerns YHWH's "preeminent sovereignty, his unrivaled power and providence."[6] Through this summons Israel's identity is established in terms of its exclusive relationship to YHWH, a relationship that is acted out in terms of Torah obedience. Third, the summons to *love* YHWH again refers to a wholehearted, unreserved loyalty that is expressed in obedience. In recent time it has become clear to scholars that *love* in covenantal context means primary adherence to commandments in obedience, thus an injunction befitting the affirmation of verse 4.[7] Jacqueline Lapsley, however, has rightly insisted that love understood as *obedience* without an *affective dimension* likely misses the passionate urgency of the claim: "Actions devoid of feeling and love, even those that fulfill commandments, are morally suspect."[8]

There is, of course, nothing morally suspect about the covenantal commands of Deuteronomy. They bind Israel as the people of YHWH and they bind YHWH as the God of Israel whose domain stretches across all of creation.

The second text that stands at the core of Israel's confession of YHWH is Exodus 20:2-3 that is reiterated in Deuteronomy 5:6-7. The command in verse 3 is absolute and precludes other gods from the horizon of Israel. In such a preclusion, of course, the existence, reality, and attractiveness of other gods are acknowledged. Thus the command verse of Exodus 20:3

is not a statement of monotheism; exactly the opposite. It is, along with Deuteronomy 6:4 when rendered as "only YHWH," a declaration for YHWH in the context of polytheism. But the banishment of other gods, and in Exodus 20:4-6 their images, amounts to a completely exclusionary claim for YHWH, not only in the life of Israel but in the world of divine powers. In this text Moses does not take the trouble to situate the other gods, as they are declared to be out of bounds and of no interest for Israel. The singularity of YHWH as the one loyalty of Israel, moreover, is given substance and energy by the defining formulation of Exodus 20:2: YHWH is the God of exodus deliverance. This motif dominates Old Testament theology and provides the central contrast to other gods who have no power to save. YHWH is entitled to singular loyalty because this is the only God who can save.

In later traditioning, the Old Testament uses some energy to contrast YHWH and the other gods, partly by doxological affirmation of YHWH and partly by mocking sarcastic dismissal of the other gods:

■ In Jeremiah 10:1-16, the other gods are dismissed as powerless products of human manufacture who can do nothing and who warrant no loyalty or devotion (vv. 3-5, 9, 14-15). By contrast, YHWH the incomparable (v. 7) has power as the creator to generate newness:

> It is he who made the earth by his power,
> who established the world by his wisdom,
> and by his understanding stretched out the heavens.
> When he utters his voice, there is a tumult of waters in the heavens,
> and he makes the mist rise from the ends of the earth.
> He makes lightnings for the rain,
> and he brings out the wind from his storehouses. (Jeremiah 10:12-13; see 51:15-16)

This massive, cosmic sovereign, moreover, is "the portion of Jacob," peculiarly committed to Israel with all the power of the creator and with all the capacity to transform that is evidenced in the exodus (v. 16).

■ Isaiah 44:9-20 in great detail traces the act of "god production," gods who are a "fraud" (v. 20) and in fact "*tohu*," before negating chaos (v. 9). By contrast, YHWH is the one who actively creates (v. 24), who founds and sustains Jerusalem (v. 26), and who summons foreign rulers to perform divine purposes (v. 28). The contrast is total.

Psalm 115 provides a mock song against the impotent gods of the nations who have no power to create or save:

> Their idols are silver and gold,
> the work of human hands.
> They have mouths, but do not speak;
> eyes, but do not see.
> They have ears, but do not hear;
> noses, but do not smell.
> They have hands, but do not feel;
> feet, but do not walk;
> they make no sound in their throats. (Psalm 115:4-7)

The contrast with YHWH is complete, for YHWH has the power to create and to bless in full fidelity (vv. 1, 12-13).

Thus in Exodus 20:2-3, the attestation to the exodus serves to contrast YHWH with the other gods who are no gods, because they have no power to save.

In the remarkable theological exchange of Isaiah 36:13-20, the Rabshakeh of Assyria is exhibited as a poor theologian who does not "get it" about YHWH. The reason he does not understand the God of Israel is that he reasons from a generic notion of God to the particularity of YHWH. This reasoning, as Israel has always known, will not work because YHWH does not fit any generic notion of godness; Israel's attestation to YHWH, rather, is always about the oddness and singularity of YHWH who resists any location or any religious taxonomy. Thus the Assyrian likens YHWH to the gods of Hamath, Arpad, and Sepharvaim; none of these have saved from Assyria or can save from Assyria. YHWH is like them; *ergo*, YHWH also cannot save from Assyria. Except YHWH is not like those other gods. The difference is exactly YHWH's capacity to do "whatever he pleases," and what he pleases is to save, deliver, and rescue that which has been by YHWH's divine power created.

If we extrapolate as the Old Testament does from the summary of Deuteronomy 6:4 and the first command of Exodus 20:1-2, YHWH is celebrated as the one whom Israel trusts and serves because YHWH has demonstrated—in "nature" as in "history"—generative power to make new:

> But the LORD is the true God;
> he is the living God and the everlasting King.
> At his wrath the earth quakes,
> and the nations cannot endure his indignation. (Jeremiah 10:10)

This claim is articulated in Israel's *historical tradition*, in Israel's prophetic literature that situates Israel in the international community over which YHWH presides, and in the wisdom traditions that concern the hidden, inscrutable governance of YHWH. The speeches of YHWH in the whirlwind of the book of Job are, to be sure, long removed from the Sinai traditions I have cited (Job 38–41). In the final form of the text, however, they are of a piece. The opening questions of defiance by the God of the whirlwind are designed to put theological probe and dissent in proper perspective:

> Where were you when I laid the foundation of the earth?
> Tell me, if you have understanding.
> Who determined its measurements—surely you know!
> Or who stretched the line upon it?
> On what were its bases sunk,
> or who laid its cornerstone
> when the morning stars sang together
> and all the heavenly beings shouted for joy?
>
> Or who shut in the sea with doors
> when it burst out from the womb?—
> when I made the clouds its garment,
> and thick darkness its swaddling band,
> and prescribed bounds for it,
> and set bars and doors,
> and said, "Thus far shall you come, and no farther,
> and here shall your proud waves be stopped"? (Job 38:4-11)

The question asked is, "Where were you?" And the answer is, "Nowhere." Nowhere until the creator God gives life and permission to live. Thus the adamant and uncompromising claims of the Sinai covenant tradition stretch well beyond the scope of Moses. What seems sometimes reducible to moral calculus in the covenantal traditions is, in the poetry of Job, blown open beyond moral calculus to the astonishing godness of God who fits none of the categories preferred either in moral religion or in philosophic reasoning. The one with whom Israel—and creation—has to do is *God*!

> Do not address your mind to criticism of the Creator,
> do not pretend to know His categories,
> Do not take His Universe in your hand, and point out

its defects with condescension.
Do not think He is a greater potentate, a manner of
President of the United Galaxies,
Do not think that because you know so few human beings,
that He is in a comparable though more favorable position.
Do not think it absurd that He should know every
sparrow, or the number of the hairs of your head,
Do not compare Him with yourself, not suppose your
human love to be an example to shame Him.
He is not greater than Plato or Lincoln, nor superior to
Shakespeare and Beethoven,
He is their God, their powers and their gifts proceeded
from Him,
In infinite darkness they pored with their fingers over the
first word of the Book of His Knowledge.[9]

It is no wonder that Israel's Psalter ends with the cumulative rhetorical force of doxology:

The LORD sets the prisoners free;
the LORD opens the eyes of the blind.
The LORDl ifts up those who are bowed down;
the Lord loves the righteous.
The LORD watches over the strangers;
he upholds the orphan and the widow,
but the way of the wicked he brings to ruin. (Psalm 146:7c-9)

Sing to the LORD with thanksgiving;
make melody to our God on the lyre.
He covers the heavens with clouds,
prepares rain for the earth,
makes grass grow on the hills.
He gives to the animals their food,
and to the young ravens when they cry.
His delight is not in the strength of the horse,
nor his pleasure in the speed of a runner;
but the LORD takes pleasure in those who fear him,
in those who hope in his steadfast love. (Psalm 147:7-11)

Praise him, sun and moon;
praise him, all you shining stars!
Praise him, you highest heavens,

> and you waters above the heavens!
> Let them praise the name of the LORD,
> for he commanded and they were created.
> He established them forever and ever;
> he fixed their bounds, which cannot be passed.
>
> Praise the LORD from the earth,
> you sea monsters and all deeps,
> fire and hail, snow and frost,
> stormy wind fulfilling his command!
>
> Mountains and all hills,
> fruit trees and all cedars!
> Wild animals and all cattle,
> creeping things and flying birds! (Psalm 148:3-10)

What else could Israel do? How else could Israel speak? It is to be noted, of course, that these sweeping acts of praise characteristically culminate with an affirmation about the particularity of Israel, about Zion (Psalm 146:10), Jerusalem and Israel (Psalm 147:2), statutes and ordinances in Israel (Psalm 147:19): "He has not dealt thus with any other nation; / they do not know his ordinances. / Praise the Lord!" (Psalm 147:20; see Psalms 148:14; 149:2).

In Israel's doxological acknowledgment of YHWH's sovereignty, there is no unbearable tension between large cosmic claims and the particularity of YHWH's devotion to Israel. Everywhere it is YHWH who is fully sovereign. At its best, Israel is glad . . . and invites all creation to be glad at YHWH's sovereign rule. At its best, Israel is obedient and knows that all creation finally must obey this sovereign who is a warrior, king, judge, and father.

The sketch of YHWH's sovereignty over Israel, the nations, and all creation just offered is the dominant affirmation of the Old Testament in all its parts. That claim for YHWH's sovereignty is rooted in old songs and narratives, and is echoed and reiterated in both the "hot" discourse of prophetic oracle where YHWH's sovereignty is immediate and direct, and in the "cool" discernment of sapiential reflection wherein YHWH's sovereignty is hidden and long term. While that account of sovereignty is surely the intent of the final form of the text, work in Old Testament theology requires that we take into full account as well the more complex judgment of critical scholarship concerning the character and role of

YHWH. It is clear from a critical perspective that YHWH's sovereign rule is reached as a theological conviction and conclusion only through a long disputatious interpretive process, evidence for which is amply available in the Old Testament text itself.[10] While Old Testament theology must deal finally with the canonical intention of the Old Testament, it cannot be innocent or uninformed about the fuller evidence of the text itself.

It is clear in critical scholarship that religious belief and practice in the culture out of which the Old Testament arose is fully and resiliently polytheistic. A great deal of evidence in the Old Testament text itself indicates that YHWH had to make a way in the midst of the complex world of the gods; extrabiblical evidence such as the texts from Ugarit, moreover, indicate that YHWH's locus among the gods has important parallels in the mythological drama between the high god El with whom YHWH tends to be equated and the young god, Baal, with whom YHWH in the Old Testament is in profound dispute. The usual critical account of the "rise of YHWH" is that YHWH was a tribal God who, through a series of contested interpretations, came to be dominant for Israel among the gods and eventually—as late as the sixth century—gained hegemony until Israel in doxology could attest YHWH as the only God before whom no other gods had any power or vitality or capacity to guarantee new life.

One hypothesis of the "origin" of YHWH famously proposed by Frank Moore Cross is that a theological formula, "El the high God creates" provided the verb *create* in Hebrew *hayah*, and that verb became the term YHWH.[11] There are technical problems with the hypothesis, but it has the merit of linking YHWH to the high God El and of connecting the proper noun YHWH with the dynamism of the verb, *cause to be*.[12] Thus YHWH, through an interpretive process, was able to claim the features, role, and authority of El, or Elyon, who was a very old god in that culture. According to some accounts the disputes with Baal, reflected for example in the book of Hosea and the reforms sponsored by King Hezekiah and King Josiah, exhibit a process whereby YHWH became the lead God until in the poetry of Second Isaiah wherein YHWH is proclaimed as the only God, the one who will defeat even the great state gods of the Babylonian Empire (Isaiah 42:8; 43:10-13; 45:5; 48:11). It is observed that this God, unlike other gods, was attached from the outset to persons and then to the community of Israel by way of covenantal commitment.[13] This covenantal commitment to a people (rather than to a state or to a place) assured that YHWH would be a God deeply involved in the vagaries and risks of the historical process. Over time functions that had been assigned in religious interpretation to a variety of gods accrued to the person of YHWH who was then understood as a complex character with a rich internal life (reflected in prophetic poetry), capable of rage and anger, capable of newness and forgiveness, and deeply moved by pain and alienation. That rich plethora of divine capacity, however, was reached only through a long interpretive process made possible by hard-nosed determined teachers, attentive scribes, and imaginative poets.

The *sovereignty of YHWH* and the *reality of polytheism* is a given of Old Testament religion, reflective of the cultural environment of Canaan and of the ancient Near East more generally. In its long disputatious development, the Old Testament takes YHWH's sovereignty seriously but is not able to—or perhaps is not interested in—completely eliminating the claim and reality of other gods:[14]

1. The primary interpretive strategy for negotiating this issue is through the "divine council," a "mythological phenomenon ubiquitous in the polytheistic world of ancient Near Eastern religions."[15] According to this imaginative scenario, there was an assembly of many gods who convened in heaven, the divine residence, in order to adjudicate divine purposes that were to be enacted in the earth. In Israelite imagination, YHWH was the presiding officer (high God) who had subjugated the other gods who were then compliant with YHWH and who became instruments through which the will of YHWH was decided and enacted. This assumption about YHWH as the presiding officer over the divine assembly is evident in the plural articulation of Genesis 1:26, in the development of "Satan" in the book of Job 1–2, in the scheme against King Ahab (1 Kings 22:19-23), and more especially in Psalm 82 where the high God sits in judgment over the lesser gods who fall short of YHWH's expectation of justice for the poor and needy. The presentation of YHWH in 1 Kings 22 and Psalm 82 evidence a way in which YHWH is known to be politically engaged in a partisan way in the world: "The mythopoeic symbol of the divine assembly not only served the radical integration of the divine world in the figure of Yahweh, but also gave to the reality of the divine a highly political shape."[16]

2. The divine council, moreover, is the launching pad for prophetic messages, so that the prophets are characteristically understood to utter messages that are not their own, but messages they have received from the "divine council." Thus the "call of Isaiah" in Isaiah 6:1-10 places the prophet in the council (see also Isaiah 40:1-11; Jeremiah 23; Amos 3:7).

The characteristic prophetic formula, "thus saith the Lord," the so-called messenger formula is a rhetorical device to mark the claim that the prophet speaks a word other than his own. It is Jeremiah's polemic against his prophetic opponents that they do not carry such divine messages, but are in fact speaking their own unauthorized message:

> I did not send the prophets,
>   yet they ran;
> I did not speak to them,
>   yet they prophesied.
> But if they had stood in my council,
>   then they would have proclaimed my words to my people,
> and they would have turned them from their evil way,
> and from the evil of their doings. (Jeremiah 23:21-22)

By the time of Isaiah in the exile, there are still marks of the divine council, as reflected in the plural imperative of Isaiah 40:1-2 wherein YHWH addresses members of the divine council.[17] But their function has now been completely demoted, so that YHWH can claim that it was only YHWH, without an associate of any kind, who has enacted the "gospel" of the end of the exile:

> I first have declared it to Zion,
>   and I give to Jerusalem a herald of good tidings.
> But when I look there is no one;
>   among these there is no counselor
>   who, when I ask, gives an answer. (Isaiah 41:27-28)

To be sure, the complexity of the divine council wells up with new vigor in the angelology of the apocalyptic literature, but that lies at the very edge of the Old Testament. And even where there is such a developed imagery, there is no doubt that YHWH presides over all, sometimes with compliance from the lesser parties, sometimes in rebellion, but always in the end, in the service of YHWH.

3. The recalcitrant "facts on the ground" required that the Old Testament, in its interpretive processes, must take heed of alternative religious claims. Given that, however, it is nonetheless the case that the Old Testament moved determinedly to exhibit "YHWH alone" as the God of Israel and creator of the world, a claim already voiced in Deuteronomy 6:4-5 and Exodus 20:2-3. The affirmation of the canon is simply a recognition of the truth in Israel that YHWH is the one God

who is to be loved, feared, trusted, served, and obeyed. In critical study, the ultimate triumph of YHWH over the gods is said to be an interpretive accomplishment of the "YHWH alone" party that worked incessantly that YHWH should be singularly the object of Israel's obedience.[18] In that view, the claims of any other power should be dismissed as illegitimate.

This advocacy against a more open theism was surely widespread and long term in Israel. There is no doubt, nonetheless, that the advocacy for "YHWH alone" is especially featured in the book of Deuteronomy and in the traditions derivative from the book of Deuteronomy. This pertains not only to Deuteronomy 6:4-5 noted above, but to the exclusionary rhetoric and general perspective of Deuteronomy that is harsh toward theological compromise and insistent on singular obedience. Deuteronomy envisions the forceful rejection of other religious options:

> Do not intermarry with them, giving your daughters to their sons or taking their daughters for your sons, for that would turn away your children from following me, to serve other gods. Then the anger of the LORD would be kindled against you, and he would destroy you quickly. But this is how you must deal with them: break down their altars, smash their pillars, hew down their sacred poles, and burn their idols with fire. For you are a people holy to the LORD your God; the LORD your God has chosen you out of all the peoples on earth to be his people, his treasured possession. (Deuteronomy 7:3-6)

Deuteronomy never wearies of urging such intense loyalty to YHWH: "The LORD your God you shall follow, him alone you shall fear, his commandments you shall keep, his voice you shall obey, him you shall serve, and to him you shall hold fast" (Deuteronomy 13:4). Finally the tradition confronts Israel with a radical either/or that is echoed in the Elijah traditions:

> See, I have set before you today life and prosperity, death and adversity. If you obey the commandments of the LORD your God that I am commanding you today, by loving the LORD your God, walking in his ways, and observing his commandments, decrees, and ordinances, then you shall live and become numerous, and the LORD your God will bless you in the land that you are entering to possess. But if your heart turns away and you do not hear, but are led astray to bow down to other gods and serve them, I declare to you today that you shall perish; you shall not live long in the land that you are crossing the Jordan to enter and

> possess. I call heaven and earth to witness against you today that I have set before you life and death, blessings and curses. Choose life so that you and your descendants may live, loving the LORD your God, obeying him, and holding fast to him; for that means life to you and length of days, so that you may live in the land that the LORD swore to give to your ancestors, to Abraham, to Isaac, and to Jacob (Deuteronomy 30:15-20)

> Elijah then came near to all the people, and said, "How long will you go limping with two different opinions? If the LORD is God, follow him; but if Baal, then follow him." The people did not answer him a word. (1 Kings 18:21; see Joshua 24:14-15)

The same programmatic intentionality is carried out in the *Deuteronomic History*. We may call attention to three explicit statements of the claim:

■ In 1 Kings 11, Solomon is severely condemned for his theological compromise that violates the first commandment of Sinai:

> King Solomon loved many foreign women along with the daughter of Pharaoh: Moabite, Ammonite, Edomite, Sidonian, and Hittite women, from the nations concerning which the LORD had said to the Israelites, "You shall not enter into marriage with them, neither shall they with you; for they will surely incline your heart to follow their gods"; Solomon clung to these in love. Among his wives were seven hundred princesses and three hundred concubines; and his wives turned away his heart. For when Solomon was old, his wives turned away his heart after other gods; and his heart was not true to the LORD his God, as was the heart of his father David. For Solomon followed Astarte the goddess of the Sidonians, and Milcom the abomination of the Ammonites. So Solomon did what was evil in the sight of the LORD, and did not completely follow the LORD, as his father David had done. (1 Kings 11:1-6)

■ Eventually the demise of the northern kingdom of Israel is explained in terms of the same intolerable compromise:

> This occurred because the people of Israel had sinned against the LORD their God, who had brought them up out of the land of Egypt from under the hand of Pharaoh king of Egypt. They had worshiped other gods and walked in the customs of the nations whom the LORD drove out before the people of Israel, and in the customs that the kings of Israel had introduced. The people of Israel secretly did things that were

> not right against the LORD their God. They built for themselves high places at all their towns, from watchtower to fortified city; they set up for themselves pillars and sacred poles on every high hill and under every green tree; there they made offerings on all the high places, as the nations did whom the LORD carried away before them. They did wicked things, provoking the LORD to anger; they served idols, of which the LORD had said to them, "You shall not do this." (2 Kings 17:7-12)

■ And in the end the Deuteronomic literature celebrates King Josiah as a "YHWH only" reformer who, unlike his grandfather Manasseh, adhered solely to YHWH: "Before him there was no king like him, who turned to the LORD with all his heart, with all his soul, and with all his might, according to all the law of Moses; nor did any like him arise after him" (2 Kings 23:25). The cadences of the basic theological claims of Deuteronomy are unmistakable in celebration of the faithful king who almost overcame the disobedience of his community . . . but not quite (see vv. 26-27)!

The same tradition from Deuteronomy is evident in at least the prose section of Jeremiah that is heavily shaped by the tradition of Deuteronomy. Thus the "temple sermon" of the prophet includes a massive threat against Jerusalem because of the worship of other gods:

> The children gather wood, the fathers kindle fire, and the women knead dough, to make cakes for the queen of heaven; and they pour out drink offerings to other gods, to provoke me to anger. . . . Yet *they did not obey or incline their ear*, but, in the stubbornness of their evil will, they walked in their own counsels, and looked backward rather than forward. (Jeremiah 7:18, 24, italics added)

The narrative of Jeremiah 44:15-23 is strongly reminiscent of Deuteronomy concerning the core indictment against Jerusalem.

4. A second, perhaps more positive assertion of "YHWH alone" is in the repeated use of the "formula of incomparability" that we have already seen in Exodus 15:11.[19] This formula can be variously a question, "Who is like you?" with the intended answer, "No one." Or the formula can be a simple declarative statement, "There is no one like YHWH." Either way, as question or as declaration the assertion is not that there is no other god; rather, of all the other gods that might be acknowledged there is none that can compete with YHWH and, therefore, none that is entitled to Israel's attentiveness.

The contrast between YHWH and the other gods is characteristically cast in terms of two criteria. First, there is no other god like YHWH *in power*, in the capacity to intervene and make a difference. This is clearly the import of Exodus 15:11-12 that is lyrical about the massive defeat of Pharaoh's army. The second criterion is that no other god is *committed to the weak, the needy, and the marginal*:

> All my bones shall say,
>   "O LORD, who is like you?
> You deliver the weak
>   from those too strong for them,
>   the weak and needy from those who despoil them." (Psalm 35:10)

It is clear in the study of these formulae that the two criteria cannot be separated. *Divine power* without *divine compassion* might yield only ruthlessness; *divine compassion* without *divine power* might result only in sympathy. But of course YHWH is attested to be unparalleled in *both power and compassion*. It is the combination that Israel has discerned in the founding miracle of the exodus and it is the same combination upon which Israel relies in its many prayers; the prayers in the Psalter are recurringly the voice of the needy and powerless who appeal to YHWH as their only source of comfort and strength. It is this incomparability that is featured in Israel's doxologies. Sometimes the formula is utilized explicitly; but even when it is not explicit, it may be rightly inferred. It is only YHWH who has such power, only YHWH who is capable of such solidarity, only YHWH who mobilizes such power on behalf of such compassionate, transformative solidarity. It is *only YHWH* in the songs and prayers of Israel because behind such utterance it has been *only YHWH* in the life and experience of Israel. No other god has done or can do what YHWH has done and therefore it follows no other god can be appropriately served, honored, or feared. It is only YHWH, the singular subject of Israel's most unrestrained doxologies and Israel's most desperate petitions.

The *strategies of the "divine council,"* the *uncompromising claims of the tradition of Deuteronomy* and the *lyrical assertion of incomparability* all converge into theological-liturgical practice of Israel to claim sovereignty for YHWH. Given that primal intention of the final form of the text of the Old Testament, I will mention three critical facets of current interpretive work in the Old Testament that are of great importance and that must be taken into account in future work in the discipline.

1. It is judged in critical scholarship that the impetus toward "YHWH alone" is a theological passion in ancient Israel that is not innocent or disinterested. The pressure toward "one YHWH" reflected in the book of Deuteronomy is likely allied with the centralization of worship and the centralization of power and wealth in the Jerusalem establishment. Thus critical Old Testament scholarship may at least entertain the thought that the passion for "YHWH alone" is in part a vehicle for power among the urban elites that gathered around monarchy and temple and that enjoyed the benefits of hegemony in the community.[20] After the fall of Jerusalem and the returned exilic community, moreover, the leadership of scribes and priests in the stead of kings engaged a similar monopoly of authority (under imperial aegis) and, in their effort to maintain "holy seed," set parameters on what was legitimate theologically, liturgically, and ethically (Ezra 9:2; Nehemiah 9:2). It is always a difficult question about the extent to which Old Testament theology should practice "suspicion," and certainly the so-called canon critics would eschew such a question. And even if one entertains suspicion about how such a claim for sovereignty came to be made, this does not perforce invalidate the claim. It does nevertheless alert us to the fact that the articulation of faith, in the Old Testament as elsewhere, does not happen in a social vacuum, but is always to some extent response to context and no doubt to the interest of the interpretive voice. This likely connection between "only YHWH" and the controlling sociopolitical interests that may evoke more sympathy for the counter-movement in Israel that did not so vigorously subscribe to that claim. That is, the counter-movement concerned political and economic matters as well as theological affirmations.

2. Every Old Testament interpreter must acknowledge the violence that is present in the Old Testament that is seemingly without much irony assigned to YHWH. This violence that is attached to YHWH is present in (a) the narrative of the death of the Egyptians at exodus, (b) the slaughter of the Canaanites in the tradition of the land entry, and (c) the prophetic threats that are made in turn against Israel and against the other states. YHWH as agent and perpetrator of violence or YHWH as legitimator of violence that is otherwise enacted through human agents stands at the center of the narrative and cannot be extricated from the narrative of violence, lest the narratives themselves will collapse. For the purpose of this discussion, it does not matter much, in my judgment, whether divine violence is enacted "supernaturally" and directly or through human agents. Either way, because of YHWH's commitment to

Israel that causes violence to others or because of divine anger at disobedience, YHWH is deeply enmeshed in the practice of violence.

3. There are two recurring explanatory strategies that are regularly employed to deal with the acute awkwardness of violence as a trait of YHWH. First, the evolutionary assumption about Israel's faith (earlier enshrined in "the documentary hypothesis" still influential in latent forms) found it possible to admit that YHWH in "primitive traditions" was violent, but as Israel's faith became more sophisticated and humane, these marks of YHWH are overcome. There is of course some truth to this reading of the data; the problem is that such a perspective is inherently supercessionist in a way that imagines the old claims are "superceded" and left behind.[21] That clearly will not do theologically, for tradition does not work in such a way. The community continues to rely upon old testimonies as nonnegotiable claims and premises.

Second, given more modern subjective consciousness, it is tempting to claim that in such violent readings of YHWH the text-making community simply projected by human text-makers upon YHWH its own land-hungry passion against previous landowners or projected its moral-covenantal expectation upon those who did not adhere to the required discipline. The operational word in either case is *projected*, so that the literary character of YHWH falls victim to the projections of human urgency. But of course such an explanatory effort subscribes too easily to "subjective consciousness" as though there were no "real" YHWH in the narrative. It does so, moreover, without reckoning with the slippery slope that our preferred YHWH may also be a projection, a point of course scored by Ludwig Feuerbach and Sigmund Freud.

More likely we must learn from Regina Schwartz in her much disputed claim that monotheism ("YHWH alone") breeds violence by its exclusionary assumptions and its readiness to eliminate all that do not subscribe to or conform with hegemonic claim.[22] As Schwartz demonstrates, the singular loyalty to Israel, singular legitimacy of the land promise, the singular claim of ethnic purity... all provide warrant for judgment, anger, and elimination.

The *violence* perpetrated through a *monopoly of claim* or a *monopoly of interpretation* is indeed evident in the Old Testament, though it is a subject that has only recently come to occupy scholarship.[23] The reason Old Testament theologians must take up the issue is abundantly apparent in current U. S. society with its ready "Christian" threat for violence and vengeance against any who do not subscribe to the exclusionary claims of the United States and particularly against Muslims who subscribe to an alternative faith that the President of the United States has termed *evil.* In lesser scope, but no less urgent in it is viciousness, is the wrath of the heterogeneous monopoly against the human claims of gays and lesbians in U. S. society, and in many other places in the world, the high religious claims of exclusivism reach down in violence against the disqualified. Our reading of the Old Testament will suggest that our contemporary potential for savagery in the name of religious loyalty is *deja vu* from this old tradition. As will be evident in what follows, the Old Testament itself moves against this propensity of YHWH, but the move against cannot be fully recognized or appropriated until we have taken into full account the centrality of violence for the character of YHWH. It is not plausible that the singers of YHWH's "incomparability" or the advocates of "YHWH alone" intended such practical and destructive consequences to their testimony. Old Testament theology nonetheless must, in our time of immense brutality, turn fresh to a consideration of the ways in which exclusive claims for YHWH generate exclusivism in attitude, policy, and action.[24]

4. One of the ways in which the monopolistic dimensions of monotheism are mitigated in the Old Testament is by way of a rich, complex, and varied range of metaphors used to characterize YHWH. I have spent considerable time on the dominant metaphors for YHWH, namely, warrior, king, judge, and father. Each of these and the sum of all of them issue in an affirmation of uncontested sovereignty, for the most part given us in quite masculine language, rhetoric that may evoke a macho presentation of YHWH. And of course much of the assertion of YHWH's wonders concerns macho acts of intervention and transformation, both negative and positive.

Such a characterization, taken by itself as it regularly is in some interpretive circles, yields high authority that indifferently imposes itself without regard for context or circumstance. When the impulse toward violence is recognized in such macho metaphors, we may then appreciate the counter-metaphors that also occur in the Old Testament in its characterization of YHWH. The field of such metaphors may include, as I have done in my more extended exposition, artist, healer, gardener-vinedresser, shepherd, and mother.[25] Here I wish only to note that the narrative of YHWH's *pathos* stands as a counterpoint to YHWH's *sovereignty*. By *pathos* I refer to the capacity to feel, notice, and care in ways that put YHWH at risk in solidarity, thus a readiness for suffering along with another in vulnerability and weakness.[26] It is the wonder of the Old Testament that it can feature these dimensions of YHWH alongside the characterization of strength and authority. I will refer to three texts that are most commonly cited concerning YHWH's pathos that gives nuance to YHWH's sovereignty:

■ In Hosea 11:1-9, the poet has articulated the emotive extremities that concern YHWH in relationship to Israel. In verses 1-4, YHWH, according to the prophetic oracle, remembers passionate, tender caring for the vulnerable child Israel. YHWH is portrayed as a devoted parent. But in verses 5-7, YHWH emotes in immense anger toward recalcitrant Israel and is prepared to abandon Israel to its sorry fate. But then in verses 8-9, YHWH is caught up short by concern for Israel and breaks off the negative binge against Israel:

> How can I give you up, Ephraim?
>   How can I hand you over, O Israel?
> How can I make you like Admah?
>   How can I treat you like Zeboiim?
> My heart recoils within me;
>   my compassion grows warm and tender.
> I will not execute my fierce anger;
>   I will not again destroy Ephraim;
> for I am God and no mortal,
>   the Holy One in your midst,
>   and I will not come in wrath. (Hosea 11:8-9)

YHWH comes to recognize that YHWH is not able to give up on Israel or to hand Israel over to desolation. YHWH, in the midst of the poem, now recognizes the powerful, deep urge for compassion that interrupts the anger and rage. It is YHWH's self-awareness about care and concern, according to the poet, that causes a reversal of the field and that protects Israel from the justifiable wrath of YHWH.

■ In the later, perhaps derivative text, YHWH experiences the same reversal of emotion (Jeremiah 31:20).[27] YHWH may "speak against" Israel, as YHWH has often done in the prophets, and immediately in the tradition of Jeremiah. But again, in the midst of such anger, YHWH disrupts YHWH's own justified propensity in place of more "speaking against," YHWH *really remembers* (as in Hosea 11:1-4) and is *really compassionate*. These two lines of the poem use affinitive absolutes, each time to articulate the intensity of YHWH's disposition toward Israel. Because of this self-discovery by YHWH, we now have the answer to the opening question of the unit: *Yes*, Ephraim is my dear son. *Yes*, he is the child of my delight. *Yes*, YHWH cares for Israel and will not reject. YHWH speaks a *yes* to Israel even though Israel's conduct merits a harsh *no*. (See derivatively, 2 Corinthians 1:19.) While we may say theologically that this is an articulation of God's grace, in fact the poem exhibits for us the wellspring of emotional turmoil out of which YHWH's grace comes. In this moment of self-disclosure made possible through poetic imagination, YHWH is more like a generous, attentive mother than a remote king or judge.[28] It is evident here, as in Hosea 11:8-9, that YHWH's godness consists in solidarity with and generous compassion toward YHWH's covenant partner.

■ In still a later text, the poet begins by reiterating Israel's exilic complaint: "But Zion said, 'The LORD has forsaken me, / my Lord has forgotten me' " (Isaiah 49:14; see Lamentations 5:20). YHWH responds to the complaint of exilic Israel with a question that seems to require a negative answer: "Can a woman forget her nursing child, / or show no compassion for the child of her womb?" (Isaiah 49:15ab). But then YHWH, via the poet, surprises in the answer. Yes, it is possible that a nursing mother may forget a suckling child; one could imagine that the answer is no, because the breast of a nursing mother would eventually become very painful. YHWH, however, will do better than a nursemaid; YHWH will never forget! The remarkable urgency of this voice likens YHWH to a nursing mother who is vulnerable and attentive, and therefore Israel in its need will be cared for.

All of these three texts—Hosea 11:8-9, Jeremiah 31:20, and Isaiah 49:14-15—attest to YHWH's mothering qualities. To be sure, in none of these texts is YHWH called *mother*, because that is to expect too much in that patriarchal world. And yet in all three texts, the mothering propensity of YHWH is unmistakable. These are the sorts of texts—not so many to be sure but enough for the case—that tell powerfully against the macho sovereignty of YHWH that is all too readily evoked in heated, interpretive matrixes of ideology. From these texts it can be argued, as in recent feminist hermeneutics, that the feminine dimension of YHWH's character is attested by Israel.[29]

More broadly, however, these texts make clear concerning the *relatedness* of YHWH who is impacted and impinged upon by the status and address of the covenant partner. (It should be noted that Christians, by appeal to the Trinity, too readily and facilely divide sovereignty and relatedness, assigning sovereignty to the Father, relatedness to the Son.) But an embrace of *perichoresis* suggests that the whole of YHWH is fully sovereign, the whole of YHWH is fully related, and thereby sovereignty of another sort is offered as the dominant metaphors by themselves might suggest.[30] It is the multiplicity of metaphors for YHWH that prevents the testimony of the Old Testament about YHWH from becoming idolatrous. The rich field of metaphors utilized must be taken altogether without being homogenized. The consequence is a self-correcting and deconstructive dynamism that precludes the fixity of a stable image or the finality of any formulation. YHWH is said and heard to be a fully personal agent engaged in an interactive process with YHWH's creaturely partners. Such a God is a practitioner of mutuality that is qualified by the incommensurability between YHWH and YHWH's partners. It is an unresolvable interpretive enigma of biblical faith that YHWH's incommensurability is enacted through mutuality.

It is clear that Israel's attestation concerning YHWH is open, dynamic, and fluid. This is not to say it is "relativistic," because the texts in their particularity are to be taken "literally," that is, with serious attention to *what is said* and *how it is said*. The *wide field of metaphors* reflective of the *plurality of voices* that speak through the text reflect many different, even competing interests; it is for that reason that Old Testament theology remains open for dialogic engagement. Indeed the long history of *normative* interpretations attest that there is no closed, final way to characterize what is said and known here about YHWH.

In concluding this discussion of YHWH in the Old Testament, I call attention to three issues that are left open and that require ongoing interpretive work. Each of these issues concerns the character and disposition of YHWH toward Israel and toward creation:

1. YHWH is peculiarly *the God of Israel* and majestically the *God of all creation*! There is no doubt that the Torah and the Moses traditions are preoccupied with YHWH as the one who has chosen Israel to be YHWH's own people and YHWH's special covenant partner. That claim scarcely requires exposition, for the text is clear. Yet, even if the core of the Sinai tradition is YHWH claims Israel, YHWH also proclaims, "The whole earth is mine" (Exodus 19:5). It is only in the last several decades that Old Testament scholarship has recovered the horizon of creation that had been largely neglected in the so-called Biblical Theology Movement featured by Gerhard von Rad and G. Ernest Wright.[31] Crucial in the recovery of that larger horizon was especially the work of Claus

Westermann who saw that the *God who saves* Israel is also the *God who blesses* all of creation.[32]

At its best the theological traditions of Judaism and Christianity have always understood that YHWH —the God named in the Christian tradition as Trinity—is not contained in or preoccupied with the community of faith (Israel or the church), but is concerned to "mend" the whole world.[33] The remarkable reality of the Old Testament is that this twofold concern of Israel and the world is held together, in some tension to be sure, but without any sense of contradiction:

■ The opening chapters of Genesis clearly attest YHWH is creator of heaven and earth and is ruler over all creation (Genesis 1–9). The genealogy of Genesis 10, moreover, indicates YHWH's governance of the entire human world of political communities. Specifically the flood narrative and the covenant of Genesis 9:8-17 presents YHWH as Lord of all, capable of *uncreating* and *recreating*, capable of care and fidelity over the creation. It is for good reason that Judaism has found in the covenant with Noah the commands that pertain to the human community beyond Israel.[34] It is clear that creation and then restored creation operate according to YHWH's blessing, the divine assignment of life abundant to all creation.

■ The ancestral narratives of Genesis have as one of their prominent themes the assertion that Abraham and his family is a means whereby "all the families of the earth shall be blessed" (Genesis 12:3). In this assertion it is affirmed that Israel—and Israel's life with YHWH—constitute an important way in the bestowal of YHWH's blessing on all of the peoples as YHWH intends.[35] The same motif is evident in Isaiah 42:6 and 49:6 in which Israel is a "covenant" and a "light" for the nations. The intentionality of YHWH in these texts is the well-being of the nations.

■ In prophetic discourse there is, of course, an intense preoccupation with Israel. It is clear, however, that YHWH's governance is large in scope. World leaders, notably Sennacarib and Nebuchadnezzar may serve as instruments of YHWH's intention. More programmatically the Oracles Against the Nations evidence the rule of YHWH over the nations and, in a few remarkable promissory passages, the future well-being of other peoples is a concern of YHWH (see Isaiah 2:2-4; 19:24-25; Micah 4:1-4; and the narrative of Jonah). These texts have no compunction about YHWH's concern for other nations for whom YHWH wills and intends good.[36]

■ In the wisdom tradition it is commonly recognized that this instructional and reflective material is for the most part not explicitly Israelite but generically human, the discourse that is common in the international community. Here the focus on YHWH is not as Lord of Israel but as the creator to whom all human communities are responsible.[37] Israel is able to participate fully in this critical reflection upon the moral structure of reality, but it can claim no special privilege or preeminence. Rather Israel stands alongside all of the peoples before the inscrutable mystery and wisdom of creaturely reality that is governed by the Lord of all.

■ In the Psalter, finally, Israel's doxologies summon all peoples to join in praise to YHWH:

> Declare his glory among the nations,
> his marvelous works among all the peoples. (Psalm 96:3)

> The LORD is king; let the peoples tremble!
> He sits enthroned upon the cherubim; let the earth quake! (Psalm 99:1)

> Praise the LORD, all you nations!
> Extol him, all you peoples! (Psalm 117:1)

In the venue of the Jerusalem temple it is clear, as surely Solomon intended, that YHWH is not simply God of Israel. YHWH is Lord of all nations; the cosmic imagery and symbolism of the Jerusalem temple require that worship be, in large scope, befitting the Lord of all nations.[38]

In every part of the Old Testament, YHWH is known to be Lord of all. YHWH has an intention for all peoples, and none can fully thwart that purpose. Thus, for example,

> The LORD of hosts has sworn:
> As I have designed,
> so shall it be;
> and as I have planned,
> so shall it come to pass:
> I will break the Assyrian in my land,
> and on my mountains trample him under foot;
> his yoke shall be removed from them,
> and his burden from their shoulders.
> This is the plan that is planned
> concerning the whole earth;

> and this is the hand that is stretched out
>   over all the nations.
> For the LORD of hosts has planned,
>   and who will annul it?
> His hand is stretched out,
>   and who will turn it back? (Isaiah 14:24-27)

The rule of YHWH here defiantly resists a challenge from the nations; that defiant challenge is matched in Job 38–41 with the same defiant claim concerning power as the Lord of creation. Thus in every part of the Old Testament, Israel's testimony concerns YHWH's rule. Of course none of this diminishes YHWH's commitment to Israel; it does, however, place Israel's covenant with YHWH in a context that requires a move beyond Israel (or the church) in order to recognize the expansive rule of YHWH. Such an expansiveness is especially important in the time of ideological passion and selfish anxiety in which nation-states (and most specifically the United States) and the compliant church too easily claim too much of the biblical God exclusively for themselves.

This delicate affirmation of both the rule of Israel and the rule of the nations is given delicate nuance by Patrick Miller. On the one hand Miller concludes:

> The nations are a part of the created order, the outcome of the blessing of God in the completion of creation. The restoration of the creation after the Flood involves also the restoration of humanity as a part of that creation and of the renewal of the blessing (Genesis 8:17; 9:1, 7) through the lineage of Noah (Genesis 9:19). So also the establishment of covenant with Noah is an establishment of covenant with all of humankind. The text makes this point repeatedly and thus with much emphasis. The universal covenant with humankind as a way of perpetuating and maintaining the creation incorporates the nations of which Israel is a single part.
>
> The nations, therefore, are susceptible to the same divine *blessing*, *mercy*, and *redemption* as is Israel.[39]

In this connection, Miller mentions especially YHWH's blessing to Ishmael (Genesis 17:2-3, 16), the narrative of Jonah, and the prophetic oracles of Amos 9:7 and Isaiah 19:20:

> The covenant with Noah, therefore, has incorporated the whole creation, including the nations, in the blessing, the compassion, and the redemption of God rising out of the promise to maintain the creation. Mosaic covenant does not stand against that or mark out a special place for Israel. That raises the question, quite naturally, of what that covenant does mean for Israel if the Noachic covenant is the larger framework that both establishes a natural order as the matrix of human and historical existence, and creates the conditions for God's compassionate and redemptive activity to become available for "every living creature."[40]

That claim, of course, is balanced, as Miller properly recognizes, with a claim for Israel:

> But there is a particular role that Israel is to play that is not necessarily a part of the universal covenant with the nations. That role is not given a uniform definition in the biblical literature. But it does seem to have to do with the nations, both implicitly and explicitly. Amos speaks of a special relation the Lord had with Israel: "You only have I known of all the families of the earth" (Amos 3:2). He seems to have in mind the election of Israel "to keep the way of the Lord by doing righteousness and justice," an election that is set in the context of the promise to bring blessing to Abraham that he and his seed after him may be the means of blessing for the nations (Genesis 18:17-19).[41]

Miller particularly mentions Isaiah 19:3-6 and Isaiah 42:1-4; 49:6 to which I have made reference. Israel's role, vis-à-vis the nations, is as a "royal priesthood" (on which see 1 Peter 2:9-10) and as a covenant. YHWH's rule is open and passionate enough both to *choose*, but then to *choose all* in time to come.

2. YHWH is the *demanding God of Sinai* and *the guaranteeing God of Jerusalem*. There is no doubt that the core claim of Old Testament faith is the disclosure of YHWH at Sinai. Through the terror of theophany, YHWH meets Israel and is found to be *holy*, *awesome*, *fearsome*, and *demanding*. YHWH is one who *will be obeyed* (*shema*). Thus the character and will and purpose of YHWH are described in terms of Torah, and Israel at Sinai assents to obedience. The great "if" of Exodus 19:5, echoed repeatedly in Deuteronomy, clearly makes the status of Israel as YHWH's covenant people conditional upon obedience to Torah.[42] The negative sanctions of covenant curses articulate the profound risk in disobedience, a risk that is many times reiterated in the prophetic speeches of judgment.

The appearance of David—and the forming of the monarchy and the establishment of the Jerusalem temple—introduce theological *novum* in Israel.[43] In Nathan's initial oracle of legitimization for David as king, the divine promise to David is that YHWH's commitment is ultimately unconditional. There will, to be sure, be punishment for disobedience. But punishment is not the last word, because YHWH's *khesedh* toward David and his family will persist in and through and beyond punishment:

> I will be a father to him, and he shall be a son to me. When he commits iniquity, I will punish him with a rod such as mortals use, with blows inflicted by human beings. But I will not take my steadfast love from him, as I took it from Saul, whom I put away from before you. Your house and your kingdom shall be made sure forever before me; your throne shall be established forever. (2 Samuel 7:14-16)

The same unconditional promise to the house of David is lavishly reiterated in lyrical form in Psalm 89:

> I have found my servant David;
>   with my holy oil I have anointed him;
> my hand shall always remain with him;
>   my arm also shall strengthen him.
> The enemy shall not outwit him,
>   the wicked shall not humble him.
> I will crush his foes before him
>   and strike down those who hate him.
> My faithfulness and steadfast love shall be with him;
>   and in my name his horns shall be exalted. (Psalm 89:20-24)
>
> Forever I will keep my steadfast love for him,
>   and my covenant with him will stand firm.
> I will establish his line forever,
>   and his throne as long as the heavens endure.
> If his children forsake my law
>   and do not walk according to my ordinances,
> if they violate my statutes
>   and do not keep my commandments,
> then I will punish their transgression with the rod
>   and their iniquity with scourges;
> but I will not remove from him my steadfast love,
>   or be false to my faithfulness.
> I will not violate my covenant,

or alter the word that went forth from my lips.
Once and for all I have sworn by my holiness;
I will not lie to David.
His line shall continue forever,
and his throne endure before me like the sun.
It shall be established forever like the moon,
an enduring witness in the skies. (Psalm 89:28-37)

Again it is recognized that "forsaking Torah" and violating the statutes of YHWH will evoke divine punishment. But again that punishment is not the last word. The last word that abides is YHWH's *khesedh* and *ʾemunah*: "But I will not remove from him my steadfast love, / or be false to my faithfulness" (Psalm 89:33). This oracle concerning the dynasty came to be matched in the temple theology of Jerusalem with the conviction that Zion is the holy residence of YHWH and therefore Jerusalem has YHWH as abiding patron (1 Kings 8:12-13). Thus see also the deep assurance of Psalm 46, the most obvious of the "Songs of Zion."[44]

Scholarship has long noticed the contrasting accents of the Sinai and the Jerusalem traditions; in the two cases YHWH is articulated very differently and, consequently, Israel's prospects for the future are very different as well. For the most, scholars have been preoccupied with the distinction between "conditional" and "unconditional" and have noted the tension if not the contradiction.

It is the merit of Jon Levenson to have considered carefully the relationship of "Sinai and Zion." Levenson agrees that the different "nuances the scholars detect are real."[45] He rightly resists that these different traditions are "north and south" geographically. But the differences should not be overstated and it is clear that the theologies can "coexist."[46] With particular reference to the appearance of both theologies in the book of Micah, Levenson concludes:

> The Davidic surely did not displace the Sinaitic in Micah, where the latter is still dominant, as Beyerlin emphasizes. But was the Sinaitic heard differently because of the presence of a Davidic oracle of deliverance? There is, to be sure, a logical contradiction between the prediction that "Zion shall be plowed as a field/And Jerusalem shall become a heap of ruins" (3:12) and the assurance that a Davidic ruler "will deliver us from Assyria/If it invades our country" (5:5b). But we have no evidence that Micah's audience recognized the logical contradiction and therefore relied upon his Davidic promise for insurance against his Sinaitic threat of destruction. In other words, there is no empirical basis

> upon which to assert that the Davidic theology blunted the impact of Micah's covenantal preaching. In fact, it may be the case that each of the two streams of tradition came to the fore alone, in a different period of the prophet's career.[47]

I derive from Levenson's careful judgment the conclusion that the two traditions, with very different accents, were championed either by different circles of traditionists or even by the same traditionists in different circumstances.

However the origin and transmission of the traditions are to be understood, it is unmistakable—as Levenson grants—that they carry very different theological accents and portray YHWH very differently. The contrast of conditional and unconditional is a major issue that makes for rich theological reflection and ongoing interpretation. Given the tension, I make three derivative points:

First, it is clear that the traditions of Moses and David function as important theological resources for the faith of Israel as Israel believed differently in different contexts. Thus in the monarchal period that is perforce also the period of the great prophetic critique of the monarchy, it is the covenant tradition of Sinai and the Torah commandments that are crucial. That is, the characteristic prophetic critique is that the monarchy, the temple priests, and the entire Jerusalem establishment have violated Torah and so stand under judgment. The Jerusalem establishment was not only urban, but also urbane. This means that it was committed to a quite broad theological horizon that chafed at the particularity of the Sinai traditions. Thus it is possible to make a general correlation between the *commands of Sinai and prophetic indictments* and *between the sanctions of Sinai and prophetic sentences*. The prophets are acutely aware of *realpolitik* but characteristically assert that the decisive factor in the security and well-being of Israel is adherence to the Torah of YHWH.

Conversely, after the destruction of Jerusalem and the deportation, the tradition of conditionality from Sinai is not of much appeal, for the conditions manifestly have not been met. Thus in the exilic period, it is the memory of Abraham and the reality of the prophetic promise that provide bearing, hope, and expectation for Israel.[48] The two traditions serve, Sinai as judgment upon the prosperous and complacent, and David (Abraham) as assurance to the dislocated and despairing. It is important to see that the canonical tradition preserves for later use traditions that in any particular circumstance might seem unhelpful or irrelevant. This is an important recognition in an ideological context when partisan interpretation would like to scuttle the parts of the text that it resists or rejects. The "canonical" memory of Israel preserved more than was immediately useful or valid in any particular context.

Second, while the matter of *conditional and unconditional* is clear enough in the two traditions, such labels should not be overstressed. The truth of the matter is that both traditions are more complex and "thick" than such a summary labeling might suggest. Thus the *conditional* tradition of Sinai knows from the outset that the covenant of Sinai is a *broken* covenant (Exodus 32). For that reason, even the possibility of a future for the covenant depends not necessarily on meeting the conditions of Torah, but on the unconditional readiness of YHWH to forgive. Thus after the broken tablets and the broken covenant of Exodus 32, YHWH can respond to Moses' urgent petition for pardon: "I hereby make a covenant. Before all your people I will perform marvels, such as have not been performed in all the earth or in any nation; and all the people among whom you live shall see the work of the LORD; for it is an awesome thing that I will do with you" (Exodus 34:10). YHWH begins again without conditions being met. That truth about the Sinai covenant is surely reflected in the tradition of Jeremiah that, by way of Deuteronomy, is rooted in Sinai:

> The days are surely coming, says the LORD, when I will make a new covenant with the house of Israel and the house of Judah.... No longer shall they teach one another, or say to each other, "Know the LORD," for they shall all know me, from the least of them to the greatest, says the LORD; for I will forgive their iniquity, and remember their sin no more. (Jeremiah 31:31, 34)

> I will restore the fortunes of Judah and the fortunes of Israel, and rebuild them as they were at first. I will cleanse them from all the guilt of their sin against me, and I will forgive all the guilt of their sin and rebellion against me. (Jeremiah 33:7-8)

Forgiveness as a basis of future covenant means, even in the tradition of Sinai, that YHWH's generosity overrides the many demands of Torah conditionality.

In like manner, it is not adequate to characterize the Davidic tradition as unconditional, for the facts on the ground led to the judgment that the unconditional promise of YHWH did not hold. To be sure, Israel belatedly returned to the Davidic promises in messianic form. But as the dynasty was destroyed, the claim of unconditionality had to be treated with candor and doubt. This is unmistakably the case in Psalm 89. As we have seen, that psalm in its primary voice affirms YHWH's unconditional commitment to the dynasty. In verse 38, however, historical reality catches up with Jerusalem theology. Verses 38-51 are apparently a response to the disaster of 587 B.C.E. when Jerusalem—monarchy and temple—was destroyed. That destruction inevitably raised hard issues about YHWH's fidelity that now was seen to be deficient:

> How long, O LORD? Will you hide yourself forever?
>   How long will your wrath burn like fire?...
> Lord, where is your steadfast love of old,
>   which by your faithfulness you swore to David? (Psalm 89:46, 49)

To be sure, the psalm does not explicitly reject the theological claim of unconditionality; but it clearly recognizes that the claim is now in jeopardy with concrete evidence against it.

As the unconditionality of Sinai moves toward *forgiveness* and as the unconditionality of David moves toward *wretchedness and doubt*, it is clear that the two traditions are not fortune-cookie formulations. They are rather ongoing interpretive positions that move and develop in context. It is clear, in the faith and lived history of Israel, that YHWH is not an automatic *quid pro quo* judge nor a predictable guarantor. Israel always had to struggle and imagine afresh its characterization of YHWH in new circumstance.

Third, these two traditions in the text itself remain dynamic and open to developing nuance. In long-term theological project, however, they are treated with some reductionism, most particularly in Christian tradition. Thus as early as Paul in his reflection about the Torah and its place in the life of Gentile Christians, Paul can juxtapose Abraham as the father of faith in distinction from the law (Romans 4:13-25). In his allegory in Galatians, Paul can contrast "Jerusalem" that is faith apart from the law and Sinai that is faith through the law:

> Now this is an allegory: these women are two covenants. One woman, in fact, is Hagar, from Mount Sinai, bearing children for slavery. Now Hagar is Mount Sinai in Arabia and corresponds to the present Jerusalem, for she is in slavery with her children. But the other woman corresponds to the Jerusalem above; she is free, and she is our mother. For it is written,

> "Rejoice, you childless one, you who bear no children,
> burst into song and shout, you who endure no birthpangs;
> for the children of the desolate woman are more numerous
> than the children of the one who is married."
>
> Now you, my friends, are children of the promise, like Isaac. But just as at that time the child who was born according to the flesh persecuted the child who was born according to the Spirit, so it is now also. But what does the scripture say? Drive out the slave and her child; for the child of the slave will not share the inheritance with the child of the free woman. So then, friends, we are children, not of the slave but of the free woman. (Galatians 4:24-31)

It is clear that "the law" in Paul's discussion is not the text of Sinai, but its own circumstance of Judaism.

In any case the model Paul articulates easily posed as opposites: *Abraham* (grace without law, that is, unconditional) and *Moses*, the conditional. In this kind of reductionism, subsequent Christian propensity, read through Luther, has given the "conditional" tradition to Jews and retained the "unconditional" tradition as the gospel.[49] The practical effect has been the Christian caricature of the Sinai tradition in Judaism as stereotypical legalism fails to understand the commandments in a context of covenant that is premised on forgiveness.

Our learning, in consideration of this tension, is that we are not permitted as biblical interpreters to take one-half of the tension as the whole of biblical faith. Taken alone, the conditional tradition may lead to despair or to a "successful" works righteousness. Taken alone, the unconditional tradition may result in cheap grace, a point to which Paul was immediately alert. Thus the tension offers a self-correcting dialectic that is faithful to the nature of a genuinely interactive relationship that includes dimensions of both requirement and guarantee. In the biblical tradition it is fair to judge that this rich pattern of relationship offered by YHWH becomes a model for all serious relationships that inescapably include dimensions of the conditionality and unconditionality. In interpretive work, it is plausible to suggest that in every case we pay primary attention to the tradition we sense to be most difficult for our own interpretive understanding.

The tension that has become a deep contestation between Jews and Christians in the matrix of Paul is an old tension in the Old Testament itself. But the tension is not to be resolved in the Old Testament, or perhaps even after. The tension, rather, is the very grist of faith and provides the ongoing task of interpretation. We may conclude with the judgment of Harmut Gese that the "Torah of Sinai" has become the "Torah of Zion," an argument made with reference to Isaiah 2:2-4 and Micah 4:1-4:

> According to Isaiah 2:2-4 and Micah 4:1-4 the peoples will of their own accord flow to Zion, which has become the center of the cosmos, and from which there issues forth the Torah that will bring eternal peace. In contrast to the old Sinai revelation, the new, eschatological revelation is addressed to all peoples, and they will become aware of the kingship of God. The Torah therefore describes the state of *shalom* in a more comprehensive manner, and this revelation is given, not at Sinai, but on Mount Zion. We can state it briefly by saying the Sinai revelation has become the eschatological Zion revelation, and the Torah of Sinai and that of Zion are different.
>
> In the light of the dynamic development of Torah that we have observed, it is not surprising that the Zion Torah is more than just a quantitative expansion of the Sinai Torah. The Old Testament provides illustrations of a qualitative change in Torah.[50]

YHWH is the *majestic God* of uncompromising glory and the *merciful God* capable of response and acute pathos. There is no doubt that YHWH is a God of surpassing power and wonder who will brook no rival, who will be worshiped and obeyed, and who commands the powers of the earth and of the cosmos. In narrative form, this large claim for YHWH is powerfully articulated in the exodus narrative. YHWH is the one who "made fools of the Egyptians" (Exodus 10:2), the one like whom there is no other (Exodus 15:11). The concreteness of narrative results in sweeping doxology about this majestic, sovereign God:

> The LORD brings the counsel of the nations to nothing;
> he frustrates the plans of the peoples. (Psalm 33:10)
>
> He makes wars cease to the end of the earth;
> he breaks the bow, and shatters the spear;
> he burns the shields with fire. (Psalm 46:9)
>
> For great is the LORD, and greatly to be praised;
> he is to be revered above all gods.
> For all the gods of the peoples are idols,
> but the LORD made the heavens.
> Honor and majesty are before him;
> strength and beauty are in his sanctuary. (Psalm 96:4-6)

Who gives food to the hungry.

The LORD sets the prisoners free;
the LORD opens the eyes of the blind.
The LORD lifts up those who are bowed down;
the LORD loves the righteous.
The LORD watches over the strangers;
he upholds the orphan and the widow,
but the way of the wicked he brings to ruin.

The LORD will reign forever,
your God, O Zion, for all generations.
Praise the LORD! (Psalm 146:7b-10)

All nations, all creatures, all elements of creation join in praise of the creator and ruler of all.

That affirmation of YHWH then was utilized in exilic poetry as Israel asserted and celebrated the sovereign authority of YHWH, even over the Babylonians. While the historical evidence is unclear, in canonical form there is little doubt that such doxological assertion provided grounds in the exile for hope, for the recovery of identity and courage, and finally for the capacity to depart the empire:

Have you not known? Have you not heard?
Has it not been told you from the beginning?
Have you not understood from the foundations of the earth?
It is he who sits above the circle of the earth,
and its inhabitants are like grasshoppers;
who stretches out the heavens like a curtain,
and spreads them like a tent to live in;
who brings princes to naught,
and makes the rulers of the earth as nothing. (Isaiah 40:21-23)

To whom then will you compare me,
or who is my equal? says the Holy One.
Lift up your eyes on high and see:
Who created these?
He who brings out their host and numbers them,
calling them all by name;
because he is great in strength,
mighty in power,
not one is missing. (Isaiah 40:25-26)

> Sing to the LORD a new song,
> his praise from the end of the earth!
> Let the sea roar and all that fills it,
> the coastlands and their inhabitants.
> Let the desert and its towns lift up their voice,
> the villages that Kedar inhabits;
> let the inhabitants of Sela sing for joy,
> let them shout from the tops of the mountains.
> Let them give glory to the LORD,
> and declare his praise in the coastlands.
> The LORD goes forth like a soldier,
> like a warrior he stirs up his fury;
> he cries out, he shouts aloud,
> he shows himself mighty against his foes.
>
> For a long time I have held my peace,
> I have kept still and restrained myself;
> now I will cry out like a woman in labor,
> I will gasp and pant.
> I will lay waste mountains and hills,
> and dry up all their herbage;
> I will turn the rivers into islands,
> and dry up the pools.
> I will lead the blind
> by a road they do not know,
> by paths they have not known
> I will guide them.
> I will turn the darkness before them into light,
> the rough places into level ground.
> These are the things I will do,
> and I will not forsake them. (Isaiah 42:10-16)

> Sing, O heavens, for the LORD has done it;
> shout, O depths of the earth;
> break forth into singing, O mountains,
> O forest, and every tree in it!
> For the LORD has redeemed Jacob,
> and will be glorified in Israel. (Isaiah 44:23)

While YHWH receives Israel's praise, it is also evident that YHWH is known to have powerful self-regard, so that YHWH can declare concerning YHWH's self:

I am the LORD, that is my name;
    my glory I give to no other,
    nor my praise to idols.
See, the former things have come to pass,
    and new things I now declare;
before they spring forth,
    I tell you of them. (Isaiah 42:8-9)

For my own sake, for my own sake, I do it,
    for why should my name be profaned?
    My glory I will not give to another. (Isaiah 48:11)

That same self-regard is on exhibit in YHWH's speeches from the whirlwind that assert the spectacular power of YHWH as creator:

Where were you when I laid the foundation of the earth?
    Tell me, if you have understanding.
Who determined its measurements—surely you know!
    Or who stretched the line upon it?
On what were its bases sunk,
    or who laid its cornerstone
when the morning stars sang together
    and all the heavenly beings shouted for joy?

Or who shut in the sea with doors
    when it burst out from the womb?—
when I made the clouds its garment,
    and thick darkness its swaddling band,
and prescribed bounds for it,
    and set bars and doors,
and said, "Thus far shall you come, and no farther,
    and here shall your proud waves be stopped"? (Job 38:4-11)

While the self-praise of YHWH is as a defiant question to Job, the obviously implied answer to that question always acknowledges YHWH's peculiar and unparalleled capacity in power and beauty.

The majesty of YHWH is everywhere celebrated in the Old Testament. At the same time, however, YHWH is said to be deeply engaged with and available for Israel in its need. This capacity of YHWH for empathy, solidarity, and mercy with Israel in its need is especially apparent in Israel's lament psalms that characteristically evoke YHWH's attention and response, a response celebrated in Israel's songs of thanksgiving. The capacity of YHWH to be engaged in something like mutuality is evident in YHWH's responses to Abraham (Genesis 18:22-33), to Moses (Exodus 32:11-14; Numbers 14:13-20), to Jeremiah (Jeremiah 12:5-6; 15:19-21), and eventually to Job in the speeches just cited. But it is especially in the Psalms that YHWH's pathos-filled responsiveness is most central:[51]

> In my distress I called upon the LORD;
> to my God I cried for help.
> From his temple he heard my voice,
> and my cry to him reached his ears. (Psalm 18:6)

> I sought the LORD, and he answered me,
> and delivered me from all my fears.
> Look to him, and be radiant;
> so your faces shall never be ashamed.
> This poor soul cried, and was heard by the LORD,
> and was saved from every trouble. (Psalm 34:4-6)

> I waited patiently for the LORD;
> he inclined to me and heard my cry.
> He drew me up from the desolate pit,
> out of the miry bog,
> and set my feet upon a rock,
> making my steps secure. (Psalm 40:1-2; see also Lamentations 3:55-57)

And because YHWH's engagement on behalf of the needy and weak is reliable, Israel can even anticipate the next divine response. Thus in Psalm 35, the psalmist proposes to YHWH what needs to be said from the divine throne:

> Draw the spear and javelin
> against my pursuers;
> say to my soul,
> "I am your salvation." (Psalm 35:3)

In these texts Israel takes YHWH's sovereign power for granted; what counts now is YHWH's peculiar capacity to be caring and responsive, a capacity that we already have seen in the exodus narrative (Exodus 2:23-25).

The wonder of YHWH's dialogical character, moreover, is that *YHWH's sovereign power* and *YHWH's compassionate engagement* are not in tension, but are taken together in Israel's life and praise and prayer. It is this quality of *sovereign relatedness* that characteristically sums up Israel's testimony concerning YHWH. I cite two texts in which this convergence of power and passion are offered in metaphorical articulation. In Deuteronomy 1:29-31, YHWH is portrayed as *decisive warrior* and as *sustaining nursemaid*:

> I said to you, "Have no dread or fear of them. The LORD your God, who goes before you, is the one who will fight for you, just as he did for you in Egypt before your very eyes, and in the wilderness, where you saw how the LORD your God carried you, just as one carries a child, all the way that you traveled until you reached this place." (Deuteronomy 1:29-31)

In this articulation, the sketch of *divine power* is rooted in the exodus (see Exodus 14:13-14, 25) and the image of *divine compassion* is rooted in the wilderness tradition (see Numbers 11:12; Psalm 78:23-29). Clearly the tradition of Deuteronomy finds no problem in juxtaposing these two very different metaphors.

The same judgment is evident in Isaiah 40:10-11:

> See, the Lord GOD comes with might,
> and his arm rules for him;
> his reward is with him,
> and his recompense before him.
> He will feed his flock like a shepherd;
> he will gather the lambs in his arms,
> and carry them in his bosom,
> and gently lead the mother sheep. (Isaiah 40:10-11)

YHWH is mighty warrior; YHWH is gentle shepherd. In this usage, both images pertain to the processional departure from exile in Babylon (see Isaiah 55:12-13). As everywhere in Second Isaiah, these verses draw upon older memory, so that the departure from Egypt is imagined both as *exodus* made possible by the warrior God and as *wilderness sojourner* made possible by the sustaining God who cares. This is indeed the "God of grace, God of glory." Both affirmations belong crucially to this God who is *utterly beyond* historical vagaries and splendor and who is *utterly engaged* amid such vagaries. The articulation of this divine wonder requires in Israel both *sweeping doxology* and *needy prayer*; both characteristic acts of speech are founded in Israel's memory, for YHWH has always been the Lord *beyond* and the savior *among*.

Chapter Eight

THE NARRATIVE OF THE GOD OF MIRACLE AND ORDER

The discussion that follows concerns the fact that Old Testament attestation to YHWH as savior of Israel and creator of heaven and earth characteristically is cast with narrative particularity.[1] In its *narrative casting*, Israel's testimony eschews every form of closure and resists the articulation of universals. The grounding of faith in Israel is in the retelling of *stories* that amount in some to *a story* in which YHWH is inescapably the lead and decisive character. Thus it is rightly asserted that there is a peculiar match between the *concrete substance* of Israel's faith and the *narrative mode* of its articulation, for in the narratives of particularity the lead character may be and do many things that would violate any conventional logic. The narrative casting makes certain that the freedom of YHWH, freedom to act in peculiar ways, is preserved, celebrated, and trusted.

I have organized this discussion around the themes of *miracle* and *order*, themes not dissimilar to the themes of *deliverance* and *blessing* in the work of Claus Westermann.[2] "Miracle," or as the Hebrew might better say, "wonder," is an act of power whereby something is made new, terminated, or transformed in ways that violate normal expectation and is accomplished beyond conventional explanatory capacity. Miracles attested in Israel's life concern the acts of making possible what has characteristically been regarded as impossible; and because they are regarded as *impossible* they are invested, as Martin Buber so nicely puts it, with "abiding astonishment."[3] Israel continues to ponder and respond to such miracles. We may see the play on "possible-impossible" in two texts. First, in Genesis 18:14 the holy visitor taunts Abraham with the question, "Is anything impossible for YHWH?"[4] The particular case is the birth of a son to an old lady, a birth that would be regarded as *impossible*. The question is left unanswered in the narrative, and left unanswered until the birth of Isaac in Genesis 21:1-7. Such a birth would be commonly regarded as impossible; however, it is exactly the peculiar capacity of YHWH to make it possible. It is this *impossibility* that sustains the life of Israel.

In Jeremiah 32, the same term is used twice. In the prophetic prayer of verses 16-25, it is asserted that, "Nothing is too hard for you" (v. 17). In the divine oracle that follows, the question is posed by YHWH with a clearly implied negative answer, "Is anything too hard for me?" (v. 27). Both the prophetic prayer and the divine assertion concern the deconstruction and reconstruction of Israel, clearly an impossibility that by YHWH's powerful resolve is seen to be possible.[5]

From these particularities, it is evident that Israel's faith, in its most elemental articulation, precisely concerns this God who enacts such impossibilities in the midst of Israel's life, before the eyes of all the nations. As the Torah is a report on the founding miracles of YHWH, so the prophetic texts are an articulation of YHWH's capacity to *unmake* and *remake* Israel before the eyes of the nations.[6] (The narratives of Elisha in 2 Kings 2–10 constitute a series of miracles that are enacted through human agency; on other occasions there is no human agent in such miracles accomplished directly by YHWH.)[7] Such testimony is perforce always quite particular and refuses any generic extrapolation from the specificity reported.

In a very different mode, Israel also attests that YHWH is a God who orders the world, maintains that order, and offers sanctions against those who violate that order. This mode of testimony is grounded in narrative discourse as in the creation narratives of Genesis (Genesis 1:1-2, 4a; 2:4b-24), the doxologies that present YHWH as the subject of active verbs (Job 9:4-10; 5:9-16), and the self-declaration that YHWH in the speeches of the book of Job (Job 38–41). It is entirely possible to take the substance of such sweeping doxological formulation as *miracle*, except that the scope of the claim is so large that it lacks some of the concreteness of the miracles cited above. In sum, however, even the great acts of creation are "impossibilities," for they are beyond human capacity or human understanding.[8] In reflection upon the consequent order of creation, moreover, the sapiential material no longer seems to take the form of narrative. The subject who enacts the order now seems to have receded in the presentation, so that creation as an orderly process seems almost to be self-regulating.[9] But the proverbial articulation of the assured ordering of creation is, in Israel's testimony, always in the context of the great doxologies.

Thus in a derivative sense, even the most one-dimensional articulation of the guaranteed order of the world in proverbial form is rooted in narrative particularity. The Old Testament can, of course, make the intellectual move toward generalization; as it makes that move, however, the agency of YHWH becomes less visible. We can, on the one hand, insist that articulations of YHWH's *miracles* and YHWH's *order* are both rooted in *narrative*; on the other hand, we can recognize that discourse concerning that order is much less directly narrative than is the discourse on miracle. Both modes of testimony concern the inscrutable character of YHWH as the decisive agent who initiates and upholds and who is beyond human explanation. In what follows I will consider the narrative mode of testimony in six parts of the Old Testament canon that reflect different genres of discourse.[10]

1. The largest scoped narrative of YHWH in Israel's testimony is of the God who can create and recreate in purposeful fashion.[11] The creation accounts in Genesis 1–2 are so well known and so much reviewed that they do not require extended comment here. Of Genesis 1:1–2:4a, the following comments will suffice:

- Here as everywhere in the Old Testament, creation is not *ex nihilo*; it is rather the imposition of a life-serving order on the preexistent mass of chaos. Israel exhibits no curiosity about that preexistent chaos, but regards it not only as disordered but as a disordering force that seeks to negate YHWH's will for life.[12]
- The imposition of an order for life is accomplished by YHWH through the work of YHWH's wind-spirit and by the utterance of the divine word that decrees order.
- The opening phrase of Genesis 1:1 indicates that creation is an ongoing process, made necessary by the resilient power of chaos that must repeatedly be rebuked and swept back.[13]
- The work of creation is to order and to infuse blessing into creation so that, by the gift of YHWH, the force of life is intrinsic to creation itself.[14]

- The human couple, in the image of God, is to rule and order creation, in YHWH's stead, for the possibility of life. The role of the human couple is celebrated in the derivative text of Psalm 8.
- The culmination of creation is the sabbath for both YHWH and for creation, indicating that creation is not intended by YHWH to be an arena for restlessness, anxiety, or endless productivity.[15]

The second creation narrative works differently but to the same effect (Genesis 2:4b, 25). Here as well the creation works from preexistent material, in this case, *soil* (*'adamah*) from which came "the man." The man is assigned responsibility for creation and has boundaries set upon him that bar him from the Tree of Knowledge. It is clear that the man, as in Genesis 1, is to exercise dominion and receives the woman as partner and helpmate only late in the narrative.[16]

While there are important tensions and differences in the two narratives, they witness together to the claim of YHWH upon creation, to the life-giving capacity of creation, and to the distinctive role of humanity in the ordering and governing of creation. The two texts attest to the dependence of the creation upon the creator and to the life-giving potential of the creation itself. It is clear beyond dispute, of course, that the texts have no interest in or relevance for the evolution-creationism debate, even if *creationism* is now fancied up as *intelligent design*. The interpretive tradition of synagogue and church has always found ample room in the narratives for the interplay of faith and science.[17]

Behind these best-known narratives is a long, well-established doxological tradition that appropriates much from the common creation myths of the ancient Near East. The most important point is that the appropriated tradition, while having narrative aspects, is characteristically doxological in style. That is, creation faith is not explanatory but rather a liturgical engagement of awe, wonder, praise, and thanksgiving to the creator, because the creation is found to be "good," that is, beautiful, well ordered, and generative of life.

This doxological tradition is evident in three clusters of texts. First, the *Psalms of creation* include Psalms 33, 104, and 145. The fullest of these is Psalm 104 that celebrates the life-giving order of creation with special provision for ample water to sustain all of life.[18] The psalm acknowledges ample food to nourish and sustain all of life:

These all look to you
    to give them their food in due season;
when you give to them, they gather it up;
    when you open your hand, they are filled with good things. (Psalm 104:27-28)

The psalm asserts, moreover, that chaos has been completely tamed (vv. 25-26) and that the world depends completely upon the *rûach* (breath, spirit) of YHWH for its existence. Psalm 145 witnesses to YHWH's sustaining fidelity that makes life possible for all:

The LORD upholds all who are falling,
    and raises up all who are bowed down.
The eyes of all look to you,
    and you give them their food in due season.
You open your hand,
    satisfying the desire of every living thing.
The LORD is just in all his ways,
    and kind in all his doings.
The LORD is near to all who call on him,
    to all who call on him in truth.
He fulfills the desire of all who fear him;
    he also hears their cry, and saves them. (Psalm 145:14-19)

This sustaining power of YHWH that guarantees an ordered, secure, joyous life is utilized by Isaiah in the exile as a poetic polemic against the Babylonian gods and as an assurance to the displaced Israelites in exile (Isaiah 40:12-26; 45:18-19; 48:12-19). The primary stress in this poetry is upon the sovereign power and incomparability of YHWH, an incomparability that exposes the Babylonian gods as null and void:

To whom then will you liken God,
    or what likeness compare with him?
An idol?—A workman casts it,
    and a goldsmith overlays it with gold,
    and casts for it silver chains.
As a gift one chooses mulberry wood
    —wood that will not rot—
then seeks out a skilled artisan
    to set up an image that will not topple.

Have you not known? Have you not heard?
    Has it not been told you from the beginning?
    Have you not understood from the foundations of the earth?
It is he who sits above the circle of the earth,
    and its inhabitants are like grasshoppers;
who stretches out the heavens like a curtain,
    and spreads them like a tent to live in;
who brings princes to naught,
    and makes the rulers of the earth as nothing. (Isaiah 40:18-23)

YHWH is identified as the great enemy of chaos:

For thus says the LORD,
who created the heavens
    (he is God!),
who formed the earth and made it
    (he established it;
he did not create it a chaos,
    he formed it to be inhabited!):
I am the LORD, and there is no other.
I did not speak in secret,
    in a land of darkness;
I did not say to the offspring of Jacob,
    "Seek me in chaos."
I the LORd speak the truth,
    I declare what is right. (Isaiah 45:18-19)

Listen to me, O Jacob,
    and Israel, whom I called:
I am He; I am the first,
    and I am the last.
My hand laid the foundations of the earth,
    and my right hand spread out the heavens;
when I summon them,
    they stand at attention. (Isaiah 48:12-13)

Carroll Stuhlmueller has shown how this creation theology is tilted consistently toward the rescue and deliverance of Israel.[19] (As a subtheme, it is evident that "creation" in Second Isaiah pertains not only to the earth, but to Israel as well. YHWH is the creator of Israel.[20]

Creation faith in Job 38–41 has as its function the relocation of the human project to its proper place and the defeat of any temptation to pride. The God who speaks in this text shows how the splendor of creation and the wonder of creation override and completely dispose of every human management of the world, a temptation that Israel practiced through a tightly drawn moral calculus. In the modern world, the temptation is not likely to be a moral calculus, but rather a technological ambition of Promethean proportion. The poem of Job that culminates in the self-congratulations of the creator functions as a deconstruction of every such ambition, ancient or contemporary.[21]

Given its doxological posture toward the creator, Israel nonetheless knows that all is not well in creation, and that creation does not meet the intention of the creator. The Old Testament has no sense of a "fall" that looms so large in Christian theology; it does, however, know very well that the earth as it is is not YHWH's intention. Thus the completion of "creation faith" in the Old Testament consists in lyrical anticipations of YHWH's "new creation" when YHWH will act as decisively in time to come as YHWH has acted in the remembered creation.[22] In Isaiah 11:6-9, the poetry anticipates complete reconciliation of all of the elements of a strange creation. What makes possible such a new matrix of life is that "knowledge of YHWH," that is, covenantal commitment to YHWH, will permeate all of creation:

> They will not hurt or destroy
>   on all my holy mountain;
> for the earth will be full of the knowledge of the LORD
>   as the waters cover the sea. (Isaiah 11:9)

Whereas Isaiah 11:6-9 focuses on the realm of the animals, Isaiah 65:17-25 more directly concerns the new, healed arrangement of the human community in which flawed and troubling aspects of contemporary society will all be corrected and overruled by the will and act of the creator.

Thus the imagination of Israel is stretched between creation and new creation. But the terms of doxological articulation are not remote from reality; they are rather informed by historical reality, namely, the destruction of Jerusalem that amounts symbolically to the failure and death of creation. Thus the "primary narrative" of Genesis 1 to 2 Kings 25 stretches from creation in Genesis to exile in 2 Kings 24–25. After the "null point" of termination and symbolic obliteration, Israel could only wait and hope.[23] The God who creates and will create again is the God who can deconstruct creation. The preexilic prophets characteristically anticipate the undoing of creation because of disobedience to Torah. I cite two clear examples in prophetic proclamation. In Hosea 4:1-3, Israel is convicted of violating the Decalogue: "Swearing, lying, and murder, / and stealing and adultery break out; / bloodshed follows bloodshed" (Hosea 4:2). The consequence of such violation is the ending of creation, for creation depends upon Torah obedience:

> Therefore the land mourns,
> and all who live in it languish;
> together with the wild animals
> and the birds of the air,
> even the fish of the sea are perishing. (Hosea 4:3)

Jeremiah 4:23-26, in a dramatic poetic pattern, anticipates the dismantling of creation. Indeed interpreters generally see in this poem a point-by-point deconstruction of the process of creation that is detailed in Genesis 1:1–2:4a.[24] The prophet, imagining YHWH to be alienated from Israel, can further imagine YHWH engaged in the willful termination of creation.

Thus Israel's creation faith is patterned as creation—de-creation (in exile)—re-creation. That full dramatic scenario is lined out in the wondrous poem of Hosea 2:2-23:[25]

- Verses 2-13 articulate YHWH's anger at Israel's infidelity and YHWH's consequent withdrawal of the power of life from creation:

> Therefore I will take back
> my grain in its time,
> and my wine in its season;
> and I will take away my wool and my flax,
> which were to cover her nakedness. (Hosea 2:9)

Infidelity will produce the failure of creation, a failure precisely and directly enacted by YHWH.

- Verses 14-15 provide an interlude whereby the creator God who has rejected creation will now recognize in love recalcitrant Israel as the object of covenant making.
- As a consequence, verses 16-20 anticipate a renewal of covenant made in righteousness, in justice, in steadfast love, in mercy, and in faithfulness.
- And then in verses 21-23, the poet anticipates the full resumption of fruitfulness that is nothing less than a new creation.

The text of Hosea 2 traces the drama of creation from *initial creation* through a *de-creation* to a *new creation.* At every point, it is the creator God who presides over the process. Unmistakably the "history of creation" traced in this text is parallel to the history of Israel, both reaching a "null point" and both relying completely upon the creator God to make a newness. While the outcomes of divine action are regularly decisive for creation, the agency of drama in every case is YHWH. Israel cannot narrate the history of creation without focus upon the creator whose story it is. Creation is everywhere on the receiving, consequent end of YHWH's action of giving, taking back, and giving again.

2. There is no doubt that the Mosaic corpus and the Torah (Pentateuch) is decisive for the faith of Israel and for the characterization of YHWH in the Old Testament. As much is indicated through my extended reflection on the primal narratives of Exodus 2:23–4:17, Exodus 19–24, and Exodus 32–34. (See above, chapters 2–4.) The larger corpus concerning Moses breaks roughly into three unequal parts, in each of which we may identify the features of the God of the Old Testament:

(a) In the exodus narrative of *Exodus 1–15*, YHWH is featured as *deliverer, savior, and rescuer.* The narrative of Exodus 1–15 is a statement concerning Israel's move from slavery to exultant freedom. YHWH as the key character in the drama exhibits the authority, the power, and the resolve to transform the circumstance of the slave community and, at the same time, to alter decisively the rule of Pharaoh whose kingdom is now decisively destabilized.[26]

The narrative of deliverance evidences a double agency in the accomplishment of the emancipation of Israel. On the one hand, Moses is summoned as an agent in the divine intention as we have seen in Exodus 3:10. On the other hand, the plagues enacted in Exodus 7–11 are massive acts of supernatural power. They are narratively at the behest of Moses, but they are clearly YHWH's own show of power. This double agency, human and divine, becomes characteristic in Old Testament faith, evidenced as well in the prophetic discourse that "enacts" divine intention, but a divine intention that comes to fruition both directly and through other human agents such as Sennacharib, Nebuchadnezzar, and Cyrus.

The intention and the outcome of the exodus deliverance is the establishment of YHWH's authority over both Israel and Egypt. That is, the consequence of the miracle of deliverance is the enhancement of YHWH's sovereignty in the eyes of YHWH's subjects. On the one hand, this show of power is in order that Israel may *know* that YHWH is God:

"I will take you as my people, and I will be your God. *You shall know* that I am the LORD your God, who has freed you from the burdens of the Egyptians" (Exodus 6:7, italics added; see Exodus 10:2). On the other hand, the exodus is in order that Pharaoh and Egypt may acknowledge YHWH's sovereignty and accept status as a vassal of YHWH:

> The Egyptians shall know that I am the LORD, when I stretch out my hand against Egypt and bring the Israelites out from among them. (Exodus 7:5)

> Moses said to him, "As soon as I have gone out of the city, I will stretch out my hands to the LORD; the thunder will cease, and there will be no more hail, so that *you may know* that the earth is the LORD's. But as for you and your officials, I know that you do not yet fear the LORD God." (Exodus 9:29-30, italics added; see Exodus 7:17; 8:10, 22; 9:14; 11:7; 14:4, 17)

It is clear in such texts as Exodus 14:4, 17 that the ultimate purpose of the deliverance is not simply emancipation for the Israelite slaves, but the glorification of YHWH as one who has the power to overturn the force of chaos that in sociopolitical form is enacted as oppression and exploitation. The verb *know*, moreover, evidences an acknowledgement of sovereignty. Thus all, including Pharaoh, are to recognize the regime change accomplished by a show of divine power.

While the exodus narrative of deliverance serves liberation theology well with its commitment to socioeconomic justice, it is also evident that the exodus deliverance has, in larger scope, the effect of "righting" creation according to the will of the creator. Frank Moore Cross has seen that the exodus narrative is the "recrudescence" of the creation myth, and Terence Fretheim has shown that the exodus narrative is yet another presentation of the ancient struggle of creation versus chaos.[27] The outcome of the exodus is that by this miracle of deliverance, creation can function again as a fruitful system of life, a function that has been disrupted by the environmental destructiveness of Pharaoh's regime.[28]

There is no doubt that the exodus narrative that attests YHWH as *deliverer* has become paradigmatic in Israel's faith; as a consequence, many subsequent transformations are presented as yet other exoduses. In Joshua 4, for example, the crossing of the Jordan into the land of promise is "as" the exodus:

> For the LORD your God dried up the waters of the Jordan for you until you crossed over, as the LORD your God did to the Red Sea, which he dried up for us until we crossed over, so that all the peoples of the earth may know that the hand of the LORD is mighty, and so that you may fear the LORD your God forever. (Joshua 4:23-24)

The intent of that wonder again is that all may "know" and Israel may "fear." In Second Isaiah, the exodus functions as a model for emancipation and departure from Babylon:

> Thus says the LORD,
> who makes a way in the sea,
> a path in the mighty waters,
> who brings out chariot and horse,
> army and warrior;
> they lie down, they cannot rise,
> they are extinguished, quenched like a wick:
> Do not remember the former things,
> or consider the things of old.
> I am about to do a new thing;
> now it springs forth, do you not perceive it?
> I will make a way in the wilderness
> and rivers in the desert.
> The wild animals will honor me,
> the jackals and the ostriches;
> for I give water in the wilderness,
> rivers in the desert,
> to give drink to my chosen people,
> the people whom I formed for myself
> so that they might declare my praise. (Isaiah 43:16-21)[29]

In this poetic scenario, Israel's attention is drawn from *old exodus* to *new exodus* and in Amos 9:7, it is imagined that YHWH is the enactor of many exoduses for many peoples, including Israel's most immediate and perennial adversaries.[30] The creator continues, by acts of deliverance, to reassert governance over creation that has become recalcitrant and idolatrous. From Pharaoh at the outset of Israel's narrative to Nebuchadnezzar at the conclusion, human power that distorts divine purpose is seen to be idolatrous and stands under acute judgment.[31] In the Christian tradition, the exodus theme of YHWH as deliverer eventuates in a Christology of *Christus victor*, wherein Jesus is said to be the one through whom God defeats the powers of Satan, sin, and death.[32] In closer narrative fashion, the presentation of Jesus exhibits him as the one who defeats the demons. In his performance of deliverance miracles through healing, the culmination of the narrative is often a response of "amazement," that is, an acknowledgment that the sovereignty of God given in the narrative conforms to none of the antecedent categories of interpretation (Mark 2:21-28; 5:1-20).

(b) In *Exodus 16–18* and *Numbers 11–36*, YHWH is featured as *leader and sustainer*. The long trek in the wilderness is the narrative "connector" between *deliverance from Egypt* and *entry into the land of promise*. While it is a subordinate theme in the larger narrative of Moses, this narrative plays its part in the articulation of YHWH. The sojourn tradition consists in a loose connection of disparate materials; nonetheless we are able to identify two themes that bear upon the identity and character of YHWH. It is clear that YHWH is the *leader* of Israel in the wilderness. Thus at the departure of Israel from Sinai in Numbers 10–11, YHWH leads by presence in a cloud; and in Numbers 10:35-36, YHWH leads as the invisible God seated on the ark-throne. The narrative of Numbers 13–14, moreover, makes clear that when Israel does not follow YHWH's leadership it runs directly into destructive disaster.

Second, YHWH is *nourisher and sustainer*. On this theme we may focus on two narratives. Most important, the manna narrative of Exodus 16 occurs immediately upon the departure of Israel from Egypt. The "wilderness" is found to be a place without a viable life-support system. That deficiency evokes in Israel a wish to return to its slavery (v. 3) and a general disgruntlement with Moses' leadership. In response to the complaint of Israel, YHWH answers with manna and quail:

> In the evening quails came up and covered the camp; and in the morning there was a layer of dew around the camp. When the layer of dew lifted, there on the surface of the wilderness was a fine flaky substance, as fine as frost on the ground. When the Israelites saw it, they said to one another, "What is it?" For they did not know what it was. Moses said to them, "It is the bread that the LORD has given you to eat." (Exodus 16:13-15)

> Yet he commanded the skies above,
> and opened the doors of heaven;
> he rained down on them manna to eat,
> and gave them the grain of heaven.

Mortals ate of the bread of angels;
    he sent them food in abundance.
He caused the east wind to blow in the heavens,
    and by his power he led out the south wind;
he rained flesh upon them like dust,
    winged birds like the sand of the seas;
he let them fall within their camp,
    all around their dwellings.
And they ate and were well filled,
    for he gave them what they craved. (Psalm 78:23-29)

The gift of bread, meat, and water indicates that the fruitfulness of creation disrupted by Pharaoh has been restored.[33] Creation now functions with an abundance—even in the wilderness—because the creator God has acted in a characteristic way to feed and sustain.

In Numbers 11:1-15, we are given a second narrative that reiterates the theme of disgruntlement and complaint, and a divine response of nourishment. Again, in response to the complaint YHWH gives manna and eventually quail to sustain Israel:

> Now the manna was like coriander seed, and its color was like the color of gum resin. The people went around and gathered it, ground it in mills or beat it in mortars, then boiled it in pots and made cakes of it; and the taste of it was like the taste of cakes baked with oil. When the dew fell on the camp in the night, the manna would fall with it. . . . Then a wind went out from the LORD, and it brought quails from the sea and let them fall beside the camp, about a day's journey on this side and a day's journey on the other side, all around the camp, about two cubits deep on the ground. So the people worked all that day and night and all the next day, gathering the quails; the least anyone gathered was ten homers; and they spread them out for themselves all around the camp. (Numbers 11:7-9, 31-32)

In contrast to Exodus 16, we may note two particular features in this text, both of which reflect deep dispute. First, in verses 11-15, there is a dispute between YHWH and Moses. In Moses' remarkable challenge to YHWH, Moses asserts by way of a rhetorical question that YHWH conceived and birthed Israel. It has been often noticed that in the challenge Moses issues to YHWH, Moses uses verbs that are connected with maternal functions, thus presenting a mothering image for YHWH. The point of the daring imagery is that this "mothering" God is responsible from the outset for Israel, and so is obligated to provide sustenance. It is characteristically a deep concrete crisis that pushes Israel's theological rhetoric in daring new directions. In the end, YHWH accepts the responsibility that Moses assigns.

Second, the larger conflict is not only with Moses but with Israel. In a defiant tone, YHWH poses a rhetorical question to Moses: "The LORD said to Moses, 'Is the LORD's power limited? Now you shall see whether my word will come true for you or not'" (Numbers 11:23). The gift of food and sustenance is taken as an acknowledgment of the capacity of YHWH's "hand," the same "hand" that delivered from Egypt (see Deuteronomy 26:8). YHWH is seen, in these two narratives, as both powerful enough and committed enough to Israel to override circumstance and to create a new condition for Israel, a condition of adequate nourishment. The narrative exhibits the creator God managing creation in ways that provide and deeply sustain.

There is no doubt that in the fuller tradition of the Old Testament, the wilderness traditions are utilized and reformulated as a theological reflection on the sixth century exile, a time said to be without a viable life-support system for Israel. Given the decisiveness of the sixth century, the time of the exile, as the context for the formation of the covenantal literature, it is most plausible to conclude that the wilderness tradition, with YHWH as leader and sustainer, is connected directly to that experience of dislocation. This articulation of YHWH is offered as a way to defy and override the overwhelming experience of dislocation. There is no doubt that the offer of free water, wine, milk, and bread in Isaiah 55:1-2 is an exact parallel to the manna story. Exile, like wilderness, is a place of sustaining presence:

> Ho, everyone who thirsts,
>   come to the waters;
> and you that have no money,
>   come, buy and eat!
> Come, buy wine and milk
>   without money and without price.
> Why do you spend your money for that which is not bread,
>   and your labor for that which does not satisfy?
> Listen carefully to me, and eat what is good,
>   and delight yourselves in rich food. (Isaiah 55:1-2)

In Christian tradition the memory of YHWH as feeder reappears in the feeding miracles of Jesus.[34] In Mark 6:30-42, the feeding of the five thousand is in "a deserted place" where Jesus has "compassion." In Mark 8:1-9, it is again "here in the desert" where Jesus has "compassion." In both instances there is an abundance of food left over. The narrative offers clear allusions back to the manna narrative, thus affirming Jesus as *nourisher and sustainer* who does what YHWH does. In John 6, the narrative of the feeding miracle is again repeated (vv. 1-14) followed by a theological reflection wherein Jesus as *feeder* becomes *the bread* (John 6:23). All of these narratives depend on and derive from the initial testimony concerning YHWH as nourisher and sustainer.

(c) In *Exodus 19–24* and the derivative traditions YHWH is portrayed as the *one who commands*. I have already explicated the *Sinai pericope* at some length (see chapter 3). We have seen that the commandments of YHWH are offered as an alternative to the commands of Pharaoh. With assent to the commands of YHWH through a covenant oath (Exodus 24:3, 7), Torah becomes the condition and prerequisite of a viable and abundant life in YHWH's world. It is clear in the derivative *Priestly tradition* and the extrapolation of the traditions of Deuteronomy, that YHWH as the one who gives commands continues to give commands in every new time and place and circumstance, in order that all of life—familial and public, civic and cultic—shall come under the aegis of YHWH who is sovereign of all.[35] Thus in every aspect of Israel's life, response to Torah becomes the hallmark of Israel's life in the world:

■ In the final form of the text there is no doubt that the prophetic speech of judgment, the characteristic preexilic oracle, is based in Torah requirements that Israel has violated.[36]

■ As James L. Mays has shown, the Torah Psalms are decisive for the shape of the Psalter.[37] By the placement of Psalms 1, 19, and 119, the Psalms intend to foster a "Torah piety" whereby the faithful "meditate day and night" on the Torah (Psalm 1:2). Patrick Miller, moreover, has shown how "Torah piety" in the Psalter is primally related to the commands of Deuteronomy, the foremost covenant teaching in the Old Testament.[38]

■ In the wisdom traditions, the Torah is much less central. There is, nonetheless, no doubt that the wisdom traditions assume a divine ordering of reality, all social and "natural" reality that requires a certain conduct that is termed *wise*. Thus wise behavior will lead to life and foolish behavior will result in death (Proverbs 8:32-36). In this usage, the Torah to which appeal is made concerns not simply the pronouncement of Sinai but the structures that are intrinsic to creation. But as Erhard Gerstenberger has suggested, the Sinai commands with their "Thou shalt not" are perhaps closely related to the demands and prohibitions of wisdom teaching.[39] It is well known that by the time of Ben Sira there is a convergence of Torah and wisdom. Before that, however, the text of Deuteronomy 4:5-8 suggests that Torah in Israel is reckoned to be a version of what is wise and just that had also been discerned by the wisdom teachers:[40] "For what other great nation has a god so near to it as the LORD our God is whenever we call to him? And what other great nation has statutes and ordinances as just as this entire law that I am setting before you today?" (Deuteronomy 4:7-8).

■ It is the merit of the work of H. H. Schmid to have seen that the horizon of "righteousness" in the Old Testament points to the ordering of all of creation, so that Torah is linked to the structure of creation.[41] Unfortunately Schmid's work remains untranslated; attention should be paid to Rolf Knireim and his reflection on the ordering of the cosmos according to the will of the Torah-giving God.[42]

■ It is on the basis of this understanding of the cosmos according to divine will that the rabbis understood the *Noachic Covenant* as a statement of the Torah to which Gentiles are obligated.[43] The outcome of such interpretation is that all human persons, not only Israel, are accountable to the commands of the creator God. It is for this reason that Isaiah in exile can declare that the coastlands wait for "his Torah" (Isaiah 42:4; see Isaiah 2:2-4).

On all counts Israel knows itself—and the world—to be under the command of YHWH. In Christian tradition the motif is picked up in the teaching of Jesus. Thus in Matthew 5, the rhetorical pattern of "of old.... But I say" reflects the dynamism of Torah teaching and interpretation. There is no doubt that Jesus' instruction to his disciples, including the "new commandment" of John, stands fully in the Torah tradition and presents Jesus as the one who continues the work of the God who demands.

The sum of Mosaic teaching, in three strands, testifies to YHWH as the one who *rescues and delivers*, who *leads and sustains*, and who *commands*. This is the core testimony of the Torah. The Moses tradition, of course, is in the context of creation faith and is bounded by the *promissory* tradition of the ancestral stories in Genesis and the *covenant traditions* of Deuteronomy. Taken altogether, the Torah yields a full portrait of the sovereign God whose governance is conducted in a dialogical, interactive way.

3. In the prophetic literature YHWH is the God who *judges and restores* Israel. By implication this same twofold action pertains to *individual persons* and to other *nations* as well. Nations rise and fall at the behest of YHWH, and individual persons are cast down and raised up to new life.[44]

The prophetic corpus of the Old Testament consists in two units. The first is the "former prophets" that is constituted by the four "historical" books: Joshua, Judges, Samuel, and Kings. The second is the "latter prophets" that consists in Isaiah, Jeremiah, Ezekiel, and the twelve Minor Prophets. With reference to the themes of *judgment and restoration*, I will consider each in turn.

The "Former Prophets" (Joshua, Judges, Samuel, and Kings) consists in a variety of narratives, poems, and records of various kinds from many sources. In the final form of the text, this literature is reckoned by critical scholarship to be a single, more or less coherent account of the story of Israel from its entry into the land of promise to the termination of the city of Jerusalem and the Davidic monarchy in 587 B.C.E. at the hands of the Babylonian army.[45] In sum, this long narrative is reckoned to be an account of loss, defeat, and failure for Israel in the land, a failure that is understood in narrative form as the judgment of YHWH. While the historical vagaries that beset Israel, Judah, and Jerusalem might be understood in other ways, in this literature the theme of divine judgment is definitional. Thus the God to whom this literature testifies is a God of judgment.

Out of this mass of material, I will mention the following characteristic articulations of judgment:

- In the central section of the book of Judges, the fourfold formula articulates the full philosophy of history (see Judges 3:7-11).[46] The distress of divine judgment is enacted because of Israel's disobedience (v. 7) and takes the form of oppression at the hands of an adversarial kingdom (v. 8). The narrative assumes that oppression is willed and affected by YHWH, though the narrative exhibits no interest in how that judgment came about. The formula of verses 9-11 goes beyond judgment to rescue, but that lies beyond our present concern.
- The David narratives in 1 and 2 Samuel are wondrously subtle and cunning, especially about David's actions.[47] In a clear, even heavy-handed oracle of judgment in 2 Samuel 12, the prophet Nathan can declare to the king: "Now therefore the sword shall never depart from

your house, for you have despised me, and have taken the wife of Uriah the Hittite to be your wife" (2 Samuel 12:10). Nathan's judgment is terse and without exposition. There is no suggestion of direct divine intervention; there is also no mention of human agency, though we may take "sword" to be a reference to a coming human military threat. The wording seems to suggest that the deed itself evokes the consequence of punishment, a way of thinking that distinguishes the point from both supernaturalism and human agency, though the latter may be implied.

■ The divine judgment uttered against Solomon in 1 Kings 11:1-11 is much more direct and heavy-handed. In a characteristic prophetic speech of judgment, Solomon is indicted for his violation of the first commandment of the Decalogue. The judgment to follow is quite terse: "Therefore the LORD said to Solomon, 'Since this has been your mind and you have not kept my covenant and my statutes that I have commanded you, I will surely tear the kingdom from you and give it to your servant'" (1 Kings 11:11). Unlike 2 Samuel 12:10, here the language is direct, anticipating the direct action of YHWH. The threat, however, is that Solomon will lose the kingdom, a threat that surely will be enacted in and through the historical process.

■ The summary statement of 2 Kings 17:7-23 comments on the defeat and termination of the northern kingdom:

> Therefore the LORD was very angry with Israel and removed them out of his sight; none was left but the tribe of Judah alone.... The LORD rejected all the descendants of Israel; he punished them and gave them into the hand of plunderers, until he had banished them from his presence. When he had torn Israel from the house of David, they made Jeroboam son of Nebat king. Jeroboam drove Israel from following the LORD and made them commit great sin. The people of Israel continued in all the sins that Jeroboam committed; they did not depart from them until the LORD removed Israel out of his sight, as he had foretold through all his servants the prophets. So Israel was exiled from their own land to Assyria until this day. (2 Kings 17:18, 20-23)

The pronouncement utilizes a series of strong verbs: "removed... reject...punish...gave in to the hand...torn...remove...exiled." All the verbs but one suggest YHWH's direct action, an action that culminates in the deportation that happened in 721 B.C.E. The single exception is the verb "give in to the hand," so that the "plunder" that happened to city and state is clearly by human agency, in this case the Assyrians. It is clear that the rhetoric of judgment is not very concerned to distinguish *direct divine action* and *authorized human agency*. In the thinking of the traditionists, it is all of a piece. That YHWH can "dispatch" the Assyrians goes readily with other modes of divine activity. Judgment occurs within the historical process, but for that it is no less a direct action of YHWH.

■ In 2 Kings 23:26-27, the speech of judgment against Judah concerns "the fierceness of his great wrath," and is carried by the verbs now familiar to us, "remove" and "reject." The statement implies direct divine action, but the narrative of 2 Kings 24–25 makes it clear that it is Babylon that is the instrument and agent of divine judgment.

In all these cases, the rhetoric is open and does not "explain" the mode of judgment. It is unmistakably clear in this purview that violation of Torah evokes YHWH's anger that eventuates in disastrous human loss. The whole story of Israel-Judah, a story of disobedience, becomes a narrative of termination.

The Former Prophets (Deuteronomistic) as a corpus is notorious for its lack of a statement of divine restoration. The account ends with the demise of the city.[48] In general, the promise to David in 2 Samuel 7 hovers over this history as noted in 1 Kings 11:12. This promise evokes the great divine "yet" that persists, though in the end this promise seems to be exhausted. The only other concrete act of restoration in the Former Prophets that is much commented upon is the concluding paragraph of 2 Kings 25:27-30. Though other scholars make less of it, Gerhard von Rad regarded this passage as a promissory note concerning the future possibility of the monarchy even after the disaster of divine judgment in 587 B.C.E.:

> One has to appreciate the dilemma into which the Deuteronomist was driven by the actual course of the history, in that it ended with the catastrophe of 587. On the basis of his theological presuppositions he had certainly no reason to lighten the darkness of this judgment. On the other hand, he could never concede that the saying about the lamp which was always to remain for David had now in fact "failed." As to any goal to which this saving word was coming he had nothing to say: the one thing he could do was just, in this direction, not to close the door of history, but to leave it open. This he did in the reflective conclusion of his work (2 Kings xxv. 27ff.). His reference to Jehoiachin, and not to Zedekiah, as the last king of Judah could be connected with the fact that in his time Jehoiachin, and not Zedekiah, was regarded as the last king of Judah.[49]

Even if von Rad is correct, however, the theme of restoration is greatly muted in the Former Prophets. The sum of the corpus is about the God who judges severely, in history, against the violation of Torah commandments.

The matter is much more complex in the Latter Prophets, the second part of the prophetic canon that is constituted by the books of Isaiah, Jeremiah, Ezekiel, and the twelve Minor Prophets. While the literature of these books is a collage of prophetic oracles, likely rooted in great prophetic personalities but combined with additional materials from ongoing traditioning processes, the final form of the text in each case has a general shape of judgment and restoration; thus an ordering according to that theological theme has been imposed on material that appears to be more-or-less ad hoc in its collection:

> In such fashion we can at least come to understand the value and meaning of the way in which distinctive patterns have been imposed upon the prophetic collections of the canon so that warnings of doom and disaster are always followed by promises of hope and restoration. . . . We must see that prophecy is a collection of collections, and that ultimately the final result in the prophetic corpus of the canon formed a recognizable unity not entirely dissimilar from that of the Pentateuch. As this was made up from various sources and collections, so also the Former and Latter Prophets, comprising the various preserved prophecies of a whole series of inspired individuals, acquired an overarching thematic unity. This centered on the death and rebirth of Israel, interpreted theologically as acts of divine judgment and salvation.[50]

We are able to see the themes of judgment and restoration in each of the four prophetic scrolls, each of which consistently bears witness to the God who judges and saves.

The book of Isaiah is a meditation upon the Holy City of Jerusalem, the temple, and the monarchy. It concerns the Holy City that was faithful (Isaiah 1:21), stands under judgment (1:24-25), and only "afterward" will be restored as faithful and righteous (1:26). According to common critical assumption, the book of Isaiah is divided into chapters 1–39 and 40–55. Brevard Childs has suggested that the "old thing" of Isaiah is constituted by chapters 1–39 and its message of destruction and deportation (see Isaiah 39:6-7) and the "new thing" is the anticipated restoration of Jerusalem voiced in chapters 40–66.[51] It is exactly YHWH, the God of Sinai, who dispatches alien armies against the city (Isaiah 10:5-6; see

28:21; 39:6-7). It is precisely the God of all creation who "stretches out the heavens" (Isaiah 44:24), who dispatches Cyrus the Persian as messiah to restore the city (Isaiah 44:28; 45:1). This is indeed the God who does both judgment and restoration: "I form light and create darkness, / I make weal and create woe; / I the LORD do all these things" (Isaiah 45:7). The import of this God is to send Jerusalem and God's people into alien territory and then to restore them to their place. The criterion for judgment, as for hope, would seem to be the enactment of righteousness and justice (Isaiah 5:7; 56:1).[52]

The same twofold theme of judgment and restoration is more explicitly lined out in the book of Jeremiah with a programmatic statement issued to Jeremiah in his call:

> See, today I appoint you over nations and over kingdoms
> to pluck up and to pull down,
> to destroy and to overthrow,
> to build and to plant. (Jeremiah 1:10)

That theme is mostly expressed in prose and is imposed upon poetic oracles in the book of Jeremiah (18:7-10; 24:6; 31:28; 45:4); but the imposed theme resonates completely with the originary prophetic utterance. YHWH is the God who "plucks up and tears down" even the institutions of the city of Jerusalem that YHWH has invested with such primal significance. Thus the book of Jeremiah can reiterate, in many variant forms, the demise of Jerusalem at the hands of the Babylonians, a demise understood in prophetic poetry as divine judgment. It is this same YHWH who will "build and plant" a future city for which the book of Jeremiah hopes, an anticipation actualized in the events around Haggai and Zechariah and Ezra and Nehemiah. Again, as in the book of Isaiah, the book of Jeremiah portrays a God who brings chosen Jerusalem to its nadir of defeat and then brings the city back to the brink of restoration, well-being, and joy. This is the God who can "reverse the destiny" of that over which YHWH presides.

This same twofold accent on judgment and restoration is especially decisive for the arrangement of the book of Ezekiel, even though that literature is primarily concerned with the temple. Chapters 1–24 trace the judgment against the city that has become infested with cultic "abominations." Conversely, the second half of the book anticipates restoration, culminating in the revival of the temple and the Holy Land around the temple (Ezekiel 40–48). The God who has absented God's self from the temple is, in the end, the God who is present there (Ezekiel 48:35).

The three great prophetic books, albeit in quite distinct idioms, constitute a common conviction about the city that is derived from a common manifestation of YHWH. YHWH is the God who judges most severely YHWH's own covenant partner; YHWH is the God who remains faithful to the people and the city that are judged. As a consequence, the ultimate voice of the prophetic tradition is one of hope; YHWH is the God who presides over the earth to bring it to fruition. What the creator has begun, the creator will now bring to fullness. Israel is led by this God deep into tears; in the end, however, all such tears fade before joy, which comes in the morning (Psalm 30:5).[53]

The teaching offered in the three great prophetic books is not different in the scroll of the Book of the Twelve. In current critical scholarship, there is now a readiness to view the twelve Minor Prophets as a single unified literary corpus.[54] Given such an assumption, the corpus moves from the judgment of YHWH (Hosea, Joel, and Amos) to the hope of restoration (Haggai, Zechariah, and Malachi). It is the same God with the same characteristic work who is evident in these utterances. The corpus stands, in its final form, as testimony to the God who will not quit until God's own people come to well-being, wherein Torah is embraced (Malachi 4:4) and the human community is reconciled (Malachi 4:5-6).

4. After the Torah traditions wherein the God of Israel *creates and recreates* and *saves, leads, and commands*, and after the prophetic traditions wherein the God of Israel *judges and restores*, consideration of the wisdom traditions is a wholly different enterprise. According to canonical claim, here we still have to do with the God of Israel; in this tradition, however, the God of Israel for the most part does none of the acts that characterize the narrative of the Torah and oracles of prophetic traditions. A leap from these traditions to the wisdom materials has been, for a long time, a major problematic of Old Testament theology. As long as Old Testament theology was focused on *historical traditions*, as it was through the twentieth century, the wisdom traditions were, at best, neglected and, at worst, declared outside the pale of faith.[55] A major shift occurred in Old Testament theology in the 1970s, largely through the work of Claus Westermann, who saw most clearly that the God who *saves* is, at the same time, the God who *blesses* and generates life-sustaining order of creation.[56] Thus in the wisdom materials that are represented in the canon primarily by the books of Proverbs, Job, and Ecclesiastes, we have testi-

mony to a God in a very expansive horizon in which the peculiar faith claims of Israel voiced in the Torah and prophets are much less prominent. Here we meet a God who *governs, orders, and sustains* but who does not, for the most part, intervene in natural processes or contravene against the givenness of the created order.[57]

The book of Proverbs provides testimony that is the accumulation of the best, most decisive learning of the community of Israel as a part of the larger human community concerning the givenness, limits, requirements, and permits of God's created order.[58] Thus wisdom teaching is creation theology, an affirmation that it is God who has ordered the world so that it is life-giving, fruitful, and blessing-bestowing;[59] but the creation is life-giving, fruitful, and blessing-bestowing only within limits that must be respected and according to conduct that is required. It is the conviction of the wisdom teachers that this ordering is hidden and inscrutable, but by slow, steady observation and faithful critical reflection, one can move from particular experience to more general ethical claims that provide the material for instruction to the young in the way of life.

The simplest and most direct of the proverbial sayings feature an "either/or" statement that confronts the addressee with two options and that requires a decision between them (see, for example, Proverbs 11:1, 3, 5). Sometimes the contrast between the two ways is between *the righteous and the wicked*, more often it is between *the wise and the foolish.* The wise are those who conform their lives to the given ordering of creation and so receive the gifts of life bestowed by creation in all of its abundance; conversely, the foolish are those who violate and defy that given order, and so bring trouble and eventually death upon themselves and upon their community. The task of wisdom instruction is to be clear about limits, requirements, and choices. The task of wisdom performance is to choose a way of existence that is in sync with the nonnegotiable ordering of creation. Thus wisdom speaks:

> And now, my children, listen to me:
>   happy are those who keep my ways.
> Hear instruction and be wise,
>   and do not neglect it.
> Happy is the one who listens to me,
>   watching daily at my gates,
>   waiting beside my doors.
> For whoever finds me finds life
>   and obtains favor from the LORD;

> but those who miss me injure themselves;
> all who hate me love death. (Proverbs 8:32-36)

It is clear that wisdom teaching, insofar as it ponders the givenness of creation and the will of the creator that is encoded in creation, is a theological enterprise that is preoccupied with YHWH's governance of creation that makes life possible. (There was a time in the twentieth century when some scholars judged that "early wisdom" was secular and without a theological reference; but such a notion is now everywhere rejected.)[60]

Thus it is that *good choices of conduct* that cohere with the *will, purpose, and order of YHWH* eventuate in an abundant life. Conversely, *bad (foolish) choices of conduct* that contradict the will, purpose, and order of YHWH eventuate in a failed life and culminate in the wretchedness and alienation of death. Thus notion of the "two ways" is central to wisdom teaching and is variously reflected in the teaching of Deuteronomy (Deuteronomy 30:15-20), and in Psalm 1:

> Happy are those
> who do not follow the advice of the wicked,
> or take the path that sinners tread,
> or sit in the seat of scoffers;
> but their delight is in the law of the LORD,
> and on his law they meditate day and night. . . .
> The wicked are not so,
> but are like chaff that the wind drives away. (Psalm 1:1-2, 4)

The same teaching reappears in early Christian tradition in the *Didachae* that faithfully echoes the old Israelite conviction.

The teaching of the book of Proverbs is focused upon the responsibility and capacity of the human person to be an agent of freedom in making choices for the sake of the well-being of the human community and the world that the human community inhabits. That charter for responsibility and freedom, however, is not without limit. For that reason the wisdom tradition is aware that human agency is always and everywhere penultimate, situated as it is in the larger agency of divine governance. While most of the proverbs focus upon human choice and decision making whereby the future is chosen for life or for death, some few proverbs acknowledge that these human choices are always in the context of divine order and divine mystery. Gerhard von Rad has helpfully and famously identified a brief series of proverbs that witness to YHWH's grand capacity to have the last word concerning the human future:[61]

> The human mind may devise many plans,
> but it is the purpose of the LORD that will be established. (Proverbs 19:21)
>
> The human mind plans the way,
> but the LORD directs the steps. (Proverbs 16:9)

Finally, wisdom teaching moves beyond ethical instruction to wonder and awe before YHWH's sustenance of the world:

> The LORD by wisdom founded the earth;
> by understanding he established the heavens;
> by his knowledge the deeps broke open,
> and the clouds drop down the dew. (Proverbs 3:19-20)

Von Rad has noticed the move from ethical instruction to theological grandeur in the wisdom teaching and concludes:

> Its proverbs are marked by the same tension between a radical secularization on the one hand and the knowledge of God's unlimited powers on the other. At one point, man's life was seen to be bound up in orders which themselves were not entirely free from a certain amount of control. Then, again, it was seen to be entirely dependent on a wholly personal attitude of benevolence on God's part. It would be easy to suppose that it must have been difficult for the wise men to maintain this tension in their teachings without loss in one direction or the other. But of this there is no trace. With effortless ease they devote themselves to the broad sweep of all that can be known. Confidently, they evaluate what has been experienced and bring every didactic aid into service in order to bring the pupil, too, to the point of trusting the evidence of the teaching in question.[62]

It is the reality of God and God's governance that curbs human freedom and ambition and that guards against human autonomy that will, in the end, be destructive. Such a guard against human autonomy was no doubt urgent in the ancient world; in the contemporary world it is equally urgent as we observe Promethean efforts to have the world on our own terms. Such Promethean ambition von Rad, in commenting upon the notion of "foolishness," terms "practical atheism."[63] While that curb takes the form of uncompromising ethical warning, in the end the curb is not heavy-handed intervention but rather the working of the inscrutable mystery of God the creator of whom the wisdom teachers are deeply aware.

The eventuality of life or death according to human choices might be taken to mean, as in the book of Deuteronomy, that God "rewards" the wise with abundant life and "punishes" the foolish with misery and death. For the most part, however, God, in sapiential attestation, does not so directly impinge upon creation or upon the human scene. In this regard wisdom teaching is quite unlike prophetic discourse in which God's impingements are characteristically direct or directly mediated through human agents. Not so in wisdom teaching. Klaus Koch has insisted, in a persuasive way, that wisdom teaching—and derivatively other traditions as well—operates with a construct of "deeds-consequences" whereby certain deeds of themselves produce certain consequences because the creation has been ordered through a system of inviolate interconnections.[64] In such an ordered world there is no direct divine intervention, no use of active verbs that describe YHWH's intervention. Rather the deeds themselves are situated in a "sphere of destiny" wherein the future is given in deed or choice itself. Thus in Proverbs 16:9, cited above, the verb is "direct" (*kun*), but the exact force of the verb is elusive. And in Proverbs 19:21, it is asserted that YHWH's decrees "endure" (*qum*), but there is no direct action. A related text is 2 Samuel 17:14 in which YHWH has "ordained" a certain outcome, but it is not clear how such a purpose is implemented. In all these cases, the wisdom traditions keep the way of the purpose of YHWH mostly hidden. For all of that, of course, they do not doubt YHWH's sustaining governance that is not, in the end, open to compromise.[65]

In the book of Job, the teaching of Proverbs is assumed and then placed in profound crisis. The "friends of Job" give voice to the dominant theology of the book of Proverbs that has now become hardened into an explanatory system without room for play or exception. Thus the drama of the book of Job turns on their conviction that Job suffers because Job has violated the will of the creator:

> Think now, who that was innocent ever perished?
> Or where were the upright cut off?
> As I have seen, those who plow iniquity
> and sow trouble reap the same.

By the breath of God they perish,
 and by the blast of his anger they are consumed. (Job 4:7-9)

As for me, I would seek God,
 and to God I would commit my cause. . . .
How happy is the one whom God reproves;
 therefore do not despise the discipline of the Almighty. (Job 5:8, 17)

Does God pervert justice?
 Or does the Almighty pervert the right?
If your children sinned against him,
 he delivered them into the power of their transgression.
If you will seek God
 and make supplication to the Almighty,
if you are pure and upright,
 surely then he will rouse himself for you
 and restore to you your rightful place. (Job 8:3-6)

These statements, echoing the claims of the book of Proverbs, assert that Job and all human persons live in a tightly ordered world where deeds produce consequences. The friends have simply inverted that reasoning: They observe the consequences and are fully prepared to imagine the foolish deeds that have produced such consequences. The poignancy of the drama is rooted in the fact that Job fully shares the assumption of his friends. He also believes in "deeds-consequences," but is not convinced, as are they, that he has committed deeds that properly produce such consequences. Thus his long plea of innocence in chapter 31 culminates in the conviction that if he can get a hearing in the divine court, he will surely be acquitted:

Oh, that I had one to hear me!
 (Here is my signature! let the Almighty answer me!)
 Oh, that I had the indictment written by my adversary!
Surely I would carry it on my shoulder;
 I would bind it on me like a crown;
I would give him an account of all my steps;
 like a prince I would approach him. (Job 31:35-37)

Job asserts his innocence but continues to trust in the framework of "deeds and consequences," convinced as he is that he will merit other consequences from God than the ones under which he now suffers.

The deconstruction in the poem of Job occurs when the God of Israel—not named as "YHWH" since the beginning prose chapters—breaks the silence and voices a massive self-announcement in response to the petitions of Job. The speeches of YHWH from the whirlwind offer a vigorous assertion of YHWH as the creator God who, in largest scope, is an agent of massive power and awesome sovereignty (Job 38–41). The outcome of the divine self-assertion is that YHWH has no interest or patience with the small-time moral calculus of Job and his friends, even though they have inherited that small-time moral calculus from the traditions of the book of Proverbs. The God who speaks here does not bother to respond to Job's questions or protests and exhibits no interest in Job's suffering. These are all matters of complete divine indifference.

It is to be noted that while YHWH, in this tradition, has no interest in the close moral calculus reflected by Job and his friends, YHWH the creator God nonetheless is the God who orders and governs, albeit in ways that are well beyond human discernment. It is for that reason that Job is reduced to silence (42:6), albeit a silence that is marked by profound ambiguity.[66]

While the drama of the poetry of Job culminates in the divine self-announcements of chapters 38–41, we may finally turn to Job 28, a meditation upon the wisdom of God the creator; there is wisdom whereby the world is ordered, but it is wisdom that is unavailable for human scrutiny:

> But where shall wisdom be found?
> And where is the place of understanding?
> Mortals do not know the way to it,
> and it is not found in the land of the living. (Job 28:12-13)

The work of creation credited to YHWH in this chapter is congruent with that of the speeches in the whirlwind; both texts assert YHWH's transcendent ordering of reality, and both texts acknowledge that human efforts to penetrate the purposes of creation are bound to fail. But then, given that assertion and that acknowledgment, the chapter concludes with counsel to "humankind." It is to be noted that there is no address to Israel; the address rather is to all human creatures, befitting the utterance of the creator God: "And he said to humankind, / 'Truly, the fear of the Lord, that is wisdom; / and to depart from evil is understanding'" (Job 28:28). The verse leads humanity away from ambitious speculation back to the daily routine of responsible discipline. In fact the teaching returns to the most elemental instruction of the book of Proverbs:

Do not be wise in your own eyes;
fear the Lord, and turn away from evil.
It will be a healing for your flesh
and a refreshment for your body. (Proverbs 3:7-8)

In both cases in the books of Proverbs and Job, the positive reference point is "fear of YHWH," the admission of the penultimate place of human capacity:

> Israel attributes to the fear of God, to belief in God, a highly important function in respect of human knowledge. She was, in all seriousness, of the opinion that effective knowledge about God is the only thing that puts a man into a right relationship with the objects of his perception, that it enables him to ask questions more pertinently, to take stock of relationships more effectively and generally to have a better awareness of circumstances.[67]

The negative counterpoint is "turn away from evil," that is, to avoid violation of God's ordering of created reality.

Thus we begin with the teaching of limit and obligation in the practice of freedom in the book of Proverbs. Given that background, the book of Job is a venturesome foray that seeks to go beyond and behind that code of conforming behavior. Such a venture, however, cannot succeed because the God who orders and governs is indeed God; for that reason after such daring venture, Israel (and all humanity) are summoned back to existence within a reliable ordering that yields life. Humankind can receive life that is given reliably and generously, but it cannot penetrate into the source. It can only live in dutiful, joyous response. This is, in Proverbs, not at all a posture of resignation. It is rather a buoyant acceptance of one's proper locus *in the world before God.*

The third sapiential book of the Old Testament canon, Ecclesiastes, lives at the edge of Israel's faith. It belongs in the tradition of proverbial wisdom and itself offers some conventional proverbs (see Ecclesiastes 7:1-14). For the most part, however, the book of Ecclesiastes carries on a dispute with conventional wisdom teaching, challenging the simplistic assurances of "deeds-consequences" in offering a sense of futility about the alleged joys of a blessed life.[68]

The book shares with the speeches of YHWH in the book of Job that YHWH's rule is transcended. It also supports the conviction of the book of Job that YHWH is fundamentally indifferent to any conventional moral calculus of reward and punishment. It does not doubt the rule of YHWH; that rule, however, is not only not knowable, but it is indifferent and unrelated to moral claim:

> I said in my heart with regard to human beings that God is testing them to show that they are but animals. For the fate of humans and the fate of animals is the same; as one dies, so dies the other. They all have the same breath, and humans have no advantage over the animals; for all is vanity. All go to one place; all are from the dust, and all turn to dust again. Who knows whether the human spirit goes upward and the spirit of animals goes downward to the earth? (Ecclesiastes 3:18-21)

From that premise that YHWH *governs and orders* but in ways that bespeak transcendence and indifference, this teaching draws two conclusions. First, the human agent should make the most of what is given without seeking ultimate explanations:

> So I saw that there is nothing better than that all should enjoy their work, for that is their lot; who can bring them to see what will be after them?... Go, eat your bread with enjoyment, and drink your wine with a merry heart; for God has long ago approved what you do. (Ecclesiastes 3:22; 9:7)

Life is brutish and contested; the best enjoyment is to deal with the gifts and tasks of the day. Second, the conclusion drawn is not an invitation to hubris or autonomy or self-indulgence. It is rather that the human actor should get along in conventional conformity to the claims of God and to the powers that be: "The end of the matter; all has been heard. Fear God, and keep his commandments; for that is the whole duty of everyone" (Ecclesiastes 12:13). There is judgment before the God of all order, but simple conventional morality and piety constitute the best response to the God who governs.

We are able to see in the movement from the *reliable teaching* of the book of Proverbs to the *dissent* of the book of Job to the *resignation* of the book of Ecclesiastes that the governance of God can be experienced and articulated in a very different nuance. Nonetheless, all three texts finally agree that there is a *givenness* to created reality and one must come to terms with that givenness. For all the differences among these several literatures, the sovereign governance of YHWH yields an ordered world that must be accepted and respected:

> Do not be wise in your own eyes;
> fear the LORD, and turn away from evil.
> It will be a healing for your flesh
> and a refreshment for your body. (Proverbs 3:7-8)
>
> And he said to humankind,
> "Truly, the fear of the Lord, that is wisdom;
> and to depart from evil is understanding." (Job 28:28)
>
> The end of the matter; all has been heard. Fear God, and keep his commandments; for that is the whole duty of everyone. (Ecclesiastes 12:13)

The ongoing tradition of wisdom teaching grows toward "futility." It does not, however, yield to futility. In sum, rather, it consists in dealing with a governance that cannot be outflanked. In terms of response to this indifferent administration, the more probing traditions do not move away from the convictions of the most ancient wisdom. This tradition lives very close to the claims of the book of Deuteronomy about choosing life or death. It is asserted that YHWH makes life possible; and because YHWH is a God of freedom, Israelites—and all human persons—must pay attention to the ways in which that freedom is enacted because it is always freedom *before God*.[69]

5. The book of Psalms is a rich poetic compendium of the several strands of Israel's faith which are sometimes in tension and sometimes complimentary. As a result, the Psalter offers a rich summary statement concerning the God of Israel who is addressed, praised, and attested to according to the many varied ways in which YHWH has disclosed YHWH's own character and purpose in the history of Israel and in the life of the world.

(a) In the Psalter *YHWH is the creator* of heaven and earth. This claim is everywhere assumed in the Psalms but is voiced with passionate conviction in the Psalms that concern the wonder of creation:

- In Psalm 33, YHWH has created, as in Genesis 1, by word (vv. 6, 9), and presides over the heavens and the waters (vv. 6-7), and over the nations (vv. 10-12). The creator God is king (v. 14), [potter] (v. 15), and warrior (v. 16) to be feared and trusted as the ground of all hope (vv. 18-21).
- In Psalm 104, YHWH the creator God has provided water for all creatures (vv. 10-13), and wine, oil, and bread for human joy (v. 15), has

defeated the powers of chaos (vv. 25-26), has assured the earth of food supply (vv. 27-28), and has guaranteed adequate breath for living (vv. 29-30). The earth is a safe, life-giving place because of YHWH's gifts.

■ In Psalm 145, the beneficence of the creator extends toward all creatures that are kept safely and well, as they trust God. All three psalms attest to the steady, reliable, generous governance of the creator.

(b) In the great psalms of historical memory, the saving, leading miracles of YHWH in the time of Moses are celebrated as paradigmatic for life in the world of God's deliverance:[70]

■ In Psalm 136, after the wonders of creation (vv. 4-9), it is the deliverance from Egypt (vv. 10-15) and guidance in the wilderness (vv. 16-22) that dominate Israel's memory, attesting to YHWH's decisive fidelity.

■ In Psalm 105, the Moses memory occupies the center of the psalm (vv. 26-42), affirming YHWH's power and promise that have given Israel a life alternative to life under Pharaoh.

■ In Psalm 106, the memory of the exodus and wilderness are again most prominent (vv. 6-26); in this reading Israel's recalcitrance is highlighted, but that rebellion is possible only because of YHWH's faithful presence.

Israel's doxological imagination remains focused in the great deliverances that have made life possible for the ex-slaves.

(c) In the so-called prophetic Psalms, Israel is rebuked for covenant violation and summoned back to Torah obedience in a tone very like that of the great prophetic traditions:

■ Psalm 50 is a summons back into covenant that calls Israel to "hear," the same "hear" that marks urgent prophetic speeches of judgment (v. 7). The critique of self-indulgent religion echoes prophetic critique (Isaiah 1:12-15) and rebukes "covenant talk" that is absent of "covenant walk" (vv. 16-17 on which see Jeremiah 7:8-11).

■ The same "hear" is sounded in Psalm 81:8 after Israel is rebuked for "not hearing" (v. 11). The God of covenant promises to "satisfy" Israel (v. 16). When Israel has listened and walked in the way of the Torah (v. 13).

■ Psalm 95:7b-11 again calls Israel to listen, but then does a riff on "hardness of heart" that is the antithesis of obedient listening. In not listening, the addressed generation is like the generation of Moses that also did not listen. The text teems with contemporaneity that is characteristically prophetic. All these texts assert that listening to the will and command of the covenant God is the basis for all viable life in the world. The Psalms, cast in liturgical form, echo exactly the rebuke and hope of prophetic faith.

(d) While there is some dispute about what constitutes "wisdom Psalms," there can be no doubt that Psalms 37 and 49 reflect the experienced-based faith and characteristic rhetoric of wisdom tradition:

- Psalm 37 is a series of proverbial instructions that assure that the "meek," the righteous and the obedient will prosper in the land (vv. 11, 21, 29, and 34). The psalm, without any divine agency, reflects the "deeds-consequences" framework of wisdom.
- Psalm 49 is a meditation concerning the limit of death that functions as a great equalizer. The critique of "pomp" (vv. 12, 20) is reminiscent of the list of those who are "stately in their stride" in Proverbs 30:29-31.

Human initiative cannot outflank the givenness of the created world. Wisdom, as in Psalm 37, is a willing submission to the boundaries, limits, and givens of the governing God who is decisive, even if not visible, for life in the world.

(e) I have cited these particular psalms to indicate that Israel's Psalter is an offer of many voices of faith, all of which are necessary to the full utterance of the God who orders, who leads, saves and commands, who judges and restores, and who governs in hidden ways. While these liturgical and pedagogical traditions in the Psalter vary in their ways of speaking, all are agreed that a life of faith is response to the reality of the God who shows up in many modes in every part of the life of the world and in every part of Israel's rhetoric of faith.[71] For that reason, the Psalter that invites attention to many voices is introduced by Psalm 1, which is a Torah summons. The two ways of Torah obedience (Psalm 1:2) or the alternative of "wickedness" (Psalm 1:4) dominate the imaginative horizon of Israel. In all these variations, the several traditions all call Israel to Torah obedience.[72] All through the Psalter the interpretive cadences of Psalm 1 are never far away. Torah obedience is the clue to Israel's "prosperity," for God who commands is the one who makes life possible.

6. It is clear that the traditions of faith in the Old Testament range from *full, direct, immediate engagement* by YHWH to *hidden hovering* that governs and upholds the world and all those in it. In Westermann's language, this is faith in the *God who delivers* and the *God who blesses*.[73] My own language for this is "miracle and order"; "miracle" pertains, first of all, to YHWH's direct intervention in the historical process in ways that cause transformation, even though the term *wonder* may also point to the miracle of creation. "Order" as it is enacted in liturgy and discerned in wisdom teaching, pertains to the steady, reliable structuring of reality that is guaranteed by the decree and governance of YHWH. Both miracle and

order are essential to the faith of Israel and both are given wide play in the cadences of Israel's Scripture.

The rich semantic field of "miracle" is voiced in the doxological affirmation of Psalm 145:

> One generation shall laud your works to another,
> and shall declare your mighty acts.
> On the glorious splendor of your majesty,
> and on your wondrous works, I will meditate.
> The might of your awesome deeds shall be proclaimed,
> and I will declare your greatness.
> They shall celebrate the fame of your abundant goodness,
> and shall sing aloud of your righteousness. (Psalm 145:4-7)

The primal terms are *wondrous works* (*pelaʾoth*) and *awesome deeds* (*norʾoth*) that refer to any divine action that is beyond the understanding, explanation, or control of human knowledge. The characteristic recital of Israel's faith is preoccupied with the stable inventory of miracles that are organizing and fundamental for Israel's life and destiny. YHWH is a God who does miracles and Israel is a people that lives from YHWH's miracles. The world beyond Israel, moreover, is open to and beneficiary of the same miracles of YHWH.

The testimony to YHWH's ordering of creation according to guaranteed patterns and limits is reflected in the lyrical texts of creation and is assumed by the wisdom tradition. This claim for YHWH is much less dramatic and much less distinctively Israelite, for every culture can notice the regularities of life that are here credited to YHWH. It is that ordered regularity that makes life livable, that guarantees the security and nurture of all creatures, and that makes stable management of historical and "natural" realms possible. This tradition of order is reflected in the postflood decree of Genesis 8:22:

> As long as the earth endures,
> seedtime and harvest, cold and heat,
> summer and winter, day and night,
> shall not cease. (Genesis 8:22)

That conviction about the regularity of reality comes to expression, for example, in two quite remarkable prophetic poems. In Hosea 2:21-23, after the withdrawal of the fruitfulness of creation (vv. 9-13), the new promise of YHWH is that the earth will again function regularly to assure the production of the staples of grain, wine, and oil:

> On that day I will answer, says the LORD,
>   I will answer the heavens
>   and they shall answer the earth;
> and the earth shall answer the grain, the wine, and the oil,
>   and they shall answer Jezreel. (Hosea 2:21-22)

The language of the text indicates that the revised ordering of creation is a function of renewed covenant.[74]

More spectacularly, the tradition of Jeremiah finally appeals to the ordering of creation as a way to voice assurance concerning YHWH's commitment to Israel:

> Thus says the LORD,
> who gives the sun for light by day
>   and the fixed order of the moon and the stars for light by night,
> who stirs up the sea so that its waves roar—
>   the LORD of hosts is his name:
> If this fixed order were ever to cease
>   from my presence, says the LORD,
> then also the offspring of Israel would cease
>   to be a nation before me forever.
>
> Thus says the LORD:
> If the heavens above can be measured,
>   and the foundations of the earth below can be explored,
> then I will reject all the offspring of Israel
>   because of all they have done, says the LORD. (Jeremiah 31:35-37)

The historical guarantees to Israel are compared to the cosmic guarantees of the "fixed order" (*hûqôth*), the moon and the stars, a fixed order as sure as "the heavens above" and "the foundations of the earth beneath." There is nothing here about intervention or transformation. It is all about steady regularity that is found in Israel's testimony to be compellingly trustworthy.[75]

YHWH is God of *order and miracle* and both articulations are crucial for Old Testament faith. It is the case, largely at the behest of Gerhard von Rad under the influence of Karl Barth, that Old Testament theology in the twentieth century was largely preoccupied with *miracles* as they occurred "in history."[76] The effect was to minimize and fail to appreciate the ordered regularity of creation as a theological datum. After that passionate interpretive tilt, only at the end of the twentieth century did Old Testament scholarship begin to appreciate a fresh creation theology and this accent in faith.[77]

I wish in conclusion to call attention to a remarkable discussion of David Hartman. Hartman compares the two rabbinic authorities, Judah Halevi and Maimonides, in order to make a statement about Jewish faith as it pertains to the contemporary policies of Israel. On the one hand is Judah Halevi who waits for a miracle from God that will make all things new:

> The Creation story in the Bible is not told solely for its own sake. What is its point? According to Nahmanides, the point is that the cosmos is in order when Israel is in its land. The Creation story is a prolegomenon, a preamble, to the Jewish claim of will. It is the underpinning of the belief in miracle. The Creation story enables us to say that when we live in this land, we live under divine protection. Israel is a people defined by divine and not by human causality.
>
> So also when we consider our coming home today, the category that we use to explain it is miracle. I would say that the interpretive category of Zionism is miracle, but the success of Zionism is reality. We interpret what we do in the category of surprise and wonderment. When we think of Auschwitz, and then think of that decimated people coming home, we think of Ezekiel and the resurrection of the dry bones.
>
> Given that sense of history and national identity, it is understandable that many Israelis should reject realism as a value....
>
> So, in Israel they use the word "Zionism" to mean "to do the impossible, not the realistic." To be a Jew is to believe in miracles.[78]

Such a view, according to Hartman, is to live in a utopian land of unreal expectations that is thick with ideology; and on the basis of ideology, one can immediately move to legitimate and aggressive violence.

As counter to this understanding of Jewish faith, Hartman cites Maimonides who shuns hope in a miracle and instead counts on the reliable course of the world under the good rule of God:

> However, there is another voice in our tradition, that of a great teacher who passionately hated dependency on miracles. Every time he read about a miracle in the Bible, he sought a natural explanation. This is the voice of Maimonides. In contrast to Halevi, Maimonides believed that the story of Creation was not meant to teach the principle of will; rather, Creation was only a founding catalytic moment to be absorbed by the principle of necessity.[79]

That faith does not wait for miracles, but goes about the human task of caring and managing and modestly doing what is given. Hartman's judgment is that faith that waits for miracles produces fanaticism that generates unreal expectations that in turn evokes aggressiveness and violence. By contrast, Maimonides found the power of God not in surprises but in patterns of order and meaning.

These two traditions of hope, according to Hartman, issue respectively in *utopian ideology* and in *historical realism*. While we wait and will not do without miracle in our account of faith, the temptation to ideology (now so powerful in U.S. religion) is checked and limited by a realism that is also crucial in the faith of Israel. In the end, the *God of order* persists in constancy, a constancy that outflanks and overrides every surge of chaos and death. The God of the Bible is located in this dual assertion, the one who makes *all things new*, the one who abides with *everlasting arms*. How we adjudicate this tension in the character of God depends upon which texts we read. That in turn depends upon the inclination of the interpreting community and the requirements of fidelity in any particular context.

IV. THE COMMUNITY OF PRAISE AND OBEDIENCE

CHAPTER NINE

ISRAEL AS A COMMUNITY OF PRAISE AND OBEDIENCE

There is no doubt that YHWH—creator of heaven and earth, deliverer of Israel—dominates the faith of the Old Testament, sometimes in direct ways, sometimes in hidden ways. YHWH, however, is never God alone or apart from the world that YHWH has created. Or more precisely, YHWH is never alone and apart from Israel, the community that YHWH has chosen, formed, and summoned to be in covenant with YHWH. For that reason a second emphasis of Old Testament study—completely subordinated to and derivative from the reality of YHWH—is Israel as the community of YHWH.

I

The Old Testament, everywhere except in the wisdom traditions that eschew historical particularity, is permeated with the conviction and affirmation that YHWH has taken the initiative in summoning and designating Israel to be in a peculiar relationship with YHWH. That conviction is pervasive in the Old Testament, but it is made most consistently explicit in the traditions of Deuteronomy where it is affirmed that Israel's existence is a gift and a summons to maintain a distinctive reality in the world:

> For you are a people holy to the LORD your God; the LORD your God has chosen you out of all the peoples on earth to be his people, his treasured

> possession. It was not because you were more numerous than any other people that the LORD set his heart on you and chose you—for you were the fewest of all peoples. It was because the LORD loved you and kept the oath that he swore to your ancestors, that the LORD has brought you out with a mighty hand, and redeemed you from the house of slavery, from the hand of Pharaoh king of Egypt. Know therefore that the LORD your God is God, the faithful God who maintains covenant loyalty with those who love him and keep his commandments, to a thousand generations, and who repays in their own person those who reject him. He does not delay but repays in their own person those who reject him. (Deuteronomy 7:6-10)

> When the LORD your God thrusts them out before you, do not say to yourself, "It is because of my righteousness that the LORD has brought me in to occupy this land"; it is rather because of the wickedness of these nations that the LORD is dispossessing them before you. It is not because of your righteousness or the uprightness of your heart that you are going in to occupy their land; but because of the wickedness of these nations the LORD your God is dispossessing them before you, in order to fulfill the promise that the LORD made on oath to your ancestors, to Abraham, to Isaac, and to Jacob. (Deuteronomy 9:4-5)

> Although heaven and the heaven of heavens belong to the LORD your God, the earth with all that is in it, yet the LORD set his heart in love on your ancestors alone and chose you, their descendants after them, out of all the peoples, as it is today. (Deuteronomy 10:14-15)

This tradition, echoed particularly in the pathos of Hosea and Jeremiah, is completely unambiguous that there is nothing about Israel that evokes the divine choice, not size or virtue or anything else. The proximate explanation for the divine choice in the narrative of Moses is the promise made to the Genesis ancestors; that, of course, only pushes the question one step backward. Another proximate explanation is that Israel receives the blessing of the land from YHWH by default, because of YHWH's rejection of the wicked nations. But behind such proximate explanations, finally the choice of Israel is an act of divine freedom that defies explanation and that can only be understood as a divine impulse of affection.[1] Thus the verb "set his heart" (*hashaq*) lets the ground of choice remain hidden in YHWH's emotional commitment to Israel (Deuteronomy 7:10; 10:15). Israel is YHWH's chosen people by the free act of YHWH's love.

It is impossible to overstate the significance of the divine choice of Israel for Old Testament theology. That choice places a "scandal of particularity" at the center of faith. That choice places YHWH by implication in the midst of the vagaries of history, for the chosen people are an identifiable people in history who will not be explained away as a theological idea. That choice has placed in international history a distinct community with an odd theological grounding that is unwilling and unable to accommodate itself easily to any "normal" political claim. That choice as a recurring *novum*, a protesting inconvenience, and a carrier of surprising historical possibility has, in the latter part of the Old Testament, eventuated in the Jewish people and in the faith of Judaism as a people of Torah who eschew idolatry and who claim concrete turf promises in the world. (After and alongside the Jewish people that same "choosing God" has, in Christian confession, placed a secondary promissory people in history that, at its best, also refuses every accommodation to the ways of the world.) Given that choice that is defining for Old Testament faith, it is not only the case that Israel is known among the nations as *the people of YHWH*; it is equally the case that YHWH is known among the nations first and foremost as *the God of Israel*. (See the misperception of the Assyrians in this regard who construe YHWH as one more tribal God; Isaiah 36:18-20.)

II

YHWH's choice of Israel, a core datum of Old Testament theology, dominates the memory and confession of Israel, though the instance of divine designation is variously understood:

1. The initial divine address to what became Israel is the terse speech of YHWH in Genesis 12 that comes without preparation or antecedent. The address is spectacular in its abruptness:

> Now the LORD said to Abram, "Go from your country and your kindred and your father's house to the land that I will show you. I will make of you a great nation, and I will bless you, and make your name great, so that you will be a blessing. I will bless those who bless you, and the one who curses you I will curse; and in you all the families of the earth shall be blessed." (Genesis 12:1-3)

The abruptness of divine address is made even more acute by the fact that Sarah is "barren," a woman without a future (Genesis 11:30). This initial address places the family of Abraham under divine promise; the family of Abraham is guaranteed a prominent place in history and a secure land in time to come. The divine utterance also situates this community vis-à-vis the nations. The coming community of Israel will not exist in a historical vacuum, but with a connection to other nations whereby Israel mediates the blessing of the creator God to all of the others. Thus at the very outset the community is given a *promise* and a *task*; that peculiar designation is everywhere the case for Israel in the Old Testament, though various verses variously accent promise or task. Israel is never without both divine promise and divine task.[2]

It remains an important initial question whether the address to Abraham in fact constitutes the beginning of Israel. On historical grounds it is commonly thought that the narratives of the Genesis ancestors belong to the "preparation" for Israel that is only belatedly formed. While that may be true historically, there is no doubt that in the remembering and traditioning of Israel this is indeed the beginning. Most particularly the promise of the land that pervades the Genesis narratives continues to be an important accent point for Jews even until contemporary Jewish self-understanding. The address to Abraham gives a subsequent community a peculiar identity and vocation in the world.[3]

2. A second narrative beginning of Israel is in the encounter of Moses with YHWH in the midst of Egyptian slavery. This encounter has a texture very different from that of Abraham in Genesis 12. In the narrative text of Exodus 2–4, YHWH is not mentioned until Exodus 2:23. That mention of "God," moreover, is in response to the cry of wretchedness on the lips of the slaves. In this account the initiation for contact with YHWH, unlike that of Genesis 12, is taken by human agents and not by YHWH. That initiative, of course, is one made without awareness of YHWH; for the slaves, it is remembered, simply "cried out." They did not address the cry to anyone and certainly not to YHWH. They simply cried out of human anguish. The ones who cry are defined in the text as "the Israelites," but in truth it is likely that the cry was a ragtag band of needy, powerless slaves who are preoccupied with their own suffering. If this band of slaves constituted Israel, then in this instant Israel is a sociological entity of those who suffer the abuse of being cheap, exploited labor in the Egyptian Empire.

The key interpretive point, however, is that the cry addressed to no one in particular "rose up to God." It is the cry that reaches YHWH that mobilizes YHWH to take action for the exodus deliverance. We are not told why YHWH received the cry. Perhaps it is because YHWH is able to recognize that the slaves who cry out are indeed heirs to the Genesis narratives; in that case this encounter is an anticipation of the later prophetic promise: "Before they call I will answer, / while they are yet speaking I will hear" (Isaiah 65:24).

Or conversely this God, unlike other gods, is peculiarly attentive to the cries of the wretched and the poor, whoever they may be.[4] Thus this beginning of Israel that eventuates in the exodus may be given a theological tilt (children of Abraham) or a sociological tilt (the cry of the wretched).[5] Either way, we are not told why YHWH received the cry. We are, however, told of the response YHWH made to the cry and the ground of the response. Upon hearing the cry—a cry that is paradigmatic in Israel—YHWH responds by attentive engagement and full involvement in the neediness of those who cry. The ground of such engagement is that God *remembered*, all the way back to the narrative of Genesis.[6] On the basis of old promises of the book of Genesis, YHWH now acts in decisive fidelity for the slaves and against the power of Pharaoh. This "second beginning of Israel" has a sociopolitical dimension of conflict, confrontation, power, and transformation that is not present in the Genesis narrative. This latter way of telling the story of YHWH with Israel is much more characteristic of what follows in the Old Testament, for the life of Israel in the world with YHWH is recurrently one of dispute, trouble, and transformation.

3. But of course the initiation of the relationship at the outset of the exodus narrative is largely promissory; the report anticipates what will happen in time to come. For that reason a third moment in the tradition may also be reckoned as the beginning of Israel's life in the world, namely, the covenant at Sinai. As we have seen, the divine announcement in Exodus 19:4-6 pivots on the "now therefore" of verse 5 wherein with the condition of radical obedience. Israel will now and in time to come, "be my people": "Now therefore, if you obey my voice and keep my covenant, you shall be my treasured possession out of all the peoples. Indeed, the whole earth is mine, but you shall be for me a priestly kingdom and a holy nation. These are the words that you shall speak to the Israelites" (Exodus 19:5-6).

The rhetoric suggests that up until now Israel was not yet fully the Israel of God. Three aspects of this text merit attention. First, that Israel is YHWH's people is situated among all the peoples and, as in Genesis 12:3, is given a role vis-à-vis the other nations. Second, the way in which Israel is to exist among the nations is by being "a holy nation," that is, one set apart for and defined by total, uncompromising loyalty to YHWH. Third, the way in which that holy status is maintained and exhibited is by *hearing the voice* of the covenant God and *keeping covenant*, that is, keeping covenant commandments.[7] The meeting at Sinai thus identifies Israel as a community of full and glad obedience to the commandments yet to be given. That is the warrant for Israel's existence in the world; Israel is to live not by bread alone but by every word that comes from the mouth of the Lord (Deuteronomy 8:4). And what comes from the mouth of the Lord is precisely commandment. Israel lives by attention to YHWH's commands!

4. If one follows current critical opinion, it is possible to conclude that Israel as an intentional self-conscious historical community originated only in the land of Canaan. On this view it emerged as a revolutionary alternative to the presiding Canaanite societal system and did so by gathering around the power and promise of YHWH as giver of land.[8] In this view the antecedent traditions of ancestors, exodus, sojourn, and Sinai are theological referents whereby Israel's historical claim is held in abeyance until the crossing of the Jordan River.

Taken theologically the land traditions of the book of Joshua as an originary point for Israel witness to YHWH as *land giver* and Israel as *land receiver*, indeed, as receiver of land that was already occupied by non-Israelites.[9] The tradition evidences awareness of the existence of the Canaanites who were ethnically and linguistically akin to the Israelites. What distinguishes Israel in such a cultural environment is precisely adherence to YHWH and the derivative conviction—voiced in Deuteronomy—that the *land of promise* can be reorganized in *covenantal, neighborly terms*. The covenant-making ceremonies described in Joshua 8:30-35 and 24:1-28 evidence the way in which the tradition draws the promised and given land into the orbit of YHWH's covenant. Even more important is the remarkable confession of Joshua 4:23-24 wherein the *crossing of the Jordan River* is understood "as" the *crossing of the Red Sea*. While the crossing of the Red Sea dominates the imaginative memory of Israel, the crossing of the Jordan connects Israel to the concrete reality of the land in which Israel understood itself to be entitled.

These four beginning points make clear that it is not possible to identify a single moment of Israel's origin. Israel is relentlessly coming into existence through the recall, reiteration, and reappropriation of these several traditions, however they may be rooted in historical reality. The four beginning points I have noted provide Israel's most characteristic theological markings,

- as a recipient carrier of *YHWH's promise*;
- as the beneficiary of *YHWH's delivering capacity*;
- as the community bound in *covenantal obedience*;
- as the people *entitled to the land*.

The accent points of promise, *deliverance*, *covenant and Torah*, and *land* constitute the primary data of Israel's faith, the primary initiatives toward Israel, and Israel's primary distinguishing marks in the world.[10]

III

We may reflect on the way in which the community of Israel is to be understood in the Old Testament. That self-understanding is clearly a complex and dialectical one that leaves Old Testament theology with an assignment that is wondrously, intriguingly, and maddeningly beyond any clear resolution.

It is clear that Israel is to be understood *theologically*, that is, as a people defined by an intense and singular relationship with YHWH. It is loyalty to YHWH, readiness to praise YHWH, and eagerness to obey YHWH's commands that mark Israel distinctively. That theological sensibility is clearly present at the beginning of the Sinai pericope envisioning Israel as "a priestly kingdom and a holy nation" (Exodus 19:6). The more expansive tradition of Deuteronomy anticipates that other peoples will notice and be dazzled by Israel's singularity: "For what other great nation has a god so near to it as the LORD our God is whenever we call to him? And what other great nation has statutes and ordinances as just as this entire law that I am setting before you today?" (Deuteronomy 4:7-8). The two ingredients of theological identity are "a God so near" and "a Torah so just."[11] That same claim is prominent in exilic prophets who appeal to the "covenant formula": "They shall be my people and I will be their God" (Jeremiah 24:7; 30:22; 31:33; Ezekiel 11:20, 14:11, 36:28;

37:23, 17).[12] While the formula seems to belong to exilic material, there is no doubt that Israel's tradition indicates that this covenantal formula be understood as definitional from the outset of the community.

That singular covenantal-theological claim, however, is made more complex by the fact that Israel—as YHWH's community—emerges within the historical process and is subject to the conditions and demands of history. Thus alongside the *theological* we may identify three ways of thinking of Israel as a *historical* community, three ways that are roughly chronological:

- Much current interpretation understands early Israel as the emergent of a social upheaval, a movement of protest against exploitative Canaanite practices that provided an alternative covenantal community. The historical data for this claim is difficult, but even if such a notion as an economic-political revolution cannot be fully sustained, we are still able to see such a claim as a subtext in the exodus narrative, which voices acute socioeconomic awareness.[13] Israel understands itself as a *sociological* political alternative to the rapacious, exploitative socioeconomic practice of a command economy. And while the initial hypothesis of Norman Gottwald may have been too laden with modern interpretive theory, one can nonetheless see that the tradition is shot through with impulses that suggest a *sociological alternative*. It is not possible to understand Israel theologically unless its theological claims are rooted in and connected to socioeconomic practice, as these claims seem to have been from the beginning.
- The view that Israel emerged as sociological protest and alternative is presented—in the books of Judges and Samuel—as a community finding its way and still short of any stable political organization or infrastructure. It is only with the rise of the monarchy under David and more fully under Solomon that Israel acquires a sustainable political identity.[14] Whatever may be the historical reality, the tradition presents a self-conscious political emergent in the monarchy that features a bureaucracy, a standing army, and a solidified administration. As a result Israel is a political entity that engages in the usual interactions with neighboring states and suffers the usual indignities and humiliations at the hands of the superpowers.
- With the termination of the Davidic regime in 587 B.C.E. at the hands of the Babylonians, Israel could no longer appeal to a stable political identity. It seems in the late period of the Old Testament to have gravitated toward an *ethnic* identity so that genealogy and pedigree become increasingly important. This mode of self-consciousness is evident, for

example, in the arrival of other peoples into Samaria in a way that adumbrated the Jew-Samaritan conflict of later generations (see 2 Kings 17:24-41). More especially, it is the attentiveness to "holy seed" that leads Israel in the late Old Testament period to guard against pollution and against the intrusion of the alien other into the community (Ezra 9:2; Nehemiah 9:2). This concern is likely at work in Genesis 17 that is probably an exilic text:

> I will establish my covenant between me and you, and your offspring after you throughout their generations, for an everlasting covenant, to be God to you and to your offspring after you. And I will give to you, and to your offspring after you, the land where you are now an alien, all the land of Canaan, for a perpetual holding; and I will be their God.
>
> God said to Abraham, "As for you, you shall keep my covenant, you and your offspring after you throughout their generations. This is my covenant, which you shall keep, between me and you and your offspring after you: Every male among you shall be circumcised. You shall circumcise the flesh of your foreskins, and it shall be a sign of the covenant between me and you. Throughout your generations every male among you shall be circumcised when he is eight days old, including the slave born in your house and the one bought with your money from any foreigner who is not of your offspring." (Genesis 17:7-12; see Numbers 16:40)

And with more historical grounding, the work of Ezra and Nehemiah is committed to such communal purity that leads inevitably to the expulsion of foreign wives (Ezra 10:6-44; Nehemiah 13:23-27):

> For they have taken some of their daughters as wives for themselves and for their sons. Thus the holy seed has mixed itself with the peoples of the lands, and in this faithlessness the officials and leaders have led the way. (Ezra 9:2)

> Then those of Israelite descent separated themselves from all foreigners, and stood and confessed their sins and the iniquities of their ancestors. (Nehemiah 9:2)[15]

Now it is the case that the featuring of *sociological, political and ethnic* dimensions of the community cannot be arranged chronologically as though they are distinct from each other or sequential. Nor is it the case that such embodiments of Israel eliminated the covenant-theological reference point that is constant through the long career of Israelite tradition. Notice of these three dimensions of Israel's life, however, alerts us to the fact that Israel as an *embodied* people of YHWH is never theologically pure and is never immune to the pressures, requirements, and seductions of the historical process. It is always a "both-and," and never an "either-or" concerning *covenantal, theological* on the one hand and concerning *sociological, political, and ethnic* on the other hand. From this it follows that Israel's theological attestation is always impinged upon by historical reality so that faith always comes amid ideology. That is, concrete, bodied vested interest is inevitably at work in the theological tradition and there is no possibility of extracting "pure faith" from embodied reality. Both this *mystery of faith* and *embodied life in the world* are together characteristic of Jewishness; in Christian tradition and practice this same reality may alert us to the inescapable ideological dimension that is present in our best interpretive efforts. It cannot be otherwise, for Jews or for Christians, in a tradition that, on the one hand, imagined a *land of promise* that is recurrently a land beset by threats and potentials for the land and, on the other hand, by an *embodied messiah* who is crucified and raised from the dead. There is no place for romantic naiveté in understanding what it means, in ancient times or until now, to be *God's people in history.*

Having said that, it is nonetheless the case that Israel, for all its sociological engagement, its political ambition, and its ethnic anxiety, is nonetheless a *people under command.* It is for that reason that I have begun my discussion with the Moses-Sinai materials, for these materials eventuate in a people sworn to allegiance to a God who in immediate and mediated ways continues to declare a purpose and an insistent will for the life of the world. It is for this reason that the Psalms, the working theological tradition of Israel, begins in Psalm 1 with an insistence that Israel should "mediate on the Torah day and night" (Psalm 1:2).

Thus the primal mark of Israel as the people of YHWH is adherence to the Torah. For a proper understanding of the theology of the Old Testament, it is crucial that this be carefully understood, especially since much Christian interpretation of the Old Testament has grossly caricatured Israel's passion for the Torah. It is clear that Torah in Israel is no once-for-all delivered dictum, but is rather the evocation of great Yahwistic claims that are subject to the many vagaries of historical impingement and to the imaginative and venturesome task of ongoing interpretation. Thus the Torah commands of YHWH are *rooted* in the jealous propensities of YHWH but are marked by a *dynamism* that continues to give fresh measure to commands and continues to make connections to new circumstance where God's people must live faithfully. That *rooted dynamism* is marked in rabbinic Judaism by the force of "oral Torah" which keeps the rabbis working out from written tradition to ongoing tradition.[16] In Christian tradition, that *rooted dynamism* is understood to be "progressive revelation" wherein "new occasions teach new duties."

In faithful Christian tradition, it is understood that it is the work of God's spirit that leads to fresh disclosures of the forms that obedience must take in any particular time and place. In my specific church tradition of the United Church of Christ, that same rooted dynamism is formulated as "God is still speaking," a conviction specified in an excessively cute use of the *comma*, an indication that divine revelation has not yet reached the end of the sentence. In a variety of ways Jewish and Christian traditions struggle in ongoing ways with *groundedness* and *openness*. Unfortunately this ongoing process is now acutely and disputatiously divided between *conservatives* who focus on the *ground* and *liberals* who champion the *dynamism*. In fact, the matter is inescapably dialectical, for only so can a tradition be maintained over time in history, an interpretive process that is venturesome and restrained, a courageous practice of continuity and discontinuity.

Here I will note signs in the tradition of that dynamism that is deeply grounded in divine decree but that recognizes at the same time that the ongoing authority of Torah depends upon interpretive connections to immediate circumstance.

■ Already in Exodus 20, just after the completion of the divine proclamation of the Decalogue, provision is made for the mediating work of Moses; that provision is evoked because the immediacy of YHWH in the community is judged to be too ominous (Exodus 20:18-21). While the text authorizes the person of Moses, it is a common assumption of scholars that these verses legitimate a continuing *office* or role of Moses in succeeding generations, those who will mediate to Israel the ongoing will and purpose of YHWH.[17] It is clear enough, most especially in the tradition of Deuteronomy, that such mediation entails interpretation and extrapolation so that the fundamentals of the Decalogue at Sinai can be unfolded and turned to meet specific need. Most poignantly the so-called book of the covenant in Exodus 21:1–23:19 offers detailed commands that by canonical placement are offered as a derivative from the Decalogue. Clearly the interpretive work of "Moses" continues through the generations, both in rabbinic interpretation of Torah and in the

Christian tradition in the work of Jesus and the ongoing teaching authority of the church.

■ The beginning of the tradition of Deuteronomy, clearly the most dynamic and imaginative rendering of Torah in the Old Testament, asserts that Moses—in the plains of Moab and not at Sinai—"expounds this Torah." The verb *expound* is difficult but surely suggests that Torah teaching in Deuteronomy is not merely reiteration but it is the offer of derivative commands by applying Sinai to new time, new place, and new circumstance.[18]

■ Deuteronomy 5:1-5 functions as an introduction to the reiteration of the Decalogue in verses 6-21. In verse 3, the urgency of contemporaneity in Torah is articulated: "Not with our ancestors did the LORD make this covenant, but with us, who are all of us here alive today" (Deuteronomy 5:3). The emphatic form of the statement in the mouth of Moses insists that Torah is not to be "remembered" as an ancient teaching but is to be received and embraced precisely in present context. What follows in the book of Deuteronomy is an interpretive act that keeps Torah commands available and relevant to new circumstance.

■ Deuteronomy 17:18 provides that the king shall keep a "copy" of the Torah available. The term *copy* is rendered as *deuteros* (second) in Greek, from which the book receives its popular title. It is entirely possible that the term means not only a reiterated copy but rather a "second version" of the Sinai Torah. It is most likely that the reference refers to Deuteronomy itself or "this Torah," so that it is the Sinai tradition expanded and interpreted that is in focus here. The tradition of Deuteronomy is the practice and evidence of dynamism as the memory of Sinai is handled in order to keep the commands perennially linked to the present life of the community.

■ The dynamism of Deuteronomy is evident in the repeated caveat of Moses that the Torah must be taken as it is, without addition or subtraction:

> You must neither add anything to what I command you nor take away anything from it, but keep the commandments of the LORD your God with which I am charging you. (Deuteronomy 4:2)

> You must diligently observe everything that I command you; do not add to it or take anything from it. (Deuteronomy 12:32)

The statement of Moses is unambiguous; the commands of Sinai are to be taken "straight up" without tampering.

Except that in the book of Deuteronomy itself the statement is stunningly ironic, for what "Moses" does in Deuteronomy is to *add* to the Sinai Torah in rich and imaginative ways as the commands of the wilderness are repositioned for an agricultural community in the land. (It could be argued that "Moses" in Deuteronomy also subtracts from the Torah as some earlier claims are neglected; but my accent is on "add" as a practice of interpretive extension and extrapolation.) Indeed it is suggested by Stephen Kaufman that the corpus of Deuteronomy 12–25 is arranged according to the Decalogue so that the commandments in sequence are in fact exegesis or exposition that add measurably to Sinai.[19] Given the interpretive horizon of Deuteronomy, such dynamism is taken not as an addition but as a faithful articulation of Sinai. Thus the act of "adding" in Deuteronomy is perforce intrinsic to the Torah and not at all imposed.

■ This same acceptance of the interpretive dynamic is more explicitly embraced in the report of the dramatic scribal activity of Ezra. In the public reading of the Torah, Ezra, along with prominent elders and Levites, made the Torah understandable to "both men and women and all who could hear with understanding" (Nehemiah 8:2):

> Also Jeshua, Bani, Sherebiah, Jamin, Akkub, Shabbethai, Hodiah, Maaseiah, Kelita, Azariah, Jozabad, Hanan, Pelaiah, the Levites, helped the people to understand the law, while the people remained in their places. So they read from the book, from the law of God, with interpretation. They gave the sense, so that the people understood the reading. (Nehemiah 8:7-8)

Faithful to the interpretive condition of Deuteronomy and the dominant authority of Moses, Israel understood that *Torah must be interpreted* because it is a living command of a living God, and therefore interpretation is witness to the process of Torah itself.

Thus the sequence of *Sinai-Deuteronomy-Ezra* form an axis of dynamism that became characteristic in both Judaism and Christianity. It is for that reason that Robert Alter can speak of Judaism as "a culture of interpretation." It is not fundamentally different in Christian tradition, though in seasons of ideological disputes some always want to halt the ongoing process of interpretation at a preferred juncture in the tradition. That dynamism may go under many names including oral tradition, *Sensus Plenior*, new hermeneutic, or progressive revelation.[20] However it may be named, it is clear that such interpretation is a primary mark and responsibility of the community that continues to engage the enduring liveliness of the God of the covenant.

IV

The "adding" to the commands of Sinai that is the proper work of interpretation may appear to be quite random and ad hoc, as circumstance requires. Given that impression, however, we are able, at least in retrospect, to see that the dynamism of Torah interpretation developed in identifiable trajectories so that streams of tradition amount to nothing less than several alternative powerful advocacies about the primary concerns of the God of the Sinai.[21]

In large scope, we are able to see that the ongoing work of interpretation is carried on in two lines of advocacy. On the one hand there is a trajectory of interpretation of Torah that is preoccupied with Israel as YHWH's holy people: "Speak to all the congregation of the people of Israel and say to them: You shall be holy, for I the LORD your God am holy" (Leviticus 19:2). Reflective in the Priestly traditions of the Pentateuch and especially in the book of Leviticus, this interpretive horizon aims to form and maintain a community that centers in cultic worship and that is preoccupied with purity whereby the holy God can be ritually present in the midst of the community. In contemporary scholarship, the anthropologist Mary Douglas has notably suggested that "holiness" is a procedure to keep things unmixed and in their right places, because mixing pollutes and places the community in jeopardy.[22] At the most elemental level, the "mixing" to be avoided concerns the details of daily life:

> You shall keep my statutes. You shall not let your animals breed with a different kind; you shall not sow your field with two kinds of seed; nor shall you put on a garment made of two different materials. (Leviticus 19:19)

> You shall not sow your vineyard with a second kind of seed, or the whole yield will have to be forfeited, both the crop that you have sown and the yield of the vineyard itself.
>
> You shall not plow with an ox and a donkey yoked together.
>
> You shall not wear clothes made of wool and linen woven together.

> You shall make tassels on the four corners of the cloak with which you cover yourself. (Deuteronomy 22:9-11)

In larger scope, however, the same concern is to maintain an order of sacrifices and a holy priesthood that are pure enough to function effectively in the presence of the holy God. The outcome of such a passion is to produce an ordered cultic community that is preoccupied with the maintenance of itself as an adequate residence for YHWH without undue attention to the civic realm of neighborly interaction. This tradition pervades Torah teaching but is concentrated in the book of Leviticus. It is of decisive importance for the tradition of Ezekiel as well as intimately connected to the book of Leviticus; Ezekiel asserts that YHWH's departure and absence from the Jerusalem temple in the sixth century is because of cultic alienation that rendered the temple site uninhabitable by YHWH (see Ezekiel 22:26).

On the other hand, a second interpretive tradition takes as it *leitmotif* the practice of neighborly justice.[23] The key reference point in this tradition is the emancipation of slavery in Egypt to suggest that the obedience of Israel is to create a neighborly economy in which the exploitative practices of Pharaoh would be excluded. This tradition is centered in Deuteronomy and constantly invokes the exodus memory as a motivation for contemporary neighborly concern expressed as economic justice: "Remember that you were a slave in the land of Egypt, and the LORD your God redeemed you; for this reason I lay this command upon you today" (Deuteronomy 15:15). To be sure, there is reference to exodus in the book of Leviticus, but even there the reference pertains precisely to neighborly engagement (see Leviticus 19:34, 36; 35:38, 42, 55; 26:13, 45). This society is envisioned as a system that continually enacts the revolutionary transformation of the exodus. The peculiar concern of that ethic, moreover, is the "quadrilateral of vulnerability," widows, orphans, sojourners, and the poor:[24]

> Every third year you shall bring out the full tithe of your produce for that year, and store it within your towns; the Levites, because they have no allotment or inheritance with you, as well as the resident aliens, the orphans, and the widows in your towns, may come and eat their fill so that the LORD your God may bless you in all the work that you undertake. (Deuteronomy 14:28-29)

> Rejoice during your festival, you and your sons and your daughters, your male and female slaves, as well as the Levites, the strangers, the orphans, and the widows resident in your towns. (Deuteronomy 16:14)

> You shall not deprive a resident alien or an orphan of justice; you shall not take a widow's garment in pledge. Remember that you were a slave in Egypt and the LORD your God redeemed you from there; therefore I command you to do this.
>
> When you reap your harvest in your field and forget a sheaf in the field, you shall not go back to get it; it shall be left for the alien, the orphan, and the widow, so that the LORD your God may bless you in all your undertakings. When you beat your olive trees, do not strip what is left; it shall be for the alien, the orphan, and the widow.
>
> When you gather the grapes of your vineyard, do not glean what is left; it shall be for the alien the orphan, and the widow. Remember that you were a slave in the land of Egypt; therefore I am commanding you to do this. (Deuteronomy 24:17-22)

This tradition is especially linked to the book of Jeremiah, for that prophetic corpus is, to some extent, preoccupied with the same vulnerable segment of the population that is especially in need:

> Like a cage full of birds,
> their houses are full of treachery;
> therefore they have become great and rich,
> they have grown fat and sleek.
> They know no limits in deeds of wickedness;
> they do not judge with justice
> the cause of the orphan, to make it prosper,
> and they do not defend the rights of the needy. (Jeremiah 5:27-28)

> For if you truly amend your ways and your doings, if you truly act justly one with another, if you do not oppress the alien, the orphan, and the widow, or shed innocent blood in this place, and if you do not go after other gods to your own hurt, then I will dwell with you in this place, in the land that I gave of old to your ancestors forever and ever. (Jeremiah 7:5-7)

> Thus says the LORD: Act with justice and righteousness, and deliver from the hand of the oppressor anyone who has been robbed. And do no wrong or violence to the alien, the orphan, and the widow, or shed

> innocent blood in this place. (Jeremiah 22:3; see Josiah as a practitioner of this ethic, Jeremiah 22:15-16)

Thus it is possible to identify two quite distinct interpretive enterprises; it is, moreover, possible to see that this teaching clusters respectively in *Leviticus-Ezekiel* and *Deuteronomy-Jeremiah*. Having said that, a careful reading will indicate that the accent points may vary in the development of these several traditions but they cannot be easily and completely separated. In the midst of the holiness teaching of Leviticus, in Leviticus 19:18, the premiere teaching of neighbor love is stated.[25] And the radical provision for jubilee, the restitution of land that curbs aggressive acquisitiveness, is in the tradition of Leviticus (Leviticus 25). Conversely, the tradition of Deuteronomy focuses upon economic justice; but we cannot help but notice nonetheless that the book of Deuteronomy, in its preoccupation with a "holy people," is concerned for the elimination of seductive religious symbols (Deuteronomy 7:5) and the maintenance of ritual purity by the avoidance of that which pollutes (Deuteronomy 14:3-21). Indeed the annihilation of adjacent peoples who are an "abomination" may jeopardize YHWH's commitment to Israel (Deuteronomy 20).

It is important to see that different accents are indeed offered; but neither accent is offered exclusively. It is characteristically an insistence upon a "both/and" of holiness and justice and not an either/or. This is evident, for example, in the tradition of Isaiah in the prophet's initial imperatives to Jerusalem. The prophet readily holds together ritual acts of holiness and neighborly acts of justice:

> Wash yourselves; make yourselves clean;
> remove the evil of your doings
> from before my eyes;
> cease to do evil,
> learn to do good;
> seek justice,
> rescue the oppressed,
> defend the orphan,
> plead for the widow. (Isaiah 1:16-17)

And even in his famous "call" report of Isaiah 6, it is the vision of God's holiness that propels the prophet to radical social critique.

This "both/and" approach that dominates the Old Testament (even with particular points of accent) is important for two identifiable interpretive concerns. First, the dialectical tension and the dynamism of Torah interpretation has been poorly misunderstood and ill served in much Christian understanding of Judaism.[26] There has been a wholesale tendency in Christianity to conclude that Judaism belongs to a narrow tradition of holiness that was reduced to a struggle for punctilious "legalism." The effect was to retain for Christianity a wholesome projection on justice questions and to imagine that it was only Christianity—and not Judaism—that cared about God's rule in the world of the neighborhood.

Such an unfortunate characterization of Judaism, of course, has no basis in reality. For the truth of the matter is that Judaism has at its best—like Christianity at its best—understood and embraced the dialectic of *holiness and justice*, and has fully understood the indispensability of both. In contemporary religious culture, no one has more fully embraced that dialectic in a visible and practical way than has Abraham Heschel. He brought to the social crises of the latter part of the twentieth century a deep passion for social justice; but that passion was deeply rooted in the life of disciplined holiness.[27] And while Heschel is a highly visible case, he is in fact a representative figure of faithful Judaism and not at all an exception.

The failure to maintain the dialectic and the temptation to fall out on one side or the other—all justice and no holiness, all holiness and no justice—happens in Judaism and produces odd configurations of practice. But of course the same distortion of the dialectic is evident in Christian faith and the same failure to maintain the dialectic is evident in Christian practice.[28]

This leads to a second derivative observation. The maintenance of the dialectic of holiness and justice is mandated in Christian faith as it is in Judaism. It is, however, the case in the current ideological mapping of Christianity in the United States that the maintenance of the dialectic is largely forgotten and neglected. Thus the holiness tradition of the Torah has been drawn into the service of so-called conservative Evangelicalism in the same way that the prophetic tradition of justice has brought into the service of self-indulgent "liberalism." In both cases, contemporary ideological pressure and passion have taken one side of the tension that Israel, in its canonical imagination, managed to keep in a generative relationship. While it is not readily clear how either trajectory of holiness or justice ought to be articulated in contemporary terms, it is unmistakably clear that canonically it is a "both/and." Any effort at "either/or" betrays the biblical testimony.

It is clear that the task of mediation that moves from the clear divine enunciation at Sinai to a contemporary covenantal obedience is complex and inescapably disputatious. The never-ending task of mediation was begun by Moses and continued among Jews and Christians until the present hour. The long Torah-poem of Psalm 119 reflects on the defining force of obedience to Torah commandments for the life of Israel. The mood of the psalm is joyous affirmation, for in Torah commandments Israel comes to know not only about "a Torah so just"; it also knows and celebrates "a God so near" (Deuteronomy 4:7-8).

CHAPTER TEN

OBEDIENCE: RESPONSE TO THE SOVEREIGN GOD IN DIALOGIC MODES

In its imagination and in its experience, Israel is always fresh from slavery, always departing Sinai with new covenantal identity, always en route through wilderness without resources, always yet again at the edge of the new land of promise, always with old ancestral promises ringing in its ears. Israel always again travels this way as the people of YHWH entrusted with YHWH's Torah, the instruction that sustains a peculiar identity in the world. The Torah from YHWH is a summons to an alternative life marked by both joy and confidence, above all characterized by *listening*. Israel is addressed always again by the Lord of the Covenant and its work is to listen. That defining imperative, "listen" (*shema*ʿ) is of course rendered "obey." Israel is to "hear and do," or as the Sinai pledge has it, to "do and hear" (Exodus 24:7). It is in hearing that Israel becomes and remains the people of YHWH. Thus for good reason John Calvin can conclude that, "all right knowledge of God is born of obedience."[1] In such a judgment, Calvin echoes the ancient verdict of Jeremiah concerning the good king Josiah, that *obedience* constitutes knowledge of God:

> Did not your father eat and drink
>   and do justice and righteousness?
>   Then it was well with him.
> He judged the cause of the poor and needy;
>   then it was well.

Is not this to know me?
says the LORD. (Jeremiah 22:15b-16)

Broadly construed, the several elements of the Old Testament are, in a variety of ways, interpretive reflections on the central theme of *obedience to Torah*. In what follows, I will take up in turn that theme in the prophetic, sapiential, and psalmic literature.

I

The prophetic corpus of the Old Testament, in canonical perspective, is offered as a derivative from the Torah, even though in critical judgment much of the prophetic material antedates the material of the Torah. The former prophets (Joshua, Judges, Samuel and Kings) are an account of land-loss caused by disobedience that culminates in exile (2 Kings 24–25).[2] As Ronald Clements has shown, the prophetic traditions of Isaiah, Jeremiah, Ezekiel, and the Twelve are now themed around judgment and hope: "In such fashion we can at least come to understand the value and meaning of the way in which distinctive patterns have been imposed upon the prophetic collections of the canon so that warnings of doom and disaster are always followed by promises of hope and restoration."[3]

Given that overall structure of prophetic discourse that pivots on the destruction of Jerusalem, the scattering of Israel, and the anticipated recovery of the community that is to be regathered, we may see in the prophetic tradition three motifs pertinent to the theme of obedience:

1. The prophetic tradition everywhere assumes that Israel is under Torah mandate. Given that assumption, the prophetic corpus everywhere assumes that Israel stands under the *judgment of YHWH* for failure to adhere to the Torah commandments. Thus Claus Westermann has seen that the prophetic *speech of judgment* is everywhere the "basic form" of prophetic speech.[4] It is a form of rhetoric that imagines a courtroom in which Israel is *indicted* for Torah violation. That Torah violation may derive from the covenantal mandates of Deuteronomy and so focus on issues of neighbor relations and the practice of *economic exploitation*. Or it may derive from the holiness traditions of the priestly materials that focus upon the violations of holiness as pertain to *cultic purity*. Either way, the life of Israel is seen to be antithetical to the will of the God of Sinai. For that reason the speech of judgment characteristically places after the

indictment a *sentence* of punishment pronounced against Israel. The declaration of punishment may be variously articulated (a) as the direct action of YHWH against Israel, (b) as the intrusion of a historical enemy at the behest of YHWH, or (c) as the "natural" working out of the consequences of a skewed, distorted life. In the imaginative practice of the Old Testament, the judgment upon Israel for disobedience is given in many articulations, but those several articulations focus regularly upon the destruction of Jerusalem, the city that is the carrier of YHWH's presence and the betrayer of YHWH's expectations. Thus the three great prophetic traditions all anticipate the decisive action of YHWH against the recalcitrant city:

> The LORD said:
> Because the daughters of Zion are haughty
>   and walk with outstretched necks,
>   glancing wantonly with their eyes,
> mincing along as they go,
>   tinkling with their feet;
> the LORD will afflict with scabs
>   the heads of the daughters of Zion,
>   and the LORD will lay bare their secret parts. (Isaiah 3:16-17)

> Days are coming when all that is in your house, and that which your ancestors have stored up until this day, shall be carried to Babylon; nothing shall be left, says the LORD. Some of your own sons who are born to you shall be taken away; they shall be eunuchs in the palace of the king of Babylon. (Isaiah 39:6-7)

> Raise a standard toward Zion,
>   flee for safety, do not delay,
> for I am bringing evil from the north,
>   and a great destruction.
> A lion has gone up from its thicket,
>   a destroyer of nations has set out;
>   he has gone out from his place
> to make your land a waste;
>   your cities will be ruins
>   without inhabitant.
> Because of this put on sackcloth,
>   lament and wail:
> "The fierce anger of the LORD
>   has not turned away from us." (Jeremiah 4:6-8)

> Thus you shall say to Zedekiah: Thus says the LORD, the God of Israel: I am going to turn back the weapons of war that are in your hands and with which you are fighting against the king of Babylon and against the Chaldeans who are besieging you outside the walls; and I will bring them together into the center of this city. I myself will fight against you with outstretched hand and mighty arm, in anger, in fury, and in great wrath. And I will strike down the inhabitants of this city, both human beings and animals; they shall die of a great pestilence. (Jeremiah 21:4-6)

> To the others he said in my hearing, "Pass through the city after him, and kill; your eye shall not spare, and you shall show no pity. Cut down old men, young men and young women, little children and women, but touch no one who has the mark. And begin at my sanctuary." So they began with the elders who were in front of the house. Then he said to them, "Defile the house, and fill the courts with the slain. Go!" So they went out and killed in the city. (Ezekiel 9:5-7)

> Therefore thus says the Lord GOD:
> Woe to the bloody city!
> I will even make the pile great.
> Heap up the logs, kindle the fire;
> boil the meat well, mix in the spices,
> let the bones be burned.
> Stand it empty upon the coals,
> so that it may become hot, its copper glow,
> its filth melt in it, its rust be consumed.
> In vain I have wearied myself;
> its thick rust does not depart.
> To the fire with its rust!
> Yet, when I cleansed you in your filthy lewdness,
> you did not become clean from your filth;
> you shall not again be cleansed
> until I have satisfied my fury upon you. (Ezekiel 24:9-13)

And of course it is not different in the Book of the Twelve:

> Thus says the LORD;
> For three transgressions of Judah,
> and for four, I will not revoke the punishment;
> because they have rejected the law of the LORD,
> and have not kept his statutes,
> but they have been led astray by the same lies

after which their ancestors walked.
So I will send a fire on Judah,
and it shall devour the strongholds of Jerusalem. (Amos 2:4-5)

Hear this, you rulers of the house of Jacob
and chiefs of the house of Israel,
who abhor justice
and pervert all equity,
who build Zion with blood
and Jerusalem with wrong!
Its rulers give judgment for a bribe,
its priests teach for a price,
its prophets give oracles for money;
yet they lean upon the LORD and say,
"Surely the LORD is with us!
No harm shall come upon us."
Therefore because of you
Zion shall be plowed as a field;
Jerusalem shall become a heap of ruins,
and the mountain of the house a wooded height. (Micah 3:9-12)

The city has failed YHWH's summons to obedience, and obedience is the prerequisite of a viable life in the world.

2. There is no doubt that divine judgment is central in prophetic tradition. And yet in the midst of such harsh and uncompromising rhetoric there is a counterpoint motif of a *call to repentance* and an invitation to *return to YHWH in obedience.*[5] In the end the call to obedience is overwhelmed by the rhetoric of judgment. Nonetheless it appears that the prophetic tradition is able to entertain, even in its harshness, the possibility that it is not yet too late and that Jerusalem by fresh resolve can return to obedience and thereby avert the anticipated disaster that is to come.

Thus one can hear in the course of prophetic rhetoric a summons to obedience that surely assumes that obedience is still possible, and therefore it is not too late to escape divine judgment:

Wash yourselves; make yourselves clean;
remove the evil of your doings
from before my eyes;
cease to do evil,
learn to do good;

seek justice
    rescue the oppressed,
defend the orphan,
    plead for the widow. (Isaiah 1:16-17)

If you return, O Israel,
                says the LORD,
    if you return to me,
if you remove your abominations from my presence,
    and do not waver,
and if you swear, "As the LORD lives!"
    in truth, in justice, and in uprightness,
then nations shall be blessed by him,
    and by him they shall boast.

For thus says the LORD to the people of Judah and to the inhabitants of Jerusalem:

Break up your fallow ground,
    and do not sow among thorns.
Circumcise yourselves to the LORD,
    remove the foreskin of your hearts,
    O people of Judah and inhabitants of Jerusalem,
or else my wrath will go forth like fire,
    and burn with no one to quench it,
    because of the evil of your doings. (Jeremiah 4:1-4)

But if this man has a son who sees all the sins that his father has done, considers, and does not do likewise, who does not eat upon the mountains or lift up his eyes to the idols of the house of Israel, does not defile his neighbor's wife, does not wrong anyone, exacts no pledge, commits no robbery, but gives his bread to the hungry and covers the naked with a garment, withholds his hand from iniquity, takes no advance or accrued interest, observes my ordinances, and follows my statutes; he shall not die for his father's iniquity; he shall surely live. (Ezekiel 18:14-17)

Sow for yourselves righteousness;
    reap steadfast love;
    break up your fallow ground;
for it is time to seek the LORD,
    that he may come and rain righteousness upon you. (Hosea 10:12)

But as for you, return to your God,
    hold fast to love and justice,
    and wait continually for your God. (Hosea 12:6)

But let justice roll down like waters,
    and righteousness like an everflowing stream. (Amos 5:24)

In the completed form of the prophetic tradition, it may be concluded that such calls to repentance constitute a minor and subdued motif that eventually is overwhelmed by the course of events and by the savage rhetoric of termination. Israel eventually defaults on the possibility of a return to obedience. Nonetheless the motif lingers in the literature, a continuing conviction in Israel that obedience is indeed possible.

This juxtaposition of *judgment in a major key* and *repentance in a minor key* is perhaps what we would expect in a literature that is tenacious in its witness to YHWH, but tenacious in a way that allows for a pastoral sensibility. This same juxtaposition strikes one as remarkably contemporary for those who see the suicidal political enterprise of the West that is surely on a trajectory to self-destruction. Our contemporary articulation of that trajectory of self-destruction, however, almost always comes with an urgent indication that it is not yet too late and something must be done. Thus the prophetic traditions, like our own modest voicings, want always to say, "It's too late" and "It's not too late yet," and we continue that double message until in the course of events it does indeed become too late.[6]

Both the accents on *judgment* and *repentance* are in the service of *obedience*. The articulation of judgment that dominates prophetic literature is grounded in hapless recalcitrance on the part of Israel that cannot be altered:

Can Ethiopians change their skin
    or leopards their spots?
Then also you can do good
    who are accustomed to do evil. (Jeremiah 13:23)

In like manner the desperate summons to repentance is in the conviction that as obedience *must* be enacted, it *can* be enacted. Thus the prophetic tradition lives in the double-minded conviction of judgment and repentance, the same double-mindedness known by every discerning poetic observer who knows too much and yet hopes against what is surely known. The double message *failed obedience* and *possible obedience* continues until overwhelmed by events, when the discerning poetic observer is silenced and can say no more. When the tongues of such discerning poets are silenced, then the moment for obedience is past. There is no more covenantal interaction. There is only the cold silence of divine sovereignty, the one who can say with startlingly unembarrassed self-regard: "It is I who by my great power and my outstretched arm have made the earth, with the people and animals that are on the earth, and I give it to whomever I please. Now I have given all these lands into the hand of King Nebuchadnezzar of Babylon, my servant, and I have given him even the wild animals of the field to serve him" (Jeremiah 27:5-6).

In that moment, the tortured drama of covenantal engagement is swept aside. We are left with the divine self-announcement, no commandment, no Israel, no people to obey. Prophetic speech ends;[7] repentance has failed. Divine judgment prevails. There is a silence over the earth, because the divine promises have been terminated. Israel is a clay pot that cannot be repaired (Jeremiah 19:11).

3. The wonder of Israel's life and the defining miracle of Old Testament faith is this. In the silence of abandonment and termination (on which see Isaiah 54:7-8), the prophets speak again. They speak at the behest of YHWH. They break the silence of displacement and begin the speech of the gathering of the scattered, that is, the homecoming of the deported. YHWH's commitment to and passion for Israel begins again in a move of divine generosity that replicates the readiness of YHWH with Moses to begin again:[8] "He said: I hereby make a covenant. Before all your people I will perform marvels, such as have not been performed in all the earth or in any nation; and all the people among whom you live shall see the work of the LORD; for it is an awesome thing that I will do with you" (Exodus 34:10).

Indeed that divine response to Moses' petition places divine "wonder" at the heart of faith, the wonder of beginning again in the midst of termination.

The ground for renewed prophetic utterance is variously given:

- In Isaiah, after the anticipation of Babylonian intervention in Isaiah 39:5-8 and given a long silence, the Isaiah tradition speaks again. The new utterance of Isaiah 40:1-11 echoes the scenario of Isaiah 6:1-13. Again the prophetic figure has access to the divine counsel where YHWH addresses the lesser gods. Only this time, the divine address is a declaration that YHWH is back in action on behalf of Israel, even against imperial power:

> Get you up to a high mountain,
> O Zion, herald of good tidings;
> lift up your voice with strength,
> O Jerusalem, herald of good tidings,
> lift it up, do not fear;
> say to the cities of Judah,
> "Here is your God!" (Isaiah 40:9)

The God who had abandoned—in an abandonment not unlike the flood in Genesis—speaks again, with assurance concerning steadfast love, compassion, and a covenant of peace:

> This is like the days of Noah to me:
> Just as I swore that the waters of Noah
> would never again go over the earth,
> so I have sworn that I will not be angry with you
> and will not rebuke you.
> For the mountains may depart
> and the hills be removed,
> but my steadfast love shall not depart from you,
> and my covenant of peace shall not be removed,
> says the LORD, who has compassion on you. (Isaiah 54:9-10)

The failed covenant of Sinai begins again. Now it is a *covenant of shalom*. ■ In the tradition of Jeremiah, the city and the people are abandoned by YHWH and left exposed to Babylonian power, all by the design of YHWH. Israel is invited into a world of bedrooms destroyed by intruders (Jeremiah 4:20), by exposure and death on the street (Jeremiah 4:31), by the radical dismantling of creation (Jeremiah 4:23-26). Jerusalem will be "devoured" by the invaders:

> I am going to bring upon you
> a nation from far away, O house of Israel,
> says the LORD.
> It is an enduring nation,
> it is an ancient nation,
> a nation whose language you do not know,
> nor can you understand what they say.
> Their quiver is like an open tomb;

all of them are mighty warriors.
They shall eat up your harvest and your food;
they shall eat up your sons and your daughters;
they shall eat up your flocks and your herds;
they shall eat up your vines and your fig trees;
they shall destroy with the sword
your fortified cities in which you trust. (Jeremiah 5:15-17)

But then Jeremiah, at the command of YHWH, speaks again. It is a new word of expectation (Jeremiah 30–31). That word is grounded in the commitment of YHWH that there is "grace in the wilderness" wherein "wilderness" no doubt refers to the reality of deportation and displacement. Even the deportation has not diminished YHWH's gracious impulse toward Israel. Indeed YHWH's love—YHWH's covenantal commitment—to Israel is an abiding one:

Thus says the LORD:
The people who survived the sword
found grace in the wilderness;
when Israel sought for rest,
the LORD appeared to him from far away.
I have loved you with an everlasting love;
therefore I have continued my faithfulness to you. (Jeremiah 31:2-3)

We are told, moreover, that the ground of newness in the Jeremiah tradition is the quite fresh awareness of the poet of YHWH that even in YHWH's rejection of Israel, YHWH nonetheless will "still remember him":

Is Ephraim my dear son?
Is he the child I delight in?
As often as I speak against him,
I still remember him.
Therefore I am deeply moved for him;
I will surely have mercy on him,
says the LORD. (Jeremiah 31:20)

And out of that memory comes "deeply moved . . . mercy."[9] From that pathos-filled abiding and freshly voiced love comes the promissory resolve of YHWH to restore and begin again.

It is from that self-resolve on the part of YHWH that there is a unilateral declaration of a new covenant:

> The days are surely coming, says the LORD, when I will make a new covenant with the house of Israel and the house of Judah. It will not be like the covenant that I made with their ancestors when I took them by the hand to bring them out of the land of Egypt—a covenant that they broke, though I was their husband, says the LORD. But this is the covenant that I will make with the house of Israel after those days, says the LORD: I will put my law within them, and I will write it on their hearts; and I will be their God, and they shall be my people. (Jeremiah 31:31-33)

The resolution of YHWH here echoes the declaration of YHWH in Exodus 34:10. On that basis, Israel has a possible future.

In the tradition of Ezekiel, the matter is given a very different nuance. In the end, YHWH as a jealous, betrayed husband is filled with destructive rage and will enact that rage to the last ounce of violent reprisal:

> I will judge you as women who commit adultery and shed blood are judged, and bring blood upon you in wrath and jealousy. I will deliver you into their hands, and they shall throw down your platform and break down your lofty places; they shall strip you of your clothes and take your beautiful objects and leave you naked and bare. They shall bring up a mob against you, and they shall stone you and cut you to pieces with their swords. They shall burn your houses and execute judgments on you in the sight of many women; I will stop you from playing the whore, and you shall also make no more payments. So I will satisfy my fury on you, and my jealousy shall turn away from you; I will be calm, and will be angry no longer. Because you have not remembered the days of your youth, but have enraged me with all these things; therefore, I have returned your deeds upon your head, says the Lord GOD.
>
> Have you not committed lewdness beyond all your abominations? (Ezekiel 16:38-43)

It is impossible to imagine, after such a tirade, any future with YHWH. And when we turn to the new resolve of Ezekiel 36, we do not find any exhibit of the emotions of compassion or care. To be sure, YHWH will provide a new future for Israel:

> I will take you from the nations, and gather you from all the countries, and bring you into your own land. I will sprinkle clean water upon you,

> and you shall be clean from all your uncleannesses, and from all your idols I will cleanse you. A new heart I will give you, and a new spirit I will put within you; and I will remove from your body the heart of stone and give you a heart of flesh. I will put my spirit within you, and make you follow my statutes and be careful to observe my ordinances. Then you shall live in the land that I gave to your ancestors; and you shall be my people, and I will be your God. I will save you from all your uncleannesses, and I will summon the grain and make it abundant and lay no famine upon you. I will make the fruit of the tree and the produce of the field abundant, so that you may never again suffer the disgrace of famine among the nations. (Ezekiel 36:24-30)

There will be restoration, homecoming, and rebuilding. There is, however, nothing here of divine compassion or everlasting love. Rather, the impetus for newness is all in YHWH's self-regard, not at all regard for Israel. YHWH has been shamed and humiliated before the nations and now acts to recover a flawed reputation. The only way to recover that lost reputation is to rehabilitate Israel. That rehabilitation is here guaranteed, but the decisive motivation is an astonishing one: "Therefore say to the house of Israel, Thus says the Lord GOD: It is not for your sake, O house of Israel, that I am about to act, but for the sake of my holy name, which you have profaned among the nations to which you came.... It is not for your sake that I will act, says the Lord GOD; let that be known to you. Be ashamed and dismayed for your ways, O house of Israel" (Ezekiel 36:22, 32).

It is on the basis of that divine self-regard that Ezekiel can assert that YHWH will now, in the midst of cataclysmic disruption, enact an "everlasting covenant" of peace:

> They shall live in the land that I gave to my servant Jacob, in which your ancestors lived; they and their children and their children's children shall live there forever; and my servant David shall be their prince forever. I will make a covenant of peace with them; it shall be an everlasting covenant with them; and I will bless them and multiply them, and will set my sanctuary among them forevermore. My dwelling place shall be with them; and I will be their God, and they shall be my people. Then the nations shall know that I the LORD sanctify Israel, when my sanctuary is among them forevermore. (Ezekiel 37:25-28; see 34:25)

Thus we are able to see that in the three great prophetic traditions, the radical termination of the sixth century becomes the venue for newly asserted covenant, a divine act of trustworthiness that mirrors the resilience of YHWH in Exodus 34:10; this is the God who is:

> The LORD passed before him, and proclaimed,
> "The LORD, the LORD,
> a God merciful and gracious,
> slow to anger,
> and abounding in steadfast love and faithfulness,
> keeping steadfast love for the thousandth generation." (Exodus 34:6-7a)

The covenant now enacted is variously articulated:

> For the mountains may depart
> and the hills be removed,
> but my steadfast love shall not depart from you,
> and my covenant of peace shall not be removed,
> says the LORD, who has compassion on you. (Isaiah 54:10; see 55:3)

> The days are surely coming, says the LORD, when I will make a new covenant with the house of Israel and the house of Judah. It will not be like the covenant that I made with their ancestors when I took them by the hand to bring them out of the land of Egypt—a covenant that they broke, though I was their husband, says the LORD. But this is the covenant that I will make with the house of Israel after those days, says the LORD: I will put my law within them, and I will write it on their hearts; and I will be their God, and they shall be my people. (Jeremiah 31:31-33)

> I will make a covenant of peace with them; it shall be an everlasting covenant with them; and I will bless them and multiply them, and will set my sanctuary among them forevermore. (Ezekiel 37:26)

■ The matter is not different in the tradition of Hosea that establishes the themes that are to dominate the Book of the Twelve. In Hosea 2, the poetry traces the acerbic breakup of the marriage covenant between YHWH and Israel (Hosea 2:2-13). By verse 13, that relationship is decisively ended:

> I will put an end to all her mirth,
> her festivals, her new moons, her sabbaths,
> and all her appointed festivals.

I will lay waste her vines and her fig trees,
of which she said,
"These are my pay,
which my lovers have given me."
I will make them a forest,
and the wild animals shall devour them.
I will punish her for the festival days of the Baals,
when she offered incense to them
and decked herself with her ring and jewelry,
and went after her lovers,
and forgot me, says the LORD. (Hosea 2:11-13)

The end of the marriage has come! But then, in a maneuver that replicates the new beginning of covenant in Exodus 34:10—and in the postexilic covenant of Isaiah 54:10, Jeremiah 31:31-33, and Ezekiel 37:26—YHWH reengages Israel:

Therefore, I will now allure her,
and bring her into the wilderness,
and speak tenderly to her.
From there I will give her her vineyards
and make the Valley of Achor a door of hope.
There she shall respond as in the days of her youth,
as at the time when she came out of the land of Egypt. (Hosea 2:14-15)

The outcome of YHWH's fresh maneuver that is grounded only in YHWH's impulse is a new covenant that is as specific as Israel and as comprehensive as all creation. The covenant is with creation: "I will make for you a covenant on that day with the wild animals, the birds of the air, and the creeping things of the ground; and I will abolish the bow, the sword, and war from the land; and I will make you lie down in safety" (Hosea 2:18; see vv. 21-22).

But it is "for them," for Israel [who is now taken on] YHWH's new people: "And I will take you for my wife forever; I will take you for my wife in righteousness and in justice, in steadfast love, and in mercy. I will take you for my wife in faithfulness; and you shall know the LORD" (Hosea 2:19-20; see v. 23).

The relationship has indeed been terminated, but it is now repaired and restored and begins again. The fact that Hosea 2 stands at the beginning of the Book of the Twelve could suggest that in this scroll, as in the three "major prophets," the accent is upon the restoration *after judgment*. In all four prophetic scrolls, the pivot point of Israel's faith is the assertion that YHWH, God of Sinai, is willing to take a disobedient people and will say to them, "You are my people" (Hosea 2:23). This astonishing gift of newness that is at the heart of prophetic faith is adumbrated in the Sinai exchange of Exodus 34:8-10. In Exodus 34:11-26, moreover, the newly restored covenant issues in new commands from Sinai, and Israel is set for a *new obedience*. So it is in the prophetic traditions as well.

4. Thus *after* the first missed chance at obedience, *after* the failed opportunity for repentance, and *after* the inescapable severity of divine judgment, Israel now stands ready for a new obedience in a newly given covenant, a *novum* that is solely at the initiative of YHWH. Israel, in its postjudgment situation, is exactly as it was initially at Sinai, called to Torah obedience that yet again is an alternative to pharaonic obedience that is everywhere in the world palpably seductive. Thus the prophetic canon focuses not so much on failed obedience but on new obedience to the same God who has reached out in unmerited graciousness.

The *new obedience* to which Israel is now summoned is articulated variously in the several prophetic traditions. That obedience is always postjudgment, for the covenant to be obeyed is always a broken covenant that has been renewed by the mercy of YHWH.

■ In the Isaiah tradition, the destruction of Jerusalem at the hands of the Babylonians (39:5-8) has in the long run been overcome by the God who abandoned Israel for a moment (54:7-8) but who in "everlasting love" will have compassion (Isaiah 54:8). The Isaiah tradition thus moves to a "covenant of peace" which, faithful to YHWH's self-announcement at Sinai, constitutes a summons to obedience. The last major section of Isaiah begins with a summons to justice that is the ground for salvation and deliverance:

> Thus says the LORD::
> Maintain justice, and do what is right,
> for soon my salvation will come,
>   and my deliverance be revealed.
>
> Happy is the mortal who does this,
>   the one who holds it fast,
> who keeps the sabbath, not profaning it,
>   and refrains from doing any evil. (Isaiah 56:1-2)[10]

At that outset that summons is not given any particular substance. In the poetry that follows, however, the substance of the summons becomes clear. In Isaiah 56:3-7, obedience consists in a welcome inclusiveness toward eunuchs and foreigners. In 58:6-7, obedience includes justice for the oppressed and sustenance for the poor and the homeless. In 59:8-15, the poetry is preoccupied with justice (vv. 8, 9, 11, 14), peace (v. 8), righteousness (vv. 9, 14), and truth (vv. 14-15). This cluster of terms provides a mandate for the maintenance of a viable neighborly community. And in 61:1-4, the mandate concerns relief for the oppressed and for prisoners in a radical enactment of the Jubilee. In sum, this poetry anticipates a community acutely committed to the enactment of Torah justice.

■ In the tradition of Jeremiah, the new covenant is precisely to the Torah:

> But this is the covenant that I will make with the house of Israel after those days, says the LORD: I will put my law within them, and I will write it on their hearts; and I will be their God, and they shall be my people. No longer shall they teach one another, or say to each other, "Know the LORD," for they shall all know me, from the least of them to the greatest, says the LORD; for I will forgive their iniquity, and remember their sin no more. (Jeremiah 31:33-34)

The premise of a new Torah "within them" is not specified, and the Jeremiah tradition lacks a parallel to the vision of newness in the Isaiah tradition. But because the tradition of Jeremiah is so deeply connected to the book of Deuteronomy, it is most probable that the new obedience concerns adherence to the commandments of Deuteronomy. It is evident, for example, that the tradition of Jeremiah has in the purview care for widows, orphans, and the poor (see 5:28; 7:6; 22:16; on which see Deuteronomy 24:17-22) and specifically alludes to the year of release on which see Deuteronomy 15:1-18. The new obedience is surely the practice of covenantal neighborliness that binds rich and poor into a common practice of "welfare" (*shalom*), for it is such "welfare" that is on the horizon of Israel (see Jeremiah 29:7, 11).

■ In the tradition of Ezekiel, it is promised that Israel will be given by YHWH a heart and a spirit that will cause obedience to be a willing practice in time to come: "A new heart I will give you, and a new spirit I will put within you; and I will remove from your body the heart of stone and give you a heart of flesh. I will put my spirit within you, and make you follow my statutes and be careful to observe my ordinances" (Ezekiel 36:26-27).

Again, there is little specificity to the new obedience. But the tradition of Ezekiel is deeply committed to priestly concerns for cleanliness, purity, and holiness (Ezekiel 36:29):

> They shall never again defile themselves with their idols and their detestable things, or with any of their transgressions. I will save them from all the apostasies into which they have fallen, and will cleanse them. Then they shall be my people, and I will be their God. . . . My servant David shall be king over them; and they shall all have one shepherd. They shall follow my ordinances and be careful to observe my statutes. . . . Then the nations shall know that I the LORD sanctify Israel, when my sanctuary is among them forevermore. (Ezekiel 37:23-24, 28)

In this case, the "ordinances and statutes" likely are the regulations for holiness in the book of Leviticus and the avoidance of pollution and abomination. This account has as its premise a new temple in Ezekiel 40–48, for the Ezekiel tradition anticipates a coming Israel properly at worship.[11] This tradition provides guidelines pertaining to the offering of sacrifices and the celebration of festivals in time to come. The tradition of Ezekiel envisions a properly ordered, symmetrical community (Ezekiel 45:13-17, 18-25).

Though the particulars of the new obedience in Isaiah, Jeremiah, and Ezekiel vary greatly, each of them is rooted in old traditions of command from YHWH. The matter is not different in the Book of the Twelve. After the great oracles of judgment in Hosea, Amos, and Micah, the scroll of the Twelve ends with an anticipation of new obedience:

- Haggai promotes the priestly agenda of cleanness (Haggai 2:11-14).
- Zechariah at the end of the corpus echoes the early prophets in a paradigmatic imperative: "Thus says the LORD of hosts: Render true judgments, show kindness and mercy to one another; do not oppress the widow, the orphan, the alien, or the poor; and do not devise evil in your hearts against one another" (Zechariah 7:9-10).
- And in Malachi, the prophetic corpus, looking well beyond the judgment of the sixth century, culminates with a clear appeal back to the commandments of Moses at Sinai: "Remember the

> teaching of my servant Moses, the statutes and ordinances that I commanded him at Horeb for all Israel" (Malachi 4:4).

The anticipation of Elijah in Malachi 4:5-6 does not at all detract from the core appeal to the Torah of Moses as the defining appeal for Israel's future.

II

In the sapiential materials, obedience is to the sum of Israelite wisdom. It is only late that wisdom comes to be equated with Torah. But long before that convergence, wisdom had discerned YHWH's order of creation that correspondence to the ordering of covenantal life according to the Torah.[12] Thus the rhetoric and the epistemological assumptions of wisdom teaching are very different from those of covenantal Torah. But the substance would seem to be the same. In the completed traditions of wisdom in the Old Testament, that new obedience that takes the world seriously is a powerful dialectic of submissiveness and challenge. That dialectic assures that obedience in Israel is not a flat conformity, but is a dialogical transaction between the *one who orders* and the *one who discerns and practices that order*.

The truth of submissiveness to the *discerned order of creation* permeates the book of Proverbs. While the teaching of the book of Proverbs is the accumulated lore of the community, in canonical form this teaching is presented as a disclosure of YHWH's will for the world. Thus wisdom itself speaks of the choice of life or death that arises with heeding or disregarding wisdom:

> And now, my children, listen to me:
> happy are those who keep my ways.
> Hear instruction and be wise,
> and do not neglect it.
> Happy is the one who listens to me,
> watching daily at my gates,
> waiting beside my doors.
> For whoever finds me finds life
> and obtains favor from the LORD;
> but those who miss me injure themselves;
> all who hate me love death. (Proverbs 8:32-36)

The stark choice is completely parallel to the claim of Deuteronomy 30:15-20, in which obedience is the precondition of life in God's good world. The great threat to life in sapiential teaching is an arrogant autonomy that is sure to be destructive. The alternative to that threat is fear of YHWH, which keeps human freedom as a penultimate possibility:

> Do not be wise in your own eyes;
> fear the LORD, and turn away from evil.
> It will be a healing for your flesh
> and a refreshment for your body. (Proverbs 3:7-8)

Adherence to YHWH is at the same time a shunning of evil. The wisdom teachers in the book of Proverbs assume compliance to their teaching that is equivalent to submission to the truthfulness of YHWH.

But of course such submissiveness contains within itself the seductive temptation to absoluteness in which the interaction of command and obedience can be reduced to formulaic certitude. For that reason the "settled" wisdom of the book of Proverbs can never be read without at the same time attending to the book of Job. The book of Job first of all echoes the book of Proverbs in a flat reductionist way. The "friends of Job" in the book of Job are the teachers of the book of Proverbs who have become overly impressed and excessively convinced by their own teaching. As a consequence they can reverse the formula of sin and judgment from the book of Proverbs to infer causative guilt from Job's suffering (Job 5:17-27; 8:1-7). In the discourse of the book of Job, moreover, Job accepts the premise of the reductionist argument that all true wisdom has already been given in Proverbs: "And he said to humankind, / 'Truly, the fear of the LORD, that is wisdom; / and to depart from evil is understanding' " (Job 28:28; see Proverbs 3:7).

Thus far, as far as Job 31, the poem of Job agrees with the Proverbs. Job is unable to escape the trap of submissive wisdom nor can he break it open. It remains the work of YHWH who speaks in the whirlwind to break open and resist the neat formulaic wisdom shared by Job and his friends. In self-congratulatory boasting, YHWH makes clear that the almighty has no interest in or patience with the detailed moral calculations of conventional wisdom. The self-announcement of YHWH is an invitation for the reader of the book to think and live outside any reductionist wisdom and, by inference, outside any reductionist Torah requirements.

The final utterance of Job in 42:6 is notoriously enigmatic and likely intentionally so.[13] In the end, it is not clear what response is appropriate to the lyrical self-declaration of the God who is beyond moral calculation. A conventional reading of this verse tilts toward a submissive piety. But the verse also seems to permit an ironic reading that functions as an act of defiance. Given that likely enigmatic conclusion to the poetry, it is astonishing that in the end the God of the whirlwind can reject the words of conventional wisdom and can accept Job's utterance as "what is right" (Job 42:7-8). It is plausible, even probable, that YHWH's affirmation of Job is because YHWH welcomes a partner who in dialogue is free and bold enough to challenge and defy, bold enough to sustain attentive interest of the creator God. Thus as Samuel Balentine observes concerning Job 40:15, Job (and by inference all human persons) have been made like Behemoth, fierce, strong, beautiful, ferocious, and majestic.[14] It is likely that the God of the whirlwind in the end acknowledges Job to be precisely such a creature.

Proverbs and Job together provide a model for "knowing in faith" that is variously submissive and disputatious. It was not always the case that the dialectical practice of submissiveness and disputatiousness could be sustained; in the book of Ecclesiastes the dispute has collapsed into resignation. Most remarkably, that resignation that acknowledges inability to know can culminate canonically in a submissiveness that sounds too weary to dispute any longer: "The end of the matter; all has been heard. Fear God, and keep his commandments; for that is the whole duty of everyone" (Ecclesiastes 12:13).[15]

If we trace the sapiential conclusion from Proverbs 3:7-8 through Job 28:28 and eventually to Ecclesiastes 12:13, it is clear that Torah obedience (and its counterpoint in wisdom) is constant. The matter of obedience is not blind conformity but serious engagement with an ultimately mystic creator. What the wisdom teachers find in creation, the Mosaic-prophetic tradition finds focused in covenant. It is clear, of course, that *specificity of covenant* and the *wonder of creation* attest together to the God who will be obeyed. Israel knows, in its very conviction about obedience, that the relationship is not one-dimensional. It is kept open by the daring imagination and venturesome utterance of those whom YHWH commands.

III

The book of Psalms is a book of instruction and worship wherein Israel, in venturesome and lyrical ways, articulates its dialogic, committed, and vexed life with YHWH. As a *book of instruction*, it aims to inculcate Israel, by stylized repeated formulation, into the life of Torah. Thus it is now noticed by scholars that the "Torah Psalms" are strategically placed in the Psalter to provide interpretive guides for its use; and most important, of course, Psalm 1 is placed as an entry point into the Psalter and summons Israel to "meditate upon the Torah day and night" (Psalm 1:2). Patrick Miller has shown, moreover, that the Torah to which reference is made is the tradition of Deuteronomy; thus we may say that the Psalter is the summons to obedience to Deuteronomic Torah.[16]

The Psalter is a *book of worship* of YHWH as the God to whom Israel is utterly committed. The songs of the corpus attest to the singularity of YHWH who is incomparable in power and in compassionate mercy. And in commensurate fashion, as Israel witnesses to YHWH, Israel also witnesses to its own life as a counterpoint to YHWH as "the people of his pasture and the sheep of his hand" (Psalm 95:7).

It is evident that the two primary genres constitute most of the material of the Psalter. On the one hand, the Psalter is a *book of praise* voiced in the recurring genre of hymn.[17] In its praise, Israel exalts in YHWH, attests YHWH's wondrous miracles, steadfast sovereign character, and Israel summons other nations to share in the exaltation and enhancement of YHWH, especially at the expense of rival gods who are doxologically dismissed as powerless, irrelevant, and unworthy of praise (see Psalm 115:3-8). It follows of course that the one celebrated as sovereign is the one to whom Israel is summoned in obedience. The hymns reflect Israel's eager willingness to submit to and conform to YHWH's purposes for life in the world. I have suggested in an earlier discussion, that the Psalter is canonically organized in its movement from Psalm 1 with its Torah accent to Psalm 150 with its lyrical doxology as a movement from obedience to praise (Exodus 24:7).[18]

The same connection of *praise and obedience*, albeit in reverse order, is voiced in Deuteronomy 10:17-22, a passage that is closely parallel to the hymnic rhetoric of the Psalter. That characteristic text begins in a lyrical praise that affirms the sovereignty of YHWH who presides over all other gods: "For the LORD your God is God of gods and LORD of lords, the great God" (Deuteronomy 10:17a-b). The text then moves from doxology to an inventory of YHWH's character as one who practices covenant, especially toward the powerless: "Who is not partial and takes no bribe, who executes justice for the orphan and the widow, and who loves the strangers, providing them food and clothing" (Deuteronomy 10:17c-18).

And then in a movement that we would expect, the text issues a summons for an obedience in Israel that is commensurate with the character that Israel praises: "You shall also love the stranger, for you were strangers in the land of Egypt. You shall fear the LORD your God; him alone you shall worship; to him you shall hold fast, and by his name you shall swear" (Deuteronomy 10:19-20).

The [rhetoric] is completely congruent with the cadences of Israel's hymn and culminates in the assertion, "YHWH is your praise." Thus in the Torah-shaped book of Psalms, the utterance of hymn has immediate and concrete ethical import.

The second most prominent genre of the Psalter is a *lament*, voiced both in personal crisis and in communal need. The primary components of the lament, with enormous rhetorical variation, are the *complaint* that enunciates Israel's circumstance of need and the *petition*, which addresses YHWH with urgency and expects that YHWH will answer with a prompt intervention that will overcome the crisis of life and death. Perhaps the most remarkable feature of the combination of complaint-petition is the visceral assumption (a) that the situation must be freshly described for YHWH and (b) that YHWH may be addressed in urgent imperative as though to command YHWH to act.

Whereas Israel is a gladly submissive voice in the hymn, in the lament there is a provisional role reversal in which Israel (or an individual Israelite) speaks in a *voice of command* and anticipates "obedience" on the part of YHWH in response to the need of Israel. While all petitionary prayer has some dimension of this imperative, in Israel's laments and complaints the rhetoric of command is sharp and intense, so that there is no doubt that by its imperative, YHWH is "ordered" to engage sovereign power and mercy on Israel's behalf:

> Save me, O God, by your name,
>   and vindicate me by your might.
> Hear my prayer, O God;
>   give ear to the words of my mouth. (Psalm 54:1-2)

> Give ear to my prayer, O God;
>   do not hide yourself from my supplication.
> Attend to me, and answer me;
>   I am troubled in my complaint.
> I am distraught by the noise of the enemy,
>   because of the clamor of the wicked.

For they bring trouble upon me,
 and in anger they cherish enmity against me. (Psalm 55:1-2)

Deliver me from my enemies, O my God;
 protect me from those who rise up against me.
Deliver me from those who work evil;
 from the bloodthirsty save me....

Rouse yourself, come to my help and see!
 You, LORD God of hosts, are God of Israel.
Awake to punish all the nations;
 spare none of those who treacherously plot evil. (Psalm 59:1-2, 4b, 5)

It is not self-evident, to be sure, that an urgent address to YHWH in an imperative may be understood as an expectation of divine obedience. And yet I would suggest that it is exactly such daring, demanding engagement with YHWH that is the distinctive mark of Israel's obedience, a distinctiveness already enacted by Moses in his daring petitions to YHWH (Exodus 32:11-14; Numbers 11:11-15; 14:19).

In conventional, flat monarchal monotheism, obedience may be taken as an unquestioning, consistent, submissive conformity to God's mandate. But not so in Israel, because YHWH is not known in Israel to be an unengaged, demanding monarch. Rather YHWH, even as king and judge, is a dialogical, covenant-keeping partner in the life of Israel, a role enacted by YHWH in the Moses narrative of Exodus 32–34. Thus "obedience" is marked, in the Old Testament, by a challenging, insistent engagement that consists partly in *submissiveness* and partly in *challenge*.[19] Thus it is credible to judge that even laments that challenge, demand, question, and protest are acts of obedience, because they take YHWH with complete seriousness and refer all of life back to YHWH and to the covenant Israel has with YHWH.

This dialogic notion of obedience is perfectly lined out in the interface of hymn and lament, a hymn as glad *submissiveness* and lament as urgent *self-assertion*. Taken together they make possible the dynamism of this relationship that has been underway since Sinai. It is of course unfortunate that very much church theology has misunderstood or neglected this dialogic component in obedience and has resulted in a flat and stultifying understanding that negates the openness, vitality, and hard work that belong to covenantal obedience.[20] The interface of hymn and lament are an ongoing work of negotiation between the covenant partners to live a life together, a life that is a complex work of alienation and reconciliation, of trust and challenge, of submission and demand. The Torah focus of the Psalter exhibits the kind of relational engagement that is initiated at Sinai and exposited in the tradition of Deuteronomy.

The *singing of hymns* and the *utterance of laments* together constitute two quite different but powerfully related acts of obedience. The act of praise constitutes obedience that is glad, exalted, and submissive without reservation or qualification. It intends to enhance ("magnify") YHWH amid the other gods and before the nations, fully confident that YHWH's performance of order and miracle is completely reliable. On the other hand, the *act of lament and complaint* is an act of obedience "against the grain," an address of truth communicating in a quite concrete way "the human predicament" to the God of all truth. This act of obedience is submissive only in the sense that it trusts and refers all of life back to YHWH; it is not, however, submissive in any conventional sense but consists in the right to speak to YHWH and the legitimacy of the petitioner before YHWH, right and legitimacy that are grounded in a mutuality of commitments. While *praise as obedience* is a rather obvious performance of faith, it is likely that *lament as obedience* more fully exhibits the relational, dialogical, interactive notion of Israel's life with YHWH. The wonder of such obedience is that YHWH is known as one who characteristically accepts, honors, and responds to such cries of need as an appropriate exhibit of divine sovereignty.

It is the merit of Claus Westermann to have shown that the characteristic and recurring dynamism of the Psalms is the move from lament to hymn, from "plea to praise."[21] Consequently, these two very different acts of obedience are in practice intimately connected to each other. Israel's address to YHWH, as in the cry of Exodus 2:23 that we have discussed earlier, begins with regularity as a cry of need. That cry of need characteristically receives a divine response, so that Israel's prayer often turns abruptly toward praise that is acknowledgment and celebration of YHWH's transformative intervention.[22] The fact that Psalm 88 receives no divine answer and that Job receives a harsh answer of divine self-regard indicates that the pattern can be broken; but the breaking of the pattern only attests to the normative reality of the pattern.

The move from plea to praise is readily recognized in the Psalter; Psalm 22 (familiar in Christian usage because of Jesus' cry on the cross) voices in sequence the cry of need (vv. 1-21a), and a celebrative act of praise (vv. 21b-31):

> But you, O LORD, do not be far away!
>   O my help, come quickly to my aid!
> Deliver my soul from the sword,
>   my life from the power of the dog!
>   Save me from the mouth of the lion! (Psalm 22:19-21a)
>
> From the horns of the wild oxen you have rescued me.
> I will tell of your name to my brothers and sisters;
>   in the midst of the congregation I will praise you. (Psalm 22:21b-22)

More succinctly, the same movement is evident in Psalm 13:

> How long, O LORD? Will you forget me forever?
>   How long will you hide your face from me?
> How long must I bear pain in my soul,
>   and have sorrow in my heart all day long?
> How long shall my enemy be exalted over me?
>
> Consider and answer me, O LORD my God!
>   Give light to my eyes, or I will sleep the sleep of death,
> and my enemy will say, "I have prevailed";
>   my foes will rejoice because I am shaken. (Psalm 13:1-4)
>
> But I trusted in your steadfast love;
>   my heart shall rejoice in your salvation.
> I will sing to the LORD,
>   because he has dealt bountifully with me. (Psalm 13:5-6)

That same movement is reflected in Songs of Thanksgiving:

> You have turned my mourning into dancing;
>   you have taken off my sackcloth
>   and clothed me with joy,
> so that my soul may praise you and not be silent.
>   O LORD my God, I will give thanks to you forever. (Psalm 30:11-12)
>
> Their hearts were bowed down with hard labor;
>   they fell down, with no one to help.
> Then they cried to the LORD in their trouble,
>   and he saved them from their distress;
> he brought them out of darkness and gloom,

and broke their bonds asunder.
Let them thank the LORD for his steadfast love,
for his wonderful works to humankind. . . .

Then they cried to the LORD in their trouble,
and he saved them from their distress;
he sent out his word and healed them,
and delivered them from destruction.
Let them thank the LORD for his steadfast love,
for his wonderful works to humankind. (Psalm 107:12-15, 19-21)

It is evident, of course, that not all hymns follow lament. Many hymns are unqualified acts of praise that have no such statement of need on the horizon (for example, Psalms 100, 103, 117). Such acts of praise simply celebrate the wonder of life generated and guaranteed by the power and fidelity of God. Conversely, there are laments that do not lead to praise, most succinctly Psalm 88.

Nevertheless in the recurring speech patterns of Israel the two governing genres of the Psalter are regularly practiced together in Israel. We may entertain the thought, moreover, that where either occurs without the other the counterpoint may be inferred and is not far from the imagination of Israel. The reason for the inference is that Israel's obedience is characteristically a dialogical one; Israel lives under command from the God of covenant to refer its life fully back to YHWH and, at the same time, to engage fully in self-regard, a self-regard that is grounded in YHWH's reliable commitment to Israel.[23]

In this discussion I have considered the pervasiveness, depth, and rich texture of Israel's vocation as the obedient people of YHWH:

- In prophetic tradition, Israel's failed obedience is voiced, a failure that leads to judgment and punishment. The remarkable dimension of Israel's faith is that after such judgment, Israel is invited, always again, to new obedience, an obedience made possible each time by the fresh willingness of YHWH to restore the relationship by a compelling act of forgiveness: "No longer shall they teach one another, or say to each other, 'Know the LORD,' for they shall all know me, from the least of them to the greatest, says the LORD; for I will forgive their iniquity, and remember their sin no more" (Jeremiah 31:34).
- In sapiential tradition, Israel's obedience is to submit and adhere to the normative order of God's creation, a normative order that has been discerned in wise human reflection and that cannot be violated with

impunity. The remarkable dimension of Israel's obedience, however, is that Israel is not meant simply to conform to that order, but to recognize that that order is not everywhere benign and reliable. Thus the poem of Job articulates a demanding, dissenting obedience that takes God with utmost seriousness, but that will not readily submit to a God who is silent and palpably unfair. The wonder is that such demanding seriousness is received by the Holy One of Israel, in the tradition of Job, as a valued and appropriate mode of faith in YHWH. The God of the wisdom tradition who characteristically accepts submissive conformity is able, on appropriate occasion, to accept dissent as a way of being honored and taken seriously:

> After the LORD had spoken these words to Job, the LORD said to Eliphaz the Temanite: "My wrath is kindled against you and against your two friends; for you have not spoken of me what is right, as my servant Job has. Now therefore take seven bulls and seven rams, and go to my servant Job, and offer up for yourselves a burnt offering; and my servant Job shall pray for you, for I will accept his prayer not to deal with you according to your folly; for you have not spoken of me what is right, as my servant Job has done." (Job 42:7-8)

■ In the book of Psalms, praise is constitutive in Israel by the yielding acts of praise and thanks that rightly honor YHWH's power and fidelity. But the remarkable dimension of Israel's praise is that along with extravagant doxology Israel engages in truth telling about its need and about its impatience with YHWH's silence. Such truth telling that is done with insistent urgency is much expressed in the book of Psalms. Thus the psalmist can ask, "My God, my God, why have you forsaken me? / Why are you so far from helping me, from the words of my groaning?" (Psalm 22:1). In that very asking, however, this accusatory utterance is still and everywhere addressed to "my God, my God." The God accused is the one in whom Israel hopes. Israel can acknowledge that it is YHWH who smites and afflicts:

> I am silent; I do not open my mouth,
>   for it is you who have done it.
> Remove your stroke from me;
>   I am worn down by the blows of your hand. (Psalm 39:9-10)

In the same psalm, however, it is the same God who is the only ground of hope:

And now, O Lord, what do I wait for?
My hope is in you. (Psalm 39:7)

In all of these traditions—prophetic, sapiential, and psalmic—Israel's obedience to YHWH is dialogical in a way that precludes flat, one-dimensional submissiveness. This recognition is definitional for the life and faith of Israel. This feature of covenantal obedience is of enormous importance even though it is so regularly and pervasively misunderstood in contemporary faith, particularly in popular Christian faith. On the one hand, obedience to the God of biblical faith is misunderstood as *one-dimensional submissiveness* that issues in a servile moralism that is sure to produce "false consciousness" and eventually "false selves."[24] On the other hand, in reaction against such servility, there is a huge temptation *to autonomy* of an Enlightenment kind that fails to remember that human freedom and human reason are penultimate and are ultimately referred back to YHWH's sovereignty. The strange interplay of *servility and autonomy* together constitute a betrayal of authentic covenantal obedience. Of course, authentic faith has never forgotten the dialogical reality of obedience; but the distortions of *false submissiveness* and *false freedom* are everywhere apparent, most especially in the contemporary ideological wars in the U.S. church. Israel's most conspicuous conviction is that authentic obedience in a dialogic practice is the most genuine form of freedom, the very freedom intended by the liberating God of the exodus.

CHAPTER ELEVEN

YHWH AS GOD OF THE NATIONS

The covenant at Sinai, which dominates Israel's Torah (Pentateuch), assured that Israel would be a special people as YHWH's covenant partner. The life of Israel, moreover, was to consist in joyous, willing obedience to YHWH's Torah, a tradition of commandments that is constituted by an ongoing dynamic process of interpretation. As Israel entered the land and especially as the monarchy of David settled in Jerusalem, the accent concerning the Sinai covenant changed. As the focus of Israel's imagination shifted *from Sinai to Zion*, the scope of Israel's theological horizon shifted and expanded. Now the Zion traditions of temple liturgy were preoccupied with Jerusalem as the epicenter of all creation from which YHWH governed all the nations of the earth.[1] The temple in Jerusalem came to occupy the center of Israel's theological imagination, for there resided the ark of the covenant, central symbol of the old covenant. At the same time, however, the Jerusalem temple came to be understood as a residence of the cosmic king-god who presided not only over Israel but also over all nations. In the most ambitious theological claim for the temple, Israel stood alongside other peoples in the Jerusalem temple before the Lord of all creation. In terms of actual political practice, the reality of the Davidic monarchy would, of course, have assured a special place to Israel. In theological scope, however, the other nations alongside Israel are very much in purview in the temple.

Most helpful to me has been the interpretive angle of Harmut Gese who proposes that "the Sinai revelation has become the eschatological Zion revelation."[2] Above all Gese stresses, with appeal to Psalm 50, the process of a "new Torah": "Accordingly we can distinguish in the Old Testament between Zion Torah and Sinai Torah. We have found evidence for an eschatological revelation at Zion, and we see that even Torah is drawn into the eschatological dimension. At the conclusion of the process there is a new Torah."[3]

While Gese labels the Torah of Zion as "eschatological," it surely is the case that in cultic performance the Torah of Zion is known to be an actuality and not merely an expectation.

I

We may notice two accents of the New Torah of Zion:

1. In Psalm 96, the temple community celebrated the newly enacted, newly acknowledged, and newly celebrated rule of YHWH over all of the earth. This psalm asserts YHWH's defeat of all of the other gods and then boldly proclaims: "Say among the nations, 'The LORD is king! / The world is firmly established; it shall never be moved. / He will judge the peoples with equity'" (Psalm 96:10). The rule of YHWH is proclaimed "among the nations." What follows is an acknowledgment of the new rule by all creatures, a rule marked by equity, righteousness, and truth (vv. 10, 13).

We may make two observations concerning this temple affirmation. First, scholars dispute whether the Jerusalem claim is eschatological and anticipatory (as Gese) or is a contemporary cultic actualization (so Sigmund Mowinckel). It seems to be neither necessary nor possible to make the "eschatology-cult" issue into an either/or; for in fact it was both, a claim *actualized* and performed in the cult and a claim *yet to be actualized* in the world outside the cult. But, characteristically, practitioners of any cult accept the world "made" in the liturgy and taken to be more adequate to reality than the world "out there."[4]

Second, it is clear that the language of Psalm 96 does not explicitly mention Torah. But the reference to "equity, righteousness, and truth" surely belongs to the world of Torah ordering in which all creation gladly comes under the rule of YHWH and fully intends, in joyous self-actualization, to obey the will and purpose of the creator.[5]

2. The second text to note, cited by Gese, is the promissory text of Isaiah 2:1-4; Micah 4:1-5. The poetic scenario offered in these texts envisions all of the nations streaming to Jerusalem to learn the ways of YHWH and

to receive YHWH's "instruction" (= Torah; Isaiah 2:5). Norman Gottwald has nicely grasped the theopolitical implications of this oracle.

> [The oracle] represents the point of Isaiah's maximum tension with the naïve nationalism which informs most of the enthronement traditions. He envisions a confederation of the peoples of the ancient Near East in which they shall employ the religious traditions and personnel of Zion to adjudicate in their contending claims for justice so that force will no longer be necessary between nations.[6]

II

It is important in doing Old Testament theology to keep in purview the tension between YHWH as the *God of Israel* ("I shall be your God") and YHWH as *God of all peoples*. It is a tension that cannot and must not be resolved, though it is evident that the great weight of the text and of the interpretive tradition is on the side of YHWH as the God of Israel. It is evident that the God of the Bible is no tribal God, even though the God of the Bible has made and can make concrete historical commitments. This tension has been well articulated by John Levenson. Thus Levenson affirms:

1. That the universal rule of God was not displaced by a more particular commitment: "This concept of the universal availability of God and his law remained alive and was never displaced in ancient Israel by more particularistic theologies."[7]
2. That God's attachment to Israel is in some sense instrumental to the larger divine purpose: "The choice itself is neither mysterious nor autonomous. It is subordinate to a larger plan encompassing goals that extend beyond the covenant relationship itself—the essential goals of right action and justice."[8]
3. The divine choice of Israel is not fully understood as instrumental to a larger purpose, but was itself marked by an ultimacy that is not in the service of anything else. Thus any serious interpretation of the Old Testament must reckon with this tension and must pay attention to the ways in which the tension is carried into the New Testament and into Christian tradition.

III

In its fundamental texts, the tension between the *God of Israel* and the *God of the nations* is everywhere apparent:

1. The genealogical mapping of Genesis 9–11 situates Israel amid the nations. Quite clearly YHWH's rule and purposeful governance of history do not engage with Israel in these chapters, but are operative and longstanding before Israel's appearance. By these texts, Israel is situated among the nations, all of whom are in purview of YHWH's purpose.

2. Nowhere is this connection between Israel and the nations more crucial and obvious than in the divine call to Abraham in Genesis 12:1-3. There is no doubt that this startling divine promise focuses upon Abraham and the promise of the land, a promise that has exercised immense influence in the following text. But alongside the promise of the land to Abraham is the promise concerning the other nations: "I will bless those who bless you, and the one who curses you I will curse; and in you all the families of the earth shall be blessed" (Genesis 12:3). As is well known, Gerhard von Rad saw in this text a literary-theological strategy by which the *history of Israel* and the *history of the world* are intimately connected.[9] Beyond this, this text provides important grounds, as Hans Walter Wolf has shown, for the instrumental purpose of Israel in bringing a blessing upon the nations.[10] As Wolf has so nicely exposited, this promise becomes the *leitmotif* for the ancestral narratives (Genesis 18:22; 22:22; 26:4; 28:14), perhaps culminating in Exodus 12:32 wherein even the mighty Pharaoh recognizes Israel to be the source of blessing. The call of God to Abraham is not fully understood without reference to the nations.

3. The exodus narrative and its culmination in Sinai constitute—alongside the ancestral promise—the second root of the divine choice of Israel. And yet even in this primal assertion of the choice of Israel at Sinai, the "others" are on the horizon: "Now therefore, if you obey my voice and keep my covenant, you shall be my treasured possession out of all the peoples. Indeed, the whole earth is mine, but you shall be for me a priestly kingdom and a holy nation. These are the words that you shall speak to the Israelites" (Exodus 19:5-6). Israel is, with the premise of obedience, promised a peculiar status before YHWH.

Yet in the very same sentence, it is affirmed that "the whole earth belongs to me," and surely Moses would affirm with the psalmist: "The earth is the LORD's and all that is in it, / the world, and those who live in it" (Psalm 24:1). That is, the claim not only concerns creation, but the creation of peoples, all of whom are cared for by YHWH and summoned to obedience by YHWH. In the exodus narrative itself, Pharaoh is addressed by YHWH (via Moses) as a recalcitrant vassal who is subject to the will of YHWH and who is expected to obey.[11] Even in the Exodus-Sinai narrative, Israel's most particularistic account of its origin, the other nations are there as well.

4. Still continuing in the pentateuchal text, Patrick Miller has focused on the narrative and poetry in the book of Deuteronomy. He calls attention to "God's other stories" wherein it is indicated that even in the election tradition of Deuteronomy, YHWH is connected to and concerned for other peoples who belong under YHWH's sovereign rule.[12]

IV

The stories of the other peoples are present in the Deuteronomic tradition, but they do not receive primary attention. In the prophetic corpus, the matter is quite different. Here the rule of YHWH over international history is of special importance. In general, the oracles against the Nations concern the arrogance and autonomy of the nations who imagine that they are not subject to the will of the creator.[13] Of special interest in current recent scholarship, the oracles against the Nations in Amos 1–2 exhibit what scholars now want to term *natural law*. By this term, with references that are very different from those of Karl Barth on natural law, scholars mean a tacit requirement of the creator God that is intrinsic to creation itself, even without the revelatory declarations of Sinai. It is observed that in Amos 1–2, the other nations are held accountable in prophetic utterance for their practices of violence, brutality, and inhumanity. It is simply a given of existence in YHWH's world that there are limits to the brutality that can be exercised against the vulnerable. Thus for example, in Amos 1:13 the Ammonites are judged and condemned, "because they have ripped open pregnant women in Gilead." The Ammonites had no access to the Sinai covenant, but the prophetic tradition affirms that YHWH's righteousness, equity, and truth are everywhere operative in creation. Norman Gottwald, early in the scholarly discussion, could conclude:

> For example, if the Israelite social order is the peculiar province of the covenant faith of Israel, how is it possible for Amos to summon Assyria and Egypt to witness and to condemn Israel's inner decay? In some way Amos must have believed also in an inner core of "natural law" which was valid within all societies, but he has omitted all mention of this because it did not directly touch upon his urgent immediate warning to Israel.[14]

> What is astonishing about Amos is not the breadth of his knowledge, which was considerable and doubtless vaster than his brief surviving words indicate, but the scope of the intellectual framework into which he placed all the facts available to him. *The framework was simply that of a single God Yahweh related as it were in two concentric circles to all the peoples of the ancient Near East—at the center to Israel and Judah and on all sides to the peoples of the known world.*[15]

> It is logical to see in Amos solid intellectual foundations for the development of natural law and a genuine religious universalism which forms the matrix of international law.[16]

Gottwald opines that such "universalism" is assumed in Genesis 12:1-3;[17] he notes, moreover, that Andre Neher has connected the Noachic covenant to Amos. [18]

The classic discussion of Amos 1–2 is that of John Barton.[19] Barton seeks to uncover what must have been the popular operative ethical presuppositions of the community of Amos, even if this perspective was never articulated in self-conscious form. He concludes:

> All the nations of the world are bound by certain moral laws and are accountable for their conduct; and Yahweh, the god who chose Israel as his special people, exercises a vigilant control over the way they act, punishing transgressions by causing wars and so destroying sinful nations. Hence the fortunes of all nations are in Yahweh's control, and this control is exercised according to ethical criteria.[20]

The tradition of Isaiah is particularly fruitful for inquiry concerning the intrinsic moral restraints upon the world that are ordered by the creator. I will enumerate a series of texts that makes clear the large horizon of the Isaiah tradition:

1. In Isaiah 10:5-19, the oracle asserts that Assyria, the great superpower of the eighth century, has been mandated to assault "a godless

nation," Israel (v. 6). Assyria, however, misconstrues its mandate from YHWH, acted too brutally against Israel, imagined itself autonomous and uncurbed, and so forfeited its mandate (vv. 7-11, 15). For that reason, "the Sovereign, the LORD of hosts" will now devastate the empire of Assyria (vv. 16-18). The oracle does not speculate on *how* the Assyrians might have known the limit of the divine mandate. It is only clear that the mandate of YHWH was violated because Assyria thought it was autonomous and free to be as brutal as it wanted to be.

2. In Isaiah 14:24-27, "the LORD of hosts" asserts a plan to "break Assyria." It is asserted, moreover, that none can annul the plan or restore YHWH. The oracle clearly assumes YHWH's rule of the nations.

3. The remarkable exchanges between the government of Hezekiah in Jerusalem and the representatives of the Assyrian government in Isaiah 36–37 evidenced that Assyrian imperial policy has failed to reckon with YHWH as a critical and powerful agent in public history.[21] That agency, moreover, is carried by the utterance of the prophet Isaiah (Isaiah 37:22-29). The affront for which Assyria is condemned does not, in this case, pertain to Israel, but the "mocking of the living God" (Isaiah 37:4, 17). That mocking is not verbal but is exhibited in violent policies that lack the restraint willed by YHWH.

4. In Isaiah 47:6-7, in a text that echoes chapter 10, the Babylonian Empire of Nebuchadnezzar is condemned for its abuse of Israel. As the Assyrians in Isaiah 10, Nebuchadnezzar had been given a divine mandate to assault Jerusalem because YHWH was "angry with my people" (v. 6). Nebuchadnezzar acts on the divine mandate, but "showed no mercy" (v. 6) and so is condemned in prophetic utterance to destruction (vv. 11, 14-15). Again the remarkable expectation of prophetic perspective is that Nebuchadnezzar—or any superpower that meets no military resistance—should "show mercy." The assumption of the oracle is that Nebuchadnezzar should have known. The emperor should have known that the real and ultimate governor of human history is a *God of mercy* who will have human agents act in mercy. Thus the very God who *judges* is the God who has *mercy* and all nations must conform to this. To be sure, in Isaiah 10 and 47, the mercy is toward Israel; in the oracles of Amos, by contrast, the anticipated mercy is toward other peoples. But the point is clear enough and is the same in both cases.

5. In Isaiah 42:4, it is asserted that the coastlands "wait for his Torah" and in 42:6-7; 49:6, Israel (or the servant) is to be "a light to the nations." The critical questions on these texts are well known. It is not clear if

"coastlands" refers only to Jews who are now scattered or to all peoples. It is conventional in much Christian interpretation to see this as a reach to the Gentiles. Insofar as that is a proper reading, we can again see that the Torah is offered to and gladly received by the nations, surely the Torah as Gese has urged it, through the majestic vista of the Jerusalem temple.

6. At the extreme of the Isaiah tradition is a most remarkable oracle that anticipates not only the healing of Egypt (Isaiah 19:22), but a final peacefulness among the great centers of power and population in the ancient Near East: "On that day Israel will be the third with Egypt and Assyria, a blessing in the midst of the earth, whom the LORD of hosts has blessed, saying, 'Blessed be Egypt my people, and Assyria the work of my hands, and Israel my heritage' " (Isaiah 19:24-25). This text would seem to be connected to the Jerusalem vision that via Torah "neither shall they learn war any more" (Isaiah 2:4). But there is more than that here. The phrasing attached to the several peoples, "my people, the work of my hands, my heritage" are all special terms for Israel and attest to Israel's peculiar status with YHWH. But here it is anticipated that all of these peoples, most especially the greatly feared superpowers, will receive names and terms that bespeak chosenness by YHWH. In time to come YHWH will have many chosen peoples. Or perhaps better, all peoples will be YHWH's chosen peoples. None of this compromises Israel's status as "my heritage," but in time to come there will be others welcomed alongside Israel.[22]

7. Finally among the Isaiah texts I will mention, Isaiah 45:1 is most remarkable, for Cyrus of the Persian Empire is identified by YHWH as "my Messiah." It is plausible that Cyrus has now displaced the Davidic line that has run out. In such a scenario, YHWH acts in large horizon to accomplish salvific purposes. What had been peculiar to Israel is now "peculiar" to all nations as they come more fully and more directly under the aegis of YHWH.

For the most part, the discussion of the other nations in the Jeremiah tradition is parallel to the claims of the Isaiah tradition.[23] For much of the book of Jeremiah, Nebuchadnezzar and the Babylonians are understood to be agents of YHWH's purpose, which is to defeat Jerusalem. Thus Nebuchadnezzar can be termed by YHWH "my servant" who is chosen for YHWH's purposes (Jeremiah 25:9; 27:6). And yet it is clear that YHWH's utilization of Nebuchadnezzar and alliance with Nebuchadnezzar are quite provisional. When YHWH's intention to punish Jerusalem is completed, Nebuchadnezzar will be rejected by YHWH and will in turn be destroyed (Jeremiah 25:12; 27:7, 22; 51:59-64). All nations are subject to the purposes of YHWH; none may claim to be YHWH's ultimate instrument or YHWH's abiding partner.

While Norman Gottwald has done a careful and compelling study in order to relate the several oracles to geopolitical realities, it is important to recognize that all such prophetic articulation is given in poetry. Such oracles are acts of prophetic imagination, albeit prophetic imagination under the lead of YHWH's self-giving truth. The purpose of such imaginative articulation, even when it can be connected to geopolitics, is to articulate an alternative world, alternative to the given world of brutality in which "might makes right." A key feature of such an alternative vision of reality is that there is a *holy agency* that is not visible in the world of power, a holy agency that is hidden but resolved, not finally to be voided, mocked, or circumvented. This prophetic oracular imagination is not "common sense" reasoning; it begins at a different place, not from sociopolitical analysis, but from liturgic possibility. The decisive agent conjured in the affairs of all peoples is both a constructive force and a curbing limit. The *curbing limit* is to stop the excesses of unbridled power. The *constructive force* is to create time and space and circumstance wherein the covenantal possibility of mercy, justice, and righteousness may be acted out in concrete ways (see Matthew 23:23).

If we consider the "rise and fall" of worldly power traced in the traditions of Isaiah and Jeremiah, then we may conclude that these interpretive trajectories culminate, in the limits of the Old Testament, in the narrative of Nebuchadnezzar in Daniel 4.[24] In that narrative Nebuchadnezzar is the ruler who imagines he is limitless in power; he must, through the course of his deconstruction, learn that "until you have learned that the Most High has sovereignty over the kingdom of mortals and gives it to whom he will" (Daniel 4:32). When Nebuchadnezzar finally and humiliatingly experienced loss of power, his reason returned (v. 34), and he was able to render a doxology appropriate to his penultimate status before YHWH:

> At that time my reason returned to me; and my majesty and splendor were restored to me for the glory of my kingdom. My counselors and my lords sought me out, I was reestablished over my kingdom, and still more greatness was added to me. Now I, Nebuchadnezzar, praise and extol and honor the King of heaven,
>
> for all his works are truth,
> and his ways are justice;

and he is able to bring low
those who walk in pride. (Daniel 4:36-37)

His sin is hubris: "Hybris as we have defined its Old Testament sense is full rebellion against God; the effort to take control of the world and all of life and to do without any God but onself."[25] The prophetic testimony is clear. Nations that engage in hubris expressed in exploitative arrogance will in the end self-destruct. They will not prevail against the intrinsic character of human life in the world that is guaranteed by the creator God.

V

It is clear in both the pentateuchal and prophetic texts that I have cited that Israel's rhetoric concerning the rule of YHWH over the nations is decidedly supernaturalist. That is, YHWH *speaks directly* and *acts directly*. To be sure there are proximate human agents in YHWH's direct action; but nonetheless YHWH is portrayed as agent.

The wisdom traditions are characteristically the most "international" of the textual trajectories of the Old Testament. These texts bear fewer marks of the distinctiveness of Israel or the distinctiveness of its theological rhetoric. Not only are these traditions more easily understood as "international," they are at the same time the least "supernaturalist" in terms of presenting God as an acting agent. Indeed the wisdom traditions can be understood as an attempt to "rationalize" the faith of Israel, that is, to render it sensible and compelling to a learned rationality that is not responsible to the claims of "direct revelation." In the Old Testament itself, the *Zion traditions* are less militant about "direct revelation" than are the Sinai traditions, and for that reason it is cogent to see a connection between the great Jerusalem myth of creation (and the rule of the creator) and the bold sapiential efforts to discern and convey the order of creation.

It is the merit of Klaus Koch to have formulated a notion of the ethical coherence of creation under the rubric of "deeds and consequences."[26] Koch proposes that the world is ordered as God's creation to ensure that certain consequences follow from certain actions. It is not difficult to see that this mode of reason is an attempt at scientific analysis through the notice of recurring patterns of deeds and consequences that establish a probable causative relationship. If the wisdom teachers could discern such cause-effect connections in the created order, then it is clear that such connections are not peculiarly Israelite and do not await revelation at Sinai. Rather, the connections pertained everywhere and can be discerned everywhere. If the connections are guaranteed by the creator, then it follows that all nations live in a venue governed by the Lord of creation. It is on that basis that the prophet Amos, for example, can articulate a connection between the *deeds of brutality* and the *consequences of punishment*, connections that derive from YHWH's governance as creator but that can be accepted on pragmatic grounds without any heavy supernaturalist claim. In such a frame of reference, "natural law" simply means the ordered reality of "nature" (creation), the honoring of which leads to a life of well-being, the violation of which leads to misery and to death.[27]

VI

It is possible to articulate the rule of YHWH over the nations with an intense *supernaturalist* rhetoric as do the prophets, or as a *rationalized* rhetoric that adumbrates a scientific perspective as do the wisdom teachers. Either way, the rule of YHWH over the nations permits four contemporary extrapolations:

1. It is a very long way from *the oracles of Amos* against the nations who are subject to the rule of YHWH to the Helsinki Universal Declaration of Human Rights (1948). And yet a connection is, in the context of this discussion, inescapable. Walter Harrelson has dramatized that implicit connection by placing the Declaration as an appendix to his fine study of the ten commandments. Of that connection, he offers only this comment:

> In that sense, the Bible has much to say about human rights. It is possible to see in the basic understandings of human rights, reflected in, for example, the United Nations' Universal Declaration of Human Rights, a large measure of the biblical understanding of human obligation under God.[28]

The Declaration speaks of "inherent dignity" and "the equal and inalienable right of all members of the human family" that share "a common standard of enhancement for all peoples and all nations." It is of course understandable that the Declaration dare say nothing of any particular theological rootage. It is clear nonetheless that the implicit theological root of the Declaration is not far removed from the Torah of Zion, the wisdom teaching of Israel, and the affirmation that the creator God has set curbs and limits on human brutality and exploitation.

The cycles of state violence through the twentieth century stand as a major challenge to ethical thought. As I write this, the U.S. government—Congress and the White House—are conducting scarcely-to-be-believed exchange about the conditions under which U.S. torture of war prisoners might be constitutionally permissible.[29] Such a contemporary willingness to entertain state barbarism in a constitutional democracy tells powerfully about the urgency of the Declaration of Human Rights. It also invites a fresh reflection on the way in which nation states that are capable of uncurbed hubris still are subject to the nonnegotiable rules and limits of the creator God.[30] There are, so Israel's tradition of moral-theological reflection claims, some matters that are off limits and precluded, no matter what technological capacity is available and no matter what self-justifying ideological self-deception may be offered. That awareness is as "modern" as Helsinki; it is as old as Amos and the wisdom teachings. To "mock the poor" is to "insult their Maker" (Proverbs 17:5). The creator does not look kindly upon being mocked (Isaiah 37:24). Predator nations, even predator superpowers, are not free to prey upon the vulnerable, no matter what military or economic capacity might indicate.

2. Closely linked to the *givenness* of human rights, Paul Kennedy has traced the course of the rise and fall of the major western powers since 1500 C.E.... Spain and Portugal, the Netherlands, Great Britain, and now the United States.[31] Kennedy's argument turns on a calculus of population, territory, and natural resources that belong to a nation state that need to be kept in some balance in order to prosper. It is evident in his analysis that overextendedness in terms of military and economic adventurism has been, characteristically, the cause of the "fall" of every great power. Kennedy is a political scientist and would, of course, make no theological interpretation of the hard case of facts that he presents.

By contrast I am not under those restraints and so may trace out what I think are the implicit theological claims made by Paul Kennedy. The *givenness of limit* is, so Kennedy affirms, a fact of geopolitics, even if it is not obvious to practitioners of state policy. That given limit tells against the autonomy of the state that imagines it is free to do whatever its resources and technical capacity might allow. It follows that an ethical curb on such autonomy is not the special pleading of a "community of revelation"; it is, rather, the available insight of any critical reflection that allows that there is a holy mystery that curbs pragmatic human capacity. There is a givenness! Thus there is a word to Sennacherib of the Assyrians, to Nebuchadnezzar and the Babylonians, and before them, to Pharaoh and the Egyptians. Of course Israel's poets go further and insist that that givenness, guaranteed from the foundation of the world, takes the form of *mercy*.[32] But nation states in their self-confident arrogance are not much prone to mercy. It is well beyond Kennedy to claim mercy as a curb on state power; but the poets in Israel will make precisely such a case. And where such rhetoric cannot be used in policy formation, this curbing reality falls away. In the end, however, the inability to speak of mercy does not in any way vitiate the reality of mercy as a condition for effective policy, for the one who stands behind and over nation states is indeed a God of mercy.

3. From the rhetoric of the prophets to the Helsinki Declaration, the talk is of "human rights." While the matter of a sustainable "natural" environment was not much on the horizon of the ancient poets and not yet in the purview of Helsinki, the same arguments about the violation of human rights pertain to the rights of *creation* and of all of the *creatures*. When the argument is transposed in this way, then the matter is not simply state power against the weak and the vulnerable, but it is the *powerful human agency* against other vulnerable creatures that have no capacity to protect or maintain themselves. That is, it is *human* hubris of a generic variety rather than *national* hubris that is operative; but the point is the same.

The vigorous way in which Alistair McGrath understands "nature" as "creation" is much to the point.[33] Wherein Lynn White has famously faulted the Bible as the basis of the abuse of creation, Cameron Wybrow has made clear that it is Enlightenment rationality—the same Enlightenment rationality that produced nation states—that caused the reification of "nature" as a commodity to be used and exploited.[34] As the nation state may exercise hubris over weaker neighboring states, so the human agent in hubris has taken "nature" to be a usable, inexhaustible resource for human explanation. The wisdom teachers do not venture very far into this question. It is, however, easy enough to extrapolate from what they write to see that it is here, as there, that adventurism of uncurbed autonomy may bring death to "nature" as to humanity.[35]

4. It need only be noted, and scarcely exposited, that at the present time it is the United States that is the primary perpetrator of arrogant autonomy that conducts itself as a predator in the world. It is not, moreover, the *state* that is the lead character in this world assault; it is, rather, the aggressiveness of the multinational *corporations* that, in the name of new markets and new profits, can trample national boundaries and human boundaries, savaging old cultures and dismissing as worthless human persons and human communities that are not economically "viable." The lead role in arrogant autonomy is variously the nation state or the multinational corporation, but the transactions of domination are the same. The issue remains whether the raw exercise of power is subject to intrinsic limits given by the creator God. A focus on corporations, moreover, does not exempt state; for the U.S. military, as support for corporate aggressiveness, is everywhere in the world making way for markets and acquiring an ever more complete monopoly on natural resources, and thereby reducing others to economic bondage in a way not unlike the strategy of Joseph in ancient Egypt.[36]

5. It is the conviction of the prophets and the wisdom teachers in these ancient texts that no drive of arrogant autonomy can finally outflank the holy God; to challenge the holy God is to choose death. That ultimate assurance is at the center of biblical faith. It is perhaps enough to end this particular discussion with this ancient conviction except that we may be bold enough to conclude that contemporary economic-technological capacity has changed not only in degree but in kind. We are then left to wonder and to ask candidly and out loud whether the old verities concerning limits are still reliable. Can autonomous power now destroy the environment? Can uncurbed military-economic aggressiveness in fact brutalize the human community beyond recognition? We do not know, though we have come close to knowing in the twentieth century.

Against that nightmarish "possibility" we have these old texts; they concern the one who laughs at such human posturing:

> The kings of the earth set themselves,
> and the rulers take counsel together,
> against the LORD and his anointed, saying,
> "Let us burst their bonds asunder,
> and cast their cords from us."

He who sits in the heavens laughs;
the LORD has them in derision. (Psalm 2:2-4)

Perhaps the laugh of God in Psalm 2:4 is indeed an "Easter laugh," who taunts death and moves on to life:

Shall I ransom them from the power of Sheol?
Shall I redeem them from Death
O Death, where are your plagues?
O Sheol, where is your destruction?
Compassion is hidden from my eyes. (Hosea 13:14)

Perhaps!

6. Any consideration of the God of the nations will inescapably raise the question of "mission," of bringing the nations to "faith." There is virtually nothing in the Old Testament about the conversion of the nations to Yahwism. Of the great dramatic pilgrimages to Zion in Isaiah 2:1-4, Norman Gottwald can write:

> Yahweh was to serve as the supranational God to whom all nations were to pay allegiance in certain spheres of their life. The terms of the oracle do not require that the confederated nations totally embrace Yahwism.... The confession on the lips of the suppliant nations is a modest one.[37]

The "mission" was not to expand Yahwism as a political reality rooted in Israel. It was rather that the nations should "not learn war anymore," should not continue the long-established brutalizing nature of the nation state. The "conversion" of nation states is not to a religious system but to an alternative ethic that is not based on money and power.

Thus the Old Testament on "God and the Nations" permits a choice and decision that are always to be made again. The choice is enunciated in Jeremiah in an oracle that has the tone of a wisdom saying:

> Thus says the LORD: Do not let the wise boast in their wisdom, do not let the mighty boast in their might, do not let the wealthy boast in their wealth; but let those who boast boast in this, that they understand and know me, that I am the LORD; I act with steadfast love, justice, and righteousness in the earth, for in these things I delight, says the LORD. (Jeremiah 9:23-24)

Here the contrast is plain and simple: *wisdom/might/wealth* or *steadfast love/justice/righteousness*. It is an old choice in Israel, one that nations and corporations must make every day. While these two verses in Jeremiah are not directed to nations, the following two verses draw the choice of verses 23-24 toward public politics:

> The days are surely coming, says the LORD, when I will attend to all those who are circumcised only in the foreskin: Egypt, Judah, Edom, the Ammonites, Moab, and all those with shaven temples who live in the desert. For all these nations are uncircumcised, and all the house of Israel is uncircumcised in heart. (Jeremiah 9:25-26)

In these lines, Israel is unlike the other nations named, all of whom are uncircumcised; except . . . at the end of the verses, "All the house of Israel is uncircumcised in heart." Israel is incapable of listening and incapable of obeying. Israel in this text is just like all other peoples, prone to be autonomous and so resistant to the Torah claims of covenant. Obedience is an alternative to the usual ways of nation states. Nation states who go their autonomous way are, so says this textual tradition, sure to fail. History, if it could speak, would say that such nation states may not fail; but they will surely brutalize the neighborhood so that no one can "learn peace anymore."

VII

The claim that the nations over which YHWH presides must obey YHWH is best articulated in the Noachic covenant of Genesis 9:8-17.[38] The biblical text attests that after the flood, God the creator makes a covenantal commitment to remain faithful to creation so that "all flesh" may endure and prosper:

> This unilateral and unconditional covenant is an obligation that God alone assumes regarding the future of the created order; remembering this covenant is exclusively a divine responsibility and it will never need to be renewed. The point may be stated in these terms: "the creator God has a relationship of love and faithfulness toward the earth and says a fundamental and irrevocable 'yes' to *this* earth and *these* human beings." This covenant will stand forever and be as good as God is, and so human beings can rest back in its promises. This covenant will

> remain in force regardless of how human beings respond to it. Even more, God will uphold this covenant independent of the community of faith, quite apart from Israel's life and mission; all human beings, whether persons of faith or not, experience the effects of this divine promise. . . . God's good creation, necessary for the very life of "all flesh," will continue to thrive come what may in the way of sin and evil. It is helpful to say that "It is only by God's covenant with Noah, God's self-obligation to keep the creation going despite the evil in it, that one can trust the creation and its orders."[39]

It is clear that God the creator has made a commitment of fidelity to the nations that is structural to creation and that antedates, in biblical tradition, the appearance of Israel.

Whereas the covenant with Noah in Genesis 9:8-17 would seem to be unconditional, in rabbinic Judaism the interpretive tradition has been able to formulate seven new commandments of YHWH for which all human persons are accountable.[40] David Novak has provided a full exposition of the seven commandments and traced the way in which they emerged in the ongoing interpretive work of Judaism. This extrapolation from the biblical text is a means whereby Judaism can formulate human responsibility to God outside of Judaism and can acknowledge that human responsibility is not dependent upon the Sinai revelation. *Mutatis mutandis*, the *covenant with Noah* and the *Helsinki Declaration of Human Rights* move exactly in the same direction. Human persons and human power are rendered penultimate before the Holy Mystery who valorizes all creation, human and nonhuman.

V. THE HOPE OF ISRAEL AND THE HOPE OF THE WORLD

CHAPTER TWELVE

THE LAND PROMISES

The great gift of Jews to the world is the practice of hope. The Jewish practice of hope is rooted in the Old Testament that is indeed a book of hope. That book witnesses to a God who is future-creating, who promises, creates, and gives new offers of life in the world that are not derived from or extrapolated from the past, but are genuine newnesses that arise "fresh from the word" and from the faithful action of YHWH. In the long intellectual history of the West, the Jewish gift of *hope* stands in powerful tension with the Greek gift of *order* that offers coherence and continuity but imagines no agency that can give a *novum*.

It is possible to situate hope, that is, the possibility of a future, in a *quid pro quo* of more reasoning. In the tight logic of covenant in Deuteronomy or the "deeds-consequences" assumption of Wisdom teaching, good futures arise from good conduct (obedience) and result as an almost automatic outcome of the performance of duty.[1] This logic is articulated, for example, in Deuteronomy 11:26-28: "See, I am setting before you today a blessing and a curse: the blessing, if you obey the commandments of the LORD your God that I am commanding you today; and the curse, if you do not obey the commandments of the LORD your God, but turn from the way that I am commanding you today, to follow other gods that you have not known." The same assumption permeates the book of Proverbs: "The good obtain favor from the LORD, / but those who devise evil he condemns" (12:2).

In this mode of reasoning, possible futures are limited to and controlled by one's own performance.[2] But such a way of thinking and hoping is quite limited; it does not begin to suggest the reach and deep capacity of ancient Israel for hope.

By hope in the Old Testament and in Judaism, rather, is meant trust in the fresh, generous capacity of God to "accomplish abundantly far more than all we can ask or imagine" (Ephesians 3:20), the gift of a goodness beyond anything that present circumstance might offer or indicate.

I

It is worth a short pause to reflect on the ways in which hope has become critical in Old Testament interpretation and, consequently, in Christian theology. Here I will mention three decisive turns in interpretation:

1. Albrecht Alt observed a decisive contrast between the gods of the land who are attached to particular places (sanctuaries) and "the gods of the fathers" (Abraham, Isaac, and Jacob) who are attached to no place but are committed to go with and lead the ancestors into new places.[3] From this Alt sees that these several "gods" in the book of Genesis, antecedents to YHWH, are situated, according to the sagas, in time and not in space, and because in time are open to new times and new futures. Thus the "gods of the fathers" in Genesis are open to new times and lead Israel into the future. This capacity to move into new times is signaled already in the initial promise of YHWH to Abraham, to lead "to the land that I will show you" (Genesis 12:1). From this it is evident that the God of the Old Testament is a God who leads his people always to new places, with the promise that the new place will be one of *shalom*.

2. Gerhard von Rad, in his magisterial interpretation of *the Hexateuch*, showed that the literature from Genesis through Joshua is composed as a great arc of "promise to fulfillment."[4] On the one hand, von Rad observed that Genesis 12:1-3 contains the three promises that will propel and order the ancestral narratives.[5] On the other hand, in an interpretive tour de force, von Rad saw that Joshua 21:43-45 is a passage complementary to Genesis 12:1-3 that reports that YHWH has indeed kept all of the old promises.[6] The connection between *the promise of Genesis* 12:1-3 and the *fulfillment of Joshua* 21:43-45 is a major theological maneuver that required both an affirmation of YHWH's hidden governance in history and the recognition of David as the fulfillment of Abraham:

> The work of the Yahwist must be interpreted in the light of two basic facts: first the new-found recognition of the hidden activity of God in

history, secondly the relevance of the ancient territorial claims to the time of David and later. We have already seen how God's control of history is depicted only in the form of a hidden guidance, a notion totally foreign to cultic thought. If we now read the remarkable conclusion of the Yahwist's work, the lists in *Judges* I, we are at once aware of the relevance which these apparently remote memoranda of territorial history must have had for David's contemporaries and their successors.

> No one could read these stereotyped descriptions of the as yet unoccupied territories without reflecting that God had not in fact left the matter in this state of semi-fulfilment. He had continued his care for Israel and had kept all his promises, even though it was not in the time of Joshua, but not till in the time of David that this was to be seen. That is what the Yahwist's restrained mode of presentation actually invites us to read between the lines at the end of the work.[7]

At the end of his discussion, von Rad grows eloquent in making very large claims that the connection of promise and fulfillment is not only a statement about Israel, but is a statement about the world under the rule of a promise-making, promise-keeping God:

> From the creation of the world onwards, what a remarkable road, what vicissitudes, what a wealth of divine ordinances and plans lead to this one goal—the Settlement! But then the Hexateuch is not solely concerned with the religion of Israel, nor even with claiming for God all human allegiance: it aims to lay a foundation for God's kingdom on earth, and to lay it on the bedrock of all human existence.[8]

3. With frequent citations of Gerhard von Rad, Jürgen Moltmann (with important reference with Ernst Bloch) moved the conversation about promise from the realm of exegesis to Christian systematic theology.[9] Moltmann's great contribution was to show that the future-making promises of God are not to be slotted in systematic theology into a specific "doctrine" of "eschatology," but are in fact the substance of the entire project of faith. Thus Moltmann worked out in contemporary form what was surely inchoate in von Rad, that the readiness of Israel to trust in God's future constitutes the crucial theological matter of Old Testament faith.

As an addendum to the accomplishment of Moltmann, special attention may be given to *Man and His Hope in the Old Testament* by Walther Zimmerli published in 1968, three years after Moltmann's *Theology of*

Hope.[10] Zimmerli's initial page sets the context for the issue of hope in the midst of the "post-war years" that "create a new hearing for the existentialist understanding of man with its experience of anxiety and vulnerability":

> What is there about the nature of man? Is it not peculiarly marked by an existence toward death, a transiency in which man can only be said really to live in the decision of the moment? Is there any real continuity to historical life beyond the moment of decision? In the light of all this, the question about the possibility of a future for mankind must be asked in a new and more fundamental way. Does man, so deeply threatened in his own existence, confronted by new and all-embracing threats, hitherto unknown, arising as they do out of all the possibilities presented him by science and technology, seriously possess the possibility of a future and a hope?[11]

Zimmerli begins his discussion by appeal to Ernst Bloch, a statement that is accompanied by a citation of Moltmann's work:

> In this situation Ernst Bloch's great philosophical masterpiece, *Das Prinzip Hoffnung*, dealing as it does not only with mankind but also with his environment, including the surrounding natural world, its history and predisposition towards a future and towards hope, fell into well-prepared soil. This book, so richly illustrated from the whole intellectual history of mankind and not least with special reference to the Old Testament, quickly stirred up a lively discussion, particularly in the theological arena.[12]

At the end of his book, Zimmerli engages Bloch in greater detail, with particular reference to Bloch's identification of the God of Israel as *Deus Spes.*[13] Before he finishes, however, Zimmerli notices the inadequacy of Bloch's theological understanding, for Bloch makes *hope* into God, rather than *God* as the source of hope. Whereas Bloch appeals to Job as "an exodus from God," Zimmerli rightly shows that in the Old Testament it is God who is the ground of hope, for hope without God is a fantasy:

> Where this biblical God is seen, then out of the transient God with futurity as his characteristic mode of being, out of the *Deus Spes*, there arises the *Deus Spei*. This God, whose characteristic mode of being is "the first and the last", leads into a future and into the newness of the new creation, the new heaven and the new earth, into that genesis at the end. He leads into the future, which to use Bloch's beautiful con-

> cluding word, word for word in its first half, we will happily describe as "that which everyone saw in childhood but no one ever really inhabited: home."[14]

I take the trouble with Moltmann and Bloch, whose discussions lie beyond textual exposition as such, in order to indicate the ways in which the exegetical work of von Rad and Zimmerli has become pivotal for the larger theological discussion. Zimmerli, of course, is right to suggest that the climate of despair in the mid-twentieth century is indeed a crucial factor in understanding the rise of hope as a theological accent, a factor Moltmann acknowledges by reference by his own experience of the war.

II

It is important at the outset of our larger discussion of *promise* to be clear and precise about the claim of faith. *Promise* is an *utterance*, a *vow*, an *oath*. It is a word spoken to which the speaker is then committed. It is important that the Jewish tradition focuses upon *utterance*, whereas Greek tradition focuses upon *idea* and *thought*. The God of the Bible is one who speaks and who makes promises. The hope of Israel is the conviction that God's utterance is trustworthy and that God will do what God says. The vexation of Israel, most particularly in its petitionary prayers and protesting laments, is the question whether God is reliable and whether God will do what God says. It is obvious that the data of Israel's history is mixed; while there are fulfillments of promises to be celebrated, there is ample evidence to the contrary. Hope then is the human-Israelite response of continuing to trust in the utterance when the data may convince otherwise.

The utterance of *YHWH as a promise that educes hope* focuses upon two larger questions: (1) What is promised? (2) To whom is the promise addressed?

1. *What is promised?* Like many commentators, von Rad had seen that the initial address to Abraham in Genesis 12:3 contains three promises, a great nation, a land, and a blessing to the nations.[15] In the sagas of the book of Genesis, the critical preoccupation is that the family should have a *son* who would be an *heir* into the next generation. If the promise of *son* is as *heir*, then it is cogent to conclude that of all of the promises the central promise is *land*, a particular piece of real estate to which the

community has primal claim. The great propensity of Christian theology has been in the spiritualizing direction, and therefore it must be accented that the initial promise is one of *materiality*, a bodily communal existence in the world, a conviction that is belatedly expressed in the Christian creed as "communion of saint . . . the resurrection of the body." The intense materiality of God's promises looms over the whole of the Old Testament.[16]

2. *To whom is the promise addressed?* It is tautological to say, but nonetheless important, that the promise of the land is made to those who are without land and who wait with eager longing for the gift of land, since characteristically such populations have been unable to secure land for themselves. While the historical-sociological realities behind the Old Testament are much in dispute, we may identify four candidates in the Old Testament to whom the divine promise of land most plausibly is addressed:

a. *Nomads*. The older tradition of Old Testament interpretation, following the story line of the Bible, assumes that the promises are made to land-hungry nomads who yearned to enter the land for the sake of a better life and that YHWH is allied with the nomads in their hunger for land. The nomads, semi-nomads, or pastoral nomads were endlessly a source of disturbance and threat to the more settled order of the economy. While there are no doubt traces of pastoral nomadism behind the biblical narratives, at the present time this identification of the landless is not much in favor in scholarship. The term *nomad* has taken on a more-or-less romantic dimension that is unhelpful in appreciating the seriousness of the land issues. Beyond that, it is now less than clear that the entry into the land was accomplished by an outside population.

b. *Slaves*. The narrative of the exodus of course is preoccupied with state slaves in the Egyptian imperial system. Because the historicity of the exodus is now uncertain, too much should not be made of the historical specificity of the narrative. Without that specificity, however, the term *slave* may be properly used to identify cheap, exploited labor that was exceedingly vulnerable and at the mercy of the political economic power, which it could not well resist. It is possible to transpose the notion of "Egyptian slavery" into cheap labor in the Canaanite city-state system. In that system as well, such vulnerable laborers must have yearned for the security of property that land ownership would have guaranteed.

c. *Peasants*. If we transpose "Egyptian slave," as was just suggested, into Canaanite cheap labor, then we may judge that the land promises are addressed to such cheap and vulnerable labor that was dependent upon and exploited by the city-state system. As is always the case with unprotected labor, such peasantry worked to produce surplus wealth for others, the benefit of which they themselves could never enjoy.

d. *Exiles*. If we follow the current near consensus that the final form of the Old Testament text is accomplished in the sixth century exile or just after, then we may imagine that the land promises in the final form of the text are addressed to displaced and deported Jews who have been scattered into other lands and who yearn for a return home to the land. Even if the land promises are much older, in such a circumstance of the sixth century they could be re-heard in a second listening. The promises, then, are not addressed to an older population of nomads or slaves or peasants, but are addressed precisely to the Diaspora that awaits homecoming.

It is not necessary or possible to be precise about the sociology of the process of land entry. It is enough to conclude that the promises, underived from anywhere except the utterance of a future-creating God, were recurrently welcomed and received by those who are without hope in the world. It is they who find in the divine utterance a new worldly possibility for security and prosperity that in no other way would ever be granted them. The promise is not to be understood, first of all, as a great theory or as an abstract formulation, but is to be heard—and understood as heard—quite concretely as a chance in the world where there was no chance, given by a God who creates "a way out of no way."[17]

III

The divine promise of land to Israel has been thoroughly reviewed by Claus Westermann and well summarized by David J. A. Clines.[18] Of these several promises given to the several generations in various parts of the ancestral tradition, I will comment quite selectively on the following texts:

1. In the book of Genesis the promise is reiterated to Isaac (Genesis 26:3) and Jacob (Genesis 28:13), but clearly it is to Abraham that the primal promise is given:

■ Genesis 12:1-3, as we have seen, is a programmatic text for the land of promise. In the Abraham narrative, everything depends upon a son born to the barren mother, or there will be none to whom to give the land. Westermann has observed that the promise of the son in Genesis 18:1-15 is intrinsic to the family narrative so that this text is the "crucial starting point" for the connection between family sagas and the promise narrative.[19]

■ Genesis 15:18-19 is a pivotal but much contested text. YHWH makes a covenant with Abraham and promises land. Of special note here is the claim of land as "Greater Israel" from Egypt to the Euphrates. The land promise is specific and self-conscious, compared to most other promises made to Abraham.

■ Genesis 17:8 offers the land promise in the Priestly tradition. Here the specificity is "the land of Canaan." A special note is the characteristic priestly qualifier, "to perpetuity."

■ One other text merits close attention. Genesis 23 narrates the process by which Abraham purchased a burial plot for Sarah upon her death. The narrative offers an entertaining account of polite, playful, cunning bargaining whereby Abraham acquires the land from the Hittite at Machpelah. It could, of course, be that the narrative is simply about the acquiring of a burial plot. More likely this narrative attests—without mentioning the land promise—the legal way whereby Abraham becomes the owner of record for the land and holds title. To be sure the narrative concerns only a small piece of real estate; that legally acquired property, however, may be representative of Abraham's entitlement to the entire land.

2. In Exodus 3:8, 17; 6:8 the land promise is reiterated to the slave community in Egypt. The tradition is effective in linking the ancestral promise to the narrative of emancipation, thus creating the credo linkage of "out of slavery" and "into land." Emancipation from Pharaoh to land is an opportunity to escape the role of exploited, vulnerable labor, a primary impetus of the plot.

3. In the spy narrative of Numbers 13–14, the goal of the land of promise is central to the plot. As I have suggested earlier, it is plausible that *wilderness* is to be understood as a cipher for *exile* in the final form of the text. If so, then this narrative may function, in a second reading, as a tale of restoration to the land from exile (Ezekiel 47:13–48:29).

4. The tradition of Deuteronomy is replete with references to land.[20] But the tradition of Deuteronomy revises the land promises so that reception and retention of the land is intensely linked to Torah obedience. Thus the land as free gift is now given conditionally, with the inference that disobedience will lead to land loss:

> Hear therefore, O Israel, and observe them diligently, *so that* it may go well with you, and *so that* you may multiply greatly in a land flowing with milk and honey, as the LORD, the God of your ancestors, has promised you.... This entire commandment that I command you today you must diligently observe, *so that* you may live and increase, and go in and occupy the land that the LORD promised on oath to your ancestors.... Keep, then, this entire commandment that I am commanding you today, *so that* you may have strength to go in and occupy the land that you are crossing over to occupy, and so that you may live long in the land that the LORD swore to your ancestors to give them and to their descendants, a land flowing with milk and honey. (Deuteronomy 6:3; 8:1; 11:8-9, italics added)

The transposition of the *land promise* into a motivation for *Torah obedience* became central to Old Testament theology and would become the ground for prophetic speeches of judgment. *Land* joined to *Torah* now becomes crucial for Israel's faith and provides a context for the formulation of exilic theology.

IV

It is clear that the land promise is shaping the future for Israel, a claim attested in the fact that the Hebrew Bible ends with a mandate to "let him go up" and into Judah and Jerusalem:

> In the first year of King Cyrus of Persia, in fulfillment of the word of the LORD spoken by Jeremiah, the LORD stirred up the spirit of King Cyrus of Persia so that he sent a herald throughout all his kingdom and also declared in a written edict: "Thus says King Cyrus of Persia: The LORD, the God of heaven, has given me all the kingdoms of the earth, and he has charged me to build him a house at Jerusalem, which is in Judah. Whoever is among you of all his people, may the LORD his God be with him! Let him go up." (2 Chronicles 36:22-23)

This is the ultimate hope of the Hebrew Bible.

From this pivotal hope that keeps biblical faith thoroughly materialistic and grounded in historical reality, we may draw three conclusions:

1. The promise of land is so decisively foundational that it is impossible to think of Israel in the Old Testament apart from the land.[21] The actual reception of the land (on whatever theory of "conquest") is a

process permeated with violence, because no people has ever willingly given up the land, and the land of promise, from the beginning of Israel's horizon, was already occupied (see Genesis 12:6). The power of the promise in the imagination of Israel, however, more than overpowers the reported brutality on the ground, the violence seemingly taken as an inescapable dimension of the promise addressed to the materiality of historical existence. That the promise concerns such historical materiality assures that the land tradition will be characteristically violent.

As the reception of the land occupies Israel's imagination, so the loss of the land, the process of displacement, exile, and the enigma of Diaspora Judaism are decisive for the canon of the Old Testament. Indeed if it is correct, as according to current critical judgment, that the final formation of the Pentateuch occurred during the sixth century exile, then it is unmistakable that the canon functions as a pastoral resource in the midst of land loss.[22] And as we shall see in the next chapter, the reality of land loss is the matrix for a new wave of prophetic promises concerning restitution of the land, of which Ezekiel 37:13-14 is perhaps the most poignant: "'And you shall know that I am the LORD, when I open your graves, and bring you up from your graves, O my people. I will put my spirit within you, and you shall live, and I will place you on your own soil; then you shall know that I, the LORD, have spoken and will act,' says the LORD."

The Old Testament is very much preoccupied with the gift of land, the loss of land, and the prospect of restoration to the land. To be sure, the emergence of Diaspora Judaism, most especially in Babylon and Egypt, made it both necessary and possible to construe and imagine a Judaism that was funded primarily not by anticipations and promises of land, but by the practice and study of the Torah.[23] But even when Diaspora Judaism focuses on Torah rather than land, there is no doubt that a focus back toward the land, and specifically toward Jerusalem, is definitional for faith and piety:

> Regard your servant's prayer and his plea, O LORD my God, heeding the cry and the prayer that your servant prays to you today; that your eyes may be open night and day toward this house, the place of which you said, "My name shall be there," that you may heed the prayer that your servant prays toward this place. Hear the plea of your servant and of your people Israel when they pray toward this place; O hear in heaven your dwelling place; heed and forgive. (1 Kings 8:28-30)

Thus even for those not in the land or intending to return to the land, the dialectic of *land and Torah* is decisive.[24]

2. It is entirely possible to do Old Testament theology and stay within the Old Testament itself concerning the question of land. As soon as one steps outside the text and makes a move toward contemporary interpretation, however, one enters a problematic zone of immense tension. And yet it seems likely that it is irresponsible not to move toward contemporaneity, for the claims of the land of promise are of enormous power and impetus in contemporary life, not only in the Near East but by extrapolation for more general questions of peace and war. There is no doubt that the old land promises are of profound importance for contemporary Judaism and for the state of Israel. But there is also no doubt that the transposition of ancient land promises into the contemporary service of the state of Israel, with all of its military capacity, is a bold interpretive maneuver that is not (and I think cannot be made) in innocence without ideological self-awareness. It is clear that the religious claim of Judaism and the political-military claims of the state of Israel overlap in important ways, but they are not coterminous or synonymous. The transposition from one to the other involves an interpretive filtering through the mid-twentieth century *shoah* and the land claims are now invested with loss and fear and a sense of victimization that give warrant for ideological claim. The ideological claim is not that the state of Israel has a right to exist, as does every state, but that the state of Israel has a right to exist because of old land promises. A Gentile interpreter must tread very gently, for this is a claim that is not fully penetrable to a non-Jew. But even Gentile interpreters can see that the land ideology now serves military Zionism and has become a warrant for aggressive militarism that is the counterpoint to Arab resistance to the state of Israel.

Regina Schwartz, from a Jewish perspective, offers a knowing and harsh critique of the ideology of the land:

> Despite the haunting protests that frequent the biblical narratives against Israel ever becoming a nation "like the nations," and despite the frequent celebrations of nomadism that punctuate the narratives, ancient Israel has bequeathed to later generations in far-flung climes the authoritative grand myth that will be used and misused by nations, ethnic groups, and religious communities for their own purposes. [25]

But because Schwartz is interested in how power and ethics are interrelated, she makes the judgment:

> The difficulty of holding onto the land, even land bequeathed in perpetuity by Permanence itself, is not solved by recourse to transcendence after all. Instead, that inevitable precariousness is woven into a biblical theology in which the land is in serious jeopardy if Israel does not obey her god. Fidelity to the one God persistently frames the discourse of land.[26]

On her reading, the power to take and hold the land is made dependent, especially in the conditionality of Deuteronomic theology, upon fidelity. It is also clear, however, that ethics can finally be shaped, as it is in much "patriotic" U.S. Christianity, so that it serves power interests. And so she concludes, "Whether they were conquerors or oppressed victims seeking liberation, they have bequeathed a myth to future generations that is ethically problematic at best, a myth that advocates the wholesale annihilation of indigenous peoples to take their land."[27]

From a Christian perspective with an emphatic attentiveness to Palestinian claims, Gene March observes that the fruition (and maintenance) of the state of Israel concerns *realpolitik* that cannot trade on biblical promises:

> Modern Israel was so named with the deliberate intention of claiming for itself the legacy of ancient Israel, the rightful reconstitution in Palestine of a long-absent people. Some Jews may actually be able to trace their lineage back to ancient Israel, though this is highly unlikely. But modern Israel is a new geo-political organization fashioned for the most part in the past fifty years. That it is situated on land once occupied by another Israel is true, but that does not mean that when we read Israel in the Bible we should automatically and rightly think of modern Israel as the continuation of the ancient people. It is fair to say that modern Israel was created to provide haven for Jews and a place where Judaism could be lived without hindrance. . . . Israel is not biblical Israel, and any rights held by biblical Israel do not belong to modern Israel. The promises and the relationship with God claimed by biblical Israel are now part of the legacy of both Judaism and Christianity. When we read the Bible, we must be quite clear that its Israel is not the modern nation.[28]

The separation that March makes between biblical claims and the present state of Israel is, of course, a separation that not many Jews would accept in the current environment of passionate ideology. It is enough now for our purposes to notice that profound problematic, so profound that it is difficult for Jews and non-Jews (perhaps especially Christians) to converse on the subject. We simply mark it as an abiding issue, one that concerns Jews and non-Jews, but also an issue about which Jews themselves are in dispute.

Michael Prior, more than anyone else, has considered the way in which land promises have been turned to contemporary ideological service. Prior is alert to the ideological dimension of the land promises both in the formation of the text and in their contemporary interpretive force. He situates his critique of the *function* of the land traditions in the critical awareness that the land policies likely are formulated quite late and are certainly not linked to any historical "facticity." Of the biblical text itself and its continuing authority, Prior judges:

> Not only do these traditions have the capacity to infuse exploitative tendencies in their readers, but they have in practice fuelled virtually every form of militant colonialism emanating from Europe, resulting in the sufferings of millions of people, and loss of respect for the Bible. And yet, as we shall see, until recently the theme of land has been neglected in biblical scholarship.[29]

Prior's assessment and critique of biblical scholarship—including the work of this author—concerns the way in which scholarship has "innocently" signed on for the ideological slant of the textual tradition and gives the benefit of the doubt to the claims of the tradition in a largely uncritical way. Prior concludes:

> The absence in biblical scholarship of concern for "the natives" reflects the deeply ingrained Eurocentric, colonialist prejudice which characterises virtually all historiography, as well as that discipline itself (see Whitelam 1996a, 1998 and Prior 1997a, 1998a). An exegesis that is not sensitive to the dispossessed people is an accomplice by omission in the act of dispossession. In the light of the biblical exegesis discussed above, one speculates as to the relationship between epistemology and the moral character of the exegete.... Most commentators are uninfluenced by considerations of human rights, when these conflict with a naive reading of the sacred text, and appear to be unperturbed by the text's advocacy of plunder, murder and the exploitation of indigenous peoples, all under the guise of fidelity to the eternal validity of the covenant of Sinai.[30]

From that critique Prior issues an important challenge to scholars:

> Biblical scholarship must set its own house in order by articulating ethical criteria by which dispositions unworthy of a civilised person may not be accorded a privileged place as part of a sacred text.... It is high time that biblical scholars, Church people, and Western intellectuals read the biblical narratives we have discussed "with the eyes of the Canaanites."[31]

Thus far I have considered the centrality of land promises to the Old Testament and the spin-offs of these promises for continuing and contemporary Jewish life. Now I want to consider how those same land promises have reached beyond Jewish horizons in the service of other peoples as well.

On the one hand, there can be little doubt that the exodus-land traditions have provided a text that has funded many contemporary liberation movements. John Levenson has warned against careless appropriation of the "liberation" texts.[32] Levenson is concerned with two accents. First, the exodus-land tradition is *peculiarly Jewish* and must not be reduced to a generic principle that is readily applicable everywhere. Second, the emancipation from Egyptian slavery is not to a kind of an Enlightenment freedom; it is, rather, to *a new obedience* in the covenant at Sinai. And when the exodus-land traditions are taken up with reference to Enlightenment freedom, they are distorted and the intense focus on Israel is forfeited. Levenson rightly resists such "liberationist supersessionism."[33] But after he has said all of that, Levenson ends his statement with an acknowledgment that the particular is indeed paradigmatic for other uses:

> But this does not mean that the exodus is not about liberation. The liberation of which the exodus is the paradigmatic instance is a liberation from degrading bondage for the endless service of the God who remembers his covenant, redeems from exile and oppression, and gives commandments through which the chosen community is sanctified.[34]

Such a way of thinking both preserves the Jewish particularity of the tradition and acknowledges the remarkable generativity of the tradition for other communities and movements beyond Judaism.

I understand Levenson to acknowledge that there is a legitimacy about the appeal of other liberation movements to this tradition, precisely because every liberation movement, notably those in Central America and Eastern Europe, seeks to recover land and to wrest land away from rapacious economic-military systems that in one way or another may be marked as pharaonic.

In taking up Levenson's acknowledgment that tradition is "paradigmatic," we may consider the work of Michael Walzer. It is Walzer's thesis that the exodus-land narrative has become the script for the great social revolutions in the world both Leninists and social democratic.[35] Walzer notes, as Levenson accents, that exodus is a departure from *state slavery* and not *market slavery*, though in the post-industrial world it is not so obvious where one of these stops and the other one starts.[36]

The several interpretive trajectories of Levenson, Walzer, and Said attest, in their vigorous disagreement, that the interpretation of these biblical traditions in a post-colonial context is endlessly problematic. It is evident, in any case, that the revolutionary impetus that all parties find in the text will not be contained in any of our preferred readings. Others, in other contexts, "take up and read," and find energy, imagination, and courage for the crisis of the land. All around the world, not only in the Near East, but in Eastern Europe, in Central America, in Northern Ireland, and in Sri Lanka, the struggle is for land. The daring thing about the biblical tradition is that the God of heaven is known to be a party to the disputes of the earth. It is no wonder that Karl Marx could so boldly see, in his early statement the connection between religious claims and the political economy: "The criticism of heaven is thus transformed into the criticism of earth, the criticism of religion into the criticism of law, and the criticism of theology into the criticism of politics."[37] Thus the tradition serves a variety of liberation movements, because every landless people imagines, in its own way, that God wants nobody landless and that coming into land requires the overthrow of the system.

But on the other hand we must add a second recognition. The land promises have also provided a warrant for conquest movements by the powerful, whereas the traditions themselves bespeak a powerless people. Regina Schwartz pursues the thought that the tradition takes on new meanings when it is read by imperial peoples:

> Surely, there is all the difference between reading the conquest as an impossible fantasy of a disempowered people and reading it as an act of empowerment by an imperial people. And surely, a powerless people creating a myth of their liberation and subsequent conquest differs markedly from a powerful people justifying their real conquest with recourse to such a myth. But how? Are the dynamics of power always so clear-cut that the oppressed and oppressors are readily distinguishable?

> And if so, how is it possible that they both have had recourse to the same myth? That insight leads to the troubling implication that the narrative itself might assist one to become the other, that a strong cultural myth that links the Exodus to the conquest could help to turn victims into victimizers.[38]

There can be little doubt that the exodus-land tradition lies close to the conquest of North America by U.S. colonialists, and that the taking of the land was seen as a sweep of God's people into the land. In that new land, it was necessary either to pretend that the land was empty or to take an aggressively violent stand against the native populations. Either way, the new population proceeded with a sense of moral legitimacy in its violence.

Given that distorted utilization of the tradition for the taking of the land, it is even more problematic that the same assumptions now operate with the imperial militarization of the United States, currently its "mission" of bringing "democracy" to Islamic states. The symbol of the "crusades" continues to be funded by a remarkable sense of mission and the uncritical conviction that "God is with us."

This is a recurring sense among Western "Christian" imperial powers during the entire colonial movement of the eighteenth and nineteenth centuries and certainly into the twentieth century. One may well imagine that both the U.S. invasion of Vietnam and now of Iraq is a spin-off of this Christian imperial ideology.

David Gunn has provided a remarkably clear and detailed account of the British occupation of New Zealand and the consequent dispossession of the [Maori] tribes. He takes up "the place of the Bible in this ideology of Victorian colonialism" with an English version of being the "chosen people" with a "manifest destiny."[39] Gunn acknowledges that there were, in the period of British seizure, "two versions of New Zealand society—a replica of British society and a utopian one."[40] In the end, the British myth of chosen people prevailed. In contemporary New Zealand there is, happily, still an active memory and movement that seek to secure the covenantally guaranteed rights of the Maori, a movement in part led by the faithful church. Such a movement, nevertheless, is uphill against the entrenched claims of colonial interest.

These several examples are enough to exhibit the fact that the land promise is at the core of biblical faith, at the core in all of its power and in all of its unresolved problematic. There is a push toward a new land of promise, a push that is rooted in God's own utterance, a push that is marked by all of the violence that makes historical materiality:

> All of these died in faith without having received the promises, but from a distance they saw and greeted them. They confessed that they were strangers and foreigners on the earth, for people who speak in this way make it clear that they are seeking a homeland. If they had been thinking of the land that they had left behind, they would have had opportunity to return. But as it is, they desire a better country, that is, a heavenly one. Therefore God is not ashamed to be called their God; indeed, he has prepared a city for them. (Hebrews 11:13-16)

Chapter Thirteen

PROPHETIC PROMISES

The land promises dominated the imagination and memory of Israel and were taken to be fulfilled in the monarchy of David and Solomon:

> I have been with you wherever you went, and have cut off all your enemies from before you; and I will make for you a great name, like the name of the great ones of the earth. And I will appoint a place for my people Israel and will plant them, so that they may live in their own place, and be disturbed no more; and evildoers shall afflict them no more, as formerly, from the time that I appointed judges over my people Israel; and I will give you rest from all your enemies. Moreover the LORD declares to you that the LORD will make you a house. (2 Samuel 7:9-11; compare Joshua 1:43-45)[1]

The promise made to Abraham and fulfilled in David, however, was understood in Deuteronomic theology as conditioned by obedience to the Torah (see Deuteronomy 11:22-25).

I

That conditionality of Torah obedience provided an ongoing critique of royal policy and pretension, and generated a series of prophets who persistently warned that land loss and the exhaustion of the divine promise upon which David in the Jerusalem establishment counted so decisively:

Alas for those who lie on beds of ivory,
    and lounge on their couches,
and eat lambs from the flock,
    and calves from the stall;
who sing idle songs to the sound of the harp,
    and like David improvise on instruments of music;
who drink wine from bowls,
    and anoint themselves with the finest oils,
    but are not grieved over the ruin of Joseph!
Therefore they shall not be the first to go into exile,
    and the revelry of the loungers shall pass away. (Amos 6:4-7)[2]

Do not rejoice, O Israel!
    Do not exult as other nations do;
for you have played the whore, departing from your God.
    You have loved a prostitute's pay
    on all threshing floors.
Threshing floor and wine vat shall not feed them,
    and the new wine shall fail them.
They shall not remain in the land of the LORD;
    but Ephraim shall return to Egypt,
    and in Assyria they shall eat unclean food. (Hosea 9:1-3)[3]

Therefore because of you
    Zion shall be plowed as a field;
Jerusalem shall become a heap of ruins,
    and the mountain of the house a wooded height. (Micah 3:12)

Ah, you who rise early in the morning
    in pursuit of strong drink,
who linger in the evening
    to be inflamed by wine,
whose feasts consist of lyre and harp,
    tambourine and flute and wine,
but who do not regard the deeds of the LORD,
    or see the work of his hands!
Therefore my people go into exile without knowledge;
their nobles are dying of hunger,
    and their multitude is parched with thirst. (Isaiah 5:11-13)

So persistent is the dissent among these poets of Israel that the Deuteronomist, in more systemic reflection, can conclude that these several ad hoc poets in fact constituted a sequence with a single recurring message:

> Yet the LORD warned Israel and Judah by every prophet and every seer, saying, "Turn from your evil ways and keep my commandments and my statutes, in accordance with all the law that I commanded your ancestors and that I sent to you by my servants the prophets." They would not listen but were stubborn, as their ancestors had been, who did not believe in the LORD their God. They despised his statutes, and his covenant that he made with their ancestors, and the warnings that he gave them. They went after false idols and became false; they followed the nations that were around them, concerning whom the LORD had commanded them that they should not do as they did. They rejected all the commandments of the LORD their God and made for themselves cast images of two calves; they made a sacred pole, worshiped all the host of heaven, and served Baal. They made their sons and their daughters pass through fire; they used divination and augury; and they sold themselves to do evil in the sign of the LORD, provoking him to anger. Therefore the LORD was very angry with Israel and removed them out of his sight; none was left but the tribe of Judah alone. (2 Kings 17:13-18)

By the conclusion of the "canonical" account of *land history* in the Old Testament, Israel has lost the land to occupiers with deportation the fate of the leadership (2 Kings 24:13–25:21; see 23:26-27). The land promise has run its course. It is conventional to view the land history of the Deuteronomist as including the sweep from the book of Deuteronomy through 2 Kings. In broader scale a number of scholars, notably David Noel Freedman, have taken all of the corpus of Genesis through 2 Kings as a single narrative that runs from *creation* to *exile*.[4] Either way, the end result is the same.

The land promise is exhausted; according to Israel's "canonical" presentation, Torah disobedience has overrun YHWH's promise and the divine forbearance. Thus the loss of the land to the Babylonians is understood as an exercise of YHWH's sovereignty over the nations and over the land of Israel as well:

> Give them this charge for their masters: Thus says the LORD of hosts, the God of Israel: This is what you shall say to your masters: It is I who by my great power and my outstretched arm have made the earth, with the people and animals that are on the earth, and I give it to whomever

> I please. Now I have given all these lands into the hand of King Nebuchadnezzar of Babylon, my servant, and I have given him even the wild animals of the field to serve him. (Jeremiah 27:4-6)

The literary-political-theological residue of this forfeiture of the land promise is that the land and its inhabitants are left without hope. The book of Lamentations, rightly presented by Norman Gottwald as the voice of grief in those "left behind" in the land, witnesses to the failure of hope:[5]

> Zion stretches out her hands,
> but there is no one to comfort her;
> the LORD has commanded against Jacob
> that his neighbors should become his foes;
> Jerusalem has become
> a filthy thing among them.
> The LORD is in the right,
> for I have rebelled against his word;
> but hear, all you peoples,
> and behold my suffering;
> my young women and young men
> have gone into captivity. (Lamentations 1:17-18)

The culmination of this poetry in Lamentations 5:20 yields a desperate petition (v. 21), but finally in verse 22 a stark acknowledgment of loss and ending:

> Why have you forgotten us completely?
> Why have you forsaken us these many days?
> Restore us to yourself, O LORD, that we may be restored:
> renew our days as of old—
> unless you have utterly rejected us,
> and are angry with us beyond measure. (Lamentations 5:20-22)[6]

II

I have taken this long to characterize the loss and failure and the mood of despair in the sixth century, in order to turn toward the most remarkable dimension of hope in the Old Testament: It is precisely in its loss, failure, and hopelessness that Israel's canonical literature features the most remarkable, lyrical, and sweeping promises from YHWH. Exile, in Israel, is the primal venue for hope as it is articulated in the great prophetic traditions. There may be practical, pragmatic reasons for the articulation of hope in the environment of Babylonian imperialism; Gottwald judges that the imagination of Israel was "Babylonianized,"[7] but that hope reflects the ideology of privilege entitlement among Jews who were the true adherence to YHWH but who had benefited from Babylonian connections:

> It is at this juncture that the Oppressed Servant figure embodies imaginatively the costly project of staying faithful against the tide of the Babylonian hegemony and the subtle attraction of Judahites to adopt that kind of hegemonic thinking. This can only have been a compelling message if it was somehow encoded in the life of the author and in the lives of those who shared his outlook, however many or few they were (it is perhaps instructive that Isaiah 65:13-16, which continues the author's tradition in Palestine after the restoration, speaks in the plural of "servants of Yahweh"). This living witness risked suffering by persistently encouraging an attitude and line of action that split the Judahite community and invited Babylonian reprisals. For this reason the Oppressed Servant encodes personal experiences of the author and/or his associates in an active mission of persuasion and resistance, even of collaboration with pro-Persian forces. The author and his like-minded associates "hide" within the Servant figure just as the author "hides" behind the entire text and yet is everywhere present within it.[8]

Such an ideological dimension to hope should not surprise us, for this community and this tradition lived characteristically in the midst of historical materiality.

When we come to articulate a theology of the Old Testament, it will not suffice to regard such ideological privilege as a complete explanation for the possibility of hope. Clearly in, with, and under such a sense of privilege and entitlement, there is the character of YHWH who is finally an unfettered historical agent who will not be exhausted by Jerusalem ideology nor contained within imperial pretense. The sort out of ideology and faith is at best tricky, but a theology of the Old Testament can fully acknowledge an ideological dimension without reduction to ideology.[9] Thus finally as we consider *hope* in *exile*, we reckon with the freedom and fidelity of YHWH, even if that freedom and fidelity inevitably serve ideological pretensions:

> I would articulate the commanding authorial ideology as follows: the rise and fall of tributary sovereignties is in the hands of one divine being, the God of Israel who is also the unrecognized God of the world—not only unrecognized by other nations but by the Judahites as well. The former Judahite tributary system deservedly collapsed because of infidelity to its God, but it will be restored if the present Judahites commit themselves unreservedly to a readiness to return to their homeland when the opening to do so arrives in the near future. The overriding authorial ideology is sharply focused on the prospect of a Judahite restoration by the Persians and this seems to be based upon a close reading of events in the latter years of the Babylonian imperium. The extent to which this ideology was accompanied by political strategizing is uncertain, but that some specific measures of resistance and rebellion were encouraged by the author is highly probable when the text is read at the conjuncture of all the social forces described above.... It is a grandiose and aristocratic ideology which puts these Judahites "on the inside track" with Yahweh, ruler and imminent rearranger of world affairs. But, this can only come about if they are willing to suffer present risk and loss in the interests of a future vindication.[10]

In what follows, I will consider the *voice of hope* in the three great prophetic traditions, all the while mindful that this hope voiced by those outside the land who anticipate a return to the land.[11]

The Jeremiah tradition is shaped so that the principal oracles of hope are gathered in chapters 30–31, introduced by a prose oracle in 29:10-14, and followed by a narrative in 32:1-15 plus a collection of brief promises in chapter 33. In addition, other promises are scattered throughout the corpus, culminating with the anticipated demise of Babylon in chapters 50–51, together with the resulting invitation for the deportation Jews to return home to the land of promise. Whereas previous scholarship in the book of Jeremiah had focused on the judgment oracles with hope regarded that best as a belated addendum, scholarship now is much more inclined to focus on hope in the tradition as it served the sixth to the fifth-century community with the oracles of judgments more plausibly to be taken as a context and rhetorical setup for the hope passages that dominate the final form of the text.

The narrative of Jeremiah 32:1-15, not unlike the earlier narrative in Genesis 23, takes the trouble to secure a land title to property in Anathoth by the careful function of witnesses and the precise recording of the deed. The action reported is to establish a clear legal entitlement to the property in Anathoth. And while the narrative concerns only a family plot, the narrative serves as a foundation for very large communal assurances:

> Thus says the LORD of hosts, the God of Israel: Take these deeds, both this sealed deed of purchase and this open deed, and put them in an earthenware jar, in order that they may last for a long time. For thus says the LORD of hosts, the God of Israel: Houses and fields and vineyards shall again be bought in this land. (Jeremiah 32:14-15)

> Fields shall be bought for money, and deeds shall be signed and sealed and witnessed, in the land of Benjamin, in the places around Jerusalem, and in the cities of Judah, of the hill country, of the Shephelah, and of the Negeb; for I will restore their fortunes, says the LORD. (Jeremiah 32:44)[12]

The prose announcement of 29:10-14 that introduces the corpus of promise and that follows the comment on *shalom* in Babylon (29:5-7), also anticipates return to the land: "I will let you find me, says the LORD, and I will restore your fortunes and gather you from all the nations and all the places where I have driven you, says the LORD, and I will bring you back to the place from which I sent you into exile" (Jeremiah 29:14). The poetic promise anticipates a celebrative return of "merry makers" to the city along with its own "prince" (30:18-21). The poetry utilizes the imagery of "scatter" (deport) and "gather" (bring home) to declare the end of the exile and the ingathering of all Jews to the homeland:

> Hear the word of the LORD, O nations,
> and declare it in the coastlands far away;
> say, "He who *scattered* Israel will *gather* him,
> and will keep him as a shepherd a flock."
> For the LORD has ransomed Jacob,
> and has redeemed him from hands too strong for him.
> They shall come and sing aloud on the height of Zion,
> and they shall be radiant over the goodness of the LORD,
> over the grain, the wine, and the oil,
> and over the young of the flock and the herd;
> their life shall become like a watered garden,
> and they shall never languish again.
> Then shall the young women rejoice in the dance,
> and the young men and the old shall be merry.
> I will turn their mourning into joy,
> I will comfort them, and give them gladness for sorrow.

I will give the priests their fill of fatness,
and my people shall be satisfied with my bounty,
says the LORD. (Jeremiah 31:10-14, italics added)

In making the case for such an astonishing future, the poetry asserts (a) that YHWH's promise of the land is as secure as the reliabilities of creation (31:35-36, 37; 33:25-26) and (b) that the community in the land will be restored to full covenantal relationship (31:31-34).

It is the claim of the Jeremiah tradition that what was experienced as a disruption in the relationship with YHWH was in fact not a disruption, because, "I have loved you with an everlasting love" (Jeremiah 31:3b).

To be sure, there is an acknowledgment of "destroying and overthrowing," but the faithful God will "build and plant" in time to come (31:28). These divine promises, now delivered in a context of extreme trauma, are as fundamental and defining and reliable as the initial promises made to Abraham.[13] Thus the conclusion of the promissory collection alludes to the ancestral promises as the one still in effect upon which the landless in the sixth century can fully rely (Jeremiah 33:25-26).

In the tradition of Ezekiel, the promises that well up in exile are largely situated in chapters 33–48. We may divide these materials into two distinct groups. In chapters 34, 36, and 37 are a series of oracles that bespeak restoration to a viable society in the land. Chapter 34 anticipates the new rule of YHWH who will perform as a caring king who will displace the Davidic kings who have been negligent and self-serving (vv. 1-22). Most remarkably, after the failed human kings have been displaced with the new "direct rule" of YHWH, verses 23-24 nonetheless anticipate a newly authorized Davidic "prince" who will function as a caring king. These two verses likely reflect continuing royalist sentiment in the period of displacement. This oracle culminates with an announcement of a "covenant of peace" that will lead to revivification of all creation, a new creation that is peculiarly a gift to the house of Israel: "They shall know that I, the LORD their God, am with them, and that they, the house of Israel, are my people, says the Lord GOD. You are my sheep, the sheep of my pasture and I am your God, says the Lord GOD" (Ezekiel 34:30-31).

In chapter 36, the promise of YHWH assures Israel of YHWH's intention of restoration of both Israel and of creation. Of special note is the twice-announced motivation of YHWH who will act on behalf of YHWH's own reputation and not because of love for Israel: "Therefore say to the house of Israel, Thus says the Lord GOD: It is not for your sake, O house of Israel, that I am about to act, but for the sake of my holy name, which you have profaned among the nations to which you came" (Ezekiel 36:22; see v. 32). Chapter 37, perhaps the most important and certainly the best known of these oracles of restoration, concerns "the valley of the dry bones" (vv. 1-14). What may interest us the most is that the *restoration to the land* is reckoned to be a *resurrection from the grave*:

> And you shall know that I am the LORD, when I open your graves, and bring you up from your graves, O my people. I will put my spirit within you, and you shall live, and I will place you on your own soil; then you shall know that I, the LORD, have spoken and will act," says the LORD. (Ezekiel 37:13-14)

This equivalence is of immense importance for the larger theme of hope, for biblical hope is characteristically preoccupied with the return to the fullness of existence in historical materiality.[14]

The second body of promissory texts in Ezekiel is in chapters 40–48 that reflect more fully the sacerdotal vision of Ezekiel for the rehabilitation of a full and faithful temple that is free of pollution and so can host the palpable liturgical presence of YHWH. The new regime, which is a new divine gift, will consist in proper priests, proper temple administration, and proper celebration of offerings and festivals. At the end of this long divine assurance, two matters are of special interest. In 47:1-12, the new temple in Jerusalem, as a place of presence, is the new source from which flow the waters of life, thus replicating and displacing the rivers of Genesis 2:10-14. Jerusalem is established as the epicenter and source of life for all of creation.[15] Secondly, in 47:13–48:35 with a new vision of a properly ordered, fully symmetrical land of promise. It is astonishing that a tradition preoccupied with holy purity should culminate in a vision of the land. But the anticipation is the formation of a *holy people* who cannot exist without a *holy place*. It is variously said to be the *holy city*, *holy temple*, or *holy land*. In the vision of Ezekiel, the city, temple, and land are in fact coterminal. After the season of divine absence, the tradition culminates with an assurance of presence. The new, reordered land will be a fitting habitat for the holy God.

The tradition of Ezekiel is preoccupied with return to the land and understands that return, wrought by the power and will of YHWH, as the defining attestation to YHWH's power and fidelity:

> Therefore thus says the Lord GOD: Now I will restore the fortunes of Jacob, and have mercy on the whole house of Israel; and I will be

> jealous for my holy name. They shall forget their shame, and all the treachery they have practiced against me, when they live securely in their land with no one to make them afraid, when I have brought them back from the peoples and gathered them from their enemies' lands, and through them have displayed my holiness in the sight of many nations. Then they shall know that I am the LORD their God because I sent them into exile among the nations, and then gathered them into their own land. I will leave none of them behind; and I will never again hide my face from them, when I pour out my spirit upon the house of Israel, says the Lord GOD. (Ezekiel 39:25-29)

The promise of land is primary, but it is here articulated in categories that are singularly priestly in tone and nuance.

The third great prophetic tradition, that of Isaiah, is organized differently on two counts. First, the entire corpus of "Second Isaiah" (40–55) is devoted to the theme of restoration to the land that is to be accomplished by the demise of Babylon and the rise of Persia. Second and related to that, the poetry of Isaiah is much more poetically engaged and self-conscious, so that the declaration of YHWH's purpose of restoration is intimately connected with the *realpolitik* on the ground.

Whatever may be said about the political realities that lie behind and permeate the announcement, the anticipation is singularly YHWH-centered. Here speaks YHWH whose promissory word has always been reliable (see 40:8; 55:10-11), but which now becomes quite specific and palpable. The word of YHWH given through this poetry is *gospel*, good news of a genuine *novum* that is a gift of God that cannot be explained according to the normal workings of the historical process:

> Get you up to a high mountain,
> O Zion, herald of good tidings;
> lift up your voice with strength,
> O Jerusalem, herald of good tidings,
> lift it up, do not fear;
> say to the cities of Judah,
> "Here is your God!" (Isaiah 40:9)

> I first have declared it to Zion,
> and I give to Jerusalem a herald of good tidings. (Isaiah 41:27)

> How beautiful upon the mountains
> are the feet of the messenger who announces peace,

who brings good news,
    who announces salvation,
    who says to Zion, "Your God reigns." (Isaiah 52:7)

The substance of the "gospel" is variously, "Here is your God," and "Your God reigns." The gospel is the announcement that YHWH is back in play with power and resolve, the very YHWH who had summoned Babylon and whom Babylon had tried to eliminate as an effective historical agent. But now, in and through this poetic utterance, YHWH takes a new initiative in the historical process.

Much of this poetry revolves around "the new thing," the action of YHWH that creates new historical possibility for Israel, specifically the possibility of return to the land and resumption of a viable life in covenant:

See, the former things have come to pass,
    and new things I now declare;
before they spring forth,
    I tell you of them. (Isaiah 42:9)

Thus says the Lord,
    who makes a way in the sea,
    a path in the mighty waters,
who brings out chariot and horse,
    army and warrior;
they lie down, they cannot rise,
    they are extinguished, quenched like a wick:
Do not remember the former things,
    or consider the things of old.
I am about to do a new thing;
    now it springs forth, do you not perceive it?
I will make a way in the wilderness
    and rivers in the desert. (Isaiah 43:16-19)

The "new thing" is wrought solely and directly by YHWH who will override all other factors in the life of Israel and in the life of the world. That is the good news!

That good news, however, does not occur in a vacuum or in a world of religious imagination apart from history. Thus the "new thing" to be enacted for Israel will concern the reordering of geopolitics. On the one hand, the newness now to be given by YHWH requires the dismantling of

Babylonian power. Thus the Babylonian gods, in prophetic imagination, are reduced to humiliating silence (Isaiah 41:21-24). They are exposed as impotent and futile, meriting neither obedience nor honor from Israel (Isaiah 46:1-2, 5-7). As the gods of the empire are exposed as fraudulent, so also the worldly power of the empire is exposed as short-term and sure to fail. Because Babylon has postured in its arrogant autonomy (47:7-8, 10), it will be reduced to humiliating helplessness (Isaiah 47:11, 14-15).

On the other hand, the fall of Babylon as a recalcitrant servant of YHWH will be matched with the rise of Cyrus who will emancipate Jews and permit homecoming. It is Cyrus who has been "roused" by YHWH (41:2) who is summoned as YHWH's "shepherd" (= king, 44:28), and who is designated "his messiah," that is, his human agent to accomplish divine purpose (45:1). This is the one "stirred up" anticipated in Jeremiah 51:9, on which see also 2 Chronicles 36:22-23.

The God who in Judah has "loved with an everlasting love" (Jeremiah 31:3) is the one who has addressed Israel with a circumstance-altering utterance. The decisive and transformative divine "fear not" has created an environment in which Israel need no longer submit to or obey imperial power, because the claimed power of the empire has been nullified by YHWH's rule. Thus the salvation oracles are divine utterances that create a wholly new environment:

> But you, Israel, my servant,
> Jacob, whom I have chosen,
> the offspring of Abraham, my friend;
> you whom I took from the ends of the earth,
> and called from its farthest corners,
> saying to you, "You are my servant,
> I have chosen you and not cast you off";
> *do not fear*, for I am with you,
> *do not be afraid*, for I am your God;
> I will strengthen you, I will help you,
> I will uphold you with my victorious right hand. (Isaiah 41:8-10, italics added)

> But now thus says the LORD,
> he who created you, O Jacob,
> he who formed you, O Israel:
> *Do not fear*, for I have redeemed you;
> I have called you by name, you are mine. . . .
> *Do not fear*, for I am with you;

I will bring your offspring from the east,
and from the west I will gather you. (Isaiah 43:1, 5; see Jeremiah 30:10-11)[16]

Thus the rhetoric of Isaiah accomplishes a transformation of Israel's imagination that is to be matched by a historical transformation. The "barren one" is to have children (54:1-3). The humiliated wife is to be restored to well-being (54:4-6). The one abandoned is to receive compassion (54:7-8). Most remarkably, in Isaiah 54:7-8, there is divine acknowledgment that Israel was abandoned by YHWH, but only "for an instant":

For a brief moment I abandoned you,
but with great compassion I will gather you.
In overflowing wrath for a moment
I hid my face from you,
but with everlasting love I will have compassion on you,
says the LORD, your Redeemer. (Isaiah 54:7-8)[17]

That instant of divine absence and alienation is now to be answered and overwhelmed by the God of steadfast love and compassion (54:10). The language of luxurious reconstruction in 54:11-12 moves to an affirmation of YHWH's faithful covenant with David (55:3) and ultimately to an imagined processional by which Israel returns, in stylized splendor, to the land of promise, accompanied by the exuberant applause of all the other creatures (55:12-13).

III

The sum of these three prophetic traditions of promise in exuberance and in lavish style far outdistance the old land promises to the ancestors. All of them, in rich variety, come to a single, glad affirmation that YHWH is actively at work to assure the return of deported Israel to its homeland, which it has been promised, from the outset. It is evident that each of these prophetic traditions makes its articulation of YHWH's future according to its own dialect. Thus Jeremiah, *rooted in the categories of Deuteronomy*, anticipates the new land as a place where Torah is known and embraced (Jeremiah 31:33-34). Ezekiel, *rooted in priestly tradition*, imagines and expects a well-ordered holy precinct, so that all of the land is reconfigured as a sanctuary for YHWH's holiness. And Isaiah, *rooted in royal tradition*, can appeal to the image of a great royal procession of homecoming, evoked by royal decree that is received as "gospel."

The poetry in each case presents the anticipated geopolitical turn in the Near East in imaginative trope that makes the turn more than geopolitical. The accomplishment of the poets is to assure a defining theological ingredient in the public experience of Israel, a claim that what they will know of newness is lived from and toward YHWH. We may identify tag words in each case that attest to the vigor and centrality of the theological dimension of Israel's history:

■ In Jeremiah 31:3 the assurance is, "I have loved you with an everlasting love." The oracle denies that there ever was a disruption in YHWH's love for Israel. YHWH has, it is asserted, loved Israel all the way through the displacement. Here speaks the pathos-filled husband who yearns for his wayward wife (Jeremiah 3:12-14). Here speaks the urgent father who cannot break from his son, even when the son merits rejection:

> Is Ephraim my dear son?
>   Is he the child I delight in?
> As often as I speak against him,
>   I still remember him.
> Therefore I am deeply moved for him;
>   I will surely have mercy on him,
>   says the LORD. (Jeremiah 31:20; see 3:19)

Here speaks the poet who has learned from Hosea about broken, betrayed love, love that does not quit even in woundedness.

■ In Ezekiel 36:22, 32, the matter is different. In this divine utterance, there is nothing of love or compassion or pardon. Here there is only the self-regard of the Holy One who resists the cheapening of reputation that happens when the God of Israel is seen in public with this abomination-committing Israel. The utterance offers a future to Israel, but not out of any positive passion for Israel. Israel benefits as a by-product of YHWH's self-regard, and should be under no illusion about YHWH's care for Israel: "Therefore say to the house of Israel, Thus says the Lord GOD: It is not for your sake, O house of Israel, that I am about to act, but for the sake of my holy name, which you have profaned among the nations to which you came" (Ezekiel 36:22). The ground of Israel's future is YHWH's own holiness, perhaps a deeper grounding than the poetry of pathos given us in Jeremiah.

■ In Isaiah 54:7-8, the pathos and anger of the God of Jeremiah cuts even deeper. Whereas God, in Jeremiah's poetry, had declared abiding love, God in the Isaiah tradition can acknowledge abandonment, even if brief:

For a brief moment I abandoned you,
  but with great compassion I will gather you.
In overflowing wrath for a moment
  I hid my face from you,
but with everlasting love I will have compassion on you,
  says the LORD, your Redeemer. (Isaiah 54:7-8)

In this particular divine admission, there is not even any accusation against Israel, not any claim that divine abandonment is in response to Israel's recalcitrance. That cause may be inferred, but it is astonishing that it is not stated here.

It is clear that the theological underpinning of the geopolitical turn that Israel anticipates is hidden in deeply interpersonal passion, wound, caring, and self-regard. No single utterance, not even any single poetic utterance, can measure or contain the inscrutable mystery of sovereignty and compassion that provide the ground for Israel's future. Variously the newness is new covenant, new temple, new land, new thing... always newness.

It is clear that the newness that wondrously emerges for Israel in exile is completely *de novo*. And yet Israel's faith is always situated in the continuity of history and in the dialectic of memory and anticipation. Paul Hanson has nicely lined out the dialectic under the general category of "reapplication," a way of thinking that includes both continuity and discontinuity.[18] This dialectic is sharply voiced in the despairing context of Lamentations. The speaker takes into full account that the present is an unbearable wound, an impossible loss:

He has made my teeth grind on gravel,
  and made me cower in ashes;
my soul is bereft of peace;
  I have forgotten what happiness is;
so I say, "Gone is my glory,
  and all that I had hoped for from the LORD." (Lamentations
3:16-18)

But then the poem turns to memory that lies authentically behind present circumstance: "But this I call to mind, / and therefore I have hope"

(Lamentations 3:21). The substance of the memory is drawn from all parts of the tradition, but perhaps especially from the Psalter:

> The steadfast love of the LORD never ceases,
> his mercies never come to an end;
> they are new every morning;
> great is your faithfulness. (Lamentations 3:22-23)

The great triad of steadfast love, mercy, and faithfulness persist. And out of that rich and deep remembering, the community left in Jerusalem knows something different even about the present. It knows that abandonment and alienation might be real; but the God of compassionate fidelity may still be expected in the midst of abandonment. It is that confidence that propels the poets of hope to speak as they speak. It is impossible to determine the extent to which the poetry is only a knowing way of speaking about evident geopolitical futures or the extent to which the utterance is originary. The task of Old Testament theology invites an accent on the latter, on the originary quality of divine utterance. That accent may be taken with some theological innocence, but not with ignorance. The poetry sits close to observed, observable events. That is how it has been since the beginning of this people. But hope will finally not accept explanation. Rather, it aims at wonder and gratitude, and finally at courage. Thus Gottwald, even in his knowing historical criticism, can judge:

> However many of these Judahites had been incorporated into Babylonian government service, this particular writing with its insistent Judahite restoration mission could not be the expression of a new Babylonian identity. And it is highly probable that it was produced and consumed under clandestine and subversive conditions.[19]

I conclude with two references to Christian tradition. First, these several traditions (and with particular reference to Ezekiel 37:13-14) invite Christians to think again about the claim of resurrection faith. Very much silliness has been offered concerning the resurrection of Jesus in modern interpretation as it has been cast into rationalistic and/or modernistic categories.[20] In these prophetic traditions, it is clear that resurrection means to return to the disputatious materiality of history that is kept under the promise of God.

Second, Paul is clearly faithful to this odd juxtaposition of *exile* and *hope* when he writes:

> And not only that, but we also boast in our sufferings, knowing that suffering produces endurance, and endurance produces character, and character produces hope, and hope does not disappoint us, because God's love has been poured into our hearts through the Holy Spirit that has been given to us. (Romans 5:3-5)

Suffering does indeed produce hope, but only in a community where memories and promises of fidelity witness against circumstance. These prophetic traditions attest to the emergence and utterance of hope precisely amid suffering. It is for this reason that Walther Zimmerli can write of "the blessing of point zero hour."[21]

CHAPTER FOURTEEN

HOPE IN EVERY DIMENSION OF REALITY

Hope in the Old Testament concerns God, God's power, and God's generosity. Hope is confidence that God can and will *make new*, because God has the power and will to override all that is old, failed, and deathly, and because God has a generous intention to act on behalf of those whom God loves. Thus it is that my consideration of *hope in God* follows an exposition of the *God of miracle and order* and concerns the community (Israel and the world) whom God loves. Because YHWH is a future-promising, future-giving God, there is hope for Israel whom YHWH loves. Because YHWH who loves Israel is creator of heaven and earth, there is hope for all of creation, which YHWH loves. There is a promise from YHWH that all the powers of evil, whether historical or cosmic, will be defeated so that a generous creation may be restored. Where evil is defeated, all creatures—including Israel—will be able to be their true selves in response to YHWH the creator.

I have begun my discussion of *hope in God* with a close consideration of the primary clusters of the divine promises, the *ancestral narratives* and the *exilic prophets*.[1] In these two clusters of texts, we have seen that YHWH promises land to the landless. In the ancestral narratives, the promise pertains to a family without heirs who will, by the faithfulness of YHWH, have heirs to receive land. In the exilic prophets, the promises pertain to Israel in its displacement; Israel will again come to its safe, fruitful land. In both cases, the narrative and oracles of promise attest to YHWH's commitment to override current conditions (barrenness, displacement) in order to create a wholly new situation, one that neither the ancestors nor the exiles could guarantee for themselves. In what follows, I will be informed by the threefold pattern of Donald Gowan who organizes his discussion of hope in the Old Testament in a threefold pattern.[2]

I

I will deal briefly, yet again, with the promises YHWH has made to Israel concerning well-being through restoration to the land. On the one hand, it is variously asserted that Israel has lost the land because of disobedience to Torah. Land loss and displacement are understood as divine punishment against disobedient people. On the other hand, it is asserted that the land is lost because of rapacious, political-military power on the part of the empires that exceed their mandates from YHWH and that deny to Israel its rightful place in the world. Either way, by *Israel's disobedience* or by the *usurpation of adversaries*, Israel has lost the land. This is the core problem of historical Israel in the Old Testament.

According to Israel's sixth-century prophets, YHWH will act soon and decisively to restore Israel to the land. When we consider the geopolitical reality, it is probable that restoration to the land was a limited historical achievement; returning Jews were able to recover only modest amounts of territory in and around the city of Jerusalem. And even that much, it is clear, was possible only by the permit of the Persian Empire in its policy of allowing local government (see the decree of Cyrus, 2 Chronicles 36:22-23). It is clear that what control returning Jews exercised over its very limited land, they did so by leave of the empire and on the terms of the empire, including conformity to imperial colonial policy and the payment of proper taxes. Thus the promise of the land was enacted through the specifications of imperial politics and the exercise of *realpolitik*.

But, of course, the stylized promises that bespeak divine resolve are poetic and lyrical, and speak with a kind of exuberance rooted in hopeful expectation that runs well beyond the facts on the ground. That lyrical expectation of restoration has a dual focus. On the one hand, the return to the land includes images of agricultural prosperity in the land. Thus Ezekiel:

I will make with them a covenant of peace and banish wild animals from the land, so that they may live in the wild and sleep in the woods securely. I will make them and the region around my hill a blessing; and I will send down the showers in their season; they shall be showers of blessing. The trees of the field shall yield their fruit, and the earth shall yield its increase. They shall be secure on their soil; and they shall know that I am the LORD, when I break the bars of their yoke, and save them from the hands of those who enslaved them. They shall no more be plunder for the nations, nor shall the animals of the land devour them; they shall live in safety, and no one shall make them afraid. I will provide for them a splendid vegetation so that they shall no more be consumed with hunger in the land, and no longer suffer the insults of the nations. (Ezekiel 34:25-29)

I will save you from all your uncleannesses, and I will summon the grain and make it abundant and lay no famine upon you. I will make the fruit of the tree and the produce of the field abundant, so that you may never again suffer the disgrace of famine among the nations.... The land that was desolate shall be tilled, instead of being the desolation that it was in the sight of all who passed by. And they will say, "This land that was desolate has become like the garden of Eden; and the waste and desolate and ruined towns are now inhabited and fortified." (Ezekiel 36:29-30, 34-35)

But as Gowan has shown, the return to the land is matched in other texts by a return to the city of Jerusalem with an expected exultation of Zion. Zechariah 8 manages to join together images of urban recovery and the resumption of cultural life:

And I will bring them to live in Jerusalem. They shall be my people and I will be their God, in faithfulness and in righteousness.

Thus says the LORD of hosts: Let your hands be strong—you that have recently been hearing these words from the mouths of the prophets who were present when the foundation was laid for the rebuilding of the temple, the house of the LORD of hosts. For before those days there were no wages for people or for animals, nor was there any safety from the foe for those who went out or came in, and I set them all against one other. But now I will not deal with the remnant of this people as in the former days, says the LORD of hosts. For there shall be a sowing of peace; the vine shall yield its fruit, the ground shall give its produce, and the skies shall give their dew; and I will cause the remnant of this people to possess all these things. Just as you have been a

> cursing among the nations, O house of Judah and house of Israel, so I will save you and you shall be a blessing. Do not be afraid, but let your hands be strong.
>
> For thus says the LORD of hosts: Just as I purposed to bring disaster upon you, when your ancestors provoked me to wrath, and I did not relent, says the LORD of hosts, so again I have purposed in these days to do good to Jerusalem and to the house of Judah; do not be afraid. (Zechariah 8:8-15)

Perhaps the lyrical expectation should not be taken too precisely. But perhaps the poets understood that the rebuilding of the temple would require a flourishing agricultural economy. The same juxtaposition of land and city is expressed, as we have seen in Ezekiel 47:13–48:35. The final chapters of Ezekiel are primally interested in the city and, more particularly, in the temple; but the final vision is of the symmetrically recovered land.

More precisely focused upon the city and the recovery of its economy is the poetry of Isaiah 60:6-11. The city of Jerusalem will be such an active trade center that the gates of the city are kept open day and night in order to receive the flow of commodities and wealth that will make Jerusalem safe and prosperous:

> A multitude of camels shall cover you,
> the young camels of Midian and Ephah;
> all those from Sheba shall come.
> They shall bring gold and frankincense,
> and shall proclaim the praise of the LORD.
> All the flocks of Kedar shall be gathered to you,
> the rams of Nebaioth shall minister to you;
> they shall be acceptable on my altar,
> and I will glorify my glorious house.
>
> Who are these that fly like a cloud,
> and like doves to their windows?
> For the coastlands shall wait for me,
> the ships of Tarshish first,
> to bring your children from far away,
> their silver and gold with them,
> for the name of the LORD your God,
> and for the Holy One of Israel,
> because he has glorified you.
> Foreigners shall build up your walls,

and their kings shall minister to you;
for in my wrath I struck you down,
but in my favor I have had mercy on you.
Your gates shall always be open;
day and night they shall not be shut,
so that nations shall bring you their wealth,
with their kings led in procession. (Isaiah 60:6-11)

In Isaiah 62:6-9, the same image of a prosperous city is offered that is safe and able to enjoy its prosperity without threat:

Upon your walls, O Jerusalem,
I have posted sentinels;
all day and all night
they shall never be silent.
You who remind the LORD,
take no rest,
and give him no rest
until he establishes Jerusalem
and makes it renowned throughout the earth.
The LORD has sworn by his right hand
and by his mighty arm:
I will not again give your grain
to be food for your enemies,
and foreigners shall not drink the wine
for which you have labored;
but those who garner it shall eat it
and praise the LORD,
and those who gather it shall drink it
in my holy courts. (Isaiah 62:6-9)

The poets offer no comment on how this is to happen. It may well be that the expectation derives from an awareness of Persia's benign attitude toward local economy. But no hint is given in the poetry of any human agency. The newness is a gift of YHWH. The poetic traditions never doubt that YHWH is completely capable of such a glorious reconstruction and never doubts that YHWH is about to accomplish it. The accent is upon historical, material prosperity, made possible because the God who offers such promises is the creator who from the outset has intended historical, political-economic well-being. There is no escapism here to another realm, no retreat from the historicity of God's future with God's people.

II

Israel's faith views individual human persons as *members of the community* toward whom YHWH will act to create futures. Israel's text does not always focus on the larger communal agenda. Most especially in the Psalms, the future of individual persons is also brought into sharp focus. As YHWH wills good for the community, so YHWH wills good for every member of that community. In the prayer and reflection of Israel, each individual member of the community is able to evoke the great miracles and to appropriate them "for me"; the great miracles of creation and rescue, of healing and feeding, are appropriated for the life of the individual person. Thus for example, in Psalm 77, the speaker is close to despair and wonders if YHWH has forgotten (vv. 1-9). But the response (and we may well believe the antidote) to such a condition is a recall of the great saving deeds that are now seen to be pertinent to this individual person (vv. 11-20).

I will review four ways in which an Israelite might fall into helplessness, a sense of failure about the present and a sense of futility about the future. After I have offered some detail of these scenarios of futility, I will consider how it is that a future-creating God breaks the power of such futility and makes new life possible.

1. The Psalms reflect upon the reality of *human mortality*, even though it is not a major accent in the Psalter. In Israel there is an acknowledgment that human life is short and that death must be faced:

> You turn us back to dust,
> and say, "Turn back, you mortals."
> For a thousand years in your sight
> are like yesterday when it is past,
> or like a watch in the night.
>
> You sweep them away; they are like a dream,
> like grass that is renewed in the morning;
> in the morning it flourishes and is renewed;
> in the evening it fades and withers. (Psalm 90:3-6)
>
> As for mortals, their days are like grass;
> they flourish like a flower of the field;
> for the wind passes over it, and it is gone,
> and its place knows it no more. (Psalm 103:15-16)

Human life is not only limited. It is exceedingly fragile and in jeopardy; human persons are helpless before the relentless onslaught of fragility that in the end nullifies human existence. The psalmists entertain the reality that human persons disappear from the human scene and leave not a trace. Such passing is inexorable, even without any trace of punishment or negation from YHWH. It is a given of human existence.[3]

2. The Psalms are more closely focused on the reality of *human guilt*; human persons are indeed alienated from YHWH by disobedience and stand subject to the anger and punishment of YHWH. To be sure, this motif is not as central to the Old Testament as some Christian caricatures of the text might suggest. And in fact, the sacrificial system of Israel (Leviticus 1–7) with its pivot on the Day of Atonement (Leviticus 16) provided a regularized, reliable apparatus for forgiveness and reconciliation. Nonetheless, the reality of the power of sin is acknowledged. The awareness that YHWH takes sin seriously is a vexation in the Psalter. It is conventional to observe that for the most part, the burdensome reality of sin in the Psalter is limited to seven so-called penitential Psalms of which the best known of these is Psalm 51.[4] In verses 1-11 of that psalm, sin is frontally acknowledged (vv. 1-5). What is most remarkable, however, is that by verse 7, the *confession* turns to *petition* with a series of petitionary imperatives:

- purge
- wash
- hide
- blot out
- create
- put
- restore
- sustain
- deliver (vv. 7-14)

Most remarkably, the psalmist, in deep alienation, addresses precisely the God from whom he is alienated. The address is in some confidence that the God who is affronted will hear and act. Such confidence, however, is all in expectation. The act of forgiveness is here not yet in hand, and the burden of guilt persists.

3. But the life of a member of the Israelite community is not preoccupied with critical reflection about internal problems of mortality or guilt.

The Psalter makes clear that a much more representative human problematic is the existential one of *conflicted and threatening social relationships* in which the psalmist is in jeopardy from powerful, malicious, cunning enemies before whom the psalmist is himself impotent. The piety of the Psalter likely contains a dimension of paranoia, but it is the present, very powerful threat of social adversaries that drives an Israelite to appeal to YHWH for help. In the social context where one is powerless, there is a turn to YHWH who is known to be the helper who is capable of transformative intervention.

One can open the Psalter (especially the first half) at almost any place and find a characterization of enemies who threaten to undo the psalmist, sometimes by physical assault, very often by malicious slander. That ancient community, like every serious contemporary community, is a community of shame. And therefore slander, whether in court testimony or in neighborhood gossip, can destroy the reputation, the social standing, and finally the person of a neighbor. Before such assaults, the "good person" is helpless and vulnerable:

> O LORD, how many are my foes!
>   Many are rising against me;
> many are saying to me,
>   "There is no help for you in God." (Psalm 3:1-2)

> The boastful will not stand before your eyes;
>   you hate all evildoers.
> You destroy those who speak lies;
>   the LORD abhors the bloodthirsty and deceitful....

> For there is no truth in their mouths;
>   their hearts are destruction;
> their throats are open graves;
>   they flatter with their tongues. (Psalm 5:5-6, 9)

> For the wicked boast of the desires of their heart,
>   those greedy for gain curse and renounce the LORD
> In the pride of their countenance the wicked say, "God will not seek it
>   out";
>   all their thoughts are, "There is no God."
> Their ways prosper at all times;
>   your judgments are on high, out of their sight;
>   as for their foes, they scoff at them.

They think in their heart, "We shall not be moved;
 throughout all generations we shall not meet adversity."

Their mouths are filled with cursing and deceit and oppression;
 under their tongues are mischief and iniquity.
They sit in ambush in the villages;
 in hiding places they murder the innocent.

Their eyes stealthily watch for the helpless;
 they lurk in secret like a lion in its covert;
they lurk that they may seize the poor;
 they seize the poor and drag them off in their net.

They stoop, they crouch,
 and the helpless fall by their might.
They think in their heart, "God has forgotten,
 he has hidden his face, he will never see it." (Psalm 10:3-11)

Guard me as the apple of the eye;
 hide me in the shadow of your wings,
from the wicked who despoil me,
 my deadly enemies who surround me.
They close their hearts to pity;
 with their mouths they speak arrogantly.
They track me down; now they surround me;
 they set their eyes to cast me to the ground.
They are like a lion eager to tear,
 like a young lion lurking in ambush. (Psalm 17:8-12)

Such pleas are characteristically voiced by the pious poor who are vulnerable before the wicked who are unprincipled and apparently capable of exercising immense social power.

The most extreme articulation of this characteristic situation is in Psalm 109 wherein the psalmist delineates an immediate social threat:

Do not be silent, O God of my praise.
For wicked and deceitful mouths are opened against me,
 speaking against me with lying tongues.
They beset me with words of hate,
 and attack me without cause.
In return for my love they accuse me,
 even while I make prayer for them.

So they reward me evil for good,
    and hatred for my love. (Psalm 109:1-5)

The psalm then proceeds to detail for YHWH the appropriate actions that YHWH should take on behalf of the beleaguered speaker (vv. 6-20).[5]

The threat of the social enemy is the defining problematic of the psalms. The "human condition" is characteristically to be under neighborly threat. Sometimes the neighbor is a scoffing nonbeliever. Sometimes a threat is an invading enemy. But most often the threat comes from other members of the community who make a future impossible for the one who speaks.

4. The primary threats voiced in the Psalter arise from conflicted social relationships. Most remarkably, however, Israel at prayer can also, *in extremis*, entertain the reality that the *ultimate adversary is none other than YHWH* who also assaults the speaker in important and unbearable ways: "Remove your stroke from me; / I am worn down by the blows of your hand" (Psalm 39:10). The fullest articulation of such an accusation against YHWH as adversary is in Psalm 88, which ends without resolution:

You have put me in the depths of the Pit,
    in the regions dark and deep.
Your wrath lies heavy upon me,
    and you overwhelm me with all your waves.

You have caused my companions to shun me;
    you have made me a thing of horror to them.
I am shut in so that I cannot escape;
    my eye grows dim through sorrow. (Psalm 88:6-9a)

O LORD, why do you cast me off?
    Why do you hide your face from me?
Wretched and close to death from my youth up,
    I suffer your terrors; I am desperate.
Your wrath has swept over me;
    your dread assaults destroy me.
They surround me like a flood all day long;
    from all sides they close in on me.
You have caused friend and neighbor to shun me;
    my companions are in darkness. (Psalm 88:14-18)

No reason is given here for such a divine assault; nor is there any thought that the divine action is punishment for sin; nor is there any notion that such a violent "undoing" of the self can come from any but YHWH.

This readiness to accuse YHWH is taken up from the Psalter in the prayers of Jeremiah and in the protests of Job, both of whom are faithful to and consistent with the piety of the Psalms.[6] In his final prayer, Jeremiah asserts that YHWH has betrayed him and given him an assignment that evokes neighborly hostility:

O LORD, you have enticed me,
    and I was enticed;
you have overpowered me,
    and you have prevailed.
I have become a laughingstock all day long;
    everyone mocks me.
For whenever I speak, I must cry out,
    I must shout, "Violence and destruction!"
For the word of the LORD has become for me
    a reproach and derision all day long.
If I say, "I will not mention him,
    or speak any more in his name,"
then within me there is something like a burning fire
    shut up in my bones;
I am weary with holding it in,
    and I cannot.
For I hear many whispering:
    "Terror is all around!
Denounce him! Let us denounce him!"
    All my close friends
    are watching for me to stumble.
"Perhaps he can be enticed,
    and we can prevail against him,
and take our revenge on him." (Jeremiah 20:7-10)

And Job, perhaps derivative from Jeremiah, can portray God as an unjust adversary who is unfaithful and unreliable:

For he crushes me with a tempest,
    and multiplies my wounds without cause;
he will not let me get my breath,
    but fills me with bitterness. . . .
When disaster brings sudden death,

he mocks at the calamity of the innocent.
The earth is given into the hand of the wicked;
he covers the eyes of its judges—
if it is not he, who then is it? (Job 9:17-18, 23-24)

Bold as a lion you hunt me;
you repeat your exploits against me.
You renew your witnesses against me,
and increase your vexation toward me;
you bring fresh troops against me. (Job 10:16-17)

On all these counts—*mortality*, *guilt*, *neighbor as adversary*, *YHWH as adversary*—the Israelite who speaks in these psalms is cut off from the future, without hope or possibility. The individual speaker finds in his life a futility that echoes the larger futility of Israel when it faces life apart from the faithfulness of YHWH:

Yet you have rejected us and abased us,
and have not gone out with our armies.
You made us turn back from the foe,
and our enemies have gotten spoil.
You have made us like sheep for slaughter,
and have scattered us among the nations.
You have sold your people for a trifle,
demanding no high price for them.

You have made us the taunt of our neighbors,
the derision and scorn of those around us.
You have made us a byword among the nations,
a laughingstock among the peoples.
All day long my disgrace is before me,
and shame has covered my face
at the words of the taunters and revilers,
at the sight of the enemy and the avenger. (Psalm 44:9-16)

As Israel prayed to YHWH in the midst of its defeat and displacement, so an individual Israelite makes the same prayer in the midst of daily existence. Such speakers who had staked everything on the promises and presence of YHWH are now left with an unbearable question: "Why have you forgotten us completely? / Why have you forsaken us these many days?" (Lamentations 5:20). This is the prayer of every person of faith who has staked everything upon God, and now finds life at its limit without possibility.

The crisis of faith disclosed in the Psalms is to find a way into the future where there seems to be no way.[7] In its futility, Israel is reduced to silence.[8] For good reason, it is Israel's characteristic strategy of faith to *break the silence* and so to summon the absent, negligent God of promise back into active concern.[9] Israel does not doubt that if YHWH can be mobilized, YHWH is capable of creating futures. And so the assertive work of faith in the midst of unbearable futility is to speak in shrill, relentless, demanding ways, and to leverage YHWH back to YHWH's most characteristic work of creating futures.

The characteristic moment of the Psalms in the turn from *plea* to *praise* may be understood as a rhetorical, covenantal strategy for moving from a futile and unbearable present tense to a future of well-being that only YHWH can give.[10] Form critical analysis has shown that this dialogical strategy is stylized and well established; but there is immense room for imaginative variation and innovation. I will first cite two well-known *pleas* that have been given divine response so that the Psalms end in dialogical celebration of the new future that YHWH has already begun to enact.

Psalm 13, the clearest and most succinct example of this characteristic rhetorical strategy, begins in verses 1-4 with complaint that describes for YHWH the unbearable situation and a threefold petition that anticipates YHWH's intervention:

> How long, O LORD? Will you forget me forever?
>   How long will you hide your face from me?
> How long must I bear pain in my soul,
>   and have sorrow in my heart all day long?
> How long shall my enemy be exalted over me?
>   Consider and answer me, O LORD my God! (Psalm 13:1-3a)

The psalm culminates in verses 5-6 that celebrates YHWH's fidelity and speaks of a new situation of well-being already accomplished by YHWH:

> But I trusted in your steadfast love;
>   my heart shall rejoice in your salvation.
> I will sing to the LORD,
>   because he has dealt bountifully with me. (Psalm 13:5-6)

The psalm itself characteristically does not provide any account of how the move from trouble to new well-being has been accomplished. We are left to conclude that the new situation is created by YHWH's intervention who has responded to the petition of the psalmist. Such intervention may, perhaps, have been by a (mediated) verbal assurance (salvation oracle) or by some other gesture or sign.[11] In any case, the psalm evidences a new future wrought by YHWH.

The same pattern is evident in the more familiar words of Psalm 22. Verses 1-21a characterize the unbearable situation that can occur only because of YHWH's abandonment (vv. 6-8, 12-18). Life without YHWH becomes an unbearable venue of assault and threat. In this extended prayer, the psalmist issues only two brief imperatives of petition to YHWH:

Do not be far from me,
    for trouble is near
    and there is no one to help. (Psalm 22:11)

But you, O LORD, do not be far away!
    O my help, come quickly to my aid!
Deliver my soul from the sword,
    my life from the power of the dog!
    Save me from the mouth of the lion! (Psalm 22:19-21a)

The deathly situation described is because of divine absence; the speaker has no doubt that YHWH's active presence will be transformational. And so in verse 21b, the Psalm turns to glad celebration for YHWH has "rescued" ("answered") the speaker (v. 21a) and heard the prayer (v. 24). The future is opened by the responsiveness of YHWH.

Thus the Psalms report on a situation of deathliness resolved by the attentiveness of the life-giving God. There are many other psalms, however, in which the futility of the present is described but the resolution and deliverance is only in the prospect. (Thus such petitions are acts of hope.) Erhard Gerstenberger rightly concludes, "All laments of Israel hope for a breakthrough (*Durchbruch*).[12] Thus, for example, Psalm 35 complains about the force of the enemy (vv. 7-8, 11-16) and petitions YHWH for deliverance (vv. 1-3, 17, 22-26). And three times the psalm promises to praise and celebrate YHWH's deliverance, but only after the deliverance is accomplished:

> *Then* my soul shall rejoice in the LORD,
>   exulting in his deliverance.
> All my bones shall say,
>   "O LORD, who is like you?
> You deliver the weak
>   from those too strong for them,
>   the weak and needy from those who despoil them." (Psalm 35:9-10, italics added)

> *Then* I will thank you in the great congregation;
>   in the mighty throng I will praise you. (Psalm 35:18, italics added)

> *Then* my tongue shall tell of your righteousness
>   and of your praise all day long. (Psalm 35:28, italics added)[13]

That is, praise is withheld by the petitioner until the new future is given by YHWH. We may imagine, moreover, that praise is withheld from YHWH as a bargaining chip, as a way of leveraging YHWH to act because YHWH is eager to be praised. Thus YHWH is not an automaton who delivers on call; Israel receives futures from YHWH, but not "on demand." Israel must await the slow working of history wherein YHWH's newness will be given. The future is promised to those who pray to YHWH, but not always given.

I will now return to the four "failed futures" I have mentioned, and consider how in each case that failed future is addressed in faith in order to make a future from YHWH possible:

1. *Concerning mortality*. Israelites, of course, knew they were going to die. But they failed in the fidelity of YHWH an adequate and reassuring antidote to the threat of death. Thus after the crisis of mortality is voiced in Psalm 103:15-16, the psalmist utilizes an adventuresome imagination to make a theological affirmation:

> But the steadfast love of the LORD is from everlasting to everlasting
>   on those who fear him,
>   and his righteousness to children's children,
> to those who keep his covenant
>   and remember to do his commandments. (Psalm 103:17-18)

The answer to death and loss and nullification is the fidelity of YHWH that is not disruptive even by death.

We may pause over this question of mortality, because the matter of a *future beyond death* is a complex matter in the Old Testament.[14] It is the case that the Psalms speak often of the power of death and *sheol* as the power that threatens life, and regularly petition YHWH to override the power of death and restore the speaker to life. It is conventional in Old Testament studies to regard such statements about death to refer, in imaginative fashion, to all the realities of life that diminish joy and well-being, such as, poor health, weakness, bondage, persecution, social alienation. Restoration to life wrought by the power of God is the power to overcome all of these negations so that life may be abundant. Thus "to die" is to have life diminished, and to be given "life" is to have existence enhanced by food, healing, freedom, or whatever. The power and promise of YHWH is to break the negation and to enhance human existence. We may see this language in a variety of psalms:

> As for me, I shall behold your face in righteousness;
> when I awake I shall be satisfied, beholding your likeness. (Psalm 17:15)
>
> I believe that I shall see the goodness of the LORD
> in the land of the living. (Psalm 27:13)
>
> But God will ransom my soul from the power of Sheol,
> for he will receive me. (Psalm 49:15)
>
> For you have delivered my soul from death,
> my eyes from tears,
> my feet from stumbling.
> I walk before the LORD
> in the land of the living. (Psalm 116:8-9)[15]

It is also a common conclusion in Old Testament studies that this rhetoric refers metaphorically to the diminishment and enhancement of life, but it does not refer to resurrection and life after death. For the most part, scholars have judged that such a way of thinking, speaking, and believing was not on the horizon of ancient Israel, and YHWH's future-creating power had its limit there.

The primary dissent from this common opinion is that of Mitchell Dahood, together with his student Nicholas J. Tromp.[16] It is their argument that the language of faith in the Psalms does indeed at many points refer to resurrection from death taken in a literal and nonmetaphorical way. They make the argument not by appeal to YHWH or by appeal to Christian doctrine, but by the language of Ugaritic myths. Thus Dahood frequently translates "life" in the Psalms as "eternal life," affirming that YHWH will create futures even beyond death.

For the most part, Dahood and Tromp have not been followed in this venturesome interpretation. Nor would I follow their lead. I do think, nonetheless, that YHWH's capacity to make futures as concerns the *daily turmoils* and YHWH's capacity to make futures as concerns *physical death* are different not in kind but only in degree. Whether the Old Testament makes a move to the second claim or not—it is only a matter of daring, trusting faith to move from one affirmation to the other. However "death and life" are understood, the claim of faith concerns YHWH's *fidelity* that persists through every travail.[17]

2. Israel's sense of its guilt before YHWH and its awareness of alienation from YHWH is acute. But it is not as all defining as it has become in much of Christian theology under the impetus of Augustine and Luther.[18] Thus Israel can acknowledge its guilt before YHWH as in Psalm 51:1-5. But that psalm that ponders the depth of sin can move abruptly to a series of expectant imperatives, an anticipation that YHWH's mercy and generosity far outdistance such guilt. In Psalm 103, the matter of guilt is situated in the context of YHWH's mercy:

> The LORD is merciful and gracious,
> slow to anger and abounding in steadfast love.
> He will not always accuse,
> nor will he keep his anger forever.
> He does not deal with us according to our sins,
> nor repay us according to our iniquities.
> For as the heavens are high above the earth,
> so great is his steadfast love toward those who fear him;
> as far as the east is from the west,
> so far he removes our transgressions from us.
> As a father has compassion for his children,
> so the LORD has compassion for those who fear him.
> For he knows how we were made;
> he remembers that we are dust. (Psalm 103:8-14)

The operational words concerning YHWH's propensity are *steadfast love*, *mercy*, and *compassion*. The statement concludes with an allusion to Genesis 2:7 and the affirmation that human persons are made from dust (clay), and do not have great staying power. In their fragility and weakness, human persons violate YHWH; and YHWH knows this and is therefore ready to act in generosity.

The "penitential Psalms" reveal an acute sense both of guilt and of the prospect of life beyond guilt. Thus in Psalm 32 it is affirmed that an "acknowledgment of sin" is the single requirement for forgiveness, a process acted out in the forgiveness of David in the narrative of 2 Samuel 12:7-15:

> Then I acknowledged my sin to you,
> and I did not hide my iniquity;
> I said, "I will confess my transgressions to the LORD,"
> and you forgave the guilt of my sin. (Psalm 32:5)

As the psalm puts it, there is no slippage or pause between *confess* and *forgive*.

In Psalm 38, the psalmist, at some length, characterizes the lack of physical "soundness" that is a result of guilt (Psalm 38:3-8). But after such a recital, the psalm turns abruptly and forcefully to YHWH:

> But it is for you, O LORD, that I wait;
> it is you, O lord my God, who will answer....
>
> Do not forsake me, O LORD;
> O my God, do not be far from me;
> make haste to help me,
> O Lord, my salvation. (Psalm 38:15, 21-22)

The God from whom there is alienation is the God to whom there is appeal, as there is no other source of a forgiven future. And in Psalm 130:4, it is affirmed that "there is forgiveness." That is the beginning of a new life of obedience. The hope that is voiced is an active, confident one that does not doubt that YHWH will act to create a new future (vv. 5-6).

3. Conflict with adversaries that leave one powerless is resolved by appeal to YHWH who, it is not doubted, is stronger than one's adversaries. All that is required is that YHWH should be mobilized to act. For when YHWH acts, no adversary can stand. It is for that reason that YHWH is addressed with urgent imperative that YHWH should act to overcome the adversary and so make new life possible. Thus, after mention of foes and enemies, the psalmist asks: "O LORD my God, in you I take refuge; / save me from all my pursuers, and deliver me" (Psalm 7:1). After the characterization of the exploitative wicked, the petition is the same:

Rise up, O LORD; O God, lift up your hand;
    do not forget the oppressed....

Break the arm of the wicked and evildoers;
    seek out their wickedness until you find none.
The LORD is king forever and ever;
    the nations shall perish from his land.

O LORD, you will hear the desire of the meek;
    you will strengthen their heart, you will incline your ear
to do justice for the orphan and the oppressed,
    so that those from earth may strike terror no more. (Psalm 10:12, 15-18)

"Because the poor are despoiled,
    because the needy groan,
I will now rise up," says the LORD;
    "I will place them in the safety for which they long." (Psalm 12:5)

Rise up, O LORD, confront them, overthrow them!
    By your sword deliver my life from the wicked,
from mortals—by your hand, O LORD—
    from mortals whose portion in life is in this world.
May their bellies be filled with what you have stored up for them;
    may their children have more than enough;
    may they leave something over to their little ones.

As for me, I shall behold your face in righteousness;
    when I awake I shall be satisfied, beholding your likeness. (Psalm 17:13-15)

That YHWH should "arise" means that the God who has been indifferent or dormant or negligent should now become YHWH's own committed self. Rainier Albertz proposes that the work of such poetry is "to restore dignity and hope to the oppressed victims of the social crisis":

> The most important task of the piety of the poor which was developed and practised in the lower-class communities was to restore dignity and hope to the oppressed victims of the social crisis.
>
> This purpose was served, first, by the petitions and wishes directed against their oppressors, which in their uncompromising harshness and sometimes wild fantasies of vengeance nowadays terrify many delicate

> bourgeois Christian spirits. Here the dull fury and desperate sense of impotence among those who had been robbed of their rights and trampled on made itself felt; here their concerted will to resist, their refusal to be content with the hopeless situation, found words to express itself.
>
> The purpose was served, secondly, by their keen eschatological expectations of a great divine judgment that would punish the wicked rich and bring justice to the poor (9.20; 12.6; 14.5). In part they imagined this as a universal judgment which would affect not only the wicked but also the nations or the whole earth (Pss. 9.8f., 20; 82.8); this universalization of the perspectives of judgment, which is particularly striking in Pss.9f., is to be explained from the fact that for the lower-class circles the political dependence of Judah on the Persians and their exploitation by the upper-class collaborators were closely connected (cf. Isa. 56.9ff.). But in part they also envisaged an individual judgment in which the wicked would be blotted out of the Book of Life (Ps. 69.29; cf. Mal. 3.16). In any case they hoped that with such a judgment Yahweh would totally reverse the present political and social conditions of domination (Ps. 75.8), banish the hated occupiers from Judah (Ps.10.16), break the power of those who were exploiting them (75.11) and give the land as a heritage solely to them and their descendants (69.37). Yahweh would overthrow all the divine powers which now supported the oppression of the poor (Ps. 82.2-7) and establish his kingly rule on earth (10.16). Then the poor and oppressed would finally secure their rights and there would be an end to all violent human rule on earth (10.18). By incorporating the whole of this horizon of eschatological expectation on which they were working in their exegesis of the prophets into their personal piety, the religious circles in the lower class were creating the possibility of holding fast to their personal God even in their extreme, chronic distress. The unjust social conditions that largely excluded them from the personal protection and blessing of God would not last; Yahweh himself would reverse them, and again become a "citadel for the oppressed" (Ps. 9.10), in accord with the age-old experiences of personal piety.[19]

Of course, in Christian imagination the repeated imperative "rise" is drawn easily into Easter faith. Thus it is possible to take these petitionary Psalms as moves of the living God against every manifestation of death that wants to negate or cancel a good life. Israel has no doubt that when death is curbed, challenged, or defeated, a new life in the world is possible.

4. The overcoming of YHWH as adversary is not such an easy case. Of course it is easiest to imagine that one must repent of disobedience, for it

is disobedience that has made YHWH into an adversary. If, however, we go outside the Psalms to the book of Job, a man and a book that are in Hebrew named "adversary," we can see that the move toward some kind of reconciliation with YHWH is not through repentance—and certainly not through automatic pro forma repentance—but through direct, confrontive speech that calls everything into question. Job is prepared to confess his sin as soon as he knows what it is (Job 31:35-37). Until then, however, Job will hold his ground and keep his "integrity." Though the matter is far from clear, we may imagine that by the end of the book of Job, the two parties of dispute have reached a new understanding. But it has been accomplished by Job who insisted, against YHWH, on his own legitimacy as a person of faith and a man of the world. It is this Job, so says YHWH, who has spoken "what is right" (Job 42:7-8).[20]

The outcome of the transformative intervention of YHWH that is in response to Israelite insistent petition is a *new life of well-being.* God does give futures! But they are futures, so the Psalter attests, that are given only to those who risk the breaking of silence and who venture to declare their own legitimacy before YHWH. It is YHWH's gift of a new future that causes such psalms of insistent petition to end in celebration and affirmation of a new life that is marked in every dimension by well-being:

> You have turned my mourning into dancing;
> you have taken off my sackcloth
> and clothed me with joy,
> so that my soul may praise you and not be silent.
> O LORD my God, I will give thanks to you forever. (Psalm 30:11-12)

There is no doubt that it is YHWH who has created this new future, a future now marked by joy (on the recovery of joy see Psalm 51:12).

The resolve of the response to the gift of the new future is *praise*, *speech*, and *thanks*:

- *Praise* is the lyrical, exuberant *abandonment of self* in the midst of the congregation that exalts in YHWH who is all in all. The one who has been absent is now fully present in life-giving power.
- *Speech* is the characteristic resolve in Israel to *forego a silence*, either of submissiveness or of self-forgetting despair. Israel knows, as Job exemplifies, that human life requires bold self-announcement in order to have a self that may commune with the future-creating God.

■ *Thanks* is the readiness to *line out in some detail* for the community the dire circumstance of need, the transformative act, and the new gift. Thanks is to "count your blessings" with specificity, as the psalmist does in Psalm 30:7-10. The new life now lived in exuberant *self-abandonment* and vigorous *self-announcement* is a gift of YHWH, the only source of futures.

CHAPTER FIFTEEN

HOPE FOR THE WORLD

The primary hope from YHWH in the Old Testament is that YHWH will keep YHWH's promises *to Israel.* But we have seen in the foregoing section that from that defining hope for Israel, the Old Testament moves to *smaller scale* to consider hope for *the individual*, albeit as a member of Israel's promissory community. In the present section of this discussion, I will consider the way in which the Old Testament moves from the defining hope for Israel to *larger scale*, to consider hope for *the world.* It is clear that hope in the Old Testament is not confined to Israel, for the redeemer of Israel is the creator of heaven and earth. For that reason, we take up the question, what may *creation* "hope" and what promises has YHWH made to creation?

I

We may identify three premises for thinking about *hope for creation.* First, there is no doubt that YHWH as creator is articulated in the Old Testament according to the many available ancient Near Eastern myths that were utilized in the great temples of Mesopotamia in liturgical construction of the world. These liturgical narratives of creation variously account for the emergence of the world by divine purpose through combat or decree. While the "preferred" theological account of creation in the Old Testament is by YHWH's word (see Psalm 33), Jon Levenson has shown how the combat myth has left decisive traces in Old Testament's creation rhetoric.[1]

Second, the utilization of such mythic constructions of the world was readily taken up by Israel. After all, if the creation accounts of Israel are products of temple theology, it is not unreasonable that the temple leadership should have appropriated materials and religious claims from antecedent traditions of liturgic practice. At the same time, it is clear that Israel's articulation of creation faith bore the marks of YHWH's definitive and peculiar character, so that the borrowed materials are in important ways transformed and transposed into articulations of Yahwistic faith. Such new markings of the material include (a) a coherent moral intention for creation, (b) a singular divine voice and not a cacophony of intentions, and (c) consequently, the absence of jealous self-regard and self-promotion on the part of the creator God. The problem of a plurality of gods in the process of the creation of the world, a claim reflected in many of the antecedent materials, is handled through the imagery of a divine council wherein other gods are subordinated to the governing purpose of YHWH.[2] The extent to which the materials have been *borrowed* as they existed and the extent to which materials have been *transformed* in Yahwistic ways is a matter of ongoing dispute among interpreters. Interpreters who take up questions of "the religion of Israel" tend to note the similarities between the biblical material and its cultural antecedents, whereas practitioners of Old Testament theology tend to accent the distinctiveness of the Yahwistic account.

Third, it is most plausible that the several texts on creation are reflective of liturgical practice so that we must understand "myth" in terms of public liturgical performance. However that may be understood theoretically, it is the case that the liturgical performance of the great theological claims is experienced in the community of worship as effective and generative of new reality. Thus the liturgic performance is indeed "world-making."[3] We can thus entertain the view that each time Israel recited or enacted creation texts it was, in the life of the gathered community, remaking and reforming an ordered world that was reflective of YHWH's singular intentionality for the well-being and the prosperity of the world. While every performance of creation myth in any culture has that intentionality, in Israel the world performed and thereby "made" is reflective of YHWH's intentionality, likely already known in the great Mosaic memories of exodus, sojourn, and Sinai.

II

Three primary convictions are constant and recurring in much Old Testament thought about creation. First, creation is the imposition, by divine sovereignty, of a fruitful order of well-being in the world. This declaration of divine purpose is done by edict or decree, the exercise of authority by a presiding sovereign who not only reigns but rules. The will of the creator, in Old Testament tradition, is clearly that the earth should be ordered so as to give life in abundance and peaceableness for all creatures, so that all creatures might bear and give evidence of the blessing of the creator in the fulfillment of their creatureliness. Four texts may be cited as evidence of the will of the creator that is to be enacted by the creatures.

1. Genesis 1, most familiarly, exhibits the divine address to the creatures with commands, "be" (vv. 3, 6, 11), "bring forth" (vv. 11, 20, 24), "be fruitful" (vv. 22, 28) is clear that the several creatures are fully and immediately prepared to obey the command of the creator and thereby fulfill the purpose of their existence. The sum of all of these *commands* and responses in *obedience* is a luxurious, teeming, abundant ordering of life.

2. In Psalm 65:9-13, the lyrical celebration of luxurious creation is governed by five verbs of doxology, each of which has YHWH as subject: "You visit, you enrich, you provide, you water, you crown." It is all YHWH's action that produces creation, and we can see the outcomes of the action of the creator in the wonder of creation. Specifically in an arid climate the doxology celebrates the gift of water that makes all life in the world possible (see Genesis 2:10-14 and derivatively Ezekiel 47:1-12). The result of such powerful generosity is that crops grow, pastures overflow, meadows support flocks, and valleys have abundant grain. All creatureliness is at work for the well-being of an abundant, blessed earth.

3. The same accent on water given by the creator is evident in the lyric of Psalm 104:10-23. The beginning point in characterizing this wondrously working world is, "You make springs gush forth" (v. 10). The result is "the earth is satisfied" (v. 13), and every creature drinks all that is needed (vv. 11-12). The image is of a waterhole in the forest where all come repeatedly and find more than enough (see Isaiah 35:6-7). As a result the earth produces grass and plants and eventually bread, wine, and oil, the staples of human existence (Psalm 104:15). Every creature is safe, well fed, and prosperous. The reliable, generous productivity of the earth leads to gratitude for satiation:

> These all look to you
>   to give them their food in due season;
> when you give to them, they gather it up;

> when you open your hand, they are filled with good things. (Psalm 104:27-28)[4]

4. The same sort of acknowledgment is expressed in Psalm 145 that also celebrates the rule of YHWH:

> The eyes of all look to you,
> and you give them their food in due season.
> You open your hand,
> satisfying the desire of every living thing. (Psalm 145:15-16)

Second, the imposition of order to make life possible makes clear that YHWH's action is an imposition on an already extant substance that of itself is unordered and incapable of producing life. It is a truism of Old Testament scholarship that the Old Testament itself does not anywhere allow that God's creation of the world is *ex nihilo*, a claim that appears in textual tradition only belatedly at the close of the Old Testament.[5] Before that articulation it is everywhere assumed that YHWH's work of creation concerns a preexistent substance that awaits the ordering, empowering, and blessing of divine decree. The Old Testament itself has no explanation for this "preexistent" material and exhibits no curiosity about it. It is a given of lived experience, a given that is marked by recalcitrant disorder that in fact works against and seeks to negate the abundant life that YHWH would give.

It is the case, moreover, that in the Old Testament that reality of life-threatening chaos continues to be in effect and at work in the world. Thus Jon Levenson can write of "the persistence of evil," and can say of the flood narrative:

> The conclusion of the Flood story includes a divine pledge to maintain creation, but the story itself manifests a profound anxiety about the givenness of creation, a keen sense of its precariousness. On the one hand, God vows to maintain the created order. On the other hand, he does so only after having ended a state of chaos that began with his announcing that he regretted having ever authored creation in the first place. Between creation and chaos, life and death, there stands neither human righteousness (which continues to be deficient) nor God's intrinsic unchangeability (which this and many other biblical stories belie), but only God's covenantal faithfulness, his respect for the solemn pledge that he makes to Noah. Here again the endurance and stability of nature is not intrinsic; it is only a corollary of God's faith-

> fulness. Should he in his freedom choose to dishonor his covenantal pledge, the created order would vanish.[6]

The threat of chaos persists, but it is held at bay by the faithful power of YHWH. The texts suggest that the threat of chaos is not fully subdued and not eliminated, but held at bay. In the Christian tradition, moreover, the miracle of Jesus "stilling the storm" (Mark 4:35-41) indicates how that threat continues in Christian imagination and is overcome fully only in the end of time when "the sea is no more" (Revelation 21). Until then, Israel (and the other creatures) can only trust in the creator to withstand the continuing threat of chaos. Jon Levenson has provided the clearest, most compelling study of this aspect of creation faith.[7] Two other studies are to be noted as well. Fredrik Lindström, in his study of Psalms of complaint, has shown that the trouble voiced in the complaint Psalms is due to the threat of chaos that emerges when YHWH is absent or negligent or derelict in duty.[8] The intent of such psalms is to summon YHWH back into presence (in the temple), for when YHWH is actively present chaos has no chance of effect. In a quite different idiom, Karl Barth has written of *Das Nichtige*, the active, abiding presence of nothingness that seeks always to undo the work of the creator.[9] Creation faith in the Old Testament is under no romantic illusion about creation. It knows that the world in and of itself cannot sustain itself, but depends fully upon YHWH:

> The world is not inherently safe; it is inherently unsafe. Only the magisterial intervention of God and his eternal vigilance prevent the cataclysm. Creation endures because God has pledged in an eternal covenant that it shall endure and because he has, also in an eternal covenant, compelled the obeisance of his great adversary. If either covenant (or are they one?) comes undone, creation disappears.[10]

The good news in Israel's faith, however, is that YHWH as creator has totally mastered chaos. For that reason the world is safe and not under threat. It is for that reason that the creation narrative in Genesis 1 culminates in Genesis 2:1-4a with celebration of sabbath. The creator is not anxious about creation, and creation itself is peaceable and not restless. The most graphic examples of this claim and this reality is the assertion of Psalm 104:25-26 that Leviathan, the evil sea monster, "has become a play thing for YHWH":

Yonder is the sea, great and wide,
creeping things innumerable are there,
living things both small and great.
There go the ships,
and Leviathan that you formed to sport in it. (Psalm 104:25-26)

The same claim for YHWH's mastery and enjoyment of the power of chaos is the lyrical statement of YHWH to Job concerning the wonder and splendor of Leviathan that overwhelms humanity but is a welcome member of YHWH's creation:

Can you draw out Leviathan with a fishhook,
or press down its tongue with a cord?
Can you put a rope in its nose,
or pierce its jaw with a hook?
Will it make many supplications to you?
Will it speak soft words to you?
Will it make a covenant with you
to be taken as your servant forever?
Will you play with it as with a bird,
or will you put it on leash for your girls?
Will traders bargain over it?
Will they divide it up among the merchants?
Can you fill its skin with harpoons,
or its head with fishing spears?
Lay hands on it;
think of the battle; you will not do it again! (Job 41:1-8)

The way in which YHWH expresses pride in Leviathan and the way in which *Job is compared to Leviathan*, indicates the distance between creator and human creatures and the way in which YHWH the creator has taken control of all that might threaten creation.[11] As a result and without denying the latent threat, the world is safe, as safe as YHWH's own fidelity.

Thus the Jeremiah tradition can appeal to the stability of creation as a way of offering reassurance to Israel concerning YHWH's reliability:

Thus says the LORD,
who gives the sun for light by day
and the fixed order of the moon and the stars for light by night,
who stirs up the sea so that its waves roar—
the LORD of hosts is his name:

If this fixed order were ever to cease
from my presence, says the LORD,
then also the offspring of Israel would cease
to be a nation before me forever. (Jeremiah 31:35-36)

Thus says the LORD:
If the heavens above can be measured,
and the foundations of the earth below can be explored,
then I will reject all the offspring of Israel
because of all they have done,
says the LORD. (Jeremiah 31:37)

Thus says the LORD: Only if I had not established my covenant with day and night and the ordinances of heaven and earth, would I reject the offspring of Jacob and of my servant David and not choose any of his descendants as rulers over the offspring of Abraham, Isaac, and Jacob. For I will restore their fortunes, and will have mercy upon them. (Jeremiah 33:25-26)

Thus the texts may be seen in a spectrum from *threat* to *stable assurance*. The decisive component in discerning the world as under threat or assurance is readiness to take seriously the role of YHWH, a rule that changes everything about the character of the world.

Third, the creatures know that the created order is under threat and in jeopardy. But they also know about the creator God, YHWH's generous decree, enormous power, and abiding fidelity. And because the creatures know this, all of them join the human creatures in the Jerusalem temple to sing praise to YHWH.[12] Fretheim has shown how full and pervasive is the praise of YHWH by the creation:[13]

Praise him, sun and moon;
praise him, all you shining stars!
Praise him, you highest heavens,
and you waters above the heavens!

Let them praise the name of the LORD,
for he commanded and they were created.
He established them forever and ever;
he fixed their bounds, which cannot be passed.

Praise the LORD from the earth,
you sea monsters and all deeps,

> fire and hail, snow and frost,
>   stormy wind fulfilling his command!
>
> Mountains and all hills,
>   fruit trees and all cedars!
> Wild animals and all cattle,
>   creeping things and flying birds! (Psalm 148:3-10)

We may take Psalm 96:11-12 as an example of this creaturely praise:

> Let the heavens be glad, and let the earth rejoice;
>   let the sea roar, and all that fills it;
>   let the field exult, and everything in it.
> Then shall all the trees of the forest sing for joy. (Psalm 96:11-12)

In verse 10 it is affirmed "among the nations" that YHWH's royal rule has been instituted, and therefore the world will be stable. In verse 13 it is affirmed that this new rule of YHWH is characterized by righteousness and truth. Sandwiched between the announcement of the new regime in verses 10 and 13, the creatures sing. We are not told why. We may deduce, however, that the announced regime change brings elation to the creatures because the old governance of the rulers of this age was devastating for creation. Thus,

- the sea roars its approval of the new regime because it knows the practice of pollution will stop;
- the field exalts because it can imagine the termination of excessive chemical fertilizer and exploitative agribusiness by absentee owners;
- the trees applaud because they anticipate a cessation of deforestation and aggressive developers that jeopardize all trees;
- along with the sea and the fields and the trees, the birds sing and the animals growl in satisfaction; they know that under the new rule their habitats will be safe and protected.

In sum, the rule of YHWH assures that all creatures will now have opportunity and protection in order to fulfill and enact their true vocation as creatures of YHWH.

Fretheim provides a thoughtful and compelling interpretation of this nonhuman praise. I wonder, however, if we may dare to go further to entertain the possibility that nonhuman creatures, plants as well as animals, have some *consciousness* and may indeed be doxologically engaged.[14] Such a thought may strike us as primitive, given modern scientism that has reduced some creatures to inanimate objects. We may entertain such a thought not by returning to a "primitive" prescientific world, but by noticing that a *covenantal* mode of existence is an alternative to a *technological* mode of existence. In such a way of thinking, any creature is in covenant with the creator, and *doxology* as well as *obedience* belongs to such a relationship.

III

It is fair to say that these themes of *created order for life*, *jeopardy*, the *restraint of chaos*, and *responsive doxology* are constitutive of Israel's creation faith. In our discussion of hope, however, such claims only form a backdrop for our consideration. Given the wide and deep claims for creation faith, we may now turn properly to the question of *creation hope*. The context for creation hope is Israel's awareness that *creation can be undone*. The good order of the creation is not a given that is intrinsic to creation; that good order persists only by the constant attentiveness of the creator. Thus in prophetic warning and critique, Israel's dissenters can imagine that the world may be undone. It is to be recognized at the outset that among the classic covenant curses that may be evoked by disobedience is *drought*, an immense and devastating threat in an arid agricultural environment (Leviticus 26:19; Deuteronomy 28:22-24; 1 Kings 8:35-36). It may well be that such rhetoric is only hyperbole that refers to the dismantling of Israel's stable life-world: it is equally possible, however, that the rhetoric is intrinsically important, for Israel knows that the Torah (or wisdom insights) are the rules and conditions for the maintenance of the created order. When these rules are violated, creation will come unglued. Thus the prophetic warning moves from the claim that the creator upholds creation and instead avers that it is a covenant, dialogical transaction of mutual fidelity that sustains the world.[15]

The following texts articulate the imaginative claim in Israel that creation can indeed be dismantled, so that it would fail as a life-giving, life-sustaining system:

■ Hosea 4:1-3 most succinctly asserts that adherence to the commands of YHWH is a precondition of creation. This rhetorical unit is a speech of judgment that, after the summons to court (v. 1a), has the usual elements of indictment and sentence. The indictment concerns the violation of the commands of the Decalogue:

> There is no faithfulness or loyalty,
> and no knowledge of God in the land.
> Swearing, lying, and murder,
> and stealing and adultery break out;
> bloodshed follows bloodshed. (Hosea 4:1b-2)

The sentence, introduced by a characteristic "therefore," describes a drought that is so acute that wild bees, birds, and fish vanish:

> Therefore the land mourns,
> and all who live in it languish;
> together with the *wild animals*
> and the *birds* of the air,
> even the *fish* of the sea are perishing. (Hosea 4:3, italics added)

This triad of creatures is a usual one that refers to all creatures. The brief poem makes a stunning and decisive linkage between indictment and sentence. The *violation of commands* produces a *life-threatening drought.* Of course this is elliptical poetry. If we were to proceed in an explanatory mode, we would need to place between indictment and threat a chain of factors based perhaps in greed that in turn leads to deforestation that in turn produces a global warming that in turn leads to devastating storms and the disruption of urban population. My purpose here is not to offer a "scientific" explanation, but to suggest that the implied connections of elliptical poetry can be understood if we muster some explanatory data. The creation is a mystery that requires no scientific understanding; but it is not a venue of magic. It is rather a matrix for covenantal answerability.

■ In the fuller poem of Hosea 2:2-23, the rhetoric moves, in the language of creaturely faithfulness, from alienation and divorce (vv. 2-13) to reconciliation and remarriage (vv. 14-23). It is astonishing that the *covenantal* imagery of divorce and remarriage has an overlay of *creation* language concerning the loss and reinstitution of fruitfulness. Here our concern is only with verses 9-13 that are dominated by first-person verbs with the God of creation and covenant who speaks in response to the covenantal infidelity of Israel, YHWH says:

I will take back,
I will take away,
I will uncover,
I will put an end,
I will lay waste,
I will punish.

The creator God, affected by disobedience and infidelity, will withdraw from Israel the blessings and life-giving power of creation. The vitality of agricultural productivity and all the possibilities of fruitfulness will be terminated. If we ask, as the text does not ask, how YHWH does that, the most likely "strategy" is a drought, for a lack of rain will cause all the growth mentioned in verse 9 to terminate and will in turn nullify all the "mirth" of harvest that is expressed in the liturgical-agricultural cycle. The rhetoric concerning the threat of drought, moreover, appeals to Baal, the god of agricultural productivity, in verses 8 and 13. Thus the poem anticipates the implementation of the curse of drought, so that the sky whence comes rain will be "like iron and your earth like copper" (Leviticus 26:19; Deuteronomy 28:23-24). Creation will fail, and Israel will suffer until its social existence is threatened.

■ A century after Hosea and a century closer to the shutdown of Jerusalem, the rhetoric of Jeremiah is even more intense and ominous. Like Hosea before him, Jeremiah imagines the failure of creation as a divine response to the failure of the Sinai covenant:

> I looked on the earth, and lo, it was waste and void;
> and to the heavens, and they had no light.
> I looked on the mountains, and lo, they were quaking,
> and all the hills moved to and fro.
> I looked, and lo, there was no one at all,
> and all the birds of the air had fled.
> I looked, and lo, the fruitful land was a desert,
> and all its cities were laid in ruins
> before the LORD, before his fierce anger. (Jeremiah 4:23-26)

It is regularly noted concerning this passage that the movement through the fourfold "I looked" is a step-by-step undoing of the creation as given in Genesis 1. Thus verse 23 reports on the return of chaos ("waste and void") as in Genesis 1:2, and the subsequent lines move through the undoing of the lights of heaven (Genesis 1:16-18), the mountains and hills of the earth (Genesis 1:9-10), the birds, human beings, and the fruitful land (Genesis 1:20-31). The undoing of creation is at the behest of YHWH, who responds to covenantal infidelity on a cosmic scale, an undoing not only of Israel but the negation of Israel's "natural" habitat.

Two things are clear about this scenario. First, the power of chaos ("waste and void") to override ordered fruitfulness does not happen because "chaos" is an autonomous acting agent who seeks to negate life. Rather "chaos" is now a tool and instrument of YHWH's covenantal sovereignty and operates according to the intention of the creator God. Second, it is clear that the fruitful ordering of creation has no intrinsic staying power, nor can it be guaranteed and sustained even by the reassuring liturgies of the Jerusalem temple. Creation rises or falls, stays or disrupts, according to the will of the creator, the God who takes seriously the Torah obedience or disobedience of Israel upon which the future of creation hinges.

Thus the prophetic rhetoric of judgment is able to affirm at the same time (a) that creation is ordered and reliable according to YHWH's sovereignty but (b) that the divine sovereignty is covenantally operative with reference to the Torah-keeping of Israel or the Torah-failure of Israel. The prophetic logic relates *Torah* and *world orde*r in the same way as the succinct summary of Hosea 4:1-3. While it is not in prophetic rhetoric, the flood narrative of Genesis 6:5–9:17 makes the same point. It is the "wickedness of humankind" (Genesis 6:5) that evokes the flood wherein YHWH the creator unleashes the force of chaos in order to terminate a failed creation. The normal requirement that sustains creation is everywhere apparent in Israel's poetic imagination. The sum of this imaginative claim is to the effect that Israel (or the world of humanity) has failed in its vocation of world maintenance through obedience. And so the end!

The rhetoric of Jeremiah 4:23-26 bespeaks a failed world order as ominous and devastating and complete as any contemporary scenario of nuclear destruction. The rhetoric is according to the imaginable possibility of the ancient world, but that imaginative possibility is a moral-covenantal equivalence to our barely thinkable technological capacity for destruction and termination. In both cases, ancient and contemporary, the "end" is not likely to be an abrupt disruption. It is more likely to be the slow erosion of viable life order through exploitative greed that, almost without notice, compromises the generous potential of the creation. Israel, in its awareness of the jeopardy of Jerusalem in the world that Jerusalem holds together symbolically, can match the coming historical disaster to a cosmic catastrophe. In both cases and according to both modes of rhetoric, Israel and its "natural environment" reached a death point and "null point" that is indeed a point of no return.

IV

Most remarkably, the Old Testament imagines beyond "the point of no return." There was no reason to do so. There was no available data whereby Israel could imagine beyond the null point. It is clear that such speaking, imagining, and hoping beyond the "null point" are rooted in nothing more and nothing less than the God of Israel who always "makes new." Israel, in its loss of hope, can remember and therefore hope according to YHWH's fidelity:

> But this I call to mind,
> and therefore I have hope:
>
> The steadfast love of the LORD never ceases,
> his mercies never come to an end;
> they are new every morning;
> great is your faithfulness. (Lamentations 3:21-23)

While Israel's primal hope, as already indicated, is restoration of Israel to the land, Israel's rhetoric proceeds on to a larger scope to wait for a new heaven and a new earth, a new beginning wrought by the power of God who has not yet completed the work of overcoming chaos, by divine intention that has been operative from the beginning. Following Donald Gowan and Terence Fretheim, I will mention six texts on new creation, each of which attest to YHWH's abiding fidelity and YHWH's generative capacity to make new beyond "the end of the world."

■ I have already mentioned the divorce-remarriage poem of Hosea 2:22-23. After the nullification uttered in verses 9-13, the poem moves to newness that will be wrought by the very God of nullification (vv. 14-23). In that articulation of newness, YHWH will reengage Israel in righteousness, justice, steadfast love, mercy, and faithfulness (vv. 19-20). At the same time, however, YHWH reengages not only Israel, but also initiates a new future for creation: "I will make for you a covenant on that day with the wild animals, the birds of the air, and the creeping things of the ground; and I will abolish the bow, the sword, and war from the land; and I will make you lie down in safety" (Hosea 2:18; see vv. 21-23). It is plausible to think that this renewed covenant with "wild animals, birds of the air, and creeping things of the ground" is a counterpoint to the postflood covenant with "all creation" in Genesis 9:9-17. The world begins again in God's fidelity!

In Isaiah 11:1-9, the prophet anticipates a new king in Jerusalem who will act on behalf of the poor and the needy. But alongside that social possibility, the poem continues to anticipate a reconciled creation that will be absent of hurt or destruction:

> They will not hurt or destroy
> on all my holy mountain;
> for the earth will be full of the knowledge of the LORD
> as the waters cover the sea. (Isaiah 11:9)

"Knowledge of the Lord" concerns covenantal fidelity, adherence to YHWH's sovereignty, and obedience to YHWH's commands. The new world will be ordered according to YHWH's intention.

■ In the latter part of the Isaiah tradition, we reach the extreme limit of hope for creation in the Old Testament. Along with Isaiah 66:22, the extended poem of Isaiah 65:17-25 lines out a new creation. It is most interesting and most important that this vision of new possibility is not some ethereal "religious" spree; it is rather a reorganized political economy that is concerned with life and death (v. 20), property and security (vv. 21-22), childbirth and health care (v. 23), reconciliation of nonhuman creation as in Isaiah 11:6-9 (v. 25), and full communion with the creator (v. 24). It is to be noted, moreover, that the newness pivots on Jerusalem, the epicenter of newness from which will flow the rivers of life (see Ezekiel 47).[16]

■ Two texts in Ezekiel attest to the same cosmic dimension of hope. Ezekiel 34:25-31, in a text that echoes the prospects of Genesis 9:8-17, anticipates "a covenant of peace" (v. 25) so that human habitation will be completely secure. (Ezekiel 34:26 also anticipates a "covenant of peace" in rhetoric that echoes the mandate of Genesis 1:27-28.) There will be ample rain and the trees shall yield their fruit, not unlike the intention of Genesis 1. There will be "splendid vegetation" and no more hunger (v. 29). To be sure, the revived function of creation is in the service of a restored Israel. It is nonetheless a prospect for a restored creation that will enact its God-given role as YHWH's creature.

■ Ezekiel 36:29-36 matches a restored Israel to a restored creation. The central creation promise is that there will be abundant grain and no famine; again there will be abundant fruit from trees, the flourishing of creation will be "like the garden of Eden" in its abundance (v. 35). It is clear that the prophetic utterance has in purview the creation tradition; indeed the liturgical recital of Genesis 1:1–2:4a may be roughly contemporary with the anticipations of Ezekiel.

■ Finally, in the sequence of texts I cite there is no doubt that the promise of Genesis 9:8-17 looms large over all thought of new creation. As Rolf Rendtorff has shown so clearly, the postflood promise of a reliable creation is nothing short of a new beginning:[17]

> As long as the earth endures,
>   seedtime and harvest, cold and heat,
> summer and winter, day and night,
>   shall not cease. (Genesis 8:22)

The renewal of covenant with creation means that the creator God enacts a creation postflood that is equal in scope and proportion to the initial creation out of "formlessness and void." The divine promise of fidelity, marked by the rainbow, assures that creation is not only an initial act; it is an abiding attentiveness whereby the creator God continues to attend to creation in protective, guaranteeing ways. All of the texts I have cited in this discussion (Hosea 2:14-23; Isaiah 11:1-9; 65:17-25; Ezekiel 34:25-31; and 36:29-36) treat the renewal of creation as a byproduct of the restoration of Israel; to be sure, the postflood declaration in Genesis 9, the new beginning of creation, is not an addendum to an Israelite concern. It will not do to reduce new creation to an appendage to Israelite concern, for the savior of Israel is indeed the creator of the earth. One of the tasks of Old Testament theology, as a corrective to the primary models of Old Testament theology in the twentieth century, is to see that creation cannot be subordinated to covenant, but has its own intrinsic reality as a divine commitment:

> The covenant with Noah, therefore, has incorporated the whole creation, including the nations, in the blessing, the compassion, and the redemption of God arising out of the promise to maintain the creation. Mosaic covenant does not stand against that or mark out a special place for Israel. That raises the question, quite naturally, of what that covenant does mean for Israel if the Noachic covenant is the larger

framework that both establishes a natural order as the matrix of human and historical existence, and creates the conditions for God's compassionate and redemptive activity to become available for "every living creature."[18]

V

We may now reflect on the data reviewed here, first by considering three interpretive questions and then by suggesting four continuing tasks of cosmic hope.

First, this discussion invites reflection on three sorts of questions about the nature and intent of the textual material I have cited.

1. These texts are all anticipatory about a future God who will yet give. This anticipatory dimension invites us to ask whether these texts function as liturgically generative of new creation in the present tense, or whether this is in fact an eschatological hope at the close of the age. Interpreters go in different directions. From the impetus of Sigmund Mowickel, there is an important strand of Old Testament interpretation that regards liturgical performance as in fact an effective mode of generativity. This way of understanding the textual tradition is especially alive in higher liturgical traditions that experience liturgy in general as performative and not simply reportorial or anticipatory. Scholars such as Brevard Childs, in a quite self-conscious Reformed stance, view the promises as eschatological and not at all as present performance;[19] this latter judgment is in part, I believe, a resistance to the temptation to an *ex opere operato* productivity.

My quite practical judgment is that however much we may insist that the promise is quite futuristic, in fact the liturgical performance is experienced by many people who have not reflected critically on the matter as present tense reality. I suspect that the either/or of liturgical performance/eschatology is in fact an "already/not yet" reality that occurs everywhere in this faith tradition. Thus it is not a flat "either/or" but includes both *realized* and *futuristic* dimensions.

2. We may ask whether these scenarios of future gifts from YHWH the creator are to be taken "literally" or is it all metaphor for the newness God will give, that is, did they really mean it? Did Isaiah really anticipate lions and lambs bedded together? Did later Israel in fact expect a time

with no infant mortality (Isaiah 65:20)? Or is the language simply vivid, lyrical hyperbole that must not be measured too closely?

Well, it is poetry! It is surely prescientific and it does not strain for precision. And the reason it is poetic and metaphorical is that the tradition speaks of possibilities beyond explanation. The focus of attention is not upon the trees or the beasts or the rain. The focus is constantly upon the God who promises, and that God cannot be spoken of precisely or with scientific exactness, because this God does not conform to our manageable explanatory world. The God of Israel is always surging beyond the *real* to the *possible*.[20]

But if we say the rhetoric is poetic, lyrical, metaphorical, and hyperbolic, does that suggest that they did not mean it? Did they not mean children would eventually govern snakes? Did they not intend that new amber waves of grain were to be forthcoming? Well, yes, they meant exactly what they said. This poetry is exact and not slovenly or haphazard. This is exactly what they anticipated, even though they expected it from YHWH. The question, "literal or metaphorical?" surely would have been a nonsensical question to the framers of the tradition, for the subject of the tradition, YHWH, runs forcefully beyond our categories and must be tested with both seriousness and with imagination.

3. Is the anticipation of *new creation* a real expectation in Israel or is this simply an alternative way of speaking of *newness for Israel*? We have seen that in most of these texts *restored Israel* and *new creation* always come together. But our propensity to subordinate *new creation* to *new Israel* is, I suggest, given not so much in the text as it is given in our habits of reading. We are disposed, as Jews or as Christians, to think that the tradition is primally about a chosen people which, when pushed hard enough, yields a mantra-life, "No salvation outside the church synagogue." That habit of reading, however, is an imposition upon the text. Clearly in this tradition *chosen people* and *chosen world* go together in the promise of this God because *the savior* is *the creator*. God's business, so Job at the edge of the Old Testament had to learn, is the wonder of creation before which our historical particularities must yield. This large dimension is of enormous importance in a culture that now must face "other religions" beyond our own. Without any compromise of particularity, the Bible is cast in a very large scenario. Thus, *mutatis mutandis*, had the dominant Christian tradition focused on Colossians and Ephesians rather than on Romans and Galatians, the proportionality of creation and chosenness would, in the long run, have been very different.[21]

Thus I conclude that on all three questions it is *both/and* and not *either/or*:

1. Both liturgical and eschatological;
2. Both metaphorical and literal;
3. Both for Israel and for the world.

Second, we may identify four ongoing interpretive tasks that arise from the preceding discussion:

1. The current discussion of evolution and intelligent design merits continuing work. Evolution, as popularly understood, lacks the moral dimension of accountability that belongs to a prophetic understanding of creation, and perhaps does not allow for the discontinuity that is definitional for the issue of creation/new creation in the Old Testament. If evolution is understood as a blind process of "selection," then it can provide no serious basis for environmental accountability. On the other hand, the attempt to treat intelligent design with reference to a creator God as a scientific claim is an interpretive impossibility. The creation texts in the Bible never offer anything that could be counted as scientific, for the characteristic mode of articulation is lyrical, poetic, and hyperbolic. To reduce such rhetoric to scientific formulation is to miss completely the doxological intent of the tradition. The present casting of the dispute is, in my judgment, singularly unhelpful; more work is required that may evoke categories of interpretation that do not infuse theological discernment with positivistic modes of insistence.

2. The hope of new creation as it is voiced in the prophetic tradition enunciates a moral dimension of accountability in creation that is of enormous importance in considering the environmental crisis that now must be faced. Cameron Whybrow has, in my judgment, made a compelling case that it is in the Enlightenment commoditization of creation that has made the earth and its resources available for limitless exploitation.[22] The biblical tradition of creation-new creation invites an interpretation away from *commoditization* to understand *creatureliness* in terms of dialogic-covenantal categories. This dialogic transaction that constitutes creation is situated in a matrix of accountability, whether in the Torah traditions of Sinai or in the wisdom traditions of "natural law."[23] Either way, there are intransigent limits against creaturely violation of creation. Such a way of thinking, in prophetic or sapiential tradition, does not require a crass supernaturalism to resituate creatureliness in terms of praise and obedience. Such a formulation still leaves open the

question of the consciousness of the creatures, a question that has not been silenced even by the long tradition of Enlightenment commoditization.

3. The dialogical, promissory tradition of new creation invites performance and re-performance of texts in the process of "world-making" that makes hope possible. Such world-making that permits hope is a counter-process against the performance of the world that is one of illusion and despair; the latter is a product of the dominant world-making of the military-technological apparatus that governs the global economy. The biblical witness refuses to give in to such a closed world where no new gifts are to be given.

In the end, of course, we shall have to ask whether such hope-filled world-making is a matter of self-deception and whistling in the dark. Such world-making, however, does not make its primary claims about the world, but rather about the creator God. If current expectations in physics are that the world will in due course either burn up or freeze over, then surely we are driven back to God. Of course, it is not known if the God of the tradition will create new worlds beyond this world that must end. What is clear is that the expectations of physics concerning the end of this world are not without resonance in prophetic faith.[24] But beyond that world-ending, even the best physics cannot go. Thus poets dare to go where scientists may not.

4. It is most likely that the promise of new creation, as in Isaiah 65:17-25, characteristically takes Jerusalem as the epicenter of that newness and as the venue for its liturgical performance. That is, "new creation" is not utopian and generic. It is quite context specific. From that textual focus, the ongoing work of interpretation and anticipation may lead us to recognize that such articulations of the future are to be done in specific venues, most especially in the work of liturgical imagination. Such an accent may serve to remind us that most liturgy in the conventional West is much too parochial in its horizon, much too focused on sin and forgiveness, and not enough on chaos and the order-giving life of God. The new creation is where war is not learned anymore, a genuine enactment of peace. The liturgical enactment of such a world is an urgent counteroffer in a world of violence, brutality, and revenge. Such a counteroffer is precisely the offer of this textual tradition.

CHAPTER SIXTEEN

HOPE IN ALTERNATIVE MODES

The Old Testament is a book of hope:

- Its hope is in the God of creation and exodus who characteristically creates new futures that the world imagines to be "impossible."
- Its hope is funded by old memories that have a dimension of normativeness, so that Israel could ground its future in what came to be a canonical past.
- Its hope arises, characteristically, at a null point of hopelessness, when all the historical data tells against new possibility, most especially in the sixth-century deportation and displacement.[1]

Given these features—a future-generating God, a vibrant, generative historical memory, and a historical experience that cries for newness—it is not any wonder that the Old Testament is permeated with anticipations of what YHWH will yet do.

But because hope is trust in a future that God has not yet given, the articulation of hope is inescapably elusive: "Now faith is the assurance of things hoped for, the conviction of things not seen" (Hebrews 11:1). Such hope defies every precise formulation, evokes figuration, poetic rhetoric, and requires a multilayered articulation with many variants. When one considers the articulation of hope in the Old Testament, one is inevitably struck with the rich diversity of voices and utterances that bear witness to the divine promises yet to be enacted. While the articulation is rich and varied, it is possible to identify certain trajectories of hope that recur in the text. Here I will explore four such trajectories of hope, no one of which can claim priority or preeminence.[2]

I

The Old Testament tradition articulates hope in one form as the anticipation of a *Messiah* who will fulfill YHWH's promises and establish rules in the earth. Both Judaism and Christianity are characterized by *messianic hope.*

The term *Messiah* and the derivative adjective *messianic* derive from the Hebrew term *msh,* which means "to anoint," that is, to mark in a sacramental way a designated human person who is to be a carrier of divine purposes. While the term *anoint* may apply to other persons, it comes in the Old Testament to pertain specifically to kings who are marked as agents of God's purposes in history (see 1 Kings 1:39; 2 Kings 9:6). Thus the term has an inescapable political dimension and refers to a human person who is engaged in an exercise of public power with sacramental legitimacy.

In the Old Testament, of course, the term *Messiah* refers specifically to David and those who come after him in that "royal line." We may mention five texts in particular that pertain to David as *Messiah*:

■ In the idyllic narrative of 1 Samuel 16:1-13, David is designated by YHWH: "Rise and anoint him; for this is the one" (v. 12). Samuel anoints David with oil; most important, with the application of oil, "the spirit of the LORD" came upon him, thus granting him power and divine legitimacy. This act is the beginning point of Davidic authority.

■ The oracle of Nathan in 2 Samuel 7:1-16 provides the substance of the divine promise to David and "his son," thus assuring the distinctive claim of David in Israel.[3] In this text, the divine promise is unconditional because YHWH will never take his steadfast love from David (2 Samuel 7:15).

■ That same claim for the anointing of David with the claim of "the spirit of the LORD" is voiced in 2 Samuel 23:1-7 as a culminating poetry of the books of Samuel. It is as though this text is placed as a confirming reprise at the conclusion of the books of Samuel.

■ The divine oracle of Isaiah 9:2-7, likely a residue of a temple liturgy of coronation, maximizes the significance of the Davidic king, so that the political interpretation is matched to theological endorsement: "The zeal of the LORD of hosts will do this" (v. 7).
■ But then the biblical text must acknowledge that the promise of YHWH to David did not hold, and the dynasty did not last. Psalm 89:1-37 makes the most sweeping claims for David, the anointed:

> I have found my servant David;
> with my holy oil I have anointed him.
> my hand shall always remain with him;
> my arm also shall strengthen him....
> Once and for all I have sworn by my holiness;
> I will not lie to David.
> His line shall continue forever,
> and his throne endure before me like the sun.
> It shall be established forever like the moon,
> an enduring witness in the skies. (Psalm 89:20-21, 35-37)

But of course the psalm does not end in verse 37. It continues in verses 38-51 and completely reverses field. It now acknowledges that the promises have been exhausted, and it wonders about the fidelity of YHWH who is nowhere evident in the horizon of royal promise. Thus as a historical reality, the "messianic" promise to David has been spent, overwhelmed by historical reality (Babylon) and negated by the judgment of YHWH against a people who have violated Torah.

II

Most remarkably, in ways that are characteristic in Israel but beyond credible explanation, as the *historical* promise to David failed, that same promise took on new life as an *eschatological* expectation.[4] Lacking a present king, Israel can expect a future king who will fulfill and enact all normative royal expectations. As for other promises in Israel, the exilic period becomes the matrix of determined royal expectation. Even Isaiah 9:2-7 that is commonly taken as an eighth-century oracle takes on futuristic expectations, as is evident in the quote of the text in Christian tradition in Matthew 4:15-16. But the generation of hope for a coming Messiah consisted not primarily in the reiteration of older texts, but rather in the articulation of new texts.[5] Thus in the Isaiah tradition that is most prominently Davidic, the royal promise of 9:2-7 is matched by 11:1-9 wherein the coming king will be powered by YHWH's spirit, will enact justice for the poor, and will reconcile all creation. In the Jeremiah tradition where we would not expect Davidic promises, moreover, the tradition pushes beyond its characteristic Deuteronomic horizon to announce a new David:

> The days are surely coming, says the LORD, when I will fulfill the promise I made to the house of Israel and the house of Judah. In those days and at that time I will cause a righteous Branch to spring up for David; and he shall execute justice and righteousness in the land. In those days Judah will be saved and Jerusalem will live in safety. And this is the name by which it will be called: "The LORD is our righteousness." (Jeremiah 33:14-16, 17; see 23:5-6)

It was expected in these traditions that there would be a full show of political, judicial, military power to enact all of the old promises; it is plausible that such expectation has enormous subversive implication as Jews had to live under the imperial domination of Babylon, Persia, and a variety of Hellenistic rulers. The import of such expectation is to counter those imperial claims and to insist that a designated empowered human agent from the community of Israel will have the capacity to overthrow the power of the empire and so to make new life possible for the community, without imperial supervision or surveillance.

That more-or-less direct political expectation, which constitutes the main force of this promissory tradition, was accompanied by other strategies as well concerning "Messianism." On the one hand, as Otto Eissfeldt has decisively urged, the reference to Davidic promises in Isaiah 55:1-5 no longer anticipates a Davidic king; rather, the utterance in the exile is redirected to concern the entire community as the carrier of the promises. Eissfeldt contrasts that mode of promise with Psalm 89:

> In Ps. 89 the content of the promise is interpreted exclusively in the continued existence of the Davidic dynasty—the current threat to which calls the validity of the promise into question. Second Isaiah, however, places the promise before the fate of Israel and its royal house and declares its eternal validity. In so doing, he relates the promise to the mission of Israel in the world, a mission which is Israel's destiny and which will bring her honor and recognition. Where Ps. 89 displays a static-rigid conception of the promise of Yahweh, Second Isaiah inter-

> prets it in a dynamic-activistic sense: he prevents its becoming involved in the collapse of the Davidic dynasty and thus ensures its permanent validity.[6]

The Davidic promises in such a reading have been dissolved into a democratic expectation for the community.

On the other hand and with a note of sober political realism, the same tradition of Isaiah knows full well that the political future belongs to the Persians and, in mid-sixth century, specifically to Cyrus. Thus the poetry alludes to Cyrus as the one roused by YHWH to fulfill divine purposes (Isaiah 41:2-3, 25). In 44:28, Cyrus is designated by YHWH as "my shepherd" (= king). And most spectacularly, in Isaiah 45:1, Cyrus is acknowledged to be YHWH's chosen and anointed historical agent:

> Thus says the LORD to his anointed, to Cyrus,
> whose right hand I have grasped
> to subdue nations before him
> and strip kings of their robes,
> to open doors before him—
> and the gates shall not be closed. (Isaiah 45:1)

This prophetic poetry boldly seizes upon the messianic title, withdraws it from the house of David, and redeploys it with reference to a non-Jewish king. The outcome of such a poetic utterance is the claim that YHWH's historical purposes do not depend upon Israelite-Jewish enactment, but outsiders to the tradition can be recruited to effect YHWH's purposes in the world. The following oracle that chides Israel leads to the conclusion that there must have been revulsion and resistance to YHWH's recruitment of a *goy* for saving purposes:

> Woe to you who strive with your Maker,
> earthen vessels with the potter!
> Does the clay say to the one who fashions it, "What are you making"?
> or "Your work has no handles"?
> Woe to anyone who says to a father, "What are you begetting?"
> or to a woman, "With what are you in labor?" (Isaiah 45:9-10)

YHWH's purposes are not confined to Israel's expectation! And that pertains even to the messianic promise that in this text is no longer Davidic! Given the reality of Persian power and Persian imperial policy, Cyrus and those after him did enact the restoration of Israel, albeit in a way severely circumscribed by imperial reality.

III

The enactment of Persian policy by Cyrus is taken, in the tradition of Isaiah, as one moment in the course of messianic expectation (see 2 Chronicles 36:22-23). But the promise and its futuristic force lived past that moment and remained generative on into the future, even until the present time. The continuing force of the messianic promise beyond the Old Testament lies outside the scope of our study. We may simply notice three factors that would belong to a close consideration of the topic:

- The content of messianic expectation is well articulated in the royal traditions of the Old Testament. The Messiah is to be an agent amid political reality with the will, capacity, and vision to enact peace, prosperity, and well-being for the community loyal to YHWH. While the motif is eschatological in its future orientation, the substance of the tradition is resolutely political in its expectation.
- It is not surprising that such a resilient, generative tradition should evoke many claimants for the role, office, and function of Messiah. Among the most prominent of such claimants is Simon bar Kosiba (Bar Kokba) who in 132–135 C.E. led a vigorous Jewish political revolt against the power of Rome. The religious energy for such a daring enterprise was the same messianic faith whereby it was expected in some circles of Judaism that God would dispatch such a political leader on behalf of the community of Israel. That moment exhibits in forceful ways the political dimension of messianic hope.
- In the context of imperial force and Jewish expectation, the appearance of Jesus and the presentation of him in the gospel narratives bring Jesus into the matrix of messianic expectation. It is clear that the New Testament witness gives evidence of the uneasy interface between the claims of Jesus and the characteristic Jewish expectation. The outcome is, according to Christian tradition, that he is the Messiah, the one to come, but he is not at all a Messiah who was expected. The issue is complex and beyond our assignment, but we may notice three characteristic ways in which the gospel traditions engage, surely inescapably engage, messianic expectation:

- In Luke 7:20-22 (see also Matthew 11:2-19), Jesus is asked "the messianic question": "Are you the one to come, or are we to look for another?" And his answer is an affirmation that he holds transformative power and does the things of the saving God: "And he answered them, 'Go and tell John what you have seen and heard: the blind receive their sight, the lame walk, the lepers are cleansed, the deaf hear, the dead are raised, the poor have good news brought to them'" (Luke 7:22). The reader is clearly invited to notice that Jesus does enact the messianic role, a political one, but not in a way that aims aggressively against Rome.
- In Mark 8:29 (see Matthew 16:13-20; Luke 9:18-20), Peter makes the church's confession of Jesus as Messiah that became the pivot of the gospel narrative: "He asked them, 'But who do you say that I am?' Peter answered him, 'You are the Messiah'" (Mark 8:29).
- In the trial narrative of John 18:33–19:16, Jesus is presented in juxtaposition to the governor Pilate, a cipher for conventional worldly power. The outcome of the narrative is that Jesus parries with Pilate and asserts his kingdom that is not of this world (John 18:36). In his haunting meditation on this text, Paul Lehmann writes:

The confrontation between Jesus and Pilate underscores the great gulf between *political realism* and *Realpolitik*. *Realpolitik* is politics with the accent upon the primacy of power over truth. *Political realism* is politics with the accent upon the primacy of truth over power. *Realpolitik* increasingly succumbs to the temptation of confusing immediate goals and gains with ultimate outcomes and options and seeks validation by increasingly dubious authority. *Political realism*, on the other hand, involves an increasing struggle against the temptation to overcome irrelevance through premature ventures to close the gap between the ultimate and the immediate, thus overdrawing on the truth in its power. Ever and again, the successors of Jesus have sought to convert the moment of truth exposed by his presence into a blend of political realism and power politics (Caesaro-papism, theocracy, sectarian withdrawal) that seeks to effect the triumph of Jesus over the "Prince of this world" in this world. Meanwhile, the successors of Pilate follow him in opting for the view that the state can have no interest in truth, i.e., in radical reality. In so doing, they convert the moment of truth exposed

> by the presence of Jesus into a politics of power that disregards the real and exalts the possible as necessary.[7]

We need now to pursue the matter no further. It is clear that the messianic claims made by the church are not direct or obvious or one-dimensional, because the authority of the one crucified and raised from the dead does not readily adapt to the hopes of raw power. Thus the Christian tradition participates in the practice of messianic expectation, but does so in a hidden and subversive way.

Because of the continuing force of messianic claims, it remains to say that messianic faith is a biblical affirmation that God's hope for the world is a hope *in the world* that is carried and enacted by a *human agent*. It is important in our pondering this hope that we not become so preoccupied with historical specificity that we fail to notice the broad and defining biblical claim that God's hopes are *for the world* and *in the world*. In this tradition the future of the world depends upon human agents that enact God's hope in ways befitting the promise for peace and justice and mercy and compassion. The messianic tradition, at least in Christian reading, is marked by a measure of fragility and vulnerability, a fragility and vulnerability that Christians have seen in Jesus of Nazareth who resisted the power modes of the world around him, the very modes of power enacted by Pilate.

IV

It is of course a long way from Old Testament promises to contemporary Judaism and Christianity. Both traditions nonetheless have taken up messianic hope and await Messiah. Both believe that eventually, in God's good time, God, through a particular agent, will bring the world to full reconciliation.

Christian hope revolves around the conviction, already confessed by Peter, that Jesus is the Messiah who has already come and begun the new rule of God. But Christians also believe that what has begun in Jesus the Messiah will be completed when Jesus Messiah returns in power. Thus Christians live in "the interim" between the first coming of Messiah "full of grace and truth," and his second coming. Christians have found in Jesus the fruition of all messianic promises.

Jews, of course, do not identify Jesus as Messiah; rather, Jews await Messiah who has not yet come but who will come in power. This dividing line between Jews and Christians on whether Messiah has come, that is, whether Jesus was Messiah, is a defining issue: *The humanly irreconcilable difference between Jews and Christians will not be settled until God redeems the entire world as promised in Scripture*.

Christians know and serve God through Jesus Christ and the Christian tradition. Jews know and serve God through Torah and the Jewish tradition. That difference will not be settled by one community insisting that it has interpreted Scripture more accurately than the other, nor by one community exercising political power over the other. Jews can respect Christians' faithfulness to their revelation just as we expect Christians to respect our faithfulness to our revelation. Neither Jew nor Christian should be pressed into affirming the teaching of the other community.[8]

Given that question, it is nonetheless of profound importance that Jews and Christians wait together for the full coming of Messiah whose work, whether begun or not, is clearly not completed. The important statement on Jewish-Christian relationships offered by Jewish theologians, *Debru Emet*, of course recognizes the deep contrast between these two traditions of hope; but it then affirms a common hope and a common possibility of obedience: ***Jews and Christians must work together for justice and peace***.

Jews and Christians, each in their own way, recognize the unredeemed state of the world as reflected in the persistence of persecution, poverty, and human degradation and misery. Although justice and peace are finally God's, our joint efforts, together with those of other faith communities, will help bring the kingdom of God for which we hope and long. Separately and together, we must work to bring justice and peace to our world. In this enterprise, we are guided by the vision of the prophets of Israel:

> It shall come to pass in the end of days that the mountain of the LORD's house shall be established at the top of the mountains and be exalted above the hills, and the nations shall flow unto it . . . and many peoples shall go and say, "Come ye and let us go up to the mountain of the LORD to the house of the God of Jacob and He will teach us of His ways and we will walk in his paths (Isaiah 2:2-3).[9]

On a lighter but no less significant note, Martin Buber, as reported by Elie Wiesel, found a way in which Christians and Jews might think together about Messiah:

> There is an anecdote about Martin Buber. Addressing an audience of priests, he said something like this: "What is the difference between Jews and Christians? We all await the Messiah. You believe He has already come and gone, while we do not. I therefore propose that we await Him together. And when He appears, we can ask Him: were You here before?" Then he paused and added: "And I hope that at that moment I will be close enough to whisper in his ear, 'For the love of heaven, don't answer.' "[10]

Both traditions hope. That hope is a of very *particular* kind that has broad and deep, even cosmic significance. That hope is that through a particular *human agent*, God's will will be fully visible in the earth. Thus at the same time messianic hope is linked to *historical reality* and to the *purposes of God* that are to be acted on the earth as in heaven. It must be recognized that such expectation is a hope, that is, an elusive, imaginative expectation that does not yield to precision or specific prediction, because "no one knows the day or the hour." Christian theology, especially in the United States, is widely vexed by a variety of forms of "dispensationalism" that appeal to Revelation 20 and its reference to a "millennium" (a thousand years). As Richard Moew has traced so closely, such millenniest thought has resulted, through the Schofield Bible, in a scheme of distinct "dispensations" of God's rule that culminate in the ultimate rule of Christ.[11] It is clear enough that such a scheme, with its immense ideological power, is a modernist imposition on the biblical text that is fundamentally alien to the nature of faith in the Bible. Thus responsible theological interpretation of the Bible must, in my perspective, resist and critique such distortions of faith and focus on the wonder that the God who makes promises can and does recruit human agents to fulfill promises in history. More than that, that by way of specification is an attempt to transpose hope into prediction and thereby into certitude. Such a transposition fails to recognize that we have to do, in the practice of hope, with a lively, free God who has not and will not succumb to our idolatrous yearning for certitude. Our age of anxiety, bewitched by the offers of technological control, craves certitude; but it is not a gift of biblical faith for either Jews or Christians.

V

Old Testament hope is articulated in YHWH's promises that arise primarily in *prophetic traditions*, so that we may properly speak of "prophetic hope" and ask how these imaginative poets who were invited into the holy presence of YHWH voiced the future that YHWH would yet create. The prophets, on the one hand, are characteristically presented as uncredentialed persons who were moved to utterance and action at the impetus of the God of the covenant who has a new word to speak. On the other hand, it is equally characteristic that these ad hoc utterers of YHWH's future claim a call from YHWH that is characteristically issued in "the council of the Gods," that is, in the venue of God's own magisterial presence.[12] The combination of *uncredentialed* and *called by God* means that the authorization and empowerment of these poetic utterers is from a locus outside the reach or supervision or surveillance of dominant culture. As a consequence, they are not in principle accountable to the power structures of society. In that sense they are free and unencumbered, though their testimonial speech is offered at a great risk and regularly collides with established truth.

While the prophets do indeed speak of the future, they are not predictors.[13] Rather, they anticipate what comes next in the historical process because they are acute "readers" of social power and *realpolitik*. Because they have been led deeply into YHWH's purpose and intention, they anticipate what will come next because they do not doubt that YHWH's rule and intention for the earth—for Israel and for the other nations—will be enacted in specific and concrete ways. It is by imaginative spirit given utterance that the prophets make a telling connection between the specificity of a historical moment and the abiding purposes of YHWH that take concrete form in particular circumstance.

The force of *prophetic promise* is recurrently offered in the sixth-century displacement when Jerusalem's primary institutions had failed and YHWH's promises were voided. Thus the most important observation of this chapter is the startling recognition that it is the null point that is the characteristic venue in the Old Testament for the articulation of God's promises. It is in the context of *hopelessness* that *hope* receives voice, precisely because it is the God of life who moves against the power of death, it is the God of freedom who moves against the power of enslavement, and it is the God of creation who moves against the negating power of chaos.

In what follows, I will consider hope as it is voiced in the four great prophetic scrolls.

VI

The book of Isaiah, in its final form, is ordered into two large themes, chapters 1–39 as judgment and chapters 40–66 on hope. This arrangement permits a focus upon the peculiar hinge between chapter 39 and the new articulation of hope in chapter 40. The end of chapters 1–39 is a prophetic anticipation of displacement and exile into Babylon: "Days are coming when all that is in your house, and that which your ancestors have stored up until this day, shall be carried to Babylon; nothing shall be left, says the LORD. Some of your own sons who are born to you shall be taken away; they shall be eunuchs in the palace of the king of Babylon" (Isaiah 39:6-7). After this oracle of closure, there must be, in the reading of the book of Isaiah, a very long pause, a pause long enough to allow for the destruction of Jerusalem at the hands of the Babylonians and then displacement of leading citizens away from Jerusalem.

Only then, after the long pause of devastation, does the voice of prophecy speak again. Now, in chapters 40–55, the new word uttered is one of "good news," a "new thing," namely, the negation of the empire and the return of Israel to its city and its land (as in 40:9; 43:16-21). The new thing, lyrically lined out, is to be wrought by the emergence of YHWH as the decisive player in world history who will overthrow the empire for the sake of Israel. The empire is judged because it did not "show mercy," the hallmark of the God of Israel who is the Lord of history (47:6).

The rhetoric of newness—homecoming and a new beginning for Israel—is voiced, as is usual in the prophets, as the direct work of YHWH who is presented as an effective agent. A closer reading of the poetry, however, shows that the Isaiah tradition does not foster much direct "supernaturalism." The most remarkable feature of hope for Israel—that entails the overthrow of Babylon—is that this hoped-for newness will be enacted through human agency. Thus in Isaiah 44:28, it is Cyrus the rising star of the Persian Empire, YHWH's "shepherd," who is to rebuild Jerusalem. More spectacularly, in Isaiah 45:1 Cyrus is "my Messiah"—my anointed human agent to effect newness so grandly understood as YHWH's own doing. In chapters 46–47, moreover, the poetry anticipates the overthrow of Babylonian gods and Babylonian power, surely by the same human agency.

As so-called Second Isaiah is preoccupied with the overthrow of Babylon and the return home for Jewish exiles, so the so-called Third Isaiah (chapters 56–66) specifies a rehabilitation of Jerusalem. Two features of this poetry are placed in remarkable juxtaposition. On the one hand, the poetry continues to speak of sweeping divine agency, especially in chapter 62 and, most dramatically, in 65:17-25. On the other hand, the poetry assumes disciplined, effective human agency whereby the new city of Jerusalem is established, first through the imperatives that are addressed to the entire community (56:1-8; 58:6-14) and then by the unnamed agent upon whom YHWH's spirit will rest (61:1-4).

If we consider the rhetoric of direct divine agency and the imperative summons addressed to human agents, we see a characteristic feature of prophetic faith, the process of *divine intentionality* enacted through *human effort*. In such rhetoric, YHWH is the legitimating, empowering, summoning force whereby those summoned become actors in their own history in order to implement the newness YHWH promises and intends. The outcome of the Isaiah tradition is that the Jerusalem that has been under judgment is now restored in peace and prosperity (66:10-13). A harbinger of the entire drama of judgment and restoration is offered at the outset in Isaiah 1:21-26 with its concluding anticipation of the future:

> And I will restore your judges as at the first,
> and your counselors as at the beginning.
> *Afterward* you shall be called the city of righteousness,
> the faithful city. (Isaiah 1:26, italics added)

There will be an *afterward* according to the tradition of Isaiah. It is an *afterward* that pivots on the return of the deportees to Jerusalem and the rehabilitation of the religious-political community in Jerusalem. That return and rehabilitation, however, spins off, in Isaianic rhetoric, in two directions. On the one hand, because the rehabilitation is lyrical and poetic, the hope extends beyond Israel in Jerusalem to take on a cosmic dimension, nothing less than the rehabilitation of creation (65:17-25). On the other hand, for all of the rhetoric of direct, supernaturalist intervention, the actual work of rehabilitation is human work, the practice of Torah that issues in welcome to "others" (56:3-7), transformative care for the powerless and negated (58:6-7), and the practice of "good news" for the needy and disenfranchised (61:1-4). Prophetic faith, for all of its deep passion for YHWH, characteristically devolves hope into covenantal responsibility for the enactment of YHWH's promise to future.

VII

The book of Jeremiah is not so clearly arranged as is the book of Isaiah. But the themes of judgment and promise are nonetheless defining for the book.[14] The poetry that is most often assigned to the prophet Jeremiah is consistently and relentlessly reprimand and anticipation of divine judgment that will take the form of the destruction of Jerusalem. That divine judgment, moreover, is to be enacted through the agency of Nebuchadnezzar who is declared to be "my servant" (25:9, 27:6). The narrative of Jeremiah's confrontation with Hananiah in chapter 28, following Jeremiah's trial in chapter 26, amounts to a dismissal and defeat of the "*shalom* prophets" and their ideological conviction that Jerusalem will be kept safe. The book of Jeremiah turns decisively in chapter 9 to reckon with the new matrix of faith, the exile in Babylon (29:1-9). In the final form of the text, that acknowledgment of Babylon as the new venue of faithful living becomes the access point for hope as the book of Jeremiah turns from judgment to hope.

In the prose passage of 29:10-14, a passage loaded with formulae of hope, it is promised that YHWH has a "plan" to "restore the fortunes" of Israel, to create *shalom* (welfare) for Israel and to bring the deportees home. This is the sum of Israel's expectation that is declared to be "a future with hope," that is, an "afterward" of positive possibility. This language, consonant with the terms of Isaiah 1:26, anticipates a time of well-being after deportation, when Israel is securely established again in Jerusalem and in the land of Judah. The same rhetoric of "hope afterward" is offered in the poetry of "The Book of Comfort" in Jeremiah 31:17:

> There is hope for your future,
> says the LORD:
> your children shall come back to their own country. (Jeremiah 31:17)

The entire corpus of Jeremiah 30–31 is preoccupied with return and rehabilitation in the land. Of special interest in this portrayal of the future are two notes at the end of chapter 31. First, the future will offer an Israel that is gladly and readily obedient to Torah, a new readiness for obedience based in YHWH's forgiveness (31:33-34). Second, YHWH's promise of return and rehabilitation of Jerusalem is as certain as the ordered reliability of creation (31:31-37; see 33:25-26). There is less affirmation of hope for creation here than in the Isaiah tradition, but clearly this voice of hope also links the recovery of Israel to the assured reality of YHWH's creation. The specificity of hope for Israel is underlined by the narrative of chapter 32 that is twice voiced as the culmination of hope:

> For thus says the LORD of hosts, the God of Israel: Houses and fields and vineyards shall again be bought in this land. (Jeremiah 32:15)

> Fields shall be bought for money, and deeds shall be signed and sealed and witnessed, in the land of Benjamin, in the places around Jerusalem, and in the cities of Judah, of the hill country, of the Shephelah, and of the Negeb; for I will restore their fortunes, says the LORD. (Jeremiah 32:44)

Again the intervention imagined by the rhetoric of the poetry is direct and portrays YHWH's own transformative agenda. The narrative promises of 32:15, 44 are articulated in a passive voice; the implied but unnamed agent of the passive verbs is clearly YHWH.

There are many indications, however, that the "supernaturalist" rhetoric of YHWH's future is grounded in concrete historical reality. This is evident first in the more-or-less historical narrative of chapters 37–44 that witnesses to real human agents in the historical process, for example, Gedeliah who must cope with the real historical crises that have real consequences. The oracles of 38:17-23 and 42:9-22 link that historicity to the nonnegotiable intention of YHWH, but the implementation of these divine purposes is through human agency.

On a larger scale, Cyrus who will permit return and restoration in Jerusalem is not mentioned in the tradition of Jeremiah as in the Isaiah tradition. We have, however, seen that Nebuchadnezzar is the specific agent of divine judgment in the Jeremiah tradition. In parallel fashion, it is clear that Cyrus, though unnamed, is clearly the human agent who, at divine behest, will overthrow Nebuchadnezzar and permit a resumption of political life in Jerusalem: "For I am going to stir up and bring against Babylon a company of great nations from the land of the north; and they shall array themselves against her; from there she shall be taken. Their arrows are like the arrows of a skilled warrior who does not return empty-handed" (Jeremiah 50:9). The text credits YHWH with "stirring up," but the human agent will do the work. As is specifically recognized in 2 Chronicles 36:22-23, the promissory utterance of the Jeremiah tradition clearly has in mind Cyrus the Persian. Thus the Jeremiah tradition, not unlike the Isaiah tradition, can match sweeping rhetoric concerning YHWH's intention with human agency that is concrete about geopolitical reality. Prophetic rhetoric presents hope as human practice in the service of divine intention, even if human agents are unwitting about that connection.

VIII

Hope in the tradition of Ezekiel is cast in a very different idiom. Whereas the tradition of Isaiah anticipates justice and prosperity for Jerusalem and the tradition of Jeremiah anticipates covenantal obedience in a safe land, the Ezekiel tradition is concerned for the acknowledgment and acceptance of YHWH's *awesome holiness*. Hope in Ezekiel is articulated in three different modes. First, in chapters 34, 36, and 37, the divine promises concern restoration to the land and the resumption of viable social infrastructure. Except for 34:23-24, no human agent is active in the restoration. The work of reestablishing society in Jerusalem is to be done by "I myself" (34:11). It is to be noted that even in these oracles, the ground of hope is YHWH's defense of YHWH's holy name (Ezekiel 36:23, 33). In a second mode, the oracles against Gog and Magog, the crisis of YHWH's sovereignty (and Israel's jeopardy), are portrayed in a much larger, even cosmic scale. The text anticipates "global mayhem."[15] YHWH, however, is unthreatened by such a challenge. YHWH will act decisively to reassert YHWH's holy sovereignty; the nations will see YHWH's glory (39:21) and the way in which that glory is exhibited is in the restoration of Israel. Thus the *glorification of YHWH* and the *rescue of Israel* are twinned, to the great benefit of Israel: "Therefore thus says the Lord GOD: Now I will restore the fortunes of Jacob, and have mercy on the whole house of Israel; and I will be jealous for my holy name" (Ezekiel 39:25).

The promise of YHWH's "spirit upon the house of Israel" (39:29) opens the way to the third way of hope, namely, the reestablishment of a pure cult in Jerusalem that can adequately host the holiness of YHWH (chapters 40–48). While priests are central to this anticipated cultic restoration, they are recipients of restoration and not its agents, for YHWH is the only agent of restoration. The culmination of the reestablishment of holiness is that the Jerusalem temple will be the source of life for all of creation (47:1-12). Israel will be safely established in a perfectly symmetrical land of well-being (47:13–48:30) and YHWH will be there (48:35). The ultimate promise is that YHWH will be present in the restored city. In a quite distinctive mode, the future expected by the Ezekiel traditions is congruent with what we have seen in the traditions of Isaiah and Jeremiah. While an opening toward new creation is not explicit, there is no doubt that, in priestly idiom, Jerusalem is reckoned as the epicenter of renewed creation. Thus *newness for Israel* and *newness for creation* are intimately linked to each other.

IX

I need only mention that in most recent scholarship the scroll of the twelve Minor Prophets is taken to be a more-or-less coherent theological statement that moves, in the sweep from Hosea to Malachi, from judgment to hope.[16] At the end of the Book of the Twelve, the tradition clearly moves to an expectation of restoration:

- In Haggai 2:20-23, the upheaval of the kingdoms is anticipated in the restoration of monarchy under Zerubbabel.
- In Zechariah 9:9-10, a text much used in Christian tradition, a returning triumphant king is anticipated; and in the later chapters of Zechariah, it is anticipated that YHWH, in all holiness, will "become king over all the earth" (Zechariah 14:9). Alongside the reestablishment of the holy king before whom all nations will bow will be "all the holy ones with him" (14:5).
- In Malachi 4:5-6, the future is left open for the reappearance of Elijah, the one filled with transformative spirit who will bring reconciliation into the human community.

In the Book of the Twelve, Israel's hope is stated in a variety of ways. All of these ways, in any case, concern the *sure rule of YHWH* and the *sure well-being of Israel.* Hope in the Old Testament concerns the resolve, the sovereign power, and the compassionate fidelity of YHWH. That conviction about YHWH is rooted in Israel's memory of faithful, powerful miracles and is carried into Israel's crisis by uncredentialed speakers who are accepted, in the final form of the text, as reliable, authorized speakers for YHWH.

We have seen two recurring "openings" in the articulation of YHWH's resolve about the future. On the one hand, there is the slippery interface between the divine intention of YHWH and the recruitment of human agents in the performance of that intention. It would seem to be a matter of little concern in the traditions whether the future is given directly or through mediation. Second, the focus is regularly upon the rehabilitation of Israel, but the scope of a future ordered by YHWH's rule is seldom limited to Israel. Rather, the anticipated rule of YHWH regularly concerns all of the nations and eventually the whole of creation.[17]

Prophetic faith in largest scope concerns the coming rule of YHWH over all of creation. That scope and dimension of hope permits a move from *prophetic* to *apocalyptic* hope. The word *apocalypse* means "revelation," that is, the disclosure of what has been kept hidden by God. Apocalyptic hope refers to the articulation of the future that is voiced in a variety of literatures that are outside the Old Testament canon in the Hellenistic period, that occupies great attention in the Dead Sea scrolls, and that shows up in the New Testament in transposed formulation. The apocalyptic literature that voices such large, radical hope is represented in the Old Testament primarily by the book of Daniel; it is apparent that the interpretive forces that produce the canonical shape of the Old Testament resisted apocalyptic thought, and for the most part were able to exclude it from the canon. We may comment on this genre in general, taking our lead from John Collins, and then comment in particular on the apocalyptic elements of hope in the book of Daniel.

Apocalyptic literature consists in oracles concerning the future that are mediated through specially designated interpreters that reveal what has otherwise been kept hidden. And what they characteristically reveal is that God's judgment on the contemporary failed world will be sudden and comprehensive, bringing the present world to a complete end; this ending will in turn make an opening for the new rule of God who will preside over a coming world of justice, security, and peace that will be offered on behalf of God's chosen community. Thus the themes of *judgment and newness* that we have seen recurring characteristically in prophetic hope are here continued, only in grander, more sweeping, more cosmic scope.

The apocalyptic literature is rich and varied; for that reason, generalization is not easy or obvious, but we may judge that the emergence of such a vision of *abrupt ending* and *radical beginning* describes convictions that arise among those who find the present world of social circumstance unbearable and are ready to relinquish what is for the sake of what will yet be given by God. The function of such literature is to entertain the notion of a complete transformation of world order and social order, so that the rule of God displaces the failed rule of the present age. John Collins has summarized scholarly judgment by suggesting five needs to which apocalyptic hope is a response, either as an offer of exhortation or as an articulation of consolation:

> An apocalypse can provide support in the face of persecution (e.g., Daniel); reassurance in the face of culture shock (possibly the Book of the Watchers) or social powerlessness (the Similitudes of Enoch); reorientation in the wake of historical trauma (*2 Baruch, 3 Baruch*), consolation for the dismal fate of humanity (4 Ezra) or comfort for the inevitability of death (the *Testament of Abraham*). The constant factor is that the problem is put in perspective by the otherworldly revelation of a transcendent world and eschatological judgment.[18]

The accent is upon the direct, powerful assertion of God's will over the world. Because this hope and expectation is sweeping and radical, it is not surprising that apocalyptic hope is characteristically available in vivid images and venturesome symbols that offer no explanation, but simply bear testimony to newness that is beyond every human explanation.

Because such literature arises in social crises, and because the intent is pastoral (exhortation and consolation) and not explanatory, this literature is not intended to offer an ontology of the coming world. Rather, it is designed to nurture and sustain the buoyancy of hope, to assert that God's sovereign power is not jeopardized or limited by any circumstance, no matter how fearful or wretched be that circumstance. Whereas some other forms of hope may *hope for the world*, this hope is precisely *hope in God*, the assertion that God can and finally will act freely to work a newness that is underived and unextrapolated from present circumstance.

The pastoral concern of such hope works on a cosmic scale. But the focus is characteristically upon the community that will be the recipient of God's newness. Thus the divine judgment that is the matrix for the new world separates sheep and goats—sheep to bliss and goats to punishment—the righteous and unrighteous, and clearly fosters a self-awareness in the community that "we," that is, the in group to whom the secret has been revealed, are the bearers of the new age. Such practical concern is a remarkable gift of buoyancy.

It takes no great interpretive acumen, moreover, to see that such "newness for us" is an interpretive venture that is readily open to ideological benefit whereby "we" are the carriers of newness and "they"—whoever they may be—are under severe and complete judgment. Such a stratagem can give assurance, but it can also yield self-deluding, self-congratulations, a temptation always at hand in a religion of radical judgment and radical expectation. This apocalyptic hope can easily run in the direction of Manichaeism, a sure notion of absolute good and absolute bad. Such absoluteness can variously show up:

- in the conviction of ancient Qumran that is evidenced in the Dead Sea scrolls;
- in any number of Christian sects over the centuries of Christian history;
- in much political thought that has a militant religious dimension;
- in current Christian passion against Islam;
- in current Christian radicalism that is championed by the "Left Behind" series;
- and in any disputatious social context where interpretation is bewitched by idolatrous self-assurance.

The book of Daniel is the primary exhibit of apocalyptic hope in the Old Testament, a literature that arises in the midst of the Hellenistic crisis of the second century B.C.E. That had evoked the military-political Jewish response of the Maccabees. While the military-political enterprise gained great force and exercised much influence, the apocalyptic offer of hope in the book of Daniel—in the same context as that of the Maccabees—is not impressed by the "little help" of human agents (Maccabees), but relies completely on the power of God to bring newness.

Without any special expertise in the book of Daniel, I will follow a conventional critical interpretation by highlighting three elements in the book of Daniel:

First, Daniel 2, through interpretation of the dream of Nebuchadnezzar, traces the "four kingdoms" that culminates in the total victory of God (vv. 36-45). It is possible to correlate the four kingdoms to the geopolitics of the Hellenistic world and such a "schedule" of the Great Powers is characteristic of an apocalyptic ordering.[19] Thus history in broad scope is a history of human pretension that is sure to fail, for history will culminate in the total victory of God over all human pretension. The footnote of this large-scale vision is that Daniel, the representative and celebrate Jew, is able to decipher the mystery of the dream and offer adequate interpretation (vv. 27-30, 47-49). That is, what is a beclouded mystery to the rulers of this age is a *revelation* extended to Jews who are the privileged insiders of this divine hope.

Second, Daniel 7 offers a parallel vision that is of particular interest in Christian interpretation. In addition to the vision of successive empires that will fail, this chapter offers the scenario of a "Son of Man" who comes on clouds to establish a new rule:

> As I watched in the night visions,
> I saw one like a human being
> coming with the clouds of heaven.
> And he came to the Ancient One
> and was presented before him.
> To him was given dominion
> and glory and kingship,
> that all peoples, nations, and languages
> should serve him.
> His dominion is an everlasting dominion
> that shall not pass away,
> and his kingship is one
> that shall never be destroyed. (Daniel 7:13-14)

This figure is a heavenly figure who remains mysterious and enigmatic; the most that can be said is that he is from God's side, that is, not a human or historical character but a heavenly being who will, in concrete ways, establish the rule of God in the earth and override all human pretensions to absolute or ultimate power. This figure—accompanied by "the holy ones of the most high," presumably the community of the faithful—will discipline all present rulers and establish a new rule (vv. 18-22).

Third, Daniel 12:2 offers one of only two clearly attested statements about the resurrection of the dead in the Old Testament.[20] It is clear that the resurrection of the dead is a subset of apocalyptic thought, a conviction that bespeaks a total break and a total discontinuity from all that has been. The locus of the *resurrection* in *apocalyptic thought* can deliver

Christian interpreters from trying to make sense of the resurrection in Easter faith apart from the radical matrix of apocalyptic thought.

Thus apocalyptic thought anticipates that God will be fully God and will enact an extreme show of sovereign power, will make a complete break with all that has gone before and thereby make all things new. That newness is cosmic but will have as its center "those who are wise" who will be like the stars forever and ever (Daniel 12). Apocalyptic is the extreme conviction that God will make all things new. This hope is, of course, resonant with messianic and prophetic faith, except that its articulation is more radical, witnesses more singularly to God's powerful resolve, and takes an even more critical view of what has been that must be rejected.

We may, as we conclude the discussion of this freighted and difficult topic, briefly trace two spin-offs from this literature. First, Ernst Käsemann has famously declared that "apocalyptic was the mother of all Christian theology."[21] In this claim he has been followed especially by Louis Martyn who has seen how Paul's theology is characteristically apocalyptic.[22] By this claim Käsemann and Martyn do not focus upon the speculative imagery that is characteristic of the literature. Rather, they interpret the central claim of New Testament faith that in Jesus Christ world history has come to a total, radical break. The coming of Jesus Christ has been and is the break whereby the rule of God is effectively under way, and the new community of blessing and obedience has been convened and empowered to new life. Very much Christian interpretation of Paul and of the whole of gospel faith has been pounded down and made into an accommodation to the world otherwise organized. Käsemann and Martyn bear witness to the radicality of the gospel that centers on the new life-giving rule of God come concretely in Jesus of Nazareth that touches every dimension of reality.

Second, there is in U.S. religion currently a great attraction to apocalyptic modes of thought and speech. That way of hope, however, has been cast into modernist modes of dispensationalism that for the most part contradicts the theological force of hope in God. Much of that current thought, prominently in the *Left Behind* Series, has an odd and disastrous alliance with right-wing politics that characteristically supports and celebrates U.S. military adventurism. This odd and widely embraced juxtaposition of apocalyptic imagery and superpower self-aggrandizement demonstrates in an unmistakable way how such daring imagery is easily pressed into the service of idolatry. The outcome of such an alliance is that the *rhetoric of hope* is matched to a *politics of despair* that intends at all cost to preserve the status quo of privilege, entitlement, and self-propelled security. Such a utilization of apocalyptic hope is a disastrous idolatry because the God to which apocalyptic hope attests stands precisely against such craven hungers of present arrangements of power and security. Hope stands as a contradiction of all such idolatries. Indeed the very superpower status of the United States, so valued in many forms of contemporary apocalyptic rhetoric, more likely stands, in the tradition of Daniel, as one of the empires that will fall rather than as an icon of the new rule of God. In the contemporary U.S. religious scene, such an idolatrous alliance of future hope and current power employs the rhetoric of hope precisely in the practice of hopelessness, bespeaking not eager trust but immense fear.

X

Otto Plöger, and after him Paul Hanson, have proposed that in the postexilic period of emergent Judaism we may trace two distinct interpretive trajectories that contributed variously to the theological and interpretive self-understanding of Jews.[23] Plöger's categories are eschatology and theocracy; Hanson's later rendition concerns *visionaries* and *hierocracy*, or following the categories of Karl Mannheim, *utopia and ideology*.[24] The analysis of Plöger and Hanson are somewhat different from each other, but for our purposes close enough to be considered together. The scheme of the two trajectories has been variously criticized by subsequent scholars and the case for such a twinning of interpretive trajectories should not be overstated. But the model is sufficient to serve as a heuristic access point for considering strategies for hope in the latter part of the Old Testament.

The trajectory of "eschatology" (Plöger) and "visionary" (Hanson) refer commonly to the emergence of apocalyptic thought, which I have considered in the previous section of this chapter. This interpretative trajectory is indeed "utopian" in the sense that it moves beyond historical realism to imagine (anticipate, construct) an alternative world toward which the community of faith may live. As we have seen, this trajectory of texts anticipates an abrupt end to the present world and the radical appearance of a new world fully resonant with the will and purpose of God.

In this section of the present chapter it remains to consider an alternative trajectory of hope that does not fit completely with Plöger's "theocracy" or Hanson's "hierocracy." In fact I take some liberties with the second trajectory, for my concern here is not the Priestly tradition which Hanson labels as "ideological," by which he means the political establishment that provided a status quo interpretation of the tradition. Rather, my focus is upon hope in *scribal* form. There is no doubt that the *priests* and the *scribes* shared some common interests, but my discussion is away from priestly domination and toward the emergence of scribal practice as a major force in the voicing and shaping of the hopes of Judaism.

The course of the emergence of scribes in ancient Israel is not very clear and the exact nature of their social location is in some dispute.[25] It is clear that the scribes are, as early as they appear, the ones who are learned in the ways of writing and who are consequently part of the urban elite and that dominated society with the rise of the monarchy. In the service of the monarchy they surely participated in the maintenance of records concerning taxes and property, and they fostered an educational enterprise of some sort. Their political role must have been of considerable importance, and Davies opines that that role eventually constituted an ideological force in the production of a canon that was an imposition of a coercive, authoritarian theological cultural norm. Here however, I will be concerned only with one sequence of texts that concerns the centers in the Deuteronomic tradition and eventuates in the work of Ezra.[26]

1. The text of 2 Kings 22 reports the finding of a scroll that evoked a radical reform on the part of King Josiah. That scroll in critical scholarship is generally taken to be some form of the book of Jeremiah. For our purposes the important thing is it is a scroll that is taken seriously and regarded as normative. The faith—and even the political life of Judah—are now linked to the scroll that must have been written, preserved, and transmitted by the learned who now emerge front and center in the life of Judah.

2. Ernest Nicholson, and many scholars after him, has seen that 2 Kings 22 is an intentional counterpoint to Jeremiah 36, also a narrative that concerns the rendering of a scroll and an official response to it. Whereas King Josiah in 2 Kings 22 responds positively to the scroll, in Jeremiah 36, King Jehoiakim responds anxiously and negatively. Of special importance is the fact that the scroll, although authored by Jeremiah, is intimately connected to Baruch the scribe, apparently representative of a highly important scribal family.[27] Thus we may take these two texts,

2 Kings 22 and Jeremiah 36, as evidence that scribes were crucial to the future of Judaism in the exilic/postexilic period when the conventional institutional supports of Jerusalem had failed. After all else had failed, there were still scrolls, and those who formed, preserved, transmitted, and interpreted the scrolls became increasingly normative for the newly emerging society.

In both of these texts the scroll and the "scroll men" now occupy a central place in the articulation of Israel. The shift of accent is away from prophetic oracle and royal leverage to the scroll that becomes the rallying point for the future of the community. George Steiner puts the matter poignantly: "The truth will out. Somewhere there is a pencil-stub, a mimeograph machine, a hand-press which the king's men have overlooked." [28]

3. It is clear that in this emergence the scribes not only preserve and transmit, they also interpret. Thus behind the two texts cited surely stands the Deuteronomic tradition and its dynamism in making the Torah of Moses newly pertinent and freshly compelling in a new circumstance. While Gerhard von Rad and Ernst Nicholson link the tradition of Deuteronomy to the prophets and Levitic tradition, I find the argument of Moshe Weinfeld compelling, that Deuteronomy arises in a scribal-sapiential tradition that advocates a stream of tradition that is authoritative but open to ongoing interpretation that is also taken as authoritative.[29] Thus at the very outset of Deuteronomy it is asserted that in Deuteronomy Moses *expounded* the Torah of Sinai (Deuteronomy 1:5). By this difficult term, *expound,* the book of Deuteronomy asserts both its *connection* to the Sinai materials and its *departure* from the Sinai materials in order to make a case for YHWH's Torah an always-new circumstance. The interpretive process of Deuteronomy, reflective in both the scroll of 2 Kings 22 and in the scroll of Jeremiah 36 evidences what Robert Alter has termed "a culture of interpretation" whereby the text tradition, given in the scroll, is open to endless refraction in ongoing interpretation.

4. That "culture of interpretation" that culminates eventually in rabbinic Judaism reaches its clear and definitive expression in the Old Testament in the work of "Ezra the Scribe" who offered the Torah afresh to the community of Jews after the return of the leadership from Babylon. In that definitive meeting, Ezra and his associates "helped the people to understand the law, while the people remained in their places. So they read from the book, from the law of God, with interpretation. They gave

the sense, so that the people understood the reading" (Nehemiah 8:7-8). It is to be especially accented "helped people to *understand*" (*bin*) "with *interpretation*" (*meforash*) so that there would be *understanding* (*bin*). The active force of this enterprise is characteristic of scribal activity. Now it may be, as Davies polemically insists, that such interpretation is an ideological imposition. Our point, however, is that it is the *free exercise of imagination concerning the text* that becomes the primal activity of the scribes. It is recognized in this mode of Judaism that the text is open, suggestive, invitational, and requires extrapolation in order that ancient text is heard as fresh summons, exhortation, and consolation. It is this textual activity that endlessly forms and reforms the community of Torah obedience for a distinct way in the world.

In order to appreciate fully Ezra (and the scribal tradition he singularly represents), reference may be made to the work of David Halivni, of which I am aware through an essay of Peter Ochs. Halivni takes Ezra as the mediating figure between Moses and the subsequent rabbinic tradition represented by Akiva. Halivni is not primarily interested in "plain sense reading," but in "pragmatic historiography" in which matters are understood according to the needs of a particular community of interpretation. Given that premise, Halivni judges that Ezra received from Moses "a wounded text"[30]; it is the work of Ezra, through imaginative interpretation, to "repair" the text so that the community may receive, embrace, and be addressed by a text of the Torah:

> . . . *the narrower range of meanings that he could consistently order into a narrative series that leads from beginning* (Moses) *to end* (*the present interpreter*) *in such a way that the series has narrative beauty and pragmatic power in his particular sub-community*. "Pragmatic power" means the power to help the sub-community repair its current crisis in a way that is arguably consistent with the narrative. *If these conditions are met, then the narrative has "pragmatic truth"*, which means, strictly, *that it represents, a priori, a reasonable means of adopting the lessons of rabbinic/scriptural reading as conditions for reparative action today. The only remaining test of the narrative would be its relative success or failure in actually contributing to the repairs its author envisions.*[31]

Thus the work of the scribe by way of interpretation is to make a text available that has the power, amid a profound social crisis, to recover the covenantal relationship with God:

> As portrayed in the Exodus narrative, Moses was an agent not only of Israel's release from slavery, but also of Israel's recovering a covenantal relation with God. As portrayed in the Ketuvim, Ezra not only shared in the restoration of Israel's polity and priesthood after the First Destruction, but also mediated the restoration of Israel's Torah. And, as portrayed in the Mishnah, Akiva was a symbol of Israel's communal as well as religious restoration after the Second Destruction.[32]

This discussion of scribes in general and Moses in particular is under the rubric of "hope." The future offered through the scribal interpretive work of Ezra is, of course, very different from hope, as we have considered it in messianic, prophetic, and apocalyptic modes. Now the community of faith is not watching external historical events for God's newness, but has eyes and ears fixed on the Torah and the interpretive process of interpretation that is generative of newness through the text. The newness expected from the text is that it will yield, by faithful imagination, new sensibility, new awareness, new truth that will transform the covenant of obedience. As a Christian interpreter, this Jewish mode of hope seems to me one that is now urgent for the recovery of biblical hope in Christian horizon. Such a work of hope coheres with George Lindbeck's cultural-linguistic, post-modern approach to interpretation that aims at the formation and sustenance of a community of faith with a coherent and intentional identity.[33] The seduction of secularism and the jeopardy of "linear thinking" that produces sectarian absolutism are twin threats that require "textual reasoning" in an intentional community in order to recover a particular identity that can move boldly, knowingly, and faithfully into the future.[34] While Ochs, following Halivni, presents this matter with reference to the Jewish community, there is no doubt that the same crisis, the same urgency, and the same possibility are before the Christian community as it seeks to find its way between secular autonomy and sectarian absolutism.

Now it may be thought that such a model of hope constitutes a withdrawal from the public scene. But this practice of scribal hope through imaginative interpretation is not at all a recipe for withdrawal from the public process. This is, rather, the nurture of faithful imaginative freedom that positions the faithful in the world differently, prepared for actions in defiance of dominant reality, actions that are themselves acts of hope, acts that cohere with expectations of justice, mercy, and compassion. Such disciplined, rooted interpretive imagination holds promise of being unafraid in the world. I judge that such faith-rooted fearlessness is most likely to come from such textual imagination, especially if mediated in sacramental practice. In recent memory, the most powerful example of such text-rooted imagination that issued in bold action is the life of Abraham Heschel, the great rabbinic scholar who gave himself over to the public crises of the Vietnam War and the Civil Rights Movement.[35] And of course Heschel was joined in that action by Christians who engaged in the same risks of obedience out of a certain and conscious faith identity. It is clear that such *praxis* is an act of hope, for they acted in defiance of dominant culture toward a world that God would surely give. This fourth mode of hope is neither an aggressive activist model nor is it a quietistic wait for transcendental miracles. It is, rather, the slow, steady act of discerning afresh and acting from what we come to see and hear and know. It is a waiting that is occupied with obedience. Thus the word of Moses in Deuteronomy 29:29 makes a distinction between the "secret things" that belong to God and the "revealed things" that are a summons to obedience: "The secret things belong to the LORD our God, but the revealed things belong to us and to our children forever, to observe all the words of this law" (Deuteronomy 29:29).[36] Textual reasoning in a scribal mode is preoccupied with the things already revealed. In such imaginative study and interpretation, practitioners find that the secret things in turn yield energy, courage, and freedom for the future.

CHAPTER SEVENTEEN

THE COMING RULE OF GOD: THROUGH FISSURES TO NEWNESS

The Old Testament is all about God, creator of heaven and earth, lover of the world, Lord, Savior, and covenant partner of Israel. The Old Testament is not about the generic gods of ancient or more recent religion and in fact carries on a relentless polemic against such generic alternatives.[1] Indeed this God is known in quite particular ways, concerning YHWH's character, actions, and commitments; consequently, there is something very particular about the modes of praise, obedience, and hope to which YHWH's creation and covenant partners are summoned. Most especially there is something profoundly particular about Israel, the people upon whom YHWH has rested YHWH's primal passion. It is because of that primal passion on the part of this future-creating God that Israel is a community of hope and that the Old Testament, Israel's book, is a book about YHWH's future.[2]

The coming rule of YHWH that is everywhere expected in the Old Testament will be a time of *shalom*, of well-being, of prosperity, security, and fruitfulness. We may take the initial recital of blessing in the covenant tradition of Deuteronomy as a representative articulation of the blessedness of life under the rule of YHWH:

> If you will only obey the LORD your God, by diligently observing all his commandments that I am commanding you today, the LORD your God will set you high above all the nations of the earth; all these blessings shall come upon you and overtake you, if you obey the LORD your God:

> Blessed shall you be in the city, and blessed shall you be in the field.
>
> Blessed shall be the fruit of your womb, the fruit of your ground, and the fruit of your livestock, both the increase of your cattle and the issue of your flock.
>
> Blessed shall be your basket and your kneading bowl.
>
> Blessed shall you be when you come in, and blessed shall you be when you go out.
>
> The LORD will cause your enemies who rise against you to be defeated before you; they shall come out against you one way, and flee before you seven ways. The LORD will command the blessing upon you in your barns, and in all that you undertake; he will bless you in the land that the LORD your God is giving you. The LORD will establish you as his holy people, as he has sworn to you, if you keep the commandments of the LORD your God and walk in his ways. All the peoples of the earth shall see that you are called by the name of the LORD, and they shall be afraid of you. The LORD will make you abound in prosperity, in the fruit of your womb, in the fruit of your livestock, and in the fruit of your ground in the land that the LORD swore to your ancestors to give you. The LORD will open for you his rich storehouse, the heavens, to give the rain of your land in its season and to bless all your undertakings. You will lend to many nations, but you will not borrow. The LORD will make you the head, and not the tail; you shall be only at the top, and not at the bottom—if you obey the commandments of the LORD your God, which I am commanding you today, by diligently observing them, and if you do not turn aside from any of the words that I am commanding you today, either to the right or to the left, following other gods to serve them. (Deuteronomy 28:1-14)

This articulation includes reference both to the domestic life of the community and to the more public history of a territorial people. In both aspects the accent is upon a material life of well-being. Upon this expectation the traditions of the Old Testament are generally agreed. At the same time, as our previous discussion has made clear, this profound confidence in God's future is articulated in a variety of voices of which we have cited four trajectories. On the main claims that define the future in terms of the purposes of YHWH, there is general agreement even given various articulations.

I

It is fair to say that biblical hope for the coming rule of YHWH characteristically proceeds on two tracks, *covenant with Israel* and *fidelity to creation.* In the first instance YHWH's promises are to Israel and for Israel that, "The LORD will make you the head, and not the tail; you shall be only at the top, and not at the bottom" (Deuteronomy 28:13). The "election tradition" of Israel's peculiar status with YHWH in the narrative memory of Israel has as its center an enormous fissure.[3]

■ There are the beginnings with Abraham and Moses, an initiative that culminates at Sinai with the giving of the Torah. This familiar memory becomes the basis of the Pentateuch (Torah), Israel's primal text.

■ This founding fidelity is decisively disrupted by the systemic infidelity of Israel that culminates in the exile and the termination of the Jerusalem establishment.[4] While the crisis of Jerusalem in exile is situated in the sixth century, the biblical narration of the crisis traces the entire *history in the land* as a history permeated with disobedience. Thus the "history" rendered by the Deuteronomic historian traces the fracture of the covenant from the crossing of the Jordan in Joshua 3:4. The course of that "history" through the monarchy is one of disobedience, the departure from covenantal fidelity of which the covenant tradition of Deuteronomy characteristically warns. The historical reality of termination, displacement, and deportation in the sixth century is simply a playing out of what was a foregone outcome of covenant requirements.

■ What concerns us here, however, is that in the very midst of that fissure, via prophetic oracles, the God of covenant fidelity moves afresh to *restoration and rehabilitation.* As we have seen, the several prophetic traditions articulate the divine gift of newness in different ways. In every case, however, *the divine gift of newness* is the stress point of prophetic faith, variously voiced in messianic, apocalyptic, and scribal modes; God *makes new* for Israel!

Thus the drama of *initial beginning, fissure*, and *belated newness* becomes the story line of Israel's faith. It is a story line that becomes with Erich Voegelin paradigmatic or with David Weiss Halivni, pragmatic historiography.[5] The same drama can be variously read beyond the sixth century in many other contexts. This same story of *fissure to newness* is the plot line of the Psalms of lament in their characteristic move *from plea to praise.* This same plot line, moreover, is reiterated in contemporary

Zionism whereby *the state of Israel* is received as God's newness after the fissure of *the shoah*. The God of Israel makes new for Israel!

II

The biblical account of God's rule in Israelite rendition, however, is not limited to newness for Israel. Israel's horizon of faith in the Old Testament recognized that its God was the God of the whole world. For that reason, Israel thinks and speaks well beyond itself concerning the coming rule of God:

■ As we have seen, Old Testament tradition is framed by creation faith. It is the savior of Israel who has transformed chaos into a life-giving system of fruitfulness that will support and sustain all creatures. As the wisdom teachers recognized, creation is ordered by the creator according to patterns of regularity and reliability that must be honored, respected, and obeyed. And when these ordered patterns are honored, life flourishes.

■ The Old Testament, in its many doxological Psalms, celebrates the good order of creation. But the faith of the Old Testament knows as well about creation disrupted—by the power of chaos, by willful human disobedience, by divine absence and neglect.[6] The Old Testament has little interest in sorting out these several explanations for the fracture of creation, but looks the recurring resurgence of chaos full in the face.[7] For that reason the flood narrative of Genesis 6–9 stands at the center of creation faith, a narrative account of the radical deathly *undoing* of creation.[8]

■ But of course the flood narrative is not the end of the story. In the Genesis tradition itself, the new covenant with "all flesh" after the flood attests to a God who reorders and renews creation and continues, after the disruption, to order creation yet again for life and well-being. That "everlasting covenant" with creation after the flood becomes a central motif of exilic prophetic promise, indicating that the new/revised covenant is not only with Israel but with all creation (Genesis 9:16):

> I will make for you a covenant on that day with the wild animals, the birds of the air, and the creeping things of the ground; and I will abolish the bow, the sword, and war from the land; and I will make you lie down in safety. (Hosea 2:18; see Isaiah 55:3; 61:8; Jeremiah 32:40; Ezekiel 16:60; 37:20; see the "Covenant of Peace" in Ezekiel 34:25; 37:26)

It is God's resolve, in the process of recovery, to accomplish, by work and by dictum, the offer of a new creation that will be free of human corruption, free of dissident chaos, and free of divine neglect.

That renewed covenant that is always coming into being is given lyrical affirmation in prophetic oracles:

> The wolf shall live with the lamb,
> the leopard shall lie down with the kid,
> the calf and the lion and the fatling together,
> and a little child shall lead them. (Isaiah 11:6; see Isaiah 65:17-25)

Because God is the Lord who brings Israel to restoration and the creator who brings the world to newness, God is also Lord of all nations. Thus it is anticipated:

■ The nations will be recipients of YHWH's saving miracles. Thus history teems with exodus deliverances:

> Are you not like the Ethiopians to me,
> O people of Israel? says the LORD.
> Did I not bring Israel up from the land of Egypt,
> and the Philistine from Caphtor and the Arameans from Kir?
> (Amos 9:7)

■ All nations will join in common worship in the cosmic arena of Jerusalem, but each in worship of its own God:

> In days to come
> the mountain of the LORD's house
> shall be established as the highest of the mountains,
> and shall be raised up above the hills.
> Peoples shall stream to it,
> and many nations shall come and say:
> "Come, let us go up to the mountain of the LORD,
> to the house of the God of Jacob;
> that he may teach us his ways
> and that we may walk in his paths."
> For out of Zion shall go forth instruction,
> and the word of the LORD from Jerusalem.
> He shall judge between many peoples,
> and shall arbitrate between strong nations far away;
> they shall beat their swords into plowshares,
> and their spears into pruning hooks;

nation shall not lift up sword against nation,
neither shall they learn war any more;
but they shall all sit under their own vines and under their own fig trees,
and no one shall make them afraid;
for the mouth of the LORD of hosts has spoken. (Micah 4:1-4)

■ All will be blessed in a special relationship with YHWH: "On that day Israel will be the third with Egypt and Assyria, a blessing in the midst of the earth, whom the LORD of hosts has blessed, saying, 'Blessed be Egypt my people, and Assyria the work of my hands, and Israel my heritage'" (Isaiah 19:24-25).

■ All persons and communities will be responsively obedient to the requirements of the Noachic covenant.[9]

Thus biblical faith offers for Israel, for the nations, and for all creation a drama of origin, disruption, and renewal.[10] The focus of the textual tradition is upon the newness that YHWH has worked, is working, and will work as the world lives in hope. We may take the poem of Hosea 2:2-23 as a witness for the future of both creation and Israel. Verses 2-13 portray the loss and the fissure. But then, beginning in verse 14, the poem testifies to a new beginning:

- a new covenant with creation: "I will make for you a covenant on that day with the wild animals, the birds of the air, and the creeping things of the ground; and I will abolish the bow, the sword, and war from the land; and I will make you lie down in safety" (Hosea 2:18).
- a new covenant with Israel: "And I will take you for my wife forever; I will take you for my wife in righteousness and in justice, in steadfast love, and in mercy. I will take you for my wife in faithfulness; and you shall know the LORD" (Hosea 2:19-20).
- a new fruitfulness in the earth:

On that day I will answer, says the Lord,
I will answer the heavens
and they shall answer the earth;
and the earth shall answer the grain, the wine, and the oil,
and they shall answer Jezreel. (Hosea 2:21-22)

- a new relationship with Israel:

And I will sow him for myself in the land.
And I will have pity on Loruhamah,
and I will say to Lomammi, "You are my people";
and he shall say, "You are my God." (Hosea 2:23)

The future of Israel and creation are twinned. The Old Testament characteristically speaks of both together, bound together because the one future-creating God is the faithful sovereign of both.

III

In the end it is important to reflect on the claims of Old Testament faith as continuing claims of worshiping communities in contemporary society. It is obvious that a great historical and critical distance exists between these ancient texts and our contemporary world, a distance that is so great that no easy connection can be made between old text and current context. That distance is occupied in the west by the enormous cultural transformations including Renaissance Humanism, the rise of science, the appearance of nation states, Enlightenment rationality, modern barbarism in scientific modes, and the emergence of postmodernism in many shadings that make larger claims of meanings intrinsically problematic. In such an environment we may rightly ask if this ancient faith, however it be nuanced, can claim a hearing and eventually an engaged response. It is a question that every community of faith rooted in this tradition must ask, and it is a wonderment that any critical analysis may evoke.

Of course the question of contemporary engagement with the tradition admits of no direct and simple answer, for a negative answer would only be *skepticism* and a positive answer would only be taken as *fideism*.[11] To pose the question in what I hope is a useful and judicious way, I have recourse to the polarity of Emmanuel Levinas between "totality and infinity."[12] By *totality* Levinas means an account of reality that is all-comprehending and that provides absolute closure. Thus totality is linked to totalitarianism, that is, a total account of reality. By contrast, Levinas uses the term *infinity* to refer to a claim of meaning and belief that are unbounded and left open, a refusal to give absolute closure.

I propose that the claims of Old Testament faith merit a hearing and an engaged response precisely because the form and substance of the textual tradition are an epitome of Levinas's *infinity*. The Old Testament does not make absolute claims that bespeak closure. Rather, in both form and substance, faith claims are left open for further reflection, interpretation, and alternative articulation; as a consequence, what is revealed remains profoundly hidden and awaits always yet one more articulation that may reveal and disclose yet again, yet again always in a way that is fresh and new.

1. This mode of *infinity* is reflected in discourse that is elusive and open to more than one reading. Obvious examples might include the enigmatic ending of Job 42:6 or the final paragraph of 2 Kings 25:27-30. This quality of elusiveness, however, is not limited to such obvious cases, but in fact pervades the whole.

2. The elusiveness of the mode of discourse is underscored by the complexity of the text in its formation and transmission. Thus what has become canonical has become so through an elongated and unrecoverable process of transmission wherein many voices speak.[13] The traditioning process, moreover, has given no effort to smoothing out, harmonizing, or reconciling these several voices, so that it is the interaction (dialogue, conversation) among the voices rather than any one or preferred voice that carries the voice of normative.

3. The elusive modes of discourse and the complexity of formation and transmission of the tradition are matched and, theologically speaking, derived from the central character, the Holy One of Israel, who is indeed elusive and irascible in a variety of settings.[14] The conventional modes of theological discourse in the church do not adequately communicate the indeterminate quality of much of the self-presentation of this God in the text.

On all counts of *modes of discourse*, *complexity of formation and transmission*, and the *elusiveness of the Subject*, the text of the Old Testament refuses closure. Indeed this is a primary characteristic of the text so that the text not only waits for a "final coming" but awaits the next interpretation and refuses any final interpretation, any "final solution."

IV

The offer of this text of openness must make its way in a culture that is much attracted to "totality," wherein there can be an articulation of a full, final, total truth. We may identify two such totalizing articulations of faith, each of which moves visibly toward totalitarian authority and control.

First, there is the narrative of *secular triumphalism* that is presented as the myth of progress. That account of reality, a product of the Enlightenment, is grounded in autonomous reason as a response to the religious wars and the divided religious truth of the seventeenth century.[15] While the origins of this perspective are philosophical and ethical, the tradition has evolved into self-justifying nation states and in the United States into a national security state that savors its "exceptionalism" and that issues in global ambitions that are a mix of technological superiority and political cynicism.[16] "Progress" now is equated with the advance of U.S. economic, political, and military hegemony, all under the banner of an innocent "democratic capitalism" that is incapable of self-criticism. This secular account of reality can readily trade upon religious (biblical, Christian) narratives, but in fact such religious reference points are only a cover for aggressive anti-neighborly policies that take self-security as an ultimate corporate project. The power of that secular narrative is so irresistible that it is able to co-opt religious and political symbols that in fact contradict the claims and practices of such absoluteness.

Second, in reaction to that secular narrative that justifies the overriding of all local traditions and social reality is *sectarian triumphalism* that more dramatically traffics in religious symbolism, but that seeks to impose a rigid exclusionary public morality in denial of the pluralism that is a fact on the ground. This account of reality appeals to the biblical traditions, but engages in reductionism that eliminates the elusiveness of the biblical claims of faith, a reductionism that issues in one-dimensional credalism that in turn produces a rigid one-dimensional notion of social reality. Like its secular counterpart, such sectarian ideology appeals to the biblical testimony, but preempts it for a mode of reality that contradicts that testimony.

Both of these claims are totalizing. *The secular account* has no patience for anything that does not fit the advance of the global market that is the glove that covers the American fist. Because there is no holy mystery to de-absolutize such arrogant power, that power goes unchecked. *The sectarian account* is totalizing in the way in which a quite particular confessional claim becomes paradigmatic and authoritative for all social reality. The two accounts, moreover, in contemporary social practice are nicely twinned, so that *the sectarian narrative* provides the broad popular political base for *the secular account* that in fact has no interest in the sectarian agenda.

Amid such powerful totalizing forces, comes this alternative biblical account of reality that is, as we have seen,

a) rooted in a holy God who issues covenant commands as a grounding for alternative,
b) pertains in particular communities of praise and obedience,
c) anticipates a full rule of the elusive God who stands over against all systems of closure.

Whether this alternative account of reality can be sustained in the face of totalizing power carried in these two narrative accounts is currently an open and unanswered question. The totalizing accounts are always seeking a "final solution" to social reality:

- the secular account seeks a "final solution" that will eliminate all resistance to democratic capitalism and its unyielding markets, dismissing all others as "rogue states";
- the sectarian account seeks a "final solution" that will eliminate all those who do not name the name of Jesus.

It has always been the burden of this alternative community to stand against such totalizing; in the Old Testament Nebuchadnezzar is a recurring cipher with a totalizing propensity that in the end is critiqued and dismissed as idolatry.[17]

V

It is clear that the practice of this alternative account of reality must perforce include hard, disciplined thought, for an intellectual case must be made for this alternative. In the end, however, it is clear that it is through *praxis* (a discipline of heart and hand) and not an abstract thought that this elusive account of reality is sustained amid other competing faith claims. That *praxis* is variously lined out in Torah, in the Priestly traditions as the *embrace of holiness*, in the Deuteronomic tradition as the *embrace of neighborliness*.[18] With the accent on *praxis*, we may appeal in particular to the oracle of Jeremiah who assaults the totalizing claims of the Davidic monarchy in the rule of Jehoiakim. Against the pretense of a monarchy, the prophet cites King Josiah, a king who was open to the elusive and primal requirements of covenant:

> Are you a king
> because you compete in cedar?
> Did not your father eat and drink
> and do justice and righteousness?
> Then it was well with him.
> He judged the cause of the poor and needy;
> then it was well.
> Is not this to know me?
> says the LORD. (Jeremiah 22:15-16)

This poetic utterance equates "knowledge of God" and "justice for the needy." And of course in the long account of Israel's life in the land, it is the rejection of such neighborly justice, according to prophetic critique, that cause the loss of the land and the totalizing dynasty, the very land that these misguided policies sought to secure.

It is important to recognize that such neighborly *praxis* consists not simply in one-to-one, face-to-face neighborly acts, though these are of crucial importance. It is clear, nonetheless, that the covenantal alternative of Sinai is more than simply a commendation of charity and kindness. Sinai does nothing less than offer a *public polity* for the ways in which public power is to be ordered and practiced.[19] It is a *public polity* chartered in the Decalogue, that is a celebration of the public good and a curbing of all autonomous ambitions (Exodus 20:1-17; Deuteronomy 5:6-21). For good reasons we may say in general that it is the public polity of Sinai that is the primal ground for the public critique of the use of power in the long history of the West. More particularly, Sinai is the ground for the paradigmatic critique of Solomon whose economic policies of exploitation are infinitely linked to distorted religious commitments.[20] Thus the covenantal-Deuteronomic-prophetic critique of distorted power, rooted in distinct religious loyalty, anticipates the key critical insight of Karl Marx: "The criticism of heaven is thus transformed into the criticism of earth, the criticism of religion into the criticism of law, and the criticism of theology into the criticism of politics."[21] Thus Israel is called to *covenantal praxis* by the Holy God to be enacted toward the neighbor in concrete acts of generosity and in public policies of justice.

As Nebuchadnezzar is the cipher for totalizing in the Old Testament, we may take the narrative figure of Daniel as a practitioner of the alternative who had to live in the empire but is on his own terms. In Daniel 1, Daniel is trained for civil service in the empire; he is trained successfully, on his own terms, in order that his Jewish identity should not be "defiled" (Daniel 1:8). Thus as Daniel Smith suggests, Daniel is a model for the faithful maintenance of Jewish identity in the midst of the empire.[22] By Daniel 3, however, the totalizing insistence of Nebuchadnezzar has become uncompromising and aggressive, so that no room was left for an identity or a practice that departed from imperial expectation. The imperial requirement to "bow down" to imperial icons is the breaking point for accommodation between empire and alternative community. The narrative ends in a defiant assertion of resistance and an affirmation of the alternative:

> Shadrach, Meshach, and Abednego answered the king, "O Nebuchadnezzar, we have no need to present a defense to you in this matter. If our God whom we serve is able to deliver us from the furnace of blazing fire and out of your hand, O king, let him deliver us. But if not, be it known to you, O king, that we will not serve your gods and we will not worship the golden statue that you have set up." (Daniel 3:16-18)

And in chapter 4 Daniel offers to Nebuchadnezzar precisely an alternative mode of praxis that resonates with Israel's most ancient covenantal mandates:

> The sentence is rendered by decree of the watchers,
>   the decision is given by order of the holy ones,
> in order that all who live may know
>   that the Most High is sovereign over the kingdom of mortals;
> he gives it to whom he will
>   and sets over it the lowliest of human beings. (Daniel 4:17)

In this insistence, Daniel echoes for the empire the oldest claim of covenant, namely, that neighborly obedience to Torah results in "prosperity" (v. 27). The model of Daniel is overstated in narrative imagination and excessively dramatic. It is nonetheless an available model for the way in which the covenant community may stand before the empire or, alternatively, for the way this elusive account of reality may stand against dominant totalizing accounts. The *praxis* that sustains an alternative account requires concrete acts of defiant conduct; alongside such concrete acts, it requires verbal testimony that makes a declaration so that concrete acts not be co-opted by the totalizing narrative.[23] That is, sustenance of this alternative narrative requires testimony that creates space for alternative living. In Christian tradition, Jesus' instruction to his disciples is in the same direction:

> But before all this occurs, they will arrest you and persecute you; they will hand you over to synagogues and prisons, and you will be brought before kings and governors because of my name. This will give you an opportunity to testify. So make up your minds not to prepare your defense in advance; for I will give you words and a wisdom that none of your opponents will be able to withstand or contradict. (Luke 21:12-15)

It has always been so with this alternative reality that remains elusive in hope and vigilant in *praxis*. This tradition yields no final solution because the God amid this tradition is not a God of finality. Rather, the tradition is constituted as an ongoing, always new interaction, the kind modeled with Moses at Sinai. In the end, the coming of the full rule of this God is elusive: "And if anyone says to you at that time, 'Look! Here is the Messiah!' or 'Look! There he is!'—do not believe it. False messiahs and false prophets will appear and produce signs and omens, to lead astray, if possible, the elect. But be alert; I have already told you everything" (Mark 13:21-23; see Matthew 24:23-27; Luke 17:20-21). The seduction of totalizing accounts of reality is that they know too much. This biblical tradition knows the elusive name of the Holy God; beyond that, it walks by faith and not by sight. Such walking by faith is inherently revolutionary, as every totalizing system eventually discovers.[24]

NOTES

1. Introduction to the Task

1. See Rudolf Bultmann, "Is Exegesis without Presuppositions Possible?" *Encounter 21* (1960): 194–200.

2. On the spectrum of current options see Walter Brueggemann, *Theology of the Old Testament: Testimony, Dispute, Advocacy* (Minneapolis: Fortress Press, 1997), 61–102; James Barr, *The Concept of Biblical Theology* (Minneapolis: Fortress Press, 1999); and Leo G. Perdue, *Reconstructing Old Testament Theology: After the Collapse of History*, OBT (Minneapolis: Fortress Press, 2005).

3. On the interface of Israelite religion and the ancient Near East in general and with Canaanite religion in particular, see Patrick D. Miller, *The Religion of Ancient Israel*, Library of Ancient Israel (Louisville: Westminster John Knox Press, 2000).

4. The classic article on common theology is by Morton Smith, "The Common Theology of the Ancient Near East," *JBL* 71 (1952): 135–47.

5. See Gerhard von Rad, *The Problem of the Hexateuch and Other Essays* (New York: McGraw-Hill, 1966), 1–78; and G. Ernest Wright, *The Old Testament Against Its Environment*, SBT (London: SCM Press, 1950).

6. On the dialectic of common theology and mutation in that commonality, see Norman K. Gottwald, *The Tribes of Yahweh: A Sociology of the Religion of Liberated Israel, 1250–1050 B.C.E.* (Maryknoll: Orbis Books, 1969), 667–75.

7. For a critical assessment of Wellhausen, see in general *Semeia* 25 (1982) and particularly Patrick D. Miller, "Wellhausen and the History of Israel's Religion," in that issue, pp. 61–73.

8. On that complexity and pluralism, see Rainer Albertz, *A History of Israelite Religion in the Old Testament Period*, 2 vols. OTL (Louisville: Westminster John Knox Press, 1994); and Erhard S. Gerstenberger, *Theologies in the Old Testament* (Minneapolis: Fortress Press, 2002).

9. An early and influential synthesis of this position is William Foxwell Albright, *From Stone Age to Christianity: Monotheism and the Historical Process* (Baltimore: Johns Hopkins Press, 1946).

10. On the development and influence of "biblical archaeology," see Thomas W. Davis, *Shifting Sands: The Rise and Fall of Biblical Archaeology* (Oxford: Oxford University Press, 2004).

11. John Van Seters, *In Search of History: History and Historiography in the Ancient*

World and the Origins of Biblical History (New Haven: Yale University Press, 1983); Thomas L. Thompson, *Early History of the Israelite People: From the Written and Archaeological Sources* (Leiden: Brill, 1992); and William G. Dever, *What Did the Biblical Writers Know and When Did They Know It?* (Grand Rapids: Eerdmans, 2001).

12. Critical study of the Bible did not move beyond Protestant circles into Roman Catholic scholarship until the papal encyclical of Leo XIII in *Divine Afflante Spiritu* (Washington, D.C.: National Catholic Welfare Conference, 1943).

13. See Walter Brueggemann, *Theology of the Old Testament*, 15–42.

14. On the later, see especially Oscar Cullman, *Christ and Time* (London: SCM Press, 1962).

15. Jon D. Levenson, "Why Jews Are Not Interested in Biblical Theology" in *The Hebrew Bible, The Old Testament, and Historical Criticism* (Louisville: Westminster John Knox Press, 1993), 33–61.

16. No scholar of the Christian Old Testament has worked more effectively at common Jewish-Christian scholarship on the Bible than has Rolf Rendtorff. See his article, "Toward a Common Jewish-Christian Reading of the Hebrew Bible," in *Canon and Theology*, OBT (Minneapolis: Fortress Press, 1993), 31–45.

17. See Perdue, *Reconstructing Old Testament Theology*, 183–238; and Barr, *The Concept of Biblical Theology*, 286–311.

18. See the phrasing of Rudolf Bultmann, "Prophecy and Fulfillment," in *Essays on Old Testament Hermeneutics*, ed. Claus Westermann (Richmond: John Knox Press, 1963), 75.

19. Perdue, *Reconstructing Old Testament Theology*, 194, refers to Levenson's programmatic question with his response, "Jews Who Do Biblical Theology."

20. See Levenson's splendid trilogy on biblical theology: *Sinai and Zion: An Entry into Jewish Theology* (New York: Winston Press, 1985); *Creation and the Persistence of Evil: The Jewish Drama of Divine Omnipotence* (San Francisco: Harper and Row, 1988); and *The Hebrew Bible, the Old Testament, and Historical Criticism: Jews and Christians in Biblical Studies* (Louisville: Westminster John Knox Press, 1993).

21. Perdue, 215, especially calls attention to the important work of Michael Fishbane. And reference may well be given to the remarkable foray of David R. Blumenthal, *Facing the Abusing God: A Theology of Protest* (Louisville: Westminster John Knox Press, 1993).

22. M. H. Goshen-Gottstein, "Tanakh Theology: The Religion of the Old Testament and the Place of Jewish Biblical Theology," in *Ancient Israelite Religion: Essays in Honor of Frank Moore Cross*, ed. Patrick D. Miller, Jr., et al. (Philadelphia: Fortress Press, 1987), 634.

23. While such humility is appropriate to its subject matter, it is clear that much U.S. Christianity of a conservative ilk has grown more shrill and is quite devoid of any humility. It is of course unfortunate that such a brand of idolatrous faith has claimed for itself the term "evangelical."

24. On an ecclesial perspective in interpretation, see Stephen E. Fowl, *Engaging Scripture: A Model for Theological Interpretation* (Malden, Mass.: Blackwell, 1998), though Fowl is not open to common work with Jewish interpreters on core theological claims.

25. See *Christianity in Jewish Terms*, ed. Tikva Frymer-Kensky et al. (Boulder: Westview Press, 2000).

26. See Brevard S. Childs, *Biblical Theology of the Old and New Testaments: Theological Reflection on the Christian Bible* (Minneapolis: Fortress Press, 1993); and Rolf Rendtorff, *The Canonical Hebrew Bible: A Theology of the Old Testament* (Leiden: Deo Publishing, 2005).

27. The term comes from Paul Ricoeur; see the discussion by Mark I. Wallace, *The Second Naiveté: Barth, Ricoeur, and the New Yale Theology*, StABH (Macon, Ga.: Mercer University Press, 1990).

28. James A. Sanders, "The Issue of Closure in the Canonical Process," in *The Canon Debate*, ed. Lee Martin McDonald and James A. Sanders (Peabody, Mass.: Hendrickson, 2002), 262–63.

29. Brevard S. Childs, *Biblical Theology of the Old and New Testaments*; over the course of his work, Childs's notion of canon and the work of canon criticism has changed and evolved in important ways. Contrast the work of 1993 with his earlier *Introduction to the Old Testament as Scripture* (Philadelphia: Fortress Press, 1979).

30. Childs, *Biblical Theology*, 95–207, 209–322.

31. Ibid., 349–716.

32. Brevard S. Childs, *The Struggle to Understand Isaiah as Christian Scripture: A Hermeneutical Study* (Grand Rapids: Eerdmans, 2004).

33. Brevard S. Childs, *Biblical Theology*, 67–68.

34. The programmatic essay for all that I have discussed here is Karl Barth, "The Strange New World Within the Bible," in *The Word of God and the Word of Man*, trans. Douglas Horton (New York: Harper & Brothers, 1957), 28–50.

35. Horst Dietrich Preuss, *Old Testament Theology*, vol. 1 (Louisville: Westminster John Knox Press, 1995), 25.

36. M. H. Goshen-Gottstein, "Tanakh Theology," 619, 621.

2. A Primal Revelation (Exodus 3:1–4:17)

1. See Patrick D. Miller, *The Religion of Ancient Israel* (Library of Ancient Israel; Louisville: Westminster John Knox Press, 2000).

2. See R. W. L. Moberly, *The Old Testament of the Old Testament: Patriarchal Narratives and Mosaic Yahwism* (Minneapolis: Fortress Press, 1992).

3. Erich Voegelin, *Order and History, vol.1, Israel and Revelation* (Baton Rouge: Louisiana State University Press, 1956).

4. On finding voice in order to reenter one's own history, see Elaine Scarry, *The Body in Pain: The Making and Unmaking of the World* (Oxford: Oxford University Press, 1985); and Judith Lewis Herman, *Trauma and Recovery: The Aftermath of Violence—from Domestic Abuse to Political Terror* (New York: Basic Books, 1992).

5. James L. Kugel, *The God of Old: Inside the Lost World of the Bible* (New York: Free Press, 2003), 134, 135–36.

6. On the "cry-save" theme, see James Plastaras, *The God of Exodus* (Milwaukee: Bruce Publishing Company, 1966); Claus Westermann, *The Praise of God in the Psalms* (Richmond: John Knox Press, 1965); and Walter Brueggemann, "Social Criticism and Social Vision in the Deuteronomic Formula of the Judges," in *Die Botschaft und die Boten: Festschrift fuer Hans Walter Wolff*, ed. by Joerg Jeremias and Lothar Perlitt (Neukirchen-Vluyn: Neukirchener Verlag, 1981), 101–114.

7. Karl Barth, *Prayer* (50th Anniversary Edition; Louisville: Westminster John Knox Press, 2002), 13.

8. See Martin Buber, *The Eclipse of God: Studies in the Relation between Religion and Philosophy* (London: Victor Gollancz, 1953); and Samuel Terrien, *The Elusive Presence: Toward a New Biblical Theology* (New York: Harper and Row, 1978).

9. Michael Fishbane, *Biblical Interpretation in Ancient Israel* (Oxford: Clarendon Press, 1985), 375–76, notes that in Exodus 12:35-38 the "mixed crowd" leaves Egypt with "jewelry and silver and gold," not unlike the departure of Abraham with many possessions.

10. This twofold accent is at the center of the influential proposal of Gerhard von Rad, *The Problem of the Hexateuch and Other Essays* (New York: McGraw-Hill, 1966), 3–8 in his exposition of Israel's "credo."

11. The theme of "reversal of fortunes" figures prominently in the exilic prophetic promises and becomes a slogan for the possibility of a YHWH-given future (Jeremiah 29:14; 30:18; 31:23; 32:44; 33:26).

12. See Walter Brueggemann, *Theology of the Old Testament: Testimony, Dispute, Advocacy* (Minneapolis: Fortress Press, 1997), 122–26, and the works cited there.

13. Von Rad, *The Problem of the Hexateuch*, 198–204.

14. The phrase is of course from Emmanuel Kant, but the "Enlightenment" mode of Karl Marx gave political-economic "body" to the phrase. Marx made sure that the revolution of Kant did not remain limited to the realm of ideas.

15. Frank Moore Cross, *Canaanite Myth and Hebrew Epic: Essays in the History of the Religion of Israel* (Cambridge: Harvard University Press, 1973), 60–75.

16. See Jean-Luc Marion, *God Without Being: Hors-Texte*, trans. Thomas A. Carlson (Chicago: University of Chicago Press, 1991). See particularly pp. 88–103 where Marion discusses 1 Corinthians 1:28 and Romans 4:17 concerning *ousia*, wherein Paul "outwits being."

17. See Walter Brueggemann, "'Impossibility' and Epistemology in the Faith Traditions of Abraham and Sarah [Genesis 18:1-15]," *ZAW* 94 (1982): 615–34.

18. Terence E. Fretheim, "The Plagues as Ecological Signs of Historical Disaster," *JBL* 110 (1991): 385–96.

19. See Walter Brueggemann, "Theme Revisited: Bread Again!" in *Reading from Right to Left: Essays on the Hebrew Bible in Honour of David J. A. Clines*, ed. Cheryl Exum and H. G. M. Williamson (London: Sheffield Academic Press, 2003), 76–89.

20. On the conviction that narrated miracle evokes faith, see also John 21:24.

21. Harvey Cox, *On Not Leaving It to the Snake* (New York: Macmillan, 1967), has sharply contrasted prophetic faith that counts on human agency with apocalyptic that appeals to supernaturalism and abdicates human agency. The issue is now an urgent one, given the apocalyptic imagery and ideology of much right-wing politics.

22. On the centrality of doxology for biblical faith, see Daniel W. Hardy and David F. Ford, *Praising and Knowing God* (Philadelphia: Westminster Press, 1985).

23. See a survey of the theme by John G. Gammie, *Holiness in Israel* (OBT; Minneapolis: Fortress Press, 1989).

24. The Priestly material in the Old Testament constitutes an important part of the whole of the corpus of the Torah and is preoccupied with the formation of a holy people (Leviticus 19:2): The tradition has obvious affinities with the tradition of Ezekiel. See Frank Crüsemann, *The Torah: Theology and Social History of Old Testament Law* (Edinburgh: T & T Clark, 1996), 277–327.

25. See Walter Brueggemann, "Pharaoh as Vassal: A Study of a Political Metaphor," *CBQ* 57 (1995): 27–51.

26. On the Oracles Against the Nations, there are a number of surveys. The best interpretation, however, is that of John Barton, "Amos's Oracles Against the Nations," in *Understanding Old Testament Ethics* (Louisville: Westminster John Knox Press, 2003), 77–129.

27. On this text and the plagues more generally, see Terence E. Fretheim, *God and World in the Old Testament: A Relational Theology of Creation* (Nashville: Abingdon Press, 2005), 113–26.

28. The same capacity of a faithful Israelite to confound the wisdom of the nations is evident in the narratives of Joseph and Daniel.

29. The practice of lament and complaint permeates Israel's text and Israel's life of faith; in addition to the "cry" as central to the discussion of Kugel cited in n. 5, see Erich Zenger, *A God of Vengeance? Understanding the Psalms of Divine Wrath* (Louisville: Westminster John Knox Press, 1996). The practice of the "cry" is fundamental to the fabric of justice in the horizon of Israel.

3. A Second Primal Revelation (Exodus 19:1–24:18)

1. Exodus 19:1–24:18, commonly referred to as the *Sinai pericope*, has been the subject of a great deal of critical study; see John J. Collins, *Introduction to the Hebrew Bible* (Minneapolis: Fortress Press, 2004), 121–37.

2. See the classic study of Dennis J. McCarthy, *Treaty and Covenant: A Study in Form in the Ancient Oriental Documents and in the Old Testament* (Second edition Analecta biblica 21A; Rome Biblical Institute Press, 1981).

3. The literature placed at Sinai runs through Numbers 10:10; of this material, however, only Exodus 19–24 and 32–34 is derived from older sources. All the rest of it is in the style and perspective of the Priestly tradition, a quite distinct voice in the larger tradition.

4. The verb "listen" (= "obey") is in the infinitive absolute, a way of expressing acute intensity in verbal form.

5. See John Davies, *A Royal Priesthood: Literary and Intertextual Perspectives on an Image of Israel in Exodus 19.6*, JSOT Supp 395 (New York: T & T Clark, 2004).

6. On the accent on "holiness" in the Priestly tradition, see John G. Gammie, *Holiness in Israel*, OBT (Minneapolis: Fortress Press, 1989), 9–70.

7. The cultic reenactment of the covenant at Sinai is plausibly reflected in Psalms 50, 81, and 95, psalms often characterized as "prophetic."

8. See Patrick D. Miller, "Israelite Religion," *The Hebrew Bible and Its Modern Interpreters*, eds. Douglas A. Knight and Gene M. Tucker (Philadelphia: Fortress Press, 1985), 211–13, who judges that concerning the uniqueness of Israel's faith, "the most likely candidates are the initial demands of the Decalogue, the claim of exclusive worship by Yahweh, and the aniconic requirement."

9. Frank Crüsemann, *The Torah: Theology and Social History of Old Testament Law* (Minneapolis: Fortress Press, 1996), 57, comments: "Sinai is, however, a utopian place. It is temporally and physically outside state authority. The association of divine law with this place is completed by steps, which the catastrophe of Israel both enabled and compelled. Sinai became the fulcrum of a legal system not connected with the power of a state and therefore not a mere expression of tradition and custom."

10. See Georg Fohrer, "The Righteous Man in Job 31," *Essays in Old Testament Ethics*, ed. James L. Crenshaw and John T. Willis (New York: KTAV, 1974), 1–22.

11. On the connections between wisdom and the covenantal traditions of Deuteronomy, see Moshe Weinfeld, *Deuteronomy and the Deuteronomic School* (Oxford: Clarendon Press, 1972).

12. See James L. Mays, *The Lord Reigns: A Theological Handbook to the Psalms* (Louisville: Westminster John Knox Press, 1994), 128–45, and Patrick D. Miller, *Israelite Religion and Biblical Theology: Collected Essays* (JSOT Supp. 267; Sheffield: Sheffield Academic Press, 2000), 318–36.

13. Hans Heinrich Schmid, *Gerechtigkeit als Weltordnung* (Tuebingen: J. C. B. Mohr, 1968).

14. Walter Harrelson, *The Ten Commandments and Human Rights* (OBT; Philadelphia: Fortress Press, 1980), 195–201.

15. I once heard a rabbi assert that at Auschwitz all Ten Commandments were systematically broken; he then observed that every time we violate all Ten Commandments systematically, we would get Auschwitz.

16. Above all it is Gerhard von Rad, *Studies in Deuteronomy*, SBT 9 (Chicago: Henry Regnery Company, 1953) who understood the dynamism of the interpretive process in Deuteronomy.

17. See Walter Brueggemann, "The Commandments and Liberated, Liberating Bonding," in *Interpretation and Obedience: From Faithful Reading to Faithful Living* (Minneapolis: Fortress Press, 1991), 145–58.

18. See Crüsemann, *The Torah*, 109–200.

19. Paul D. Hanson, "The Theological Significance of Contradiction within the Book of the Covenant," *Canon and Authority: Essays in Old Testament Religion and Theology*, ed. George W. Coats and Burke O. Long (Philadelphia: Fortress Press, 1977), 110–31.

20. James A. Sanders, "Adaptable for Life: The Nature and Function of Canon," *The Mighty Acts of God*, ed. Frank Moore Cross, et al. (Garden City: Doubleday, 1976), 531–60.

21. The case of slavery in the Bible is of course a prime and notorious example.

22. The language of "policy" and "technique" is from George Mendenhall, *Law and Covenant in Israel and the Ancient Near East* (Pittsburgh: Biblical Colloquium, 1955).

23. See Thomas B. Dozeman, *God on the Mountain: A Study of Redaction, Theology and Canon in Exodus 19–24*, SBL Monograph Series 37 (Atlanta: Scholars Press, 1989).

24. See Samuel Terrien, *The Elusive Presence: Toward a New Biblical Theology* (New York: Harper & Row, 1978).

25. On the tension, see Fernando Belo, *A Materialist Reading of the Gospel of Mark* (Maryknoll: Orbis Books, 1981).

4. A Third Primal Revelation (Exodus 32–34)

1. For a closer reading of this text, see R. W. L. Moberly, *At the Mountain of God: Story and Theology in Exodus 32–34*, JSOT Supp. 22 (Sheffield: JSOT Press, 1983).

2. On the complex history of the various priestly houses in ancient Israel, see Frank M. Cross, "The Priestly Houses of Early Israel," in *Canaanite Myth and Hebrew Epic: Essays in the History of the Religion of Israel* (Cambridge: Harvard University Press, 1973), 195-215.

3. The rhetorical pattern of indictment and sentence together constitute the recurring prophetic "speech of judgment" on which see Claus Westermann, *Basic Forms of Prophetic Speech* (Philadelphia: Westminster Press, 1967).

4. Terence E. Fretheim, *The Suffering of God: An Old Testament Perspective*, OBT

(Philadelphia: Fortress Press, 1984) has summarized and assessed the data concerning YHWH's capacity to change YHWH's mind.

5. On these verses, see Walter Brueggemann, *Theology of the Old Testament: Testimony, Dispute, Advocacy* (Minneapolis: Fortress Press, 1997), 215–28.

6. John Calvin, *Commentary on the Book of Psalms*, vol. 2 (Grand Rapids: Baker Book House, 1979), 8–9.

7. Phyllis Trible, *God and the Rhetoric of Sexuality* (OBT; Philadelphia: Fortress Press, 1978), 31–59.

8. On the related text in Numbers 14 and the problem of forgiveness, see Katherine Sakenfeld, "The Problem of Divine Forgiveness in Numbers 14," *CBQ* 37 (1975): 317–30.

9. Terence E. Fretheim, "The Plagues as Ecological Signs of Historical Disaster," *JBL* 110 (1991).

10. On this later text, see Frank Crüsemann, *The Torah: Theology and Social History of Old Testament Law* (Edinburgh: T & T Clark, 1996), 109–43.

11. This formulation has something of a belated parallel in the characteristic recital in Christian Eucharist of the "mystery of faith": Christ has died, / Christ has risen, / Christ will come again.

12. On the "unbuilding" of the Jerusalem temple and the continuing interpretive force of that event, see the book of Lamentations, and the discussions of Tod Linafelt, *Surviving Lamentations: Catastrophe, Lament, and Protest in the Afterlife of a Biblical Book* (Chicago: University of Chicago Press, 2000), and Kathleen M. O'Connor, *Lamentations and The Tears of the World* (Maryknoll: Orbis Books, 2002). Note especially the New Testament reference in John 2:19-22.

13. Ronald E. Clements, "Patterns in Prophetic Canon," *Canon and Authority: Essays in Old Testament Religion and Theology*, ed. George W. Coats and Burke O. Long (Philadelphia: Fortress Press, 1977), 49, 53.

14. On the newness of the sixth-century prophetic materials, see Gerhard von Rad, *Old Testament Theology*, vol. 2 (London: Oliver and Boyd, 1965), 188–277.

15. See the new and comprehensive study of the creation traditions in the Old Testament by Terence E. Fretheim, *God and the World in the Old Testament: A Relational Theology of Creation* (Nashville: Abingdon Press, 2005).

16. Rolf Rendtorff, *Canon and Theology*, OBT (Minneapolis: Fortress Press, 1993), 134.

17. On that pattern in the book of Psalms, see Walter Brueggemann, *The Psalms and the Life of Faith*, ed. Patrick D. Miller (Minneapolis: Fortress Press, 1995), 3–32.

18. On the pivotal function of the cry in discerning the God of ancient Israel, see James L. Kugel, *The God of Old: Inside the Lost World of the Bible* (New York: Free Press, 2003), 109–36.

19. James Plastaras, *The God of Exodus* (Milwaukee: Bruce Publishing Company, 1966) chapter 3, has most clearly exhibited the connections between the exodus liturgy and the practice of lament.

20. See Jürgen Moltmann, *The Crucified God: The Cross of Christ as the Foundation and Criticism of Christian Theology* (New York: Harper & Row, 1974).

21. See Jürgen Moltmann, *Theology of Hope: On the Ground and the Implications of a Christian Eschatology* (New York: Harper & Row, 1967).

5. YHWH as Sovereign God

1. The initial critical formulation of common theology is by Morton Smith, "The Common Theology of the Ancient Near East," *JBL* 71 (1952): 135–47.

2. On the "divine council," see E. Theodore Mullen, *The Divine Council in Canaanite and Early Hebrew Literature* (Chico: Scholars Press, 1980), and Patrick D. Miller, *Genesis 1–11: Studies in Structure and Theme*, JSOT Supp. 8 (Sheffield: University of Sheffield, 1978).

3. On Israelite "mutations" to the common theology of the ancient Near East, see Norman K. Gottwald, *The Tribes of Yahweh: A Sociology of the Religion of Liberated Israel, 1250–1050 B C.* (Maryknoll: Orbis Books, 1979), 667–91.

4. See Terence E. Fretheim, *God and World in the Old Testament: A Relational Theology of Creation* (Nashville: Abingdon Press, 2005), 62–63 and passim.

5. On creation theology in the exodus narrative, see Terence E. Fretheim, "The Plagues as Ecological Signs of Historical Disaster," *JBL* 110 (1991): 385–96.

6. See Walter Brueggemann, *Old Testament Theology: Testimony, Dispute,* Advocacy (Minneapolis: Fortress Press, 1997), 492–527.

7. Paul M. Kennedy, *The Rise and Fall of the Great Powers: Economic Change and Military Conflict from 1500 to 2000* (New York: Random House, 1987), has traced the fall of major Western powers by reference to territory, population, resources, and military adventurism. Kennedy has no explicit interest in any theological dimension of the issue; my impression, however, is that what Kennedy describes in geopolitical terms about absolute and arrogant power that is inherently self-destructive is closely parallel to the prophetic critique of major states who defy the ultimate rule of the creator God.

8. It is likely that reference to Assyria in this text, as John Calvin had already suggested, in fact refers to Babylon. On the regular "intertwining" of Assyria and Babylon in the tradition of Isaiah, see Brevard S. Childs, *Isaiah*, OTL (Louisville: Westminster John Knox Press, 2001), 124–28.

9. See Walter Brueggemann, *The Land: Place as Gift, Promise, and Challenge in Biblical Faith* (Philadelphia: Fortress Press, 1977).

10. See John van Seters, *Abraham in History and Tradition* (New Haven: Yale University Press, 1975). It is not necessary to follow van Seters in his judgment about the origin of the Abraham tradition to appreciate his accent on the cruciality of the Abraham promise in the sixth century.

11. On the continuing ideological force and function of the land promises, see the fine discussions of Michael Prior, *The Bible and Colonialism: A Moral Critique* (Sheffield: Sheffield Academic Press, 1997); and Prior, *Zionism and the State of Israel: A Moral Inquiry* (New York: Routledge, 1999).

12. See Hans Walter Wolff, "The Kerygma of the Yahwist," *Interpretation* 20 (1966): 131–58.

13. See Ellen Davis, "'And Pharaoh Will Change His Mind...' (Ezekiel 32:12): Dismantling Mythical Discourse," in *Theological Exegesis: Essays in Honor of Brevard S. Childs*, ed. Christopher Seitz and Kathryne Green-McCreight (Grand Rapids: Eerdmans, 1999), 224–39.

14. On this crucial text, see John Davies, *A Royal Priesthood: Literary and Intertextual Perspectives on an Image of Israel in Exodus 19:6* (JSOT Supp. 395; New York: T & T Clark,

2004). More broadly, see *A Royal Priesthood*, ed. Craig Bartholomew, et al. (Grand Rapids: Zondervan, 2002).

15. In Christian tradition, 1 Peter 2:9-10 represents an important usage of Exodus 19:5-6; the text in 1 Peter has exercised an enormous influence in the missional thinking of the ecumenical church.

16. In Second Isaiah, the creation theme is utilized to speak of the creation of Israel; see Carroll Stuhlmueller, *Creative Redemption in Deutero-Isaiah* (Rome: Biblical Institute Press, 1970).

17. For a general exposition of the theme of holiness in the Old Testament, see John G. Gammie, *Holiness in Israel*, OBT (Minneapolis: Fortress Press, 1989).

18. There is no doubt that this lament in the mouth of Israel in verse 20 is a quote from the liturgical cadences of Lamentations 5:20, on which see the splendid discussion of Kathleen M. O'Connor, *Lamentations and the Tears of the World* (Maryknoll: Orbis Books, 2002).

19. The point has been forcefully made by Jon D. Levenson, *The Hebrew Bible, The Old Testament, and Historical Criticism* (Louisville: Westminster John Knox Press, 1993), 145:

> I have been stressing the element of subjugation, Israel's inescapable subjugation to YHWH, because in the contemporary context, the term "liberation" can suggest something very different from what the Bible intends: it can suggest *self-determination*. For many people today, liberation means in essence an expansion of choices: the more options you have, the freer you are. Concentration on the movement out of bondage in Egypt can leave the impression that the Torah, too, endorses the modern Western agenda of self-determination in its various forms, just as concentration on covenant, a form of contractual relationship, can leave the false impression that the Torah endorses the currently popular idea that the only obligations that persons have are those they have voluntarily assumed, there being no morality independent of human will. But, as we have seen, the biblical story of the exodus is not couched in the vocabulary of freedom at all. Rather, it serves to undergird a set of obligations to the divine sovereign, who is Israel's king, their lord in covenant, and the deity to whose service they have been dedicated and consecrated.

20. On the "cry" and YHWH's characteristic response to the cry, see James L. Kugel, *The God of Old: Inside the Lost World of the Bible* (London: Free Press, 2003), chapter 5.

21. See Michael Walzer, *Exodus and Revolution* (New York: Basic Books, 1985).

22. Jorge Pixley, *On Exodus: A Liberation Perspective* (Maryknoll: Orbis Books, 1987). Levenson's critique of Pixley is cited in n. 9. On the wider usage of the Old Testament beyond Israel, it is worth noting that Erich Voegelin, *Israel and Revelation* (Baton Rouge: Louisiana State University Press, 1956), takes the Israelite narrative as "paradigmatic," a move that opens the tradition beyond the particularity of Israel. In his discussion, Voegelin works hard to negotiate between Israelite particularity and wider usage.

23. The phrase, "God's Preferential Option for the Poor" is of course a primal mantra of liberation theology, on which see, for example, Leonardo Boff and Clodovis Boff, *Introducing Liberation Theology* (Maryknoll: Orbis Books, 1987).

24. On the text see Walter Brueggemann, "'Exodus' in the Plural (Amos 9:7)," in

Many Voices One God: Being Faithful in a Pluralistic World, ed. Walter Brueggemann and George W. Stroup (Louisville: Westminster John Knox Press, 1998), 15–34.

25. See the careful delineation of the particular and the universal by Jon D. Levenson, "The Universal Horizon of Biblical Particularism," in *Ethnicity and the Bible*, ed. Mark G. Brett (New York: Brill, 1996), 143–69.

26. On YHWH's several "partners," see Walter Brueggemann, *Theology of the Old Testament*, 407–564.

27. The fullest statement of divine commitment to Israel in the ancestral narratives is in Genesis 17; but see also Genesis 15:1-20.

28. See Walter Brueggemann, *Theology of the Old Testament*, 213–28.

29. The issue of theodicy as it is regularly framed is no concern of the Old Testament, but is an issue that arises only in modern Enlightenment philosophy. See Terrence W. Tilley, *The Evils of Theodicy* (Eugene: Wipf and Stock, 2000), and behind him Michael Buckley, *At the Origins of Modern Atheism* (New Haven: Yale University Press, 1987). Such an issue as theodicy and the context of atheism do not arise when Israel practices its vigorous dialogic faith.

6. *YHWH as Sovereign—In Metaphor*

1. See Samuel Terrien, *The Elusive Presence: Toward a New Biblical Theology* (New York: Harper & Row, 1978).

2. See my fuller discussion of this field of metaphors, Walter Brueggemann, *Old Testament Theology: Testimony, Dispute, Advocacy* (Minneapolis: Fortress Press, 1997), 229–66.

3. The normative discussion of YHWH as warrior is Patrick D. Miller, Jr., *The Divine Warrior in Early Israel* (Cambridge: Harvard University Press, 1973). See also Frank Moore Cross, *Canaanite Myth and Hebrew Epic: Essays in the History of the Religion of Israel* (Cambridge: Harvard University Press, 1973), 91–144.

4. On the prophetic speech of judgment, see Claus Westermann, *Basic Forms of Prophetic Speech* (Philadelphia: Westminster Press, 1967).

5. The war poetry in Jeremiah 4–6 is representative of appeal to human agents in the intervention of YHWH. In older historical critical perspective, those poems were assigned to various identifiable enemies; see the articles by Cazelles, Childs, and Whitley in *A Prophet to the Nations: Essays in Jeremiah Studies*, ed. Leo G. Perdue and Brian W. Kovacs (Winona Lake: Eisenbrauns, 1984), 129–73. For the newer discussion that moves in very different directions, see Kathleen M. O'Connor, "The Tears of God and Divine Character in Jeremiah 2–9," *Troubling Jeremiah*, JSOT Supp. 260 (Sheffield: Sheffield Academic Press, 1999), 391–95.

6. See William L. Moran, "End of Holy War and the Anti-Exodus," *Biblica* 44 (1963): 333–42.

7. G. Ernest Wright, *The Old Testament and Theology* (New York: Harper & Row, 1969), 121–50.

8. Regina M. Schwartz, *The Curse of Cain: The Violent Legacy of Monotheism* (Chicago: University of Chicago Press, 1997).

9. Ibid., 62.

10. James L. Mays, *The Lord Reigns: A Theological Handbook to the Psalms* (Louisville: Westminster John Knox Press, 1994), 148, n. 13.

11. J. J. M. Roberts, "Mowinckel's Enthronement Festival: A Review," in *The Book of Psalms: Composition and Reception*, ed. Peter W. Flint and Patrick D. Miller, Jr. (Leiden: Brill, 2005), 97–115.

12. See E. Theodore Mullen, *The Divine Council in Canaanite and Early Hebrew Literature* (Chico: Scholars Press, 1980).

13. It was Walther Zimmerli, "The Place and Limit of the Wisdom in the Framework of the Old Testament Theology," *SJT* 17 (1964): 146–58, who first articulated the now common view that wisdom thinking is creation theology: "Wisdom thinks resolutely within the framework of a theology of creation" (148).

14. George E. Mendenhall, "Covenant Forms in Israelite Tradition," *BA* 17 (1954): 50–76.

15. See Dennis J. McCarthy, *Treaty and Covenant* (Analecta biblica 21A; Rome: Biblical Institute Press, 1978), and a summary of the scholarly discussion by Ernest W. Nicholson, *God and His People: Covenant and Theology in the Old Testament* (Oxford: Clarendon Press, 1986), 56–82.

16. Gerhard von Rad, *The Problem of the Hexateuch and Other Essays* (New York: McGraw-Hill, 1966), 26–33, had seen in an early phase of this scholarship the decisive covenantal shaping of the book of Deuteronomy.

17. On the ways in which theological claims in the Old Testament function powerfully in ongoing ways in the arena of *realpolitik*, see Michael Prior, *Zionism and the State of Israel: A Moral Inquiry* (New York: Routledge, 1999); and Prior, *The Bible and Colonialism: A Moral Critique* (Sheffield: Sheffield Academic Press, 1997).

18. See the definitive discussion of Westermann cited in n. 4.

19. See the comments of J. Clinton McCann Jr., "The Book of Psalms," *NIB* IV, on these several psalms. These psalms reflect the Mosaic tradition and articulate the theological crisis that Israel regularly faced as it sought to secure itself in the world.

20. See 2 Samuel 9 for an example of the way in which a human king can reassign land to his subjects.

21. Moshe Weinfeld, "The Covenant of Grant in the Old Testament and in the Ancient Near East," *JAOS* 90 (1970): 184–203.

22. Peter L. Berger, *The Sacred Canopy: Elements of a Sociological Theory of Religion* (Anchor Books: Garden City: Doubleday, 1969), 53–80.

23. Ibid. 59.

24. Job's statement of innocence in Job 31 constitutes a summary of the best ethic of the Old Testament; see Georg Fohrer, "The Righteous Man in Job 31," in *Essays in Old Testament Ethics*, ed. by James L. Crenshaw and John T. Willis (New York: KTAV Publishing House, 1974), 122.

25. See Walter Brueggemann, *Solomon: Israel's Ironic Icon of Human Achievement* (Columbia: University of South Carolina Press, 2005), 124–38.

26. Berger, *The Sacred Canopy*, 59–60.

27. For a discussion of the contemporary crisis of the global economy from a biblical perspective, see Ross Kinsler and Gloria Kinsler eds., *God's Economy: Biblical Studies From Latin America* (Maryknoll: Orbis Press, 2005).

28. See Walter Brueggemann, "Social Criticism and Social Vision in the Deuteronomic Formula of the Judges," *Die Botschaft und die Boten: Festschrift fuer Hans Walter Wolff*, ed. Joerg Jeremias and Lothar Perlitt (Neukirchen-Vluyn: Neukirchener Verlag, 1981), 101–14.

29. James L. Kugel, *The God of Old: Inside the Lost World of the Bible* (New York: Free Press, 2003), 110, 111.

30. Ibid., 124.

31. Ibid., 136.

32. There is no doubt that in the world of Israel's faith it is intended that human judges should imitate the divine judge. While the matter may of course have developed from the human to the divine, in the theological reckoning of Israel, the move is in the other direction.

33. See John R. Donahue, *The Gospel Parables* (Philadelphia: Fortress Press, 1988), 180–85.

34. Ibid., 181.

35. Erhard S. Gerstenberger, *Theologies in the Old Testament* (Minneapolis: Fortress Press, 2002) has made a sharp distinction between the religion of the state and the religion of the family and has insisted that these quite different practices yield very different theological outcomes.

36. See Sigmund Mowinckel, *He That Cometh* (Nashville: Abingdon Press, n. d.).

37. Otto Eissfeldt, "The Promises of Grace to David in Isaiah 55:1-5," in *Israel's Prophetic Heritage: Essays in Honor of James Muilenburg*, ed. Bernhard W. Anderson and Walter Harrelson (New York: Harper & Brothers, 1962), 206–07.

38. Donahue, *The Gospel in Parable*, 157.

39. Ibid., 159–60.

40. Sandra Schneiders, *Women and the Word: The Gender of God in the New Testament and the Spirituality of Women* (New York: Paulist Press, 1986), 47. I am indebted to John Donahue for this reference.

7. Israel's Confession of One God

1. See S. Dean McBride, "The Essence of Orthodoxy: Deuteronomy 5:6-10 and Exodus 20:2-6," *Interpretation* 60 (2006): 133–51.

2. See Patrick D. Miller, *The Religion of Ancient Israel* (Louisville: Westminster John Knox Press, 2000); and Mark S. Smith, *The Memoirs of God: History, Memory, and the Experience of the Divine in Ancient Israel* (Minneapolis: Fortress Press, 2004).

3. See J. G. Janzen, "On the Most Important Word in the Shema (Deuteronomy VI 4-5)," Vetus Testamentum 37 (1987): 280–300; and S. Dean McBride, "The Yoke of the Kingdom: An Exposition of Deuteronomy 6:4-5," *Interpretation* 27 (1973): 273–306.

4. See George Stroup, *Before God* (Grand Rapids: Eerdmans, 2004).

5. See the discussion of Patrick D. Miller, *Deuteronomy* (Interpretation: Louisville: John Knox Press, 1990), 97–104.

6. McBride, "The Yoke of the Kingdom," 278.

7. The classic discussion is by W. L. Moran, "The Ancient Near Eastern Background of the Love of God in Deuteronomy," *CBQ* 25 (1963): 77–87.

8. Jacqueline E. Lapsley, "Feeling Our Way: Love for God in Deuteronomy," *CBQ* 65 (2003): 368.

9. Alan Paton, "Meditation for a Young Boy Confirmed, *Christian Century* (Oct. 13, 1954), 1238.

10. See Bernard Lang, *The Hebrew God: Portrait of an Ancient Deity* (New Haven: Yale University Press, 2002).

11. Frank Moore Cross, *Canaanite Myth and Hebrew Epic: Essays in the History of the Religion of Israel* (Cambridge: Harvard University Press, 1973), 60–73; and Patrick D. Miller, *The Religion of Ancient Israel*, 23–29.

12. Miller, Ibid., 2–3.

13. See the discussion of El and YHWH by Rainer Albertz, *A History of Israelite Religion in the Old Testament Period: Volume I: From the Beginnings to the End of the Monarchy* (OTL; Louisville: Westminster John Knox Press, 1994), 76–79.

14. In what follows I have drawn extensively from the fine summary of Patrick Miller, *The Religion of Ancient Israel*, Chapter 1.

15. Ibid., 26.

16. Ibid., 27.

17. See Frank Moore Cross, "The Council of Yahweh in Second Isaiah," *JNES* 12 (1953): 274–77; and Christopher R. Seitz, *Zion's Final Destiny: The Development of the Book of Isaiah: A Reassessment of Isaiah 36–39* (Minneapolis: Fortress Press, 1991), 197–202.

18. See Morton Smith, *Palestinian Parties and Politics that Shaped the Old Testament* (London: SCM Press, 1987).

19. See Walter Brueggemann, *Old Testament Theology: Testimony, Dispute, Advocacy* (Minneapolis: Fortress Press, 1997), 139–144; and the basis study of C. J. Labuschagne, *The Incomparability of Yahweh in the Old Testament* (Leiden: Brill, 1966).

20. On the urban elites in ancient Jerusalem, see William G. Dever, *Did God Have a Wife? Archaeology and Folk Religion in Ancient Israel* (Grand Rapids: Eerdmans, 2005). In addition to a polemical presentation, Dever offers a comprehensive bibliography on the subject.

21. The much-noted and popular work of Rene Girard, *Violence and the Sacred* (Baltimore: Johns Hopkins University Press, 1977) is an important reference in this discussion, but surely contains elements of supersessionism in his purview.

22. Regina M. Schwartz, *The Curse of Cain: The Violent Legacy of Monotheism* (Chicago: University of Chicago Press, 1997).

23. See the recent discussion of John J. Collins, "The Zeal of Phinehas: The Bible and the Legitimization of Violence," *JBL* 122 (2003): 3–21; the fact that his paper was his presidential address to the Society of Biblical Literature indicates how important the issue of violence in the Bible has become in current interpretive conversations.

24. See my summary discussion, Walter Brueggemann, *Old Testament Theology*, 359–99.

25. Ibid., 250–261.

26. The classic discussion of the pathos of God in the Old Testament is that of Abraham Heschel, *The Prophets* (New York: Harper & Row, 1962).

27. On this text see Kazo Kitamori, *Theology of the Pain of God* (Richmond: John Knox Press, 1965).

28. Erhard Gerstenberger, *Theologies in the Old Testament* (Minneapolis: Fortress Press, 2002), has hypothesized that each of these different accents reflects and serves a different social constituency in a different social environment. His discussion is an important one, even if the distinctions he makes seem somewhat forced and overstated.

29. For a classic discussion of the subject, perhaps still the best we have, see Phyllis Trible, *God and the Rhetoric of Sexuality*, OBT (Philadelphia Fortress Press, 1978).

30. See the seminal discussion of Jurgen Moltmann, *The Crucified God: The Cross of*

Christ as the Foundation and Criticism of Christian Theology (New York: Harper & Row, 1974); and Eberhard Jungel, *God as the Mystery of the World: On the Foundation of the Theology of the Crucified One in the Dispute Between Theism and Atheism*, trans. Darrell Guder (Grand Rapids: Eerdmans, 1983).

31. See my review of this important work, Brueggemann, *Theology of the Old Testament*, 15–49.

32. Claus Westermann, *What Does the Old Testament Say About God?* (Atlanta: John Knox Press, 1979).

33. On this new accent in scholarship, see the summation by Terence E. Fretheim, *God and World in the Old Testament: A Relational Theology of Creation* (Nashville: Abingdon Press, 2005).

34. See David Novak, *The Image of the Non-Jew in Judaism: An Historical and Constructive Study of the Noahide Laws* (New York: E. Mellan Press, 1983).

35. On this theme, see Hans Walter Wolff, "The Kerygma of the Yahwist," *Interpretation* 20 (1966): 131–58.

36. For a historical critical survey of these texts, see Norman K. Gottwald, *All the Kingdoms of the Earth: Israelite Prophecy and International Relations in the Ancient Near East* (New York: Harper & Row, 1964).

37. Following Walther Zimmerli, it is now a truism among us that wisdom traditions articulate a theology of creation; see Fretheim, *God and World in the Old Testament*, 199–268.

38. On the cosmic significance of Jerusalem, see Ben C. Ollenburger, *Zion, The City of the Great King: A Theological Symbol of the Jerusalem Cult*, JSOT Supp. 41 (Sheffield: Sheffield Academic Press, 1987); and Samuel Terrien, *The Elusive Presence; Toward a New Biblical Theology* (New York: Harper & Row, 1978), 186–226.

39. Patrick D. Miller, "Creation and Covenant," *Biblical Theology: Problems and Perspectives*, ed. Steven J. Kraftchick et al. (Nashville: Abingdon Press, 1995), 166–67.

40. Ibid., 168.

41. Ibid.

42. On the "if" as a critical interpretive marker, see Walter Brueggemann, *Solomon: Israel's Ironic Icon of Human Achievement* (Columbia: University of South Carolina Press, 2005), 139–159.

43. There is no doubt that in canonical form, the memory of Abraham has had imposed upon it anticipations of David, so much so that John van Seters, *Abraham in History and Tradition* (New Haven: Yale University Press, 1975) has taken the venturesome leap to suggest that the Abraham tradition was formulated post-David . . in the exile.

44. See Ollenburger, *Zion City of the Great King*, chapter 3.

45. Jon D. Levenson, *Sinai and Zion: An Entry into the Jewish Bible* (New York: Winston Press, 1985), 192.

46. Ibid., 199.

47. Ibid.

48. So Van Seters, *Abraham in History and Tradition.*

49. See Krister Stendahl, *Paul Among Jews and Gentiles* (Philadelphia: Fortress Press, 1976), 78–96; E. P. Sanders, *Paul and Palestinian Judaism* (Philadelphia: Fortress Press, 1977); and more broadly, R. Kendall Soulen, *The God of Israel and Christian Theology* (Minneapolis: Fortress Press, 1996).

50. Hartmut Gese, *Essays on Biblical Theology* (Minneapolis: Augsburg Publishing House, 1981), 81–82.

51. See Patrick D. Miller, *They Cried to the Lord: The Form and Theology of Biblical Prayer* (Minneapolis: Fortress Press, 1994), chapter 4.

8. *The Narrative of the God of Miracle and Order*

1. See H. Richard Niebuhr, *The Meaning of Revelation* (New York: Macmillan Publishing Company, 1941); Hans W. Frei, *The Eclipse of Biblical Narrative: A Study in Eighteenth and Nineteenth Century Hermeneutics* (New Haven: Yale University Press, 1974); on Karl Barth, see David Ford, *Barth and God's Story: Biblical Narrative and the Theological Method of Karl Barth in the "Church Dogmatics,"* Frankfurt: Verlag Peter Lang, 1985); and the summary statement of Stanley Hauerwas and L. Gregory Jones, eds., *Why Narrative? Readings in Narrative Theology* (Grand Rapids: Eerdmans, 1989).

2. The programmatic statement of Claus Westermann is "Creation and History in the Old Testament," in *The Gospel and Human Destiny*, ed. Vilmos Vajta (Minneapolis: Augsburg Publishing House, 1971), 11–38.

3. Martin Buber, *Moses: The Revelation and the Covenant* (Atlantic Highlands: Humanities Press International, Inc., 1946; 1988), 75.

4. See Walter Brueggemann, "'Impossibility' and Epistemology in the Faith Tradition of Abraham and Sarah (Genesis 18:1-15)," *ZAW* 94 (1982): 615–34.

5. See Walter Brueggemann, "A 'Characteristic' Reflection on What Comes Next (Jeremiah 32.16-44)," in *Prophets and Paradigms: Essays in Honor of Gene M. Tucker*, ed. Stephen Breck Reid JSOT Supp. 229 (Sheffield: Sheffield Academic Press, 1996) 16–32.

6. The most succinct statement of this twofold process is in Jeremiah 1:10 wherein the prophet receives his twofold mandate; the formulation of this verse is reiterated in the book of Jeremiah and becomes the *leitmotif* of the canonical book of Jeremiah.

7. On these narratives, see Walter Brueggemann, *Testimony to Otherwise: The Witness of Elijah and Elisha* (St. Louis: Chalice Press, 2001).

8. This, I take it, is the point of the divine speeches in the book of Job; the ways of YHWH are beyond human comprehension; Job and his friends should desist from explanatory mode of thought.

9. See Klaus Koch, "Is There a Doctrine of Retribution in the Old Testament?" in *Theodicy in the Old Testament*, ed. James L. Crenshaw (Philadelphia; Fortress Press, 1983), 57–87.

10. These five modes overlap in important ways with the five "originary expressions of revelation" identified by Paul Ricoeur, *Essays on Biblical Revelation* (Philadelphia: Fortress Press, 1980), 73–118.

11. See the comprehensive statement on creation faith by Terence E. Fretheim, *God and the World in the Old Testament: A Relational Theology of Creation* (Nashville; Abingdon Press, 2005).

12. See Bernhard W. Anderson, *From Creation to New Creation: Old Testament Perspectives*, OBT (Minneapolis: Fortress Press, 1994), 19–41.

13. See the counter opinion of Walther Eichrodt, "In the Beginning," in *Israel's Prophetic Heritage: Essays in Honor of James Muilenburg*, ed. Bernhard W. Anderson and Walter Harrelson (New York: Harper & Brothers, 1962), 1–10.

14. See Claus Westermann, *Blessing in the Bible and the Life of the Church* (OBT; Philadelphia: Fortress Press, 1978).

15. One accent of this sabbath is that there is no productivity. YHWH does not "make" anything on the seventh day!

16. See the subversive exposition of this text by Phyllis Trible, *God and the Rhetoric of Sexuality* (OBT; Philadelphia: Fortress Press, 1978), 72–143.

17. On the "faith and science" issues in creation theology, see the trilogy of Alister E. McGrath, *A Scientific Theology* (Grand Rapids: Eerdmans, 2001, 2002, 2003).

18. It is commonly recognized that Psalm 104 is appropriated by Israel from an earlier Egyptian poem. Egyptian theology focused on the matter of order; the theme serves the claim of a life-giving order that made appropriation by Israel an easy Yahwistic move of interpretation.

19. Carroll Stuhlmueller, *Creative Redemption in Deutero-Isaiah*, AnBib 43 (Rome: Biblical Institute Press, 1970).

20. See Rolf Rendtorff, *Canon and Theology: Overtures to an Old Testament Theology* (OBT; Minneapolis: Fortress Press, 1993), 92–113. See also Patrick D. Miller, "Creation and Covenant," in *Biblical Theology: Problems and Perspectives*, ed. Steven J. Kraftchick et al. (Nashville: Abingdon Press, 1995), 155–68.

21. Terence E. Fretheim, "The Plagues as Ecological Signs of Disaster," *JBL* 110 (1991): 385–96, has shown the way in which Pharaoh is portrayed in the exodus narrative as a Promethean figure who tries to mobilize creation for his interests. The outcome of the narrative is to show that YHWH places severe limits on such Promethean efforts.

22. See Stuhlmueller, *Creative Redemption in Deutero-Isaiah*, chapter 6, and Anderson, *From Creation to New Creation*, chapter 14.

23. The phrase "null point" comes from Walther Zimmerli, *I Am Yahweh* (Atlanta: John Knox Press, 1982), 111–33.

24. See Michael Fishbane, "Jeremiah 4:23-26 and Job 3:1-13: A Recovered Use of the Creation Pattern," *VT* 21 (1971): 151–67.

25. See the close reading of David J. A. Clines, "Hosea 2: Structure and Interpretation," in *Studia Biblica 1978*, ed. E. A. Livingston (JSOT Supp 11; Sheffield: JSOT Press, 1979), 83–103.

26. Ibid.

27. Frank Moore Cross, *Canaanite Myth and Hebrew Epic: Essays in the History of the Religion of Israel* (Cambridge: Harvard University Press, 1973), 135, and the article by Fretheim cited in n. 21.

28. See Walter Brueggemann, "*Theme* Revisited: Bread Again!" in *Reading from Right to Left: Essays on the Hebrew Bible in Honour of David J. A. Clines* ed. J. Cheryl Exum and H. G. M. Williamson (London: Sheffield Academic Press Ltd., 2003) 76–89.

29. See Bernhard Anderson, "Exodus Typology in Second Isaiah," *Israel's Prophetic Heritage*, 177–95.

30. See Walter Brueggemann, "'Exodus' in the Plural (Amos 9:7)," in *Many Voices, One God: Being Faithful in a Pluralistic World*, ed. Walter Brueggemann and George W. Stroup (Louisville: Westminster John Knox Press, 1998), 15–34.

31. See Donald E. Gowan, *When Man Becomes God: Humanism and Hybris in the Old Testament* (Pittsburgh: Pickwick Press, 1975).

32. The classic discussion is by Gustaf Aulen, *Christus Victor: An Historical Study of the Three Main Types of the Idea of the Atonement* (New York: Macmillan Publishing

Company, 1969). In recent discussion, these several traditional "explanations" of the work of Christ are found to be inadequate; much new work needs to be done on the subject.

33. See my article cited in n. 28.

34. See also 2 Kings 4:42-44.

35. The normative discussion is that of Frank Crüsemann, *The Torah: Theology and Social History of Old Testament Law* (Minneapolis: Fortress Press, 1996).

36. The clearly attested cases of prophetic appeal to the Decalogue are found in Hosea 4:2 and Jeremiah 7:9.

37. James L. Mays, "The Place of the Torah-Psalms in the Psalter," *JBL* 106 (1987): 3–12.

38. Patrick D. Miller, "Deuteronomy and Psalms: Evoking a Biblical Conversation," *JBL* 118 (1999): 3–18.

39. Erhard Gerstenberger, "Covenant and Commandment," *JBL* 84 (1965): 38–51.

40. On the impact of sapiential teaching on the tradition of Deuteronomy, see Moshe Weinfeld, *Deuteronomy and the Deuteronomic School* (Oxford: Clarendon Press, 1972).

41. H. H. Schmid, *Gerechtigkeit als Weltordnung* (Tuebingen: J. C. B. Mohr, 1968).

42. Rolf P. Knierim, *The Task of Old Testament Theology: Method and Cases* (Grand Rapids: Eerdmans, 1995).

43. See David Novak, *The Image of the Non-Jew in Judaism: An Historical and Constructive Study of the Noahide Laws* (New York: Edwin Mellen Press, 1983).

44. I take YHWH's interaction with Israel as normative. On a smaller scale the same interaction is with individual persons, as is evident in the lament Psalms. On a larger scale, the same interaction is with nations, as is evident in the prophetic oracles against the Nations.

45. On the Deuteronomic history, the basic hypothesis is by Martin Noth, *The Deuteronomic History* (JSOT Supp. 15; Sheffield: JSOT Press, 1981). There are now many critical revisions of the hypothesis, but the general claim for a unified corpus still holds among scholars.

46. On the formula, see Walter Brueggemann, "Social Criticism and Social Vision in the Deuteronomic Formula," in *Die Botschaft und die Boten: Festschrift fuer Hans Walter Wolff*, ed. Joerg Jeremias and Lothar Perlitt (Neukirchen-Vluyn: Neukirchener Verlag, 1981): 101–14.

47. See the recent splendid discussion of Barbara Green, *How Are the Mighty Fallen? A Dialogical Study of King Saul in 1 Samuel* (JSOT Supp. 365; Sheffield: Sheffield Academic Press, 2003).

48. The matter is not different in 2 Chronicles 36, except there verses 22-23 supply an important dimension of restoration. Thus the restoration is to be accomplished by human agency, Cyrus the Persian. In that narrative, YHWH is ultimately responsible for the restoration. It is YHWH's verb "stir up" that is decisive for Israel's future beyond judgment. On the verb see Jeremiah 52:9 and Second Isaiah.

49. Gerhard von Rad, *Old Testament Theology*, vol. 1 (San Francisco: Harper & Row, 1962), 343, n. 22.

50. Ronald E. Clements, "Patterns in the Prophetic Canon," in *Canon and Authority: Essays in Old Testament Religion and Theology* (Philadelphia: Fortress Press, 1977), 49, 53.

51. Brevard S. Childs, *Introduction to the Old Testament as Scripture* (Philadelphia: Fortress Press, 1979), 328–30.

52. See Rolf Rendtorff, *Canon and Theology*, 181–89.

53. On the tears that precede joy, see Kathleen M. O'Connor, *Lamentations and the Tears of the World* (Maryknoll: Orbis Books, 2002).

54. See my summary discussion of recent scholarship, Walter Brueggemann, *An Introduction to the Old Testament: The Canon and Christian Imagination* (Louisville: Westminster John Knox Press, 2003), 209–14.

55. This negative reservation about wisdom in Old Testament theology was sharply voiced by G. Ernest Wright and more recently is reflected in the otherwise fine exposition of Horst Dietrich Preuss, *Old Testament Theology*, 2 vols., OTL (Louisville: Westminster John Knox Press, 1992, 1995). Gerhard von Rad, with his emphasis on "God's Mighty Deeds," had done much to marginalize wisdom in Old Testament theology; all the more then, the surprise that in his last book, *Wisdom in Israel* (Nashville: Abingdon Press, 1972), von Rad moved in a quite new direction and made a strong case for the theological importance of the wisdom traditions.

56. The initial impetus for this scholarly refocus was in the work of Claus Westermann. In addition to the essay cited in n. 2, see *What Does the Old Testament Say About God?* (Atlanta: John Knox Press, 1979). See my summary statement of the shift in scholarship, "The Loss and Recovery of Creation in Old Testament Theology," *Theology Today* 53 (1996): 177–90.

57. See Lennart Bostrom, *The God of the Sages: The Portrayal of God in the Book of Proverbs* (Coniectanea Biblica Old Testament Series 29; Stockholm: Almqvist & Wiksell International, 1990).

58. The most important and sustained exposition of these issues is by James L. Crenshaw; see especially his collected essays, *Urgent Advice and Probing Questions: Collected Writings on Old Testament Wisdom* (Macon: Mercer, 1995).

59. See Walther Zimmerli, "The Place and Limit of the Wisdom in the Framework of the Old Testament Theology," *SJT* 127 (1964): 146–58.

60. This was the premise of William McKane, *Proverbs: A New Approach* (OTL; Philadelphia: Westminster Press, 1970).

61. Gerhard von Rad, *Wisdom in Israel*, 98–102.

62. Ibid., 98–99.

63. Ibid., 65.

64. Klaus Koch, in the work cited in n. 9, spoke of these inviolate interconnections as "a sphere of destiny" that required no intervening agent for the enactment of consequences after deeds.

65. See the comment of Bostrom, *The God of the Sages*, 174, concerning the hypothesis of Koch and the "Sondergut" of Israel's teaching as understood by Harmut Gese and Horst Dietrich Preuss.

66. On the ambiguity of Job's final response, see Jack Miles, *God: A Biography* (New York: Knopf, 1995), 425, n. 324.

67. Gerhard von Rad, *Wisdom in Israel*, 67–68.

68. See Roland E. Murphy, "Qohelet's 'Quarrel' with the Fathers," in *From Faith to Faith: Essays in Honor of Donald G. Miller*, ed. Dikran Y. Hadidian (Pittsburgh: Pickwick Press, 1979), 235–45.

69. On the theme as a broad theological stance, see George Stroup, *Before God* (Grand Rapids: Eerdmans, 2004).

70. See Walter Brueggemann, *Abiding Astonishment: Psalms, Modernity, and the Making*

of History (Literary Currents in Biblical Interpretation; Louisville: Westminster/John Knox Press, 1991).

71. On the theme of "response," see Gerhard von Rad, *Old Testament Theology*, vol. 1, 355–459.

72. See Patrick D. Miller, "The Way of Torah," in *Israelite Religion and Biblical Theology: Collected* Essays (JSOT Supp. 267; Sheffield: Sheffield Academic Press, 2000), 496–507.

73. Claus Westermann, *What Does the Old Testament Say About God?* (Atlanta: John Knox Press, 1979).

74. The interface of creation and covenant is a programmatic theme for Karl Barth, *The Doctrine of Creation; Church Dogmatics*, vol. 3/1 (Edinburgh: T & T Clark, 1958).

75. This attestation to the divinely guaranteed ordering of creation is ground for "natural law" in ancient Israel, though that topic is different in important ways from the target of Karl Barth's famous polemics. The best discussion of "natural law" in the Old Testament is offered by John Barton, *Understanding Old Testament Ethics: Approaches and Explorations* (Louisville: Westminster John Knox Press, 2003), 32–44, 77–129, and *passim*.

76. See my summary of that scholarship in *Theology of the Old Testament: Testimony, Dispute, Advocacy* (Minneapolis: Fortress Press, 1997), 15–49.

77. See n. 56.

78. David Hartman, *Conflicting Visions: Spiritual Possibilities of Modern Israel* (New York: Schocken Books, 1990), 235–36

79. Ibid., 236–37.

9. *Israel as a Community of Praise and Obedience*

1. On this rhetoric, see Walter Brueggemann, *Theology of the Old Testament: Testimony, Dispute, Advocacy* (Minneapolis: Fortress Press, 1997), 414–17.

2. See Hans Walter Wolff, "The Kerygma of the Yahwist," *Interpretation* 20 (1966): 134–58.

3. Michael Prior, *The Bible and Colonialism: A Moral Critique* (Sheffield: Sheffield Academic Press, 1997); and Prior, *Zionism and the State of Israel: A Moral Inquiry* (London: Routledge, 1999) has explored the way in which these traditions not only provide identity and vocation, but then have been hardened into an ideology of self-justification for the continuing community of Israel.

4. See James L. Kugel, *The God of Old: Inside the Lost World of the Bible* (New York: Free Press, 2003), 109–36.

5. In his polemical statement, Jon D. Levenson, *The Hebrew Bible, the Old Testament, and Historical Criticism* (Louisville: Westminster John Knox Press, 1993), 127–59, is alert to the loss of Israel's particularity when the exodus narrative is interpreted as a generic account of God's rescue of the vulnerable.

6. On the cruciality of "God's remembering" for the narrative, see the several notations concerning Noah (Genesis 8:1), Lot (19:21), and Rachel (30:22), and the plea of Lamentations 5:20 and the answering assurance of Isaiah 49:14-15.

7. It is important that the imperative verb *obey* (*shema*ʾ) is stated in the absolute infinitive, underscoring its urgency.

8. See Norman K. Gottwald, *The Hebrew Bible: A Socio-Literary Introduction*

(Philadelphia: Fortress Press, 1985), 272–76. Note the references to the initial proposals of George E. Mendenhall, Norman K. Gottwald, and Marvin L. Chaney in n. 12.

9. On land as a primary theme of the Old Testament, see Walter Brueggemann, *The Land: Place as Gift, Promise, and Challenge in Biblical Faith* (Philadelphia: Fortress Press, 1977) and W. D. Davies, *The Gospel and the Land: Early Christian and Jewish Territorial Doctrine* (Berkley: University of California Press, 1974).

10. David Hartman, *Conflicting Visions: Spiritual Possibilities of Modern Israel* (New York: Schocken Books, 1990), 267–70, has poignant words about Jewish marks of hope in relation to the principal Jewish festivals. It is clear in Hartman's comments that the festivals offer not just a special people, but also a peculiar view of the entire world as God's creation.

11. See the use of the first of these phrases as the title for the Festschrift of Patrick D. Miller, *A God So Near: Essays on Old Testament Theology in Honor of Patrick D. Miller*, ed. Brent A. Strawn and Nancy R. Bowen (Winona Lake: Eisenbrauns, 2003).

12. On this covenantal formulary, see Rolf Rendtorff, *The Covenant Formula: An Exegetical and Theological Investigation* (Edinburgh: T & T Clark, 1998).

13. It is of course for this reason that the exodus narrative has been so decisive for much liberation theology. In that trajectory of interpretation, the narrative is pushed well beyond God's emancipation of the Israelites to be made contemporary for many other oppressed peoples.

14. See reviews of the claims of the narrative concerning Israel's political achievement by Walter Brueggemann, *Solomon: Israel's Ironic Icon of Human Achievement* (Columbia: University of South Carolina Press, 2005); and William G. Dever, *Who Were the Early Israelites and Where Did They Come From?* (Grand Rapids: Eerdmans, 2003).

15. See the indictment of Solomon in 1 Kings 11:1-4 and the interpretive comment of Claudia V. Camp, *Wise, Strange and Holy: The Strange Woman and the Making of the Bible*, JSOT Supp. 320 (Sheffield: Sheffield Academic Press, 2000), 144–90.

16. On the "oral Torah" see Jacob Neusner, *What, Exactly, Did the Rabbinic Sages Mean by "the Oral Torah"? An Inductive Answer to the Question of Rabbinic Judaism* (Atlanta: Scholars Press, 1998).

17. See James Muilenburg, "The 'Office' of the Prophet in Ancient Israel," *The Bible in Modern Scholarship*, ed. J. Philip Hyatt (Nashville: Abingdon Press, 1965), 74–97; note especially Muilenburg's references to Hans-Joachim Kraus.

18. For a general perspective on re-presentation of old tradition in new circumstance, see Martin Noth, "The 'Re-Presentation of the O. T. in Proclamation," in *Essays on Old Testament Hermeneutics*, ed. Claus Westermann (Richmond: John Knox Press, 1963), 76–88. Note in particular his judgment that the proclamation of the law in Deuteronomy was "always formulated in such a way as to make Israel hear the law as if it were the very first time" (p. 82).

19. Stephen Kaufman, "The Structure of the Deuteronomic Law," *Maarav* 1 (1979): 105–58.

20. See Raymond Edward Brown, *The Sensus Plenior of Sacred Scripture* (Baltimore: St. Mary's University, 1955).

21. See Odil Hannes Steck, "Theological Streams of Tradition," in *Tradition and Theology in the Old Testament*, ed. Douglas A. Knight (Philadelphia: Fortress Press, 1977), 183–214; and Walter Brueggemann, "Trajectories in Old Testament Literature and the Sociology of Ancient Israel," *JBL* 98 (1979): 161–85.

22. Mary Douglas, *Purity and Danger: An Analysis of the Concepts of Pollution and Taboo* (Boston: Ark Paperbacks, 1984), 41–57.

23. See Moshe Weinfeld, *Social Justice in Ancient Israel and in the Ancient Near East* (Minneapolis: Fortress Press, 1995); and Enrique Nardoni, *Rise Up, O Judge: A Study of Justice in the Biblical World* (Peabody: Hendrickson, 2004).

24. I owe the phrase, "quadrilateral of vulnerability" to Nicholas Waltersdorff (oral communication). On the sojourner, see Frank A. Spina, "Israelites as Gerim, 'Sojourners' in Social and Historical Context," in *The Word of the Lord Shall Go Forth: Essays in Honor of David Noel Freedman in Celebration of His Sixtieth Birthday*, ed. Carol L. Meyers and M. O'Connor (Winona Lake: Eisenbrauns, 1983), 321–35. See the critical assessment of provision for these marginal groups in the Old Testament by Harold V. Bennett, *Injustice Made Legal: Deuteronomic Law and the Plight of Widows, Sojourners, and Orphans in Ancient Israel* (Grand Rapids: Eerdmans, 2002).

25. On the position of Leviticus 19 in the larger corpus of purity laws, see Mary Douglas, "Justice as the Cornerstone," *Interpretation* 53 (1999): 341–50.

26. See the programmatic essay of R. Kendall Soulen, *The God of Israel and Christian Theology* (Minneapolis: Fortress Press, 1996).

27. The most compelling attestation from Heschel is his life of testimony; but see, among his writings, "The God of Israel and Christian Renewal," in *Moral Grandeur and Spiritual Audacity: Essays*, ed. Susannah Heschel (New York: Farrar, Straus, Giroux, 1996), 268–85.

28. Ernest P. Sanders, *Paul and Palestinian Judaism: A Comparison of Patterns of Religion* (Philadelphia: Fortress Press, 1977), has explored the ways in which Christian interpretation has misconstrued the "covenantal monism" of Judaism.

10. Obedience: Response to the Sovereign God in Dialogic Modes

1. John Calvin, *Institutes of the Christian Religion* (The Library of Christian Classics XX; Philadelphia: Westminster Press, 1960), 72. In parallel fashion, Abraham J. Heschel, *Who Is Man?* (Stanford: Stanford University Press, 1965), 111, can write, "I am commanded... therefore I am."

2. The classic statement in this textual tradition claiming that land loss is a consequence of disobedience to Torah is found in 2 Kings 17:7-23. Even though the text refers to the demise of the northern kingdom, the same theological assertion pervades the material as concerns Judah as well.

3. Ronald E. Clements, "Patterns in the Prophetic Canon," *Canon and Authority: Essays in Old Testament Religion and Theology*, ed. George W. Coats and Burke O. Long (Philadelphia: Fortress Press, 1977), 49.

4. Claus Westermann, *Basic Forms of Prophetic Speech* (Philadelphia: Westminster Press, 1967).

5. See the resistance to such a hypothesis by A. Vanlier Hunter, *Seek the Lord! A Study of the Meaning and Function of the Exhortations in Amos, Hosea, Isaiah, Micah, and Zephaniah* (Baltimore: St. Mary's Seminary & University, 1982). Hunter avers that the calls for repentance in these prophetic texts are all rejected calls that have made the only present proclamation one of judgment, having passed the point of no return.

6. This "double message" that may reflect either assertions from different times or

ambivalence in the tradition is especially clear in Jeremiah 4:27, 5:10, 18; 30:11. See Walter Brueggemann, "An Ending that Does Not End: The Book of Jeremiah," in *Postmodern Interpretations of the Bible: A Reader*, ed. A. K. A. Adam (St. Louis: Chalice Press, 2001), 117–28.

7. The loss of prophetic speech in that context is something of a parallel to the dictum of Theodore W. Adorno, *Prisms*, trans. Samuel and Shierry Weber (Cambridge: MIT Press, 1981), 34: "To write poetry after Auschwitz is barbaric." The savage loss requires silence. See my discussion of that motif in every attempt at a "final solution," Walter Brueggemann, "A Fissure Always Uncontained," in *Strange Fire: Reading the Bible after the Holocaust*, ed. Tod Linafelt (Sheffield: Sheffield Academic Press, 2000), 62–75.

8. On YHWH's passion for the "resurrection" and restoration of Israel, see Jon D. Levenson, Resurrection *and the Restoration of Israel: The Ultimate Victory of the God of Life* (New Haven: Yale University Press, 2006).

9. The term *have mercy* is in the infinitive absolute indicating the intensity of the divine resolve.

10. On the cruciality of these verses in the Isaiah tradition, see Rolf Rendtorff, *Canon and Theology*, OBT (Minneapolis: Fortress Press, 1993), 181–89.

11. On this text, see Jon D. Levenson, *Theology of the Program of Restoration of Ezekiel 40–48* (Missoula: Scholars Press, 1976).

12. The classic statement on wisdom as creation theology is that of Walther Zimmerli, "The Place and Limit of the Wisdom in the Framework of the Old Testament Theology," *SJT* 17 (1964): 146–58. More recently, see Lennart Bostrom, *The God of the Sages: The Portrayal of God in the Book of Proverbs* (Coniectanea Biblica Old Testament Series 29; Stockholm: Almqvist & Wiksell International, 1990).

13. See Jack Miles, *God: A Biography* (New York: Knopf, 1995), 425, n. 324.

14. Samuel E. Balentine, "What Are Human Beings, That You Make so Much of Them?" Divine Disclosure from the Whirlwind: "Look at the Behemoth," in *God in the Fray: A Tribute to Walter Brueggemann*, ed. Tod Linafelt and Timothy K. Beal (Minneapolis: Fortress Press, 1998), 259–78.

15. See Gerald T. Sheppard, "The Epilogue to Qoholeth as Theological Commentary," *CBQ* 39 (1977): 182–189, and Brevard S. Childs, *Introduction to the Old Testament as Scripture* (Philadelphia: Fortress Press, 1979), 584–86.

16. Patrick D. Miller, "Deuteronomy and Psalms: Evoking a Biblical Conversation," *JBL* 118 (1999): 3–18.

17. Under the large rubric of "praise" we may for convenience subsume Songs of Thanksgiving as well, even though the Songs of Thanksgiving have their own importance apart from the more generic practice of praises. For one influential opinion of the relationship of the two, see Claus Westermann, *The Praise of God in the Psalms* (Richmond: John Knox Press, 1965), 25–30.

18. Walter Brueggemann, "Bounded by Obedience and Praise: The Psalms as Canon," in *The Psalms and the Life of Faith*, ed. Patrick D. Miller (Minneapolis: Fortress Press, 1995), 189–213.

19. Jon D. Levenson, *Creation and the Persistence of Evil: The Jewish Drama of Divine Omnipotence* (San Francisco: Harper & Row, 1988), 149–156, has nicely exposited this tension under the rubric of "Argument and Obedience."

20. See Levenson, ibid., 140–148, in "The Dialectic of Covenantal Theonomy."

21. See Claus Westermann cited in n. 17.

22. James Plastaras, *The God of Exodus* (Milwaukee: Bruce Publishing Company, 1966), has most directly shown how the exodus narrative is shaped in the characteristic move from plea to praise familiarly given in the lament Psalms.

23. For a discernment of the give-and-take of YHWH-Israel with a frequent "role reversal" wherein Israel becomes provisionally the "senior partner" to the transaction, I have found most helpful the exposition of Roy Schafer, *Retelling a Life: Narration and Dialogue in Psychoanalysis* (New York: Basic Books, 1992), 94–96. It cannot be incidental that Schafer's insight concerns psychoanalysis, a theory and practice of personhood that arose from dynamic Jewish understandings of human personhood. As healthy sexual partners must practice "reversibility," so the healthy covenantal transaction of YHWH with Israel practices such provisional reversibility.

24. With this phrase I intend to make explicit reference to D. W. Winnicott, *The Maturational Processes and the Facilitating Environment: Studies in the Theory of Emotional Development* (Madison, Conn.: International Universities Press, 1965), 140–52 and *passim*. There is, in my judgment, an exact parallel between Winnicott's understanding of "false self" in the mother-child relationship and the relationship between YHWH and YHWH's partners where there is only submissiveness without the practice of freedom and challenge. Israel, in its practice of praise and lament, understood this dynamic in the most profound ways. And therefore Israel understood obedience as a dialectical process.

11. *YHWH as God of the Nations*

1. See Samuel Terrien, "The Omphalos Myth and Hebrew Religion," *VT* 20 (1970): 315–38; and Ben C. Ollenburger, *Zion the City of the Great King: A Theological Symbol of the Jerusalem Cult*, JSOT Supp. 41 (Sheffield: Sheffield Academic Press, 1987).

2. Harmut Gese, *Essays on Biblical Theology* (Minneapolis: Augsburg Publishing House, 1981), 82.

3. Ibid., 82–83.

4. On the liturgy as the work of "world construction," see Walter Brueggemann, *Israel's Praise: Doxology against Idolatry and Ideology* (Philadelphia: Fortress Press, 1988), chap. 1.

5. The point has been decisively argued by H. H. Schmid, *Gerechtigkeit als Weltordnung* (Tubingen: Mohr, 1968).

6. Norman K. Gottwald, *All the Kingdoms of the Earth: Israelite Prophecy and International Relations in the Ancient Near East* (New York: Harper and Row, 1964), 199–200.

7. Jon D. Levenson, "The Universal Horizon of Biblical Particularism," in *Ethnicity and the Bible*, ed. Mark G. Brett (Leiden: Brill, 1996), 149.

8. Ibid., 154.

9. Gerhard von Rad, *The Problem of the Hexateuch and Other Essays* (New York: McGraw-Hill, 1966), 63–74.

10. Hans Walter Wolff, "The Kerygma of the Yahwist," *Interpretation* 20 (1966): 131–58.

11. See Walter Brueggemann, "Pharaoh as Vassal: A Study of a Political Metaphor," CBQ 57 (1995): 27–51.

12. Patrick D. Miller, "God's Other Stories: On the Margins of Deuteronomic Theology," in *Israelite Religion and Biblical Theology: Collected Essays* (JSOT Supp. 267; Sheffield: Sheffield Academic Press, 2000), 593–602.

13. See Donald E. Gowan, *When Man Becomes God: Humanism and Hybris in the Old Testament* (Pittsburgh Theological Monograph Series 6; Pittsburgh: Pickwick Press, 1975). On the oracles against the Nations, see Walter Brueggemann, *Theology of the Old Testament: Testimony, Dispute, Advocacy* (Minneapolis: Fortress Press, 1997), 492–527, and Klaus Koch, *The Prophets: The Babylonian and Persian Periods* (Philadelphia: Fortress Press, 1982), 72, 171, and his notion of "metahistory" that allows for the hidden governance of YHWH in the affairs of the nations.

14. Gottwald, *All the Kingdoms of the Earth*, 116–17.

15. Ibid., 117–18.

16. Ibid., 119.

17. Ibid., 118.

18. Ibid., 118, n. 37.

19. John Barton, "Amos's Oracles against the Nations," in *Understanding Old Testament Ethics* (Louisville: Westminster John Knox Press, 2003), 77–129. On p. 83 Barton cites the study of Gottwald.

20. Ibid., 117.

21. On these texts, see Christopher R. Seitz, *Zion's Final Destiny: The Development of the Book of Isaiah: A Reassessment of Isaiah 36–39* (Minneapolis: Fortress Press, 1991).

22. On the closely related text of Amos 9:7, see Walter Brueggemann, "'Exodus' in the Plural (Amos 9:7)," in *Many Voices, One God: Being Faithful in a Pluralistic World*, ed. Walter Brueggemann and George W. Stroup (Louisville: Westminster John Knox Press, 1998), 15–34.

23. On Babylon in the Jeremiah tradition, see John Hill, *Friend or Foe? The Future of Babylon in the Book of Jeremiah MT* (Biblical Interpretation; Leiden: Brill, 1999).

24. By the phrase "rise and fall" I intend to call attention to the important work of Paul S. Kennedy, *The Rise and Fall of the Great Powers: Economic Change and Military Conflict from 1500 to 2000* (New York: Random House, 1987). Kennedy's analysis, in a contemporary secular mode, closely parallels the analysis of the prophets of Israel concerning geopolitics and national destiny.

25. Donald Gowan, *When Man Becomes God*, 127.

26. Klaus Koch, "Is There a Doctrine of Retribution in the Old Testament?" in *Theodicy in the Old Testament*, ed. James L. Crenshaw (Philadelphia: Fortress Press, 1983), 57–87.

27. See the defining article by John Barton, "Natural Law and Poetic Justice in the Old Testament," in *Understanding Old Testament Ethics*, 32–44.

28. Walter Harrelson, *The Ten Commandments and Human Rights*, OBT (Philadelphia: Fortress Press, 1980), xv. More broadly on the religious basis of human rights, see John Witte Jr., *God's Joust, God's Justice: Law and Religion in the Western Tradition* (Grand Rapids: Eerdmans, 2006).

29. On a theological critique of torture as it bears upon public ethics in the United States, see the current discussion in *Theology Today* 63/3 (2006), especially the articles by William Cavanaugh, Edward Feld, Jeremy Waldron, and David P. Gushee.

30. See the particular accent on hubris by Donald Gowan, *When Man Becomes God*, a theme that became central in the critique of U.S. public policy and discourse by Reinhold Niebuhr.

31. See the discussion of given limit that curbs state power by Paul Kennedy in the work cited in n. 24.

32. On "mercy" in geopolitics in prophetic discourse, see Isaiah 47:6; Jeremiah 6:23; 42:12; 51:42; Daniel 4:27.

33. Alister E. McGrath, *A Scientific Theology*, 3 vols. (Grand Rapids: Eerdmans, 2001, 2002, 2003).

34. Lynn White Jr., "The Historical Roots of Our Ecological Crisis," in *Western Man and Environmental Ethics*, ed. Jon G. Barbour (Reading, MA: Addison-Wisely, 1973), 18–30. Cameron Wybrow, *The Bible, Baconism, and Mastery over Nature: The Old Testament and Its Modern Misreading* (American University Studies, series 7, vol. 112 (New York: Peter Lang, 1991).

35. Attention should be paid to the work of Wendell Berry and Bill McKibben. Berry's concern is with agribusiness, as in *The Gift of the Good Land: Further Essays Cultural and Agricultural* (San Francisco: North Point Press, 1981), but it is clear that one cannot consider agribusiness without the military impulse of domination. The two together constitute an autonomous abuse of creation. See Bill McKibben, *The End of Nature* (New York: Random House, 1989).

36. In Genesis 47:13-27, Joseph designs and implements a policy of food and land monopoly in the service of Pharaoh that leads directly to the exodus narrative in what follows. Economic monopoly inevitably reduces to poverty and powerlessness, even if done in the rhetoric of "the market."

37. Gottwald, *All the Kingdoms of the Earth*, 200.

38. See Levenson, "The Universal Horizon of Biblical Particularism," 147–51.

39. Terence E. Fretheim, *God and World in the Old Testament: A Relational Theology of Creation* (Nashville: Abingdon Press, 2005), 85–86.

40. See David Novak, *The Image of the Non-Jew in Judaism: An Historical and Constructive Study of the Noahide Laws* (New York: Edwin Mellen Press, 1983).

12. The Land Promises

1. See Klaus Koch, "Is There a Doctrine of Retribution in the Old Testament?" in *Theodicy in the Old Testament*, ed. James L. Crenshaw (Philadelphia: Fortress Press, 1983), 57–87; and Walter Brueggemann, "A Shape for Old Testament Theology I: Structure Legitimation," in *Old Testament Theology: Essays on Structure, Theme, and Text* (Minneapolis: Fortress Press, 1992), 1–21.

2. Gerhard von Rad, *Old Testament Theology*, vol.1 (San Francisco: Harper and Row, 1962), 438–41, has identified six proverbs in the book that witness against the tight calculus of "deed-consequence" and allow for the freedom of God. See also von Rad, *Wisdom in Israel* (Nashville: Abingdon Press, 1972), 97–110.

3. Albrecht Alt, "The God of the Fathers," in *Essays on Old Testament History and Religion* (Oxford: Blackwell, 1966), 1–77.

4. Gerhard von Rad, *The Problem of the Hexateuch and Other Essays* (New York: McGraw Hill, 1966), 1–78.

5. Ibid., 67.

6. Ibid., 68–74.

7. Ibid., 73.

8. Ibid., 78.

9. Jürgen Moltmann, *Theology of Hope: On the Ground and the Implications of a Christian Eschatology* (New York: Harper & Row, 1967).

10. Walther Zimmerli, *Man and His Hope in the Old Testament*, SBT Second Series 20 (Naperville: Alec R. Allenson, 1971).

11. Ibid., 1.

12. Ibid.,

13. Ibid., 155.

14. Ibid., 165.

15. Gerhard von Rad, *The Problem of the Hexateuch*, 67.

16. On the cruciality of "the resurrection of the body" in Judaism, see Jon D. Levenson, *Resurrection and the Restoration of Israel: The Ultimate Victory of the God of Life* (New Haven: Yale University Press, 2006).

17. On the phrase "a way out of no way," see Andrew Young, *A Way Out of No Way: The Spiritual Memoirs of Andrew Young* (Nashville: Nelson Publishers, 1994).

18. Claus Westermann, *The Promises to the Fathers: Studies on the Patriarchal Narratives* (Philadelphia: Fortress Press, 1980), 143–49; and David J. A. Clines, *The Theme of the Pentateuch*, JSOT Supp. 10 (Sheffield: JSOT Press, 1978), 32–43.

19. Westermann, *The Promises to the Fathers*, 60–63.

20. See Patrick D. Miller, "The Gift of God: A Deuteronomic Theology of the Land," *Interpretation* 23 (1969): 451–65.

21. See Walter Brueggemann, *The Land* (Philadelphia: Fortress Press, 1977); W. D. Davies, *The Territorial Dimension of Judaism* (Berkeley: University of California Press, 1982); Norman C. Habel, *The Land Is Mine: Six Biblical Land Ideologies*, OBT (Minneapolis: Fortress Press, 1995).

22. James A. Sanders, *Torah and Canon* (Philadelphia: Fortress Press, 1972) has most acutely noticed the theological significance of the fact that the Pentateuch ends with Israel still outside the promised land, an affirmation pertinent to the displaced Jews of the sixth century whom the canonical shape served.

23. See W. D. Davies, *The Gospel and the Land: Early Christianity and Jewish Territorial Doctrine* (Berkeley: University of California Press, 1974).

24. See Habel, *The Land Is Mine*, 36–53.

25. Regina M. Schwartz, *The Curse of Cain: The Violent Legacy of Monotheism* (Chicago: University of Chicago Press, 1997), 41.

26. Ibid., 48.

27. Ibid., 62.

28. W. Eugene March, *Israel and the Politics of the Land: A Theological Case Study* (Louisville: Westminster John Knox Press, 1994), 66–67; see also 70–71.

29. Michael Prior, *Zionism and the State of Israel: A Moral Inquiry* (New York: Routledge, 1999), 165.

30. Ibid., 173, 181.

31. Ibid., 182–83.

32. Jon D. Levenson, "Exodus and Liberation," in *The Hebrew Bible, the Old Testament, and Historical Criticism* (Louisville: Westminster John Knox Press, 1993), 127–59.

33. Ibid., 157.

34. Ibid., 159.

35. Michael Walzer, *Exodus and Revolution* (New York: Basic Books, 1985).

36. Ibid., 30.

37. Karl Marx, quoted by David McLellan, *The Thought of Karl Marx: An Introduction* (New York: Macmillan Press, 1971), 22.

38. Schwartz, *The Curse of Cain*, 57–58.

39. David M. Gunn, "Colonialism and the Vagaries of Scripture: Te Kooti in Canaan (A Story of Bible and Dispossession in Aotearoa/New Zealand," in *God in the Fray: A Tribute to Walter Brueggemann*, ed. Tod Linafelt and Timothy K. Beal (Minneapolis: Fortress Press, 1998), 129.

40. Ibid., 137.

13. Prophetic Promises

1. Gerhard von Rad, *The Problem of the Hexateuch and Other Essays* (New York: McGraw-Hill, 1966), 68–74, has seen most clearly how the traditions of land promise are connected to the Jerusalem monarchy.

2. This oracle was apparently delivered in the context of northern Israel, but was then appropriated and reused to address the Jerusalem establishment.

3. Again, this is a northern oracle reused for the south through the traditioning process.

4. David Noel Freedman, *The Unity of the Hebrew Bible* (Ann Arbor: University of Michigan Press, 1993), chap. 1. His term for the corpus, Genesis–2 Kings, is "The Primal History."

5. Norman K. Gottwald, "Social Class and Ideology in Isaiah 40–55; An Eagletonian Reading," in *The Bible and Liberation: Political and Social Hermeneutics*, ed. Norman K. Gottwald and Richard A. Horsley (Maryknoll: Orbis Books, 1993), 337–40.

6. On this ending of the book, see Tod Linafelt, *Surviving Lamentations: Catastrophe, Lament, and Protest in the Afterlife of a Biblical Book* (Chicago: University of Chicago Press, 2000), 58–61.

7. Gottwald, "Social Class and Ideology in Isaiah 40–55," 331.

8. Ibid., 335.

9. On the issue see Patrick D. Miller, "Faith and Ideology in the Old Testament," in *Israelite Religion and Biblical Theology: Collected Essays*, JSOT Supp. 267 (Sheffield: Sheffield Academic Press, 2000), 629–47.

10. Ibid., 334, 335.

11. On what follows, see Walter Brueggemann, *Hopeful Imagination: Prophetic Voices in Exile* (Philadelphia Fortress Press, 1986).

12. On this text see Walter Brueggemann, "A 'Characteristic' Reflection on What Comes Next (Jeremiah 32:16-44)," in *Prophets and Paradigms: Essays in Honor of Gene M. Tucker*, ed. by Stephen Breck Reid (JSOT Supp. 229; Sheffield: Sheffield Academic Press, 1996), 16–32.

13. On biblical literature as a response of faith to situations of trauma, see the forthcoming work of Kathleen O'Connor.

14. On the interplay of material restoration and resurrection, see Jon D. Levenson, *Resurrection and the Restoration of Israel: The Ultimate Victory of the God of Life* (New Haven: Yale University Press, 2006).

15. See the discussion of Steven Tuell, "The Rivers of Paradise: Ezekiel 47:1-12 and Genesis 2:10-14," in *God Who Creates: Essays in Honor of W. Sibley Towner*, ed. William P. Brown and S. Dean McBride Jr. (Grand Rapids: Eerdmans, 2000), 171–89.

16. On the formula of "Do not fear" more broadly, see Patrick D. Miller, *They Cried to*

the Lord: The Form and Theology of Biblical Prayer (Minneapolis: Fortress Press, 1994), 135–77.

17. On the "instant" of divine abandonment, see Walter Brueggemann, "A Shattered Transcendence? Exile and Restoration," in *Problems and Perspectives: Biblical Theology in Honor of J. Christiaan Beker*, ed. Steven J. Kraftchick, et al. (Nashville: Abingdon Press, 1995), 169–182.

18. Paul D. Hanson, "Israelite Religion in the Early Postexilic Period," in *Ancient Israelite Religion: Essays in Honor of Frank Moore Cross*, ed. Patrick D. Miller Jr., et al. (Philadelphia: Fortress Press, 1987), 485–508.

19. Gottwald, "Social Class and Ideology in Isaiah 40–55," 332.

20. Levenson, *Resurrection and the Restoration of Israel*, chapter 1, is vigorous in his critique of the rationalistic propensity among "modernist" Jews; of course the same is true in modernist Christian thought among those who keep repeating the Enlightenment categories of the nineteenth century.

21. Walther Zimmerli, *I Am Yahweh* (Atlanta: John Knox Press, 1982), 133.

14. Hope in Every Dimension of Reality

1. See chapters 12 and 13.

2. Donald E. Gowan, *Eschatology in the Old Testament* (Philadelphia: Fortress Press, 1986).

3. See the dissenting exposition of Genesis 2–3 by James Barr, *The Garden of Eden and the Hope of Immortality* (Minneapolis: Fortress Press, 1992). Barr has not been followed by other scholars in this interpretation.

4. The "penitential Psalms" of classic church teaching include Psalms 6, 32, 38, 51, 102, 130, and 143. On the more general matter of sin and confession that leads to forgiveness, see Patrick D. Miller, *They Cried to the Lord: The Form and Theology of Biblical Prayer* (Minneapolis: Fortress Press, 1994), 244–61. Fredrik Lindström, *Suffering and Sin: Interpretations of Illness in the Individual Complaint Psalms* (Coneictanea Biblica Old Testament Series 37; Stockholm: Almqvist & Wiksell International, 1994) has shown that characteristically the Psalms of lament are not preoccupied with sin and do not entertain the thought that suffering is to be understood as punishment for sin.

5. It is to be noted that the usual words introducing verse 6 in English are "They said," attributing the harsh words that follow to the adversary. This is the assumption in the interpretation of Norbert Lohfink, "Three Ways to Talk about Poverty: Psalm 109," in *In the Shadow of Your Wings: New Readings of Great Texts from the Bible* (Collegeville: Liturgical Press, 2003), 120–35. Lohfink does not translate, "They said," but his reading means the same with his use of quotation marks. The effect of that rendering is to protect the voice of the psalm from saying such harsh words. In my judgment, a much more cogent and powerful reading is to let these harsh words be on the lips of the psalmist; there is no sign in the text itself to the contrary.

6. See Walter Baumgartner, *Jeremiah's Poems of Complaint* (Sheffield: Sheffield Academic Press, 1987); and Claus Westermann, *The Structure of the Book of Job: A Form-Critical Analysis* (Philadelphia: Fortress Press, 1981), 31–66.

7. I take the phrase from Andrew Young, *A Way Out of No Way* (Nashville: T. Nelson Publishers, 1994).

8. On the several silences of Israel, see Andre Neher, *The Exile of the Word: From the*

Silence of the Bible to the Silence of Auschwitz (Philadelphia: Jewish Publication Society of America, 1981).

9. Fredrik Lindström, *Suffering and Sin*, has made the case that Israel's suffering is due to YHWH's absence, for the powers of evil will occupy the vacuum left by that absence. The work of Israel's prayers then is to summon YHWH back into activity, for where YHWH is active, the powers of evil cannot function effectively. On the silence, see Walter Brueggemann, "Voice as Counter to Violence," *Calvin Theological Journal* 36 (April 2001): 22–33.

10. The move from *plea* to *praise* is given classic expression by Claus Westermann, *The Praise of God in the Psalms* (Richmond: John Knox Press, 1965).

11. On the salvation oracles, see the discussion of Patrick D. Miller, *They Cried to the Lord*, 135–77.

12. Erhard Gerstenberger, "Der klagende Mensch: Anmerkungen zu den Klagegattungen in Israel," *Probleme biblischer Theologie: Gerhard von Rad zum 70. Geburtstag*, ed. Hans Walter Wolff (Munich: Chr. Kaiser Verlag, 1971), 72.

13. It is to be recognized that in the Hebrew text the "then" in these three usages is not as strongly marked as it appears in our English translations. The sense of such an accent, however, seems certain.

14. See now the compelling theological analysis of the matter by Jon D. Levenson, *Resurrection and the Restoration of Israel: The Ultimate Victory of the God of Life* (New Haven: Yale University Press, 2006).

15. By appealing to nonbiblical parallels, Mitchell Dahood, *Psalms III 101–150* (AB 17A; Garden City: Doubleday and Co., 1970), xli–lii, has read a number of texts in terms of resurrection. The nonbiblical parallels have not been persuasive to most scholars after Dahood.

16. Along with Dahood, see the work of his student Nicholas J. Tromp, *Primitive Conceptions of Death and the Nether World in the Old Testament* (Rome: Pontifical Biblical Institute, 1969). Note also the dissent of James Barr, cited in n. 3.

17. The advance of the argument of Levenson, beyond that of Dahood, is most important and merits close attention. Whereas Dahood argued on the basis of a general religious phenomena in that culture, Levenson has made a powerful case that resurrection claims are intrinsic to the faith of ancient Israel; while the articulation of resurrection faith may have appeared later in Israel's theological development, the primal theological claims that lie behind the claim of resurrection are deep and old in Israel's faith.

18. See the classic statement of the matter by Krister Stendahl, "The Apostle Paul and the Introspective Conscience of the West," in *Paul Among Jews and Gentiles* (Philadelphia: Fortress Press, 1976).

19. Rainer Albertz, *A History of Israelite Religion in the Old Testament Period; Volume II: From the Exile to the Maccabees*, OTL (Louisville: Westminster John Knox Press, 1994), 521–22.

20. On the remarkable concluding verdict, "What is right," see the exquisite exposition of Samuel E. Balentine, *Job* (Smyth & Helwys Bible Commentary; Macon: Smyth & Helwys, 2006), 708–14.

15. Hope for the World

1. Jon D. Levenson, *Creation and the Persistence of Evil: The Jewish Drama of Divine Omnipotence* (San Francisco: Harper & Row, 1988). The most comprehensive theological

study of the creation traditions is Terence E. Fretheim, *God and the World in the Old Testament: A Relational Theology of Creation* (Nashville: Abingdon Press, 2005). Whereas Levenson takes a more or less history-of-religions approach, Fretheim works with a more frontally theological perspective. These two fine books provide the starting point for our discussion.

2. See the summary discussion on the divine council by Patrick D. Miller, Jr., *Genesis 1–11; Studies in Structure and Theme*, JSOT Supp. 8 (Sheffield: Department of Biblical Studies, University of Sheffield, 1978). On the liabilities of monotheism in the final form of the text, see Regina M. Schwartz, *The Curse of Cain: The Violent Legacy of Monotheism* (Chicago: University of Chicago Press, 1997).

3. On "world making" generally, see Peter L. Berger and Thomas Luckmann, *The Social Construction of Reality: A Treatise in the Sociology of Knowledge* (Anchor Books: Garden City: Doubleday and Co., 1967). As concerns the theme in Old Testament studies, the most important work is that of Sigmund Mowinckel, on which see J. J. M. Roberts, "Mowinckel's Enthronement Festival: A Review," in *The Book of Psalms: Composition and Reception*, ed. Peter W. Flint and Patrick D. Miller (Leiden: Brill, 2005), 97–115. For a heuristic exploration of "world making" in textual exposition, see Walter Brueggemann, *Israel's Praise: Doxology Against Idolatry and Ideology* (Philadelphia: Fortress Press, 1988).

4. In church usage this psalm, which affirms the reliability of fruitful creation, functions as a much-used table prayer of thanks for food. On the theological depth of such table prayers, see Mark Douglas, *Confessing Christ in the 21st Century* (New York: Rowman and Littlefield 2005), 235–39.

5. It is commonly agreed that the very late text of 2 Maccabees 7:28 is the first text that clearly attests creation from nothing. But see the dissent from Walther Eichrodt, "In the Beginning," in *Israel's Prophetic Heritage: Essays in Honor of James Muilenburg*, ed. Bernhard W. Anderson and Walter Harrelson (New York: Harper and Brothers, 1962), 1–10.

6. Jon D. Levenson, *Creation and the Persistence of Evil*, 14.

7. Levenson takes with theological seriousness texts concerning cosmogonic struggle that most interpreters believe have been "overcome" in the traditioning process of canonical formation. There can be no doubt what those texts say; the interpretive issue is how they function in the final form of the text. I believe Levenson's point is an important one to which attention must be paid.

8. Fredrik Lindström, *Suffering and Sin: Interpretations of Illness in the Individual Complaint Psalms* (Stockholm: Almqvist & Wiksell International, 1994).

9. Karl Barth, "God and Nothingness," in *Church Dogmatics*, vol 3/3 (Edinburgh: T & T Clark, 1960), 289–368.

10. Jon D. Levenson, *Creation and the Persistence of Evil*, 17.

11. Samuel E. Balentine, *Job* (Smyth & Helwys Bible Commentary; Macon: Smyth & Helwys, 2006), 686, comments on Behemoth, and by inference Job:

> What is perhaps most striking about all these descriptions of Behemoth is that God does *not* regard this creature as a threat to creation's order or as an opponent that God must defeat in order to be God. Instead, God commends Behemoth to Job as a model for what it means to be a creature worthy of the Creator's pride and praise. The lesson for Job seems to be that those who dare to stand before their maker with exceptional strength, proud prerogatives, and

fierce trust come as near to realizing God's primordial design for life in this world as it is humanly possible to do.

12. See Fretheim, *God and World in the Old Testament*, 249–69.

13. Ibid., 267–69.

14. See Walter Brueggemann, "The Creatures Know!" in *The Wisdom of Creation*, ed. Edward Foley and Robert Schreiter (Collegeville, Minn.: Liturgical Press, 2004), 1–12.

15. The basic study is that of H. H. Schmid. See an English summary of his thesis, H. H. Schmid, "Creation, Righteousness, and Salvation: 'Creation Theology' as the Broad Horizon of Biblical Theology," in *Creation in the Old Testament*, ed. Bernhard W. Anderson (Philadelphia: Fortress Press, 1984), 102–17. See also the several discussions of Bernhard W. Anderson in his book, *From Creation to New Creation: Old Testament Perspectives*, OBT (Minneapolis: Fortress Press, 1994).

16. On these texts, see Steven Tuell, "The Rivers of Paradise: Ezekiel 47:1-12 and Genesis 2:10-14," in *God Who Creates: Essays in Honor of W. Sibley Towner*, ed. William P. Brown and S. Dean McBride Jr. (Grand Rapids: Eerdmans, 2000), 171–89.

17. Rolf Rendtorff, *Canon and Theology: Overtures to an Old Testament Theology* (OBT; Minneapolis: Fortress Press, 1993), 125–34.

18. Patrick D. Miller, "Creation and Covenant," in *Biblical Theology: Problems and Perspectives*, ed. Steven J. Kraftchick et al. (Nashville: Abingdon Press, 1995), 168. On the relation of creation and covenant in dogmatic perspective, see Karl Barth, *Church Dogmatics*, vol. 3/1 (Edinburgh: T & T Clark, 1958), 42–329.

19. Brevard S. Childs, *Introduction to the Old Testament as Scripture* (Philadelphia: Fortress Press, 1979), 517–18.

20. Karl Barth, *Church Dogmatics*, vol. 1/2 (Edinburgh: T & T Clark, 1956), 1–44, early on has made a powerful case that the "reality" of the revealed God has priority over the "possibility" of that God. This priority is clear for the attestations of ancient Israel and matters enormously in contemporary church theology.

21. It is clear that the Western church, preoccupied with "sin and salvation," has very much to learn in this matter from the Eastern church that has thought much more consistently in the categories of the creator God. Failure on this point in the West has enfeebled the church in its contemporary struggles over "science" and "the environmental crisis."

22. Cameron Wybrow, *The Bible, Baconism, and Mastery over Nature: The Old Testament and Its Modern Misreading* (New York: Peter Lang, 1991).

23. It is for good reason that Fretheim has subtitled his important book, "A Relational Theology of Creation," for he calls sustained attention to the dialogical process that constitutes the creation. That claim can be made and sustained without the unfortunate notion of human persons as "cocreators."

24. See the several important essays on creation and "the end of the world" in *The End of the World and the Ends of God: Science and Theology on Eschatology*, ed. John Polkenhorne and Michael Welker (Harrisburg: Trinity Press International, 2000).

16. *Hope in Alternative Modes*

1. On the "null point," see Walther Zimmerli, *I Am Yahweh* (Atlanta: John Knox Press, 1982), 111–33.

2. On such an approach, see Odil Hannes Steck, "Theological Streams of Tradition," in *Tradition and Theology in the Old Testament*, ed. Douglas A. Knight (Philadelphia: Fortress Press, 1977), 183–214.

3. Jon D. Levenson, *Sinai and Zion: An Entry into the Jewish Bible* (New York: Winston Press, 1985), 187–217.

4. The classic study of these texts is Sigmund Mowinkel, *He That Cometh* (Nashville: Abingdon Press, n.d.).

5. Ibid., 17–20.

6. Otto Eissfeldt, "The Promises of Grace in Isaiah 55:1-5," in *Israel's Prophetic Heritage: Essays in Honor of James Muilenburg*, ed. Bernhard W. Anderson and Walter Harrelson (New York: Harper & Brothers, 1962), 206.

7. Paul Lehmann, *The Transfiguration of Politics* (New York: Harper & Row, 1975), 56–57.

8. "A Jewish Statement on Christians and Christianity" (*Dabru Emet*), *Christianity in Jewish Terms*, ed. Tikva Frymer-Kensky, et al., (Boulder: Westview Press, 2000), xix.

9. Ibid., xx.

10. Elie Wiesel, *Memoirs: All Rivers Run to the Sea* (New York: Knopf, 1995), 354–55.

11. Richard Moew, "Where Are We Going?" *Essentials of Christian Theology*, ed. William C. Placher (Louisville: Westminster John Knox Press, 2003), 335–47.

12. See Patrick D. Miller, Jr., *Genesis 1-11: Studies in Structure & Theme*, JSOT Supp. 8 (Sheffield: Department of Biblical Studies, 1978), 9–26.

13. The common category mistake of conservatives concerning the prophets is that they were predictors; the converse liberal common category mistake is that they were social reformers and activists.

14. See Ronald E. Clements, *Old Testament Prophecy: From Oracles to Canon* (Louisville: Westminster John Knox Press, 1996), 105–41.

15. See Margaret S. Odell, *Ezekiel* (Smyth & Helwys Bible Commentary; Macon: Smyth & Helwys, 2005), 472.

16. See my summary, Walter Brueggemann, An *Introduction to the Old Testament: The Canon and Christian Imagination* (Louisville: Westminster John Knox Press, 2003), 209–14.

17. Jon D. Levenson, *Resurrection and the Restoration of Israel: The Ultimate Victory of the God of Life* (New Haven: Yale University Press, 2006) has shown with a fine nuance the way in which restoration of Israel stands at the center of faith in the "ultimate victory" of God in the Hebrew Bible.

18. John J. Collins, *The Apocalyptic Imagination: An Introduction to the Jewish Matrix of Christianity* (New York: Crossroad, 1987), 205.

19. See Martin Noth, *The Laws in the Pentateuch and Other Essays* (Philadelphia: Fortress Press, 1967), 194–214.

20. The other text is Isaiah 26:19; more generally see the work of Levenson cited in n. 17.

21. Ernst Kasemann, *New Testament Questions Today* (London: SCM Press, 1969), 137.

22. See J. Louis Martyn, "World without End or Twice-Invaded World?" in *Shaking Heaven and Earth: Essays in Honor of Walter Brueggemann and Charles B. Cousar*, ed. Christine Roy Yoder, et al. (Louisville: Westminster John Knox Press, 2005), 117–32.

23. Otto Plöger, *Theocracy and Eschatology* (Richmond: John Knox Press, 1968); Paul

D. Hanson, *The Dawn of Apocalyptic: The Historical and Sociological Roots of Jewish Apocalyptic Eschatology* (Philadelphia: Fortress Press, 1975).

24. Karl Manheim, *Ideology and Utopia* (New York: Harcourt, Brace, and Co., 1936).

25. See Philip R. Davies, *Scribes and Schools: The Canonization of the Hebrew Scriptures* (Louisville: Westminster John Knox Press, 1998).

26. See E. W. Nicholson, *Preaching to the Exiles: A Study of the Prose Tradition in the Book of Jeremiah* (Oxford: Blackwell, 1970). On the dynamism and sweep of this tradition of discourse, see Hindy Najman, *Seconding Sinai: The Development of Mosaic Discourse in Second Temple Judaism* (Leiden: Brill, 2003).

27. See Jeremiah 51:59 on the brother of Baruch; see James Muilenburg, "Baruch the Scribe," *Proclamation and Presence: Old Testament Essays in Honour of Gwynne Henton Davies*, ed. John I. Durham and J. R. Porter (London: SCM Press, 1970), 215–38.

28. Quoted by Robert P. Carroll, *Jeremiah*: A *Commentary*, OTL (Philadelphia: Fortress Press, 1986).

29. Moshe Weinfeld, *Deuteronomy and the Deuteronomic School* (Oxford: Clarendon Press, 1972). For a severe critique of Weinfeld's thesis, see Peter T. Vogt, *Deuteronomic Theology and the Significance of Torah* (Winona Lake: Eisenbrauns, 2006).

30. See Peter Ochs, "Talmudic Scholarship as Textual Reasoning: Halivni's Pragmatic Historiography," in *Textual Reasonings: Jewish Philosophy and Text Study at the End of the Twentieth Century*, ed. Peter Ochs and Nancy Levene (Grand Rapids: Eerdmans, 2002), 133.

31. Ibid., 134.

32. Ibid., 135.

33. George A. Lindbeck, *The Nature of Doctrine: Religion and Theology in a Postliberal Age* (Philadelphia: Westminster Press, 1984).

34. Ochs, "Talmudic Scholarship," 132.

35. See Edward Kaplan and Samuel H. Dresner, *Abraham Joshua Heschel: Prophetic Witness* (New Haven: Yale University Press, 1998).

36. On this text, see R. A. Carlson, *David The Chosen King: A Traditio-Historical Approach to the Second Book of Samuel* (Stockholm: Almqvist & Wiksell, 1964), 263–67.

17. The Coming Rule of God: Through Fissures to Newness

1. The polemic against generic notions of "religion" is, of course, foundational for the work of Karl Barth. That accent of Barth, moreover, is reflected in Old Testament studies in the programmatic essay of Gerhard von Rad, *The Problem of the Hexateuch and other Essays* (New York: McGraw-Hill, 1066), 1–78, published in 1938 in the wake of the Barmen Declaration. Von Rad's accent on "credo" was to secure standing ground for a particular faith claim in the midst of "Canaanite" alternatives that, in context, are to be understood as generic claims of "German Christianity."

2. I have used the term *Old Testament* throughout this discussion because I write from a Christian perspective. That nomenclature, or any other, is problematic and we have not yet found adequate nomenclature. On the problem of such terminology, see *Hebrew Bible or Old Testament? Studying the Bible in Judaism and Christianity*, ed. Roger Brooks and John J. Collins (Notre Dame: University of Notre Dame Press, 1990).

3. On the fissure and the turn to the future in ancient Israel, see Martin Buber, *The Prophetic Faith* (Harper Torchbooks; New York: Harper & Brothers, 1949), 96–154.

4. While questions of historicity of the "exile" can be raised and contested vigorously, more interesting and more important for our purposes is the recognition that "every generation" of Jews must reenact the memory of exile and restoration; see Jacob Neusner, *Understanding Seeking Faith: Essays on the Case of Judaism* (Atlanta: Scholars Press, 1986), 137–41. Neusner also terms this memory a "paradigm" that defined all Jewish experience.

5. Erich Voegelin, *Israel and Revelation: Order and History*, vol. 1 (Baton Rouge: Louisiana State University Press, 1956); and David Weiss Halivni, *Revelation Restored: Divine Writ and Critical Responses* (Boulder: Westview Press, 1997).

6. For these several ways of understanding the disruption that features the human agents as perpetrators and/or victims, see Paul Ricoeur, *The Symbolism of Evil* (Boston: Beacon Press, 1967).

7. The notion of the fall that is central to Christian interpretation is not present in the Old Testament nor in the primary trajectories of Judaism. Nonetheless, the Jewish tradition is as aware of this crisis as is the Christian tradition, even if not articulated in such a certain and therefore problematic mode. It is plausible that what the Christian tradition has termed *the fall* is the disruption of the sixth century writ large.

8. See Rolf Rendtorff, *The Canonical Hebrew Bible: A Theology of the Old Testament* (Leiden: Deo Publishing, 2005), 17–21.

9. See David Novak, *The Image of the Non-Jew in Judaism: An Historical and Constructive Study of the Noahide Laws* (New York: Edwin Mellen Press, 1983).

10. In all spheres of life—social, cosmic, personal—Israel experienced and interpreted life through a drama of "orientation, disorientation, new orientation." See my articulation of this dramatic pattern in Walter Brueggemann, *The Psalms and the Life of Faith* (Minneapolis: Fortress Press, 1995), 3–32.

11. See my probe of these issues in Walter Brueggemann, *Theology of the Old Testament: Testimony, Dispute, Advocacy* (Minneapolis: Fortress Press, 1997), 727–50.

12. Emmanuel Levinas, *Totality and Infinity: An Essay on Exteriority* (Pittsburgh: Duquesne University Press, 1969).

13. See James A. Sanders, "Adaptable for Life: The Nature and Function of Canon," in *Magnalia Dei: The Mighty Acts of God: Essays on the Bible and Archaeology in Memory of G. Ernest Wright*, ed. Frank Moore Cross et al. (Garden City; Doubleday, 1976), 531–60.

14. See Samuel Terrien, *The Elusive Presence: Toward a New Biblical Theology* (New York: Harper & Row, 1978).

15. See Klaus Scholder, *The Birth of Modern Critical Theology: Origins and Problems of Biblical Criticism in the Seventeenth Century* (Philadelphia: Trinity Press International, 1990). It may give us pause that Zygmunt Bauman, *Modernity and Holocaust* (Cambridge: Polity Press, 1991), has urged that the holocaust is not an aberration but a logical outcome of Enlightenment rationality mediated through technological means.

16. On the mixed outcomes of "exceptionalism" with its theological rootage, see Gary Dorrien, "Consolidating the Empire: Neoconservatism and the Politics of American Domination," *Political Theology* 6 (2005), 409–28.

17. "Babylon" performs the same function in Revelation 18, a critique of all autonomous empires.

18. For the contemporary accent on *praxis*, see Dorothy C. Bass, *Practicing Our Faith: A Way of Life for a Searching People* (San Francisco: Jossey-Bass, 1997); Miroslav Volf and Dorothy C. Bass, *Practicing Theology: Beliefs and Practices in Christian Life* (Grand Rapids: Eerdmans, 2002); and Craig Dykstra, *Growing in the Life of Faith: Education and Christian Practices* (Louisville: Westminster John Knox Press, 2005).

19. S. Dean McBride, "Polity of the Covenant People: The Book of Deuteronomy," *Constituting the Community: Studies on the Polity of Ancient Israel in Honor of S. Dean McBride Jr.*, ed. John T. Strong and Steven S. Tuell (Winona Lake: Eisenbrauns, 2005), 17–33. To be sure, McBride's focus is on Deuteronomy, but we may recognize that such "constitutional" impulses are inchoately present in the Sinai traditions as well.

20. See Walter Brueggemann, *Solomon: Israel's Ironic Icon of Human Achievement* (Columbia: University of South Carolina Press, 2005), 139–59.

21. David McLellan, *The Thought of Karl Marx: An Introduction* (London: Macmillan, 1971), 22.

22. Daniel L. Smith, *The Religion of the Landless: The Social Context of the Babylonian Exile* (Bloomington: Meyer Stone, 1989), 153–78.

23. On social *praxis* as resistance, see the now classic studies of James C. Scott, *Weapons of the Weak: Everyday Forms of Peasant Resistance* (New Haven: Yale University Press, 1985); and Scott, *Domination and the Arts of Resistance: Hidden Transcripts* (New Haven: Yale University Press, 1990).

24. See the extraordinary case study of faith against totalizing system by William T. Cavanaugh, *Torture and Eucharist* (Oxford: Blackwell, 1998).

SCRIPTURE INDEX

Old Testament

Leviticus

Numbers

Proverbs

Ecclesiastes

Jeremiah

New Testament